RANGE SAFETY RULES
1. A SAFETY OFFICER IS REQUIRED FOR ALL SHOOTING.
2. TREAT EVERY FIREARM AS IF LOADED.
3. NEVER POINT A FIREARM AT ANYTHING OR ANYONE THAT YOU DO NOT INTEND ... OR IN A DIRECTION WHERE ...ENTIONAL DISCHARGE MAY D... OR HARM.
...ACE YOUR FINGER IN THE ...GUARD UNTIL YOU ARE READY ...
...OF YOUR TARGET, BACKSTOP, ...OND.
...WRAP-AROUND EYE PROTECTION IS MANDATORY.
7. EAR PROTECTION IS MANDATORY.

MAKE YOUR WEAPON SAFE:
...ALWAYS POINT YOUR FIREARM IN A SAFE ...ION WITH THE SAFETY ON (IF APPLICABLE) ...ZINE REMOVED OR CYLINDER OPEN ...LIDE, OR COCKING LEVER TO THE REAR ...LY AND PHYSICALLY INSPECT ...LEAR THE CHAMBER

100% MANDATORY ID CHECK

NO PHOTOGRAPHY OR VIDEOGRAPHY
CAMERAS WILL BE CONFISCATED

RESTRICTED AREA — AUTHORIZED PERSO...
AUTHORIZED ENTRY INSTALLATION CONSTITU... TO SEARCH OF PERSONNEL AND THE PROPERTY UNDER THEIR CONTROL
INTERNAL SECURITY ACT OF 1950 SECTION 21; 50 U.S.C. 797

फोटो, विडियो फिल्मींग या ... पीक्चर लेना मना है

COSMIC TOP SECRET

BLACK CHARLIE INTELLIGENCE CELL

IS TODAY YOUR DAY?
COMPLACENCY KILLS

NO FLIGHTLINE PHOTOGRAPHY ALLOWED
CONTACT PUBLIC AFFAIRS FOR PERMISSION FOR PHOTOGRAPHY, AT PAO 841-1314

DANGER
STAY AWAY POSSIBLE UXO
OFF LIMITS BY ORDER O... BASE COMMANDER

NAVSPECWARCEN COMBAT TRAINING TANK (FOR OFFICIAL USE ONL...

...WARCEN ...NING TANK ...USE ONLY)

WARNING
U.S. NAVY PROPERTY ...HORIZED PERSONNEL ONLY
...ED ENTRY ONTO THIS INSTALLATION CONSTITUTES CONSENT TO ...OF PERSONNEL AND THE PROPERTY UNDER THEIR CO...
INTERNAL SECURITY ACT OF 1950 SECTION 21; 50 U.S.C. 797

...R OWN RISK!!!
...TRAINING IS ...DANGEROUS!!
...ER IS VOLUNTARY AND ...ZING THE BLACKWATER ...BY ASSUMES ALL RISK ...AMAGE ARISING FROM ...R'S TRAINING FACILITY.
...ES THAT ENGAGING IN ...WATER FACILITY SHALL ...ANCE OF ALL OF THE ...AND CONDITIONS.

FALLUJAH EMERGENCY
MAIN ENTRANCE
CLEAR ALL WEAPONS
CHECK IN AT THE GUARD SHACK

DO NOT DISTURB EMERGENCIES ONLY!
If you are not having a heart attack, hemorrhaging from an artery, missing a limb or eyeball, in active labor or have a bullet lodge somewhere in your person DO NOT KNOCK ON THIS DOOR.
I will be available after 1400 for sick call. Thanks for your cooperation.
DOC POWELL

WARNING!!
TRAFFIC LAWS ARE ...MILITARY INSTALLAT... ION MAY BE PROSEC... L COURT VIOLATORS ...RISONED AND/OR F...
...1315; 18 U.S.C. 13; 32 CFR

WARNING
THIS ACTIVITY IS PATROLL... MILITARY WORK DOG TEAMS

ALL ...raphy / Video ...g / Sketching ...ohibited
السرعة...

COSMIC TOP SECRET

...TED ACCESS ...CILITY NOT ... ...ENERAL USE

RESTRICTED AREA NO VIDEO OR PHOTOGRAPHY AUTHORIZED

EXTREME DANGER
خطر شديد
STAY BACK 100 MET...
100 متر بعيداً...

WEAPON CLEARING
...TED SAFE DIRECTION, ATTEMPT TO PLACE ...
...CANNOT BE PLACED ON SAFE.
...SSING THE MAGAZINE CATCH BUTTON AND PU...
...ANDLE REARWARD, PRESS BOTTOM OF BOLT CAT...
...CH, RETURN CHARGING HANDLE TO FULL FORWAR...
...FOR LEVER ON SAFE.
...LT THE RECEIVER AND CHAMBER TO ENSURE THER...
...G TOWARD SAFE, ALLOW THE BOLT TO GO FORW...
...FIRE AND SQUEEZE THE TRIGGER, PULL THE CH...
...NG THE BOLT TO RETURN TO THE FULL FORWARD

RAWAH K-9

U.S. NAVY PROPERTY RESTRICTED AREA KEEP OUT AUTHORIZED PERSONNEL ONLY
...AVISO...
AREA PROHIBIDA
MANTENERSE FUERA
SOLO PERSONAS AUTORIZADAS

ALL Photography / Video Filming / Sketching Prohibited
السرعة
...نابيبسية عن طريق القناة...
फोटो, विडियो फिल्मींग या आधी पीक्चर लेना मना है

100% MANDATORY ID CHECK

...OUND ...IDE ...UIRED
...sidered "PROHIBITED" by the ...dministration and may not be ...board the aircraft:
...TED ITEMS
...plosives, Weapons, Martials Arts ...c or Offensive Material, War ...or Any Device That May Cause ...ion Casings, Lighter (all types), ...(strike) Matches, Soil, Soiled ...ducts to include Fresh Fruits, ...or Vegetables.
...sidered "CONTROLLED" by the ...Administration and may be ...however; MUST BE DECLARED

...ETAINEE ...N DECK ...NTAIN SILENCE ...ACTICE OPSEC

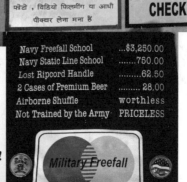

BLACKWATER
TRAIN AT YOUR OWN RISK!!!
FIREARMS TRAINING IS INHERENTLY DANGEROUS!!
TRAINING AT BLACKWATER IS VOLUNTARY AND EACH INDIVIDUAL UTILIZING THE BLACKWATER TRAINING FACILITY HEREBY ASSUMES ALL RISK OF INJURY, LOSS OR DAMAGE ARISING FROM THE USE OF BLACKWATER'S TRAINING FACILITY.
THE PARTICIPANT AGREES THAT ENGAGING IN TRAINING AT THE BLACKWATER FACILITY SHALL CONSTITUTE ACCEPTANCE OF ALL OF THE...

Navy Freefall School ...$3,250.00
Navy Static Line School 750.00
Lost Ripcord Handle 62.50
2 Cases of Premium Beer 28.00
Airborne Shuffle worthless
Not Trained by the Army PRICELESS

Military Freefall
Joe None #340 0001 9600 3250

ENTER

NO PHOTO'S OF THE HLZ PLEASE

NIKON

290 280

DANGER

"On any given day, Navy SEALs can be operating in more then 40 countries; in some areas, we are asked to be there; in other areas, people don't want us there; in some other areas, they don't know we are there; and in some parts of the world, people think we are there but we have never operated there."

Rear Admiral (SEAL) Garry J. Bonelli, USN (Ret.)
Former Deputy Commander, Naval Special Warfare Command

UNITED STATES
NAVAL SPECIAL WARFARE
U.S. NAVY SEALs

Greg E. Mathieson Sr.
Editor-in-Chief / Photographer
and

David T. Gatley
Photo Editor / Photographer

**ST. MARTIN'S
CASTLE POINT**

NEW YORK

PAGES 4–5: *Fully "locked up" tactical SEAL team operators are wearing wet suits and ready for any combat situation in this over-the-beach exercise. They carry combat equipment second to none. Their weapons systems can be individually customized for the specific mission to fit that operator's needs or comfort factor. (Photo: Dave Gatley)*

PAGE 8: *SEALs undergo a lot of water training. A program that was developed during the Vietnam War was that of drown proofing, which builds great confidence in the students of being able to survive in deep water. In this part of training, their hands are tied behind their backs and they descend to the bottom of the pool to recover their face mask with their teeth and bring it to the surface. (Photo: Greg E. Mathieson Sr. / NSW Publications, LLC)*

PAGES 14–15: *Coronado Bay, CA—The master chief takes the point ahead of his fire team as they approach through the shallows of the shoreline clandestinely in a CRRC (Combat Rubber Raiding Craft) ready for an OTB (over the beach) exercise. The CRRC is also known as an IBS (Inflatable Boat, Small) or Zodiac in recognition of its prime manufacturer. It is used for clandestine surface insertions and extractions of lightly armed amphibious forces of SEAL fire teams, such as in this group. (Photo: Greg E. Mathieson Sr. / NSW Publications, LLC)*

UNITED STATES NAVAL SPECIAL WARFARE.

Copyright © 2012, 2015 by Greg Edward Mathieson Sr. All rights reserved. Printed in China. For information, address St. Martin's Press, 175 Fifth Avenue, New York, N.Y. 10010.

www.stmartins.com

The Library of Congress Cataloging-in-Publication Data is available upon request.

ISBN 978-1-250-08614-3 (hardcover)

St. Martin's Press books may be purchased for educational, business, or promotional use. For information on bulk purchases, please contact the Macmillan Corporate and Premium Sales Department at 1-800-221-7945, extension 5442, or write to specialmarkets@macmillan.com.

Respective photos and text: © 2012 Greg Edward Mathieson Sr. / NSW Publications, LLC, © 2012 Dave Gatley / NSW Publications, LLC. All other photos copyrighted and credited to their respective copyright holders.

Originally published in the United States by NSW Publications, LLC

First St. Martin's Castle Point Edition: October 2015

10 9 8 7 6 5 4 3 2 1

CONTENTS

THE NAVY SEALS CREED

In times of war or uncertainty there is a special breed of warrior ready to answer our Nation's call. A common man with uncommon desire to succeed.

Forged by adversity, he stands alongside America's finest special operations forces to serve his country, the American people, and protect their way of life.

I am that man.

My Trident is a symbol of honor and heritage. Bestowed upon me by the heroes that have gone before, it embodies the trust of those I have sworn to protect. By wearing the Trident I accept the responsibility of my chosen profession and way of life. It is a privilege that I must earn every day.

My loyalty to Country and Team is beyond reproach. I humbly serve as a guardian to my fellow Americans always ready to defend those who are unable to defend themselves. I do not advertise the nature of my work, nor seek recognition for my actions. I voluntarily accept the inherent hazards of my profession, placing the welfare and security of others before my own.

I serve with honor on and off the battlefield. The ability to control my emotions and my actions, regardless of circumstance, sets me apart from other men.

Uncompromising integrity is my standard. My character and honor are steadfast. My word is my bond.

We expect to lead and be led. In the absence of orders I will take charge, lead my teammates and accomplish the mission. I lead by example in all situations.

I will never quit. I persevere and thrive on adversity. My Nation expects me to be physically harder and mentally stronger than my enemies. If knocked down, I will get back up, every time. I will draw on every remaining ounce of strength to protect my teammates and to accomplish our mission. I am never out of the fight.

We demand discipline—We expect innovation. The lives of my teammates and the success of our mission depend on me—my technical skill, tactical proficiency, and attention to detail. My training is never complete.

We train for war and fight to win. I stand ready to bring the full spectrum of combat power to bear in order to achieve my mission and the goals established by my country. The execution of my duties will be swift and violent when required yet guided by the very principles that I serve to defend.

Brave men have fought and died building the proud tradition and feared reputation that I am bound to uphold. In the worst of conditions, the legacy of my teammates steadies my resolve and silently guides my every deed.

I will not fail.

THE SPECIAL WARFARE COMBATANT-CRAFT CREWMAN CREED

In our nation's time of need, an elite brotherhood of Sailors stands ready off distant shores and on shallow rivers. Defending freedom, they serve with honor and distinction. I am proud to be one of these Sailors.

I am a Special Warfare Combatant-craft Crewman: a quiet professional; tried, tested and dedicated to achieving excellence in maritime special operations. I am a disciplined, confident and highly motivated warrior.

My honor and integrity are beyond reproach, my commitment unquestioned and my word trusted. The American people depend on me to carry out my mission in a professional manner.

I maintain my craft, equipment and myself at the highest level of combat readiness. I set the standard and lead by example. I am responsible for my actions and accountable to my teammates. I challenge my brothers to perform, as I expect them to challenge me.

I am ready for war. I will close and engage the enemy with the full combat power of my craft. My actions will be decisive yet measured. I will always complete the mission. I will never quit and I will leave no one behind.

My heritage comes from the Sailors who operated the PT boats of World War II and the combatant craft of Vietnam. The legacy of these warriors guides my actions. I will always remember the courage, perseverance and sacrifices made to guarantee our nation's freedom. I uphold the honor of those who have fought before me and will do nothing to disgrace my proud heritage.

On Time, On Target, Never Quit!

FOREWORD

By the Honorable John F. Lehman Jr., Secretary of the Navy, 1981–1987,
Member of the 9/11 Commission

On September 11, 2001, America and indeed the entire free world closed the book on the Cold War and entered a less certain and deeply threatening era. 9/11 marked the emergence of a destructive transnational threat driven by religious fervor and fanaticism. Our enemy is not terrorism. Our enemy is violent Islamist fundamentalism. This new enemy is not a rational or deterrable state actor, nor is it bound by traditional "rules of war." It confronts us with methods of attack that are truly heinous and for which we are ill-prepared.

As members of the 9/11 Commission, the evidence made it abundantly clear to us that much had to be done to improve the United States government's capabilities to deal with this new era. We found that our intelligence establishment was basically dysfunctional and our nation's ability to marshal and use "soft power" was also lacking.

Former Secretary of the Navy John F. Lehman Jr. surrounded by other members of the 9/11 Commission. Above in the background is fellow Commission member Senator Bob Kerrey, U.S. Navy SEAL and Medal of Honor Recipient (Photo: Greg E. Mathieson Sr. / NSW Publications, LLC)

Our nation's willingness to use economic aid, technical support, and other tools to help threatened nations was just not up to the task.

One bright spot in America's "tool kit," however, was the very substantial and growing capabilities resident in our nation's Special Operations Forces. One of the most important recommendations from the 9/11 Commission was a unanimous recommendation to preemptively capture or kill those jihadists operating against us wherever they happened to be in the world. One key to successful preemption of those extremist forces that plan and train to attack us is the highly professional unconventional forces that have been growing in each of our armed services since President Reagan began to rebuild them in the 1980s.

As a naval person, I may be forgiven the belief that the best of these excellent forces are the Navy SEALs. These super-elite commandos had their beginnings in the Underwater Demolition Teams of World War II and today are the most sought after and competitive elite Special Operations Forces in the world. Able to operate in and from the sea, the air, and the land and operating in small teams, they provide a huge multiplier effect for all of our conventional forces. In the current wars in Iraq and Afghanistan they have been able to capture or kill many key jihadist leaders; they have been able to infiltrate into enemy-controlled areas to gather critical intelligence, and they have been able to direct devastating precision air and missile strikes so that today no one in al Qaeda can ever sleep securely in the belief that they are safe. The Navy SEALs of today are supported by a larger team of specialized personnel of the Naval Special Warfare Command, and together they make up a very capable tool set available to the President and military commanders 24/7.

As part of President Reagan's buildup of Special Operations Forces, I had the pleasure of promoting Capt. Cathal

Flynn to the rank of admiral, thereby opening a path that now exists for Navy SEALs to rise to four-star command. The number of SEAL teams was expanded and each of the teams received the funding support that allowed them to have the most modern equipment and training available. In the years since the 1980s, the SEAL teams have served our nation well. Their performance in Iraq, Afghanistan, and in many other unnamed places around the globe has vindicated their expansion many times over. In today's age, it is clear that our nation's enemies and potential enemies have concluded that asymmetric warfare offers their best hope of attacking or defeating the United States. In this new world, the United States will need Special Forces capabilities on an even greater scale, and I am confident that Congress and the Executive Branch will provide the resources necessary for a further expansion not only of the SEALs but of the special operations capabilities within all of the military services.

There is another challenge, however, that must be kept in mind. Success and expansion have degraded many elite corps throughout military history. Opening of promotion to the highest level and hence the requirement for broadening and "joint tours" can easily lead to bureaucratic pressures for careerism to the detriment of real professionalism. The Goldwater/Nichols requirement for years of staff and joint duty has already eroded the professionalism of some warfare communities, often forcing warfighters to choose between building their community-unique professional skills and leadership on the one hand and checking the necessary boxes for promotion on the other.

The provision of considerably more material resources to the SEALs also carries with it perils as more of the best SEALs must be devoting ever more significant amounts of time and effort to programming, budgeting, procurement, and Pentagon politics.

Let us hope that Navy leadership will make every effort to avoid these pitfalls and will build the Navy SEALs not only in size and capabilities but in undiminished effectiveness and professionalism. The nation cannot afford less.

This book provides a unique, firsthand look at the Navy SEALs. Never before has the Navy allowed such a close-up look at the capabilities of our nation's naval special warriors. The reader will be able see SEALs and their specialized equipment in a way that was formerly available only to those with high-level security clearances. This book is the result of many years of effort on the part of highly skilled photographers who wanted our nation to have a better understanding of the dedicated men and women who help keep our families and our nation safe and secure. Our nation's SEAL teams have been shrouded in secrecy in the past for good reason. Now, however, for the first time, the SEALs and the thousands of dedicated Naval Special Warfare personnel who support them can be seen in action.

It is my hope that this book will help Americans better understand that the comfort and safety that they enjoy is, at least in part, due to the fact that some very brave and talented young men and women have been willing to dedicate themselves to a life of hardship and sacrifice in order to keep our country safe and free. Greg Mathieson and his team have traveled the globe and been with our nation's military forces on the land and on the sea and in the air. Greg has been in some of the nastiest and most dangerous places on earth, in war and peace—all to capture the images of the Navy SEALs at work and those who support them. He has done a superb job and brings great credit to all of the unsung heroes of Naval Special Warfare and the U.S. Navy SEALs.

John F. Lehman Jr.

INTRODUCTION

This project started back in 1987, at a time when Navy SEALs and Naval Special Warfare were mostly unknown and always unseen by the public.

At that time, *Life* magazine and *The New York Times Magazine* were interested in me doing a photo story. *Life* had managed to follow some Navy SEALs around in El Salvador, where they were advisors in 1981. Dave Gatley started covering BUD/S training—Basic Underwater Demolition/SEAL—in 1991, yet never got beyond that training. Getting access to a Special Operations Unit was not the easiest thing to do then, and nearly as impossible today, given the Global War on Terror. But we never gave up.

Letters were written, contacts made, meetings held, and favors cashed in. Little came of it, regardless of the coverage, restrictions promised, top name publications, and requestors. SEALs were too sensitive a subject and they wanted to remain behind that impenetrable wall of secrecy.

Ironically, at the time, one of the contributing writers of this book was then the Commander of Naval Special Warfare. I still have his letter to this day, saying that they were "always being tasked with higher priorities." It wasn't going to happen.

Then one day in 1993, the phones rang and calls went out to numerous news organizations. The Naval Special Warfare Command decided to clear their drawers of the many requests and have a "media photo day," a day in which all the requesting news organizations over the years could come out to Coronado, CA, visit, and take photos of planned events and of SEALs "cleared" to have their photos taken and do interviews. This, too, was not without restrictions. We needed to all stay together, getting the same photos and in each other's shots. That was all followed by our film having to be processed and reviewed that day by the Command's Public Affairs Officer before we could depart. In the end, we ended up with what peo-

ple thought the SEALs looked like and how they acted; guys coming out of the water, rebreather hoses in their mouths and weapons at the ready dripping with saltwater. The Hollywood version!

Over time, more and more access was allowed, but only to the same activities and locations. Different days, same pictures, which are the shots you see in numerous books on SEALs. The usual training at the water's edge carrying logs, getting wet and swimming under the watchful eye of the instructors culminating in the nighttime shots of "Hell Week." It was more "Hollywood" with everyone shooting the same photos at the same locations, just a different day of the year.

Much of this was to protect the identities of the real SEALs. You never saw who the instructors were behind those ubiquitous sunglasses that you didn't take photos of. Many of the students would go though BUD/S and pass the course, yet would undergo a physical change through training. The guy that showed up the first day would not be the same guy you might see years later with a beard and physique he never had before, like the high school freshman football player morphing into the pro football player years later. In effect, that was what really protected the identities of new recruits, in that it would be some time before they ever saw a real mission.

Finally, perseverance paid off. This book is the first of its kind. An authentic exclusive inside look at SEALs and the NSW community and its history. And, given the history of putting it together, probably the last allowed like this, given all that needed to be approved and attempted over and over again. At times, even the access and scenes shown for the first time in these pages would get approved, but the word didn't get through and it just didn't work right, due to weather, mission changes, or scheduling. But we never gave up.

One thing is for certain, none of what you are about to see would have been possible had it not been for Admiral

Joe Maguire, WARCOM Commander, Cdr. Greg Geisen, Command PAO, and my colleague, photographer Dave Gatley. All of whom I owe a great debt of thanks for their tolerance and patience in seeing this project through to the end. They all put up with my New York pushiness and attitude for almost three years. During that time, I learned to mellow out, a bit.

This book goes well beyond all the others, yet incorporates some of what has been seen before to be complete. It goes beyond the SEALs to the support staff and the men and women behind the scenes that make Naval Special Warfare and the SEALs what they are. It also shows never-before-seen documents that have been declassified for this project that show the beginnings of Navy SEALs and where the name came from. We go to the earliest days of Maritime Units of the OSS, which helped establish the need for amphibious guerrilla and counter-guerrilla operations, which led to today's SEALs.

For this project, we used a lot of specialized gear that we have also used to cover wars in Central America, Desert Shield/Storm, and the wars in Iraq and Afghanistan. Like the SEALs, we needed to be prepared for desert heat, arctic cold, and the sea. Our equipment included ballistic vests and helmets, GPS units, dive gear and waterproof items, cameras and cases of all shapes and sizes, state of the art night vision and infared lights, custom made adapters, and all the little things needed for life support, safety, and navigation. All were acquired at our expense.

We traveled the sea off Hawaii, the air over various states and nations, the land of freezing Alaska, and the heated dust storms of Iraq. Like the extraordinary men and women we accompanied, there were locations we cannot mention in highly classified rooms and centers that the public will never see outside of these pages. Most importantly, the SEALs themselves have never been seen in action, in war, and at peace as they are captured by our photos.

All the photos have been screened for security and shot under supervision. Many have been digitally altered for security purposes, having names, details, items, and some faces removed or changed that would otherwise threaten national security and personal security and breach biometric security as well. In most cases, we will not disclose the location of the shoots. If you look at the endpapers of this book you'll see the numerous security warnings and signs we encountered, always restricting photography and access. Many were surprised to see a camera in the location for the first time, making it much more time consuming and difficult for us to do this very special project.

We owe a special debt of gratitude and thanks to the people listed in the back of this book, from the President of the United States down to the unsung Sailors helping us get around. We are grateful to all the commands, SEAL operators, SWCC, and NSW staff, whose trust we had to earn every day before we clicked a photo. And a special thank you to the men of SEAL Team 3, who in the darkness of April 13, 2003, in Tikrit, a few hundred feet from Saddam Hussein's Palace, took out enemy fedayeen sneaking just feet away from my position while I was with an NBC News crew and the 3rd LAR of the U.S. Marines. They had our six.

We are still in awe of what we have seen, what we could photograph, and what we couldn't. Our country owes a great debt to the men and women of Naval Special Warfare, the SEALs, and the UDT before them who go silently into the night, around the globe, keeping us free and safe.

Many have made the ultimate sacrifice; we attended some of the funerals and ceremonies. They will always be remembered.

A special thank you to the Navy SEAL Foundation for all they do to help the families of NSW and the SEAL community, providing scholarships and help to the families of NSW in need. They need your support, so please visit them at www.NavySEALFoundation.org.

And most importantly, a special thank you to my wife, Maura, and our son, Greg Jr., who is currently serving our country in the U.S. military. They had to hear about "the book" for years and tolerate me, my travels, the piles of equipment, books, and files, and my grumbling when things were not going right. What's next?

"The only easy day was yesterday."

Greg E. Mathieson Sr.
Editor-in Chief and Photographer

OSS, Navy Combat Demolition Units, Underwater Demolition Teams, Scouts and Raiders

CDR (SEAL) TOM HAWKINS,
USN (RET)

CHAPTER 1

Navy Combat Demolition Units, Scouts and Raiders, Office of Strategic Services, Underwater Demolition Teams

Cdr. (SEAL) Tom Hawkins, USN (Ret.)

Foundations of Naval Special Warfare

A S THE UNITED STATES WAS PLUNGED INTO WORLD WAR II, YOUNG men from across the country enlisted or were drafted into the armed services. The war against Japan was raging throughout the Pacific, and Germany was raising havoc all over Europe and North Africa. This country was filled with a united sense of purpose.

It all started in November 1942 with the U.S. participation in Operation Torch, the invasion of North Africa, the first major Allied sea-air-land offensive action in the European theater during World War II.

It was in 1942 that training for assaults from the sea began, resulting in establishment of several amphibious training bases (ATBs). A major training base was located at Solomons, Maryland, at the confluence of the Patuxent River and Chesapeake Bay; another base was at Little Creek near Norfolk, Virginia, at the mouth of the Chesapeake Bay. In the early days of 1942, a joint training force made up of U.S. Army, Navy, and Marine Corps personnel was established to define and refine the art of amphibious warfare. From this early force evolved the Atlantic Fleet Amphibious Force, which developed tactics through a series of fleet landing exercises conducted in Chesapeake Bay. This is where the story of Naval Special Warfare (NSW) actually begins.

Several special naval units were formed at that time: naval combat demolition units (NCDUs), Scouts and Raiders, an Office of Strategic Services Maritime Unit (OSS MU), and the underwater demolition teams—soon to become legendary as the underwater demolition team (UDTs) of the Pacific Fleet. Of these units, only the UDTs survived after the war, when they remained organized within the Navy's amphibious force. In one fashion or another, however, all of these units contributed to the structure of today's U.S. Navy *SE*a, *A*ir, *L*and (SEAL) teams that would be formed some thirty years hence.

The Duke of Windsor, Governor of Bahamas (center white shirt), poses with Lt. Hugh McDevitt's (center front) Operational Swimmer Group II and squad of OSS operatives on the beaches of Burmuda, where the OSS did much of its mini-submersible training in the early 1940s during the war. (Photo: National Archives / NSW Publications, LLC)

First Demolitioneers

For most people, the term "underwater demolition" brings to mind the image of a swimmer placing explosives on an underwater obstacle. In the case of the first units, however, the term actually referred more to the explosives and shallow-water demolition capabilities themselves than to the action of placing them on underwater obstacles.

In September 1942 a small detachment of Sailors was picked for the first underwater demolition operation. Seventeen Navy salvage divers, led by Lt. Mark

UDT Team 21 with their welcome sign for the U.S. Marines on their arrival to Japan. (Photo: Courtesy of Tom Hawkins)

TOP, LEFT: *First Mate WOJG James H. Flynn (L) and 1st Lt. Walter L. Mess (R) were OSS Maritime Unit men, the forefathers of today's Special Boats. Both in the U.S. Army, they ran P-564, an 85-foot Air-Sea Rescue boat which was acquired for OSS service in SEAC and named the Jeanie after 1st Lt. Mess's wife. Having a hull of one-and-a-half inch plywood, the boat had been modified to quiet the engines so that they couldn't be heard over 10 feet away. The small boat could have a range of 800 miles, becoming a floating gas tank, storing thousands of gallons of 100/130 octane aviation gasoline on deck in 55-gallon drums. No one smoked on the boat. (Photo: Courtesy of Walter Mess)*

TOP, RIGHT: *Military ID card belonging to one of the first OSS Maritime Unit operators, 1st Lt. Walter Mess. During his service Lieutenant Mess would at times need to put on the uniform of a general or other senior officers while working for the OSS to get the mission done. (Photo: Greg E. Mathieson Sr. / NSW Publications, LLC)*

BOTTOM: *Army members of the Amphibious Scouts and Raiders (Joint) lift their inflatable boat to a carry position during a demonstration at their training at Amphibious Training Base, Fort Pierce, Florida, during 1943. (Photo: Courtesy of Tom Hawkins)*

Starkweather (senior in command) and Lt. James Darroch, reported from Hawaii to the ATB at Little Creek, where they began a cram course on underwater demolition methods, explosive cable cutting, and commando raiding techniques for a special mission in Operation Torch.

Their single mission in Torch was to destroy a boom and net blocking the seaward approach of the Wadi Sebou River in French Morocco. Removing it would allow the destroyer USS *Dallas* (DD-199) to move up the river, insert a group of Army Rangers, and cover them with its guns while they captured the Port Lyautey airfield. They operated at night from an open Higgins boat in thirty-foot seas and under direct enemy machine-gun fire. Several of the men were badly injured in the rough seas, but they accomplished their task on a second attempt. The mission was so demanding and critical to the success of the invasion that every demolition man in the operation was awarded the Navy Cross.

Atlantic Scouts and Raiders

It quickly became apparent in the summer of 1942 that a pre-assault reconnaissance and beach-marking capability were needed as well. A group of chief petty officers stationed in Norfolk, Virginia, responded to a request for volunteers for a new program described only as "amphibious commandos." In May 1942, they were sent to ATB Solomons, Maryland, for training in landing-craft operations. The following August, they returned to Norfolk and Little Creek, where they were combined with Army Raider–trained soldiers to form the Amphibious Scouts and Raiders (Joint), under the command of Army first lieutenant Lloyd E. Peddcord Jr. and Navy ensign John Bell, who served as his executive officer. Scouts and Raiders were trained to operate at night, reconnoitering and identifying an objective beach, marking it prior to H-hour (the time designated for the operation to begin), and then guiding assault waves to the correct landing sites.

Commissioned in October 1942, this group was first introduced into combat during Operation Torch in November of that year. During one mission Army scouts under Lt. Willard G. Duckworth launched kayaks from the submarine USS *Barb* in the first U.S. submarine–based operation of World War II involving specially trained reconnaissance personnel. Their mission was to paddle to a location off the

TOP, LEFT: *The "Chariot," an underwater submersible used by the Italian frogmen. After they changed sides during the war, Italian operatives worked with the Allies. (Photo: Courtesy of the Lambertsen Collection)*

TOP, RIGHT: *Lt. John E. Babb, USN and CPO Herman J. Becker of the OSS Maritime Unit using a British kayak to reach the P-564 after taking beach samples on Foul Island during Operation Boston in the Arakan on February 21, 1945. (Photo: Courtesy of Walter Mess)*

BARREL EXTENSIONS

SIGHT

SAFETY CATCH

CAP

DART

COMPRESSION CHAMBER

TRIGGER

SLIDING CATCH

RAMROD

GAS CYLINDER

SECRET

LEFT: *A top secret dart gun developed by the OSS's Research and Development Division, which fired a plastic dart with an effective range of 150 feet using compressed gas. (Photo: National Archives / NSW Publications, LLC)*

Jette Principal at Safi, Morocco, under cover of darkness to guide the destroyers USS *Cole* (DD-155) and USS *Bernadou* (DD-153) into the harbor.

Upon completion of the campaign in North Africa, Scout and Raider training was shifted to ATB Fort Pierce, Florida. Resources were shifted to a series of planned amphibious landings in the Mediterranean. The first, Operation Husky—the invasion of Sicily—was the start of the Allies' assault on German-occupied Europe. The British prime minister, Winston Churchill, described Sicily and Italy as "the soft underbelly" of Europe. Scout and Raider personnel already in Europe continued as an essential part of amphibious operations at Sicily and Italy and later at Normandy on the north coast of France and finally in southern France.

Later, in preparation for Operation Overlord—the planned landing at Normandy—the Scout and Raider personnel completed extensive training with British commandos, including escape and evasion, submersible operations, and other amphibious commando proficiencies. Several of the men conducted pre-assault reconnaissance at Normandy several weeks before the landing, paddling ashore at night in kayaks to collect beach samples (from which planners could determine whether heavy equipment could land).

After D-Day, on 6 June 1944, and the invasion of southern France that August, the need for Scouts and Raiders in Europe ceased; no other amphibious operations were envisioned in that theater. Many of the men returned to Fort Pierce to serve as instructors at the Scout and Raider school. Soon, because similar functions already were being performed in the Pacific by the newly formed UDTs, Army personnel were returned to their parent units, and many Navy men were reassigned to sea duty or given the opportunity to join the Pacific units.

PACIFIC SCOUTS AND RAIDERS

A second and lesser-known group of Scouts and Raiders, code-named Special Services Unit One (SSU-1), was established on 7 July 1943, in the Pacific as a joint and combined (that is, international) force, with personnel from Australia and the U.S. Army, Navy, and Marine Corps. By 18 July, the majority of the group was at Cairns Base to begin training in physical education, martial arts, hand-to-hand combat, mapmaking, rubber craft operation, jungle survival training, Pidgin English, underwater coral formations and sea creature recognition, and panoramic sketching to identify precise locations. About 28 August of that year the unit moved to a new base at Fergusson Island, off the D'Entrecasteaux Islands, New Guinea. Their first mission, in September, was at Finschafen, New Guinea. Later operations were carried out at Gasmata, Arawe, Cape Gloucester, and the eastern and southern coasts of New Britain (an island in New Guinea), all without any loss of personnel. The focus of this organization was much different from the focus of their Atlantic counterparts, who concentrated only on their amphibious missions. SSU-1 personnel collected intelligence, and trained and operated with indigenous personnel, conducting many guerrilla-warfare missions. They were later designated the 7th

ABOVE: *Scouts and Raiders, shown here in Salerno Bay, Italy, used kayaks to locate probable landing sites for Allied invasions. (Photo: Courtesy of the National Navy UDT - SEAL Museum)*

LEFT: *Special Services Unit #1 personnel formed as a joint reconnaissance group for Sansapor mission during 27–30 June 1944. Standing (l-r) Sgt. Heinnich, Sgt. Alan Lumingkewas, Sgt. Herman S. Chanley, two native scouts, COX Cal Byrd. Kneeling: Lt. (j.g.) Don Root, Maj. W.M. Chance, Lt. George Thompson (Team Leader), Lt.Col. C. G. Atkinson, Maj. F. M. Rawolle (nonparticipant). (Photo: Courtesy of Tom Hawkins)*

Amphibious Scouts and organized under staff intelligence sections, somewhat along the lines of the Atlantic Scouts and Raiders, and operating much the same way as the UDTs.

CHINA SCOUTS AND RAIDERS

Some Scout and Raider personnel returning from Europe were given special assignment with the U.S. Naval Group in China, headed by Capt. Milton "Mary" Miles. He, along with a Chinese counterpart, set up the Sino-American Cooperative Organization (SACO) for the training, equipping, and operating of guerrilla forces against Japanese occupation forces.

Pontoon boat fashioned by Scout Raider personnel from a French seaplane and used in the invasion of southern France. Circa World War II. (Photo: Courtesy of the National Navy UDT - SEAL Museum)

Scout and Raider personnel moving over the beach at Fort Pierce, Florida, back on December 10, 1943. (Photo: Courtesy of the National Navy UDT SEAL Museum)

To help bolster the work of SACO, Adm. Ernest J. King—who was both chief of the U.S. Fleet and chief of naval operations (CNO)—ordered that 120 officers and 900 men be trained for "Amphibious Roger" at the Scout and Raider School at Fort Pierce. Amphibious Roger was a cover name for the training of Navy personnel for raiding operations along the Yangtze River. Many of these men never made it to China before the war ended. Those who did, however, were used in a very dramatic way, far different from what their counterparts experienced in Europe: they trained Chinese guerrilla forces and conducted reconnaissance operations with them until the end of the war. Their primary mission was to locate and survey prospective landing beaches for a potential invasion of the China mainland and to provide weather reports for the fleet. They were frequently referred to as the "Rice Paddy Navy."

Naval Combat Demolition Units

On 6 May 1943, Admiral King issued the first orders for the organization of clearance units. Men were to be provided for "a present urgent requirement" of the Atlantic Fleet Amphibious Force; experimental work and training of permanent naval demolition units for assignment to other amphibious forces was the first order of business.

The first unit formed for naval combat demolition began with a group of volunteers from the Dynamiting and Demolition School at Camp Peary, near Williamsburg, Virginia. They were sent to ATB Solomons, where they were joined by other demolition men to form a twenty-one-man unit led by Lt. Fred Wise of the Navy Seabees (construction battalions). These men were given an intensive course in blowing channels through sandbars with explosive hose, and in placing explosive charges on underwater obstacles while working from rubber boats.

The initial operation for these men was to open channels through Sicily beaches in Operation Husky. On the morning of 10 July 1943, operations began. Finding no natural or artificial obstacles, for the next two days the men joined with Army engineers salvaging stranded boats, buoying channels through sandbars, and surveying beaches.

Many of the men of this first group remained in naval combat demolition after Husky, proceeding to Fort Pierce to serve as instructors for the tougher training that now resulted from Admiral King's directive. There they joined preparations for the still-secret cross-channel invasion of Europe at Normandy, where intelligence indicated that the Germans were placing extensive obstacles on the beaches.

On 7 May 1943, also in response to Admiral King's directive, Lt. Cdr. Draper Kauffman was ordered to set up a school that would formally train volunteers to eliminate obstacles on enemy-held beaches prior to an invasion. Kauffman had recently organized the Navy Bomb Disposal School in Washington, DC, and he brought with him several of his officers to help develop the new school.

In June 1943, the NCDU training school was established at Fort Pierce, and Lieutenant Commander Kauffman began assembling volunteers for "hazardous, prolonged, and distant duty" in what would be called NCDUs. In addition to the officers from the Bomb and Mine Disposal School, a group of Seabees from the Navy Civil Engineering Corps, both officers and enlisted men, came from Camp

TOP: *Naval Combat Demolition Unit (NCDU) trainees conduct rock portage operations during training at Fort Pierce, Florida, during 1943. The same training event is still accomplished by SEALs today. (Photo: Courtesy of Tom Hawkins)*

BOTTOM: *Men from Naval Combat Demolition Units #2 and #3. Front: (l-r) S2c James D. Sandy (NCDU #3), GM2c John N. Wilhide Jr. (NCDU #2), and S2c William L. Dawson (NCDU #2). Back: GM2c Harrison Q. Eskridge (NCDU #3), S2c Dillard E. Williams (NCDU #2), and S1c S. Pahdopony (NCDU #3). (Photo: Courtesy of Tom Hawkins)*

Peary to fill the first training classes. Each NCDU comprised one officer and five men in a single boat crew.

Area "E" at Camp Peary was subsequently established as a training base for selected NCDU volunteers. Naval demolition training there lasted for six weeks, after which men were moved to Fort Pierce for advanced NCDU training. This training pipeline extended from the early summer of 1943, through the spring of 1944.

In July 1943, the first class began training. The men called the intense second week "the week from hell." Lieutenant Commander Kauffman and his officers went through this intensive training beside the first enlisted trainees, establishing a precedent that still holds today—that officers and enlisted men demonstrate the same abilities and endure the same hardships. (Hell Week remains an essential part of SEAL basic training today.) By the end of Fort Pierce training, 65 to 75 percent of the trainees had dropped out, an overall attrition rate much as it is today. In this period Lieutenant Commander Kauffman earned his later reputation as the "father of demolition."

In September 1943, after arduous training, with primary emphasis on demolition of submerged beach obstacles, the first NCDU class graduated. Seven units were dispersed to the Third Fleet and Fifth Fleet in the Pacific, three units went to the Eighth Fleet in the Mediterranean, and one unit went to the British Fleet. The second class graduated in November, and most of these units went to England.

The first NCDU deployed for duty was from the first class; it left in August 1943, before the class actually graduated. Under Lt. (jg) Edwin Williams, it joined the assault on the Aleutian Islands but saw no action—the Japanese had already fled. The men were sent to Hawaii and became a part of UDT-1 and UDT-2, which were organized the following November.

NCDU-4, under WO Ward Cartree, and NCDU-5, under WO Ben Morris, left Fort Pierce on 8 September 1943, en route to the South Pacific. On 15 February 1944, both NCDUs participated in landings with SSU-1 at Green Island off New Guinea, between the islands of New Ireland and Bougainville.

BROHL   STEARNS   BUELL   WHITEHOUSE ADAMS STRICKLAND

NCDU-2, under Lt. (jg) Frank Kaine, and NCDU-3, under Lt. (jg) Lloyd Ande, were the first to arrive in the southwest Pacific, seeing action at the Admiralty Islands in March 1944. They were later joined by NCDU-19, NCDU-20, NCDU-21, and, after Normandy, by NCDU-24. These NCDUs served with the 7th Amphibious Force throughout the war, clearing boat channels from Biak to Borneo. These were the only groups that remained NCDUs for the war's duration; all others were re-formed into the Pacific UDTs or went to Europe.

By April 1944, thirty-four NCDUs had collected in England in preparation for Operation Overlord. Each was augmented with three Navy seamen brought from Scotland; the resulting eight-man NCDUs were integrated with Army combat engineers to form thirteen-man gap assault teams.

On D-Day, NCDUs at Omaha Beach led by Lt. Cdr. Joseph Gibbons cleared eight complete gaps and two partial gaps in the German defenses. These NCDUs suffered thirty-one killed and sixty wounded—a casualty rate of 52 pecent. NCDUs at Utah Beach, under Lt. Cdr. Herbert Peterson, met less-intense enemy fire. They cleared seven hundred yards of beach in two hours, and another nine hundred yards by the afternoon. NCDUs at Utah Beach suffered six killed and eleven wounded.

D-Day remains the single bloodiest day in the history of NSW, although not one assault demolitioneer was lost to improper handling of explosives. The NCDUs at Omaha were awarded the Presidential Unit Citation, one of only three presented for Normandy. The men at Utah Beach earned the only Navy Unit Commendation awarded for Operation Overlord.

Several of the NCDUs from Utah Beach, augmented with new units from Fort Pierce, participated at the landing in southern France, first code-named Anvil and later Dragoon. Planned originally as a simultaneous complement to Overlord, the assault actually occurred more than two months later, on 15 August, making it appear almost an afterthought to the main offensive in northern Europe. Yet the success of Anvil, the ensuing captures of the great southern French ports of Toulon and Marseilles, and the subsequent drive north up the Rhone River valley to Lyon and Dijon, were ultimately to provide critical support to the armies finally moving east from the Normandy beachhead toward the German border.

Though the NCDUs contributed greatly to the war in Europe, they were over-

shadowed by the Pacific UDTs. Indeed, some histories have it that UDTs performed at Normandy and in southern France. Actually, however, during World War II the UDTs operated only in the Pacific.

Moreover, NCDU men have often been referred to as "frogmen." But in those early days swimming was only a test of fitness and a method of physical training. The men wore full combat dress and were taught to wade ashore through the surf from rubber boats carrying explosives to exposed or partially submerged obstacles during predawn hours.

The Office of Strategic Services Maritime Unit

One of the most influential World War II forerunners of the UDTs and, subsequently, SEAL teams, was a component of the OSS. Many OSS capabilities were later adopted by the postwar UDTs, and many of the same capabilities can still be found in today's SEAL teams.

On 20 January 1943, a Marine section was established within the special operations branch of OSS with responsibility for planning covert infiltration operations from the sea. On 10 June, that section was taken from the special operations branch and reorganized as the MU, with branch status in its own right. Its responsibilities included planning and coordinating the clandestine infiltration of agents, supplying resistance groups, engaging in maritime sabotage, and developing special equipment for operations from the sea. The OSS MU was to pioneer U.S. capabilities in maritime sabotage through use of special boat infiltration operations and tactical combat, including swimming and diving using flexible swim fins and face masks, closed-circuit diving equipment, submersible vehicles, and limpet mines.

ABOVE: Present day Challenge coin of the OSS (Office of Strategic Services). (front) (Photo: Dave Gatley)

RIGHT, BOTTOM: "The Toy I" OSS SDV prototype shell being constructed in August of 1943. (Courtesy of the Lambertsen Collection)

BELOW: OSS Maritime Unit, Little Poison. (Photo: National Archives / NSW Publications, LLC)

Development of U.S. maritime sabotage capabilities began in August 1942, at Area "D," a classified OSS training base on the Maryland side of the Potomac River, across from today's Marine Corps base in Quantico, Virginia. Presumably because the British had already undertaken such capabilities, the head of OSS, Maj. Gen. William J. "Wild Bill" Donovan (Ret.), acquired the services of Royal Navy commander Herbert G. A. Woolley, DSC (Distinguished Service Cross) to direct the maritime group.

Throughout that autumn the men trained in small-boat operations and experi-

REPORT ON RAFT, SUBMERSIBLE

(DAVY'S LOCKER)

INTRODUCTION

R & D was requested by MU to build a submersible storage raft for underwater storage of a radio set and stores for an agent. Sketches of a proposed raft were submitted, and it was suggested that R & D follow the design outlined therein. The facilities of the Experimental Diving Unit at the Washington Navy Yard were made available for the work, and the cooperation of Captain O. K. O'Daniel, USN and Lieutenant Commander J. E. Morgan, USNR was secured. During the course of the work it became apparent that the original design as submitted to R & D would not have the desired characteristics, and a new one was made providing for the same volume of wet and dry storage as the original. A raft has been completed according to this design, and shows the desired characteristics. It is described herein.

DISCUSSION

In the early stages of the design it became necessary to determine the most desirable system for submerging and surfacing the raft. Four flotation chambers were necessary to provide a satisfactory degree of longitudinal and transverse stability, and the use of compressed air seemed to be the most logical means of blowing the chambers when it was desired to surface the raft. This required a piping system and manifold to get the air from the storage cylinders to the flotation chambers through the necessary valves. Non-return valves were required in each high pressure line to prevent the shifting of air from one flotation chamber to another and destroying the stability of the raft. The use of a hand pump by the operator was suggested but proved not to be practical because of the volume and pressure of air required to surface the raft. In addition, the hand pump would have to work through the high pressure lines, as they are the only lines connecting the four flotation chambers. These lines pass through a reducing block to cut the pressure down from that in the storage cylinders. Pump pressure of the order of 150-200 psi would be required to pump air through this block for surfacing the raft in any reasonably time. The volume of air required for surfacing from 30 feet is approximately 40 cubic feet.

The use of a manifolded exhaust system was tried, but trouble developed in it because of water entering the exhaust lines and blocking them. An early model had the exhaust manifolds made of 3/4" pipe, and is shown in the illustrations. The final model is of identical appearance except that the exhaust piping has been eliminated and a 1/2" valve has been placed near the end of each flotation chamber.

The final design is the result of extensive study and experiment, and the emphasis was placed on simplicity and ease of construction. Various types of special valves were suggested for surfacing the device by remote control; some of these refinements can be applied to future rafts if the need for them arises.

(76826)   -1-

DESCRIPTION

The overall length of the raft is 11 feet 2 inches, its width 7 feet 6 inches, and its height 4 feet 6 inches without the mast. Its weight empty is approximately 900 pounds and its maximum load is 400 pounds excluding two men. This load assumes storage in the dry storage compartments or high density wet storage loads; much greater loads can be carried in wet storage if the load density is approximately that of water. For transportation, the raft breaks down into sections. The largest section is 11 feet 2 inches long and of circular cross section 21 inches in diameter, weighing approximately 275 pounds. By breaking down in this fashion, the raft can pass through a standard submarine hatch. The raft consists of two pontoons which support a framework and deck between them. In the center of the deck and extending through it are the dry storage compartments, which are cylindrical cans 14 inches in diameter and 4 feet long. The wet storage compartments are located in the middle of each pontoon, between the flotation chambers which are at the ends of the pontoons. Each wet storage compartment is of square cross section, and they have a combined volume of approximately 7.0 cubic feet. The walls of the wet storage compartments are expanded metal on a structural steel framework. The doors of the wet storage compartments open upward, and are nearly flush with the deck when closed.

The flotation chambers each have a 4 inch hole in the bottom for the entrance and expulsion of water. When afloat the chambers are full of air. When it is desired to submerge the raft, the air is allowed to escape from the flotation chambers by opening four valves, one of which is located near the nose of each flotation chamber. When it is desired to surface the raft, the four flotation chamber valves are closed, and the high pressure valve opened. This valve is located near the center of the deck. This allows air or CO_2, whichever is being used, to come from the storage cylinders under the deck and to flow to the flotation chambers. This gas is at high pressure; it forces the water out of the chambers and the raft comes to the surface. Two 110 cubic foot cylinders are used for gas storage, connected in parallel to a manifold. When air is used, the raft may be surfaced 10 times from ten feet or 6 times from thirty feet if the storage cylinders are pumped to an initial pressure of 2200 psi. If CO_2 is used the capacity is 20 blows from 10 feet or 12 blows from thirty feet. If additional blows are deemed necessary, additional gas cylinders can be lashed to the raft without affecting its loading; the cylinders are nearly of neutral buoyancy in water.

In the design of the raft it was decided to use as many standard parts as possible. This was done, and all the components were obtainable in U.S. Navy yards throughout the world. The flotation chambers are exercise heads from 21 inch torpedoes; the dry storage compartments are powder cans for 14 inch guns; other components are either standard items or ones that can be readily fabricated from standard parts. A complete set of drawings and a bill of materials have been prepared, and construction of the raft in other Navy yards should be possible with a minimum of time and effort.

The raft is equipped with a transom for the use of an outboard motor (gasoline or electric) and also with a mast and small sail that may be lashed to the deck when not in use. It can also be paddled. It should be pointed out that the device was not intended for use as a boat, and that propelling machinery was desired only to get it to its point of operation.

(76826)   -2-

RADIO

One of the primary functions of the raft is to act as a base for communications and radio station. R & D was referred to Communications Branch for description of the radio equipment, and this contact was made. The TR-1 was the set recommended, and one complete radio set was obtained for use in planning the raft. The dry storage compartments were fitted with special brass racks for use with the equipment. The power supply, transmitter, and receiver fit into one rack, while the engine-generator set fits into the other. In the stored position, the racks fold down into the storage compartments, and in the operating position they extend above the top of the storage compartments and hold the radio components securely in place. The storage batteries for the radio are contained in the bottom of the dry storage compartments and a cabling schedule has been worked out for the rapid interconnection of the units. A representative of Communications Branch saw and approved the way in which the equipment was installed. Several types of antennas may be used; for short distances (100-200 miles) an insulated wire may be placed on the surface of the water and used for an antenna. There are many points at which a whip antenna may be attached to the raft, and for maximum range a balloon may be used for carrying a wire aloft for an antenna. A hydrogen cylinder is provided for inflating a balloon, and several types of balloons were available in OSS and the Army. There is room for a small amount of gear in addition to the radio in the dry storage compartments.

TESTS

The raft has been subjected to an extensive series of tests, and performed well in all of them. It was found that the tests bore out the calculations in the fact that it cannot capsize. The center of buoyancy is raised above the center of gravity by the presence of the dry storage compartments; thus the raft's only stable position is that in which the dry storage compartments are on top. The deck can assume an angle of about 45° under the worst possible conditions (one pair of flotation chambers flooded and the other pair dry), but the raft will not capsize. The position of the exhaust valves is such that the raft stabilizes itself while being submerged. Should one flotation chamber fill too rapidly, it sinks a little and the shift of the water level inside the flotation chamber shuts off the exhaust port so that no more air can escape. Thus the raft is stabilized, although some oscillations may occur. They are slow oscillations however, and the raft is easily controlled by the operator at all times.

The dry storage compartments have been pressure tested to a depth of 60 feet and no leakage or crushing occurred. This is twice the anticipated maximum operating depth of the raft. The dry storage compartments are the only components of the raft that would be subject to crushing by water pressure if the raft were attached to the exterior of a submarine for transportation. Transportation of this type could be used with the raft completely assembled if the dry storage compartments were left open and not used while in transit. The only other sealed components of the raft are the gas storage cylinders which operate at high pressure (2200 psi) and they will withstand any pressure which will be encountered at the operational depths of submarines.

(76826)   -3-

SECRET documents of the Office of Strategic Services, Maritime Unit, detailing the Submersible Raft, "Davy's Locker," one of the first known submersible vehicles used in maritime underwater special operations in the United States. (Photo: National Archives / NSW Publications, LLC)

ABOVE: *"Davy's Locker" was an OSS SECRET submersible storage raft used for underwater storage of a radio set and stores for an agent. The raft was designed to submerge and resurface through a working of valves, compression chambers, and compressed air. It submerged to a working depth of 30 feet. (Photo: National Archives / NSW Publications, LLC)*

UNDERWATER
OPERATIONS

PREPARED FOR THE
MARITIME UNIT

●

BY THE PRESENTATION DIVISION
FIELD PHOTOGRAPHIC BRANCH
OFFICE OF STRATEGIC SERVICES

●

December 1943

The entire equipment at the present time allows a trained swimmer to stay under water about an hour and a half, and to swim at least a mile. A trained man can work as deep as 50 feet, and has no connections with the surface. There are no tell-tale bubbles.

To eliminate any excess air pressure in the face piece, the swimmer merely squeezes the right tube, presses up the spit cock, and blows.

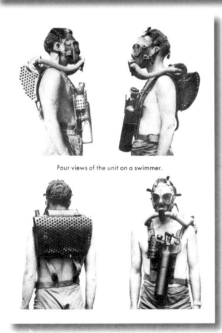

Four views of the unit on a swimmer.

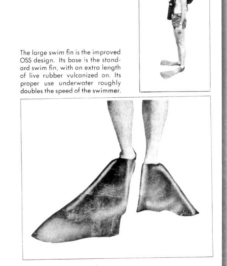

The large swim fin is the improved OSS design. Its base is the standard swim fin, with an extra length of live rubber vulcanized on. Its proper use underwater roughly doubles the speed of the swimmer.

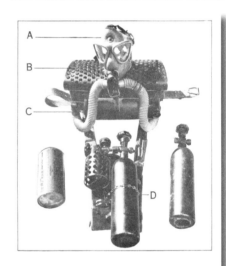

The Lambertsen Unit is a completely self-contained breathing device. Cylinder D contains the oxygen which flows into the rubber lung B. It then passes to the face piece A, where it is breathed by the swimmer. The exhaled air is passed through the canister of lime C, which absorbs the carbon dioxide. A new face piece, affording improved vision, is in process of manufacture, and will soon be standard on all units. An extra canister of lime and cylinder of oxygen are shown.

RIGHT: *The crew of OSS Maritime Unit, boat P-564, the Jeanie, named after the skipper's wife. Back (l-r) Master Sgt. Ear L. Williams, Cpl. Joseph P. Jones, Staff Sgt. Lester H. Linville, T/5 Joseph E. Viola. Front (l-r) Sgt. Willard R. Floyd, T/Sgt. Harry F. Johnson, 2nd Lt. John A Swayze, 1st Lt. Walter L. Mess (Skipper), WOJG James H. Flynn (First Mate), Sgt. Benjamin W. Brunaugh, T/Sgt. Lous K. Woodland, and Cpl. Robert L. Philpott. Their mission was to insert and recover small contingents of OSS swimmers, operators, and agents. (Photo: Courtesy of the Walter L. Mess / USASOC History Office)*

SECRET · 1

UNDERWATER OPERATIONS

The latest model of the two-man kayak. With a rubberized canvas hull, and a spray cover snapping around the cockpit, it weighs only 104 pounds, and is 16 1-2 feet long. Its beam is 34 inches, and depth 13 inches. The cockpit is 7 feet by 19 inches, the forward deck 5 feet 5 inches and the after deck 4 feet 2 inches.

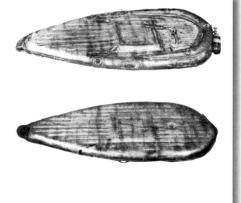

The two man surfboard presents a low silhouette on the water. Measuring 10 1-2 feet x 3 feet 7 1-2 inches, it can carry two men and their entire equipment, or about 900 pounds. A 3-4 horsepower motor can drive it at 5 or 6 knots.

The fabric hull weighs 52 pounds, and is carried in its own pack. The fabric has a tearing strength of several hundred pounds per square inch. Punctures will not run, and can easily be repaired with rubber patches and cement. The entire boat can be put together by two trained men in less than five minutes.

mented with the Lambertsen amphibious respiratory unit (LARU). The LARU was a revolutionary pure-oxygen closed-circuit underwater breathing apparatus (UBA) adapted for underwater diving and mobility. It was the invention of Dr. Christian J. Lambertsen, a medical student at the University of Pennsylvania, who in 1947, would introduce the same combat diving capabilities to the postwar UDTs. In 1942, a reserve U.S. Army Medical Corps captain, Dr. Lambertsen was recruited by OSS to integrate a program of underwater operations, including tactics, navigation, demolition, and communications. He conceived the missions, trained the operators, and designed or coordinated the design of most of the early hardware used by this first generation of U.S. combat divers. He is recognized today as the "father of U.S. combat diving."

Four swimmer groups originated from the OSS diver-training program. LARU-1 and LARU-2 were the initial units fielded, and they stayed together from 12 January through 22 June 1944. They were deployed to England, where they trained

ABOVE: *OSS Maritime Unit Operational Swimmer Group at their training base in the Caribbean during World War II. (Photo: Courtesy of the Lambertsen Collection)*

BELOW: *An OSS Maritime Swimmer wearing a Model 10 LARU, training to breach anti-submarine nets at the Guantanamo Bay, Cuba, in 1944. (Photo: Courtesy of the Lambertsen Collection)*

to infiltrate enemy harbors along the coast of France with the aim of destroying shipping and U-boat berthing pens. Never committed operationally, they later returned to the United States to help form Operational Support Groups One and Two (OSG-1 and OSG-2). These two operations support groups started training in November 1943, at Camp Pendleton, California, but were moved to Catalina Island off the coast of southern California in January 1944, and finally to warmer waters in the Bahamas in March.

TOP, LEFT: *OSS diver Donald Fulton, USCGR with an inflatable boat on the beach of Ceylon, as part of Operational Swimmer Group II (Group B). (Photo: Courtesy of the Lambertsen Collection)*

TOP, RIGHT: *USCG Lt. John Booth wearing the Lambertsen Amphibious Respiratory Unit (LARU). (Photo: Courtesy of the Lambertsen Collection)*

CENTER, LEFT AND RIGHT: *OSS Maritime Operational Swimmer Group member John Booth wearing the Lambertsen Amphibious Respiratory Unit (LARU) and full face mask during training operations in Florida during World War II. (Photo: Courtesy of the Lambertsen Collection)*

LEFT: *Members of the OSS Maritime Unit (l-r) GM3c Gordon "Salty" Soltau, USNR; MoMM2c Robert Talmadge, USCGR; and COX Gene Ward, USCGR, who were members of the initial Operational Swimmer Group (OSG) deployed as L-Unit in January 1944 to England, retrained with OSG III in the Bahamas during October 1944, and deployed to Ceylon, OSS Detachment 101 Southeast Asia Command (SEAC), in January 1945. The photograph was taken during preparation for SEAC operations in Burma. (Photo: Courtesy of Tom Hawkins)*

TOP: *OSS Maritime operatives wearing Dr. Lambertsen's rebreather unit, known as the LARU (Lambertsen Amphibious Respiratory Unit), Mark II, while manuvering on the two-man surfboard/motorized mattress which was also known as the "Water Lilly." (Photo: Courtesy of Tom Hawkins)*

CENTER, LEFT: *What looks like a power drill attached to a wet cell battery (under the flap) was the power source for moving and steering the two-man surfboard/motorized mattress. (Photo: National Archives / NSW Publications, LLC)*

CENTER, RIGHT: *The battery compartment of the two-man surfboard/motorized mattress. (Photo: National Archives / NSW Publications, LLC)*

BOTTOM: *What was referred to as a two-man surfboard or motorized mattress in the OSS Maritime manual was basically an inflatable raft used by OSS agents to insert into a shoreline. (Photo: National Archives / NSW Publications LLC)*

BELOW: *The OSS service pin was presented by the Veterans of the OSS, the predecessor to today's OSS Society, at a ceremony at the Central Intelligence Agency to members of the Office of Strategic Services who served during World War II. This one was presented to Walter Mess for his years of service in the OSS Maritime Units. (Photo: Greg E. Mathieson Sr. / NSW Publications, LLC)*

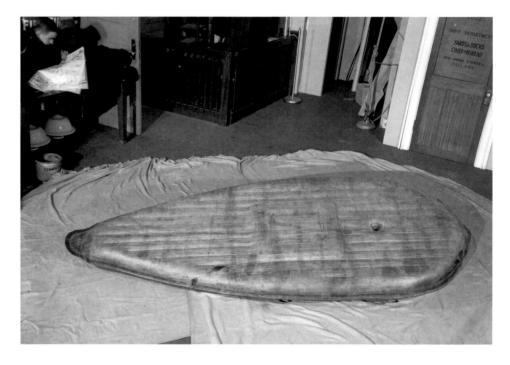

In July 1944, OSG-1 was loaned to the U.S. Navy and became the nucleus of UDT-10 in the Pacific. Five men from this group and several UDT men from Maui were assigned a special mission, the first UDT submarine NSW mission during the war. This noteworthy operation was conducted from USS *Burrfish* (SS-312) at the island of Yap in the Caroline Islands. Three members of the special mission group were captured and later killed by their Japanese captors, and their bodies

were never recovered: CPO Howard "Red" Roeder (UDT), PO Bob Black (OSS), and PO John MacMahon (OSS).

In addition to combat diving, the OSS MU developed capabilities in small-boat operations and eventually set up clandestine boat infiltrations in the Mediterranean. This was first accomplished by Lt. Jack Taylor (Navy), who acquired caïques, small indigenous wooden-hulled vessels with auxiliary sails, manned by Greek partisans and set up using partisan personnel. During the summer of 1943, Lieutenant Taylor conducted more than fourteen infiltration operations, some of them enormously successful, onto the hostile shores of Corfu, Yugoslavia, and Albania.

In December 1944, the MU was sent to the U.S. Southeast Asia Command (SEAC) and assigned to OSS Detachment (Det) 404 in Kandy, Ceylon. Here the MU trained for and conducted operations in Arakan (now named Rakhine State), an area on the western Burma coast, from December 1944 to 15 June 1945. Operations included boat infiltrations and reconnaissance operations by OSG-2 along the beaches and waterways. During the same period the swimmers trained intensively for maritime special operations in preparation for the invasion of Japan, which never happened because of President Truman's decision to use nuclear bombs.

Soon after the war, on 1 October 1945, the MU, along with the remainder of the OSS, was abolished. Thanks to Dr. Lambertsen, the MU's capabilities survived and would be resurrected two years later in the Navy's UDTs.

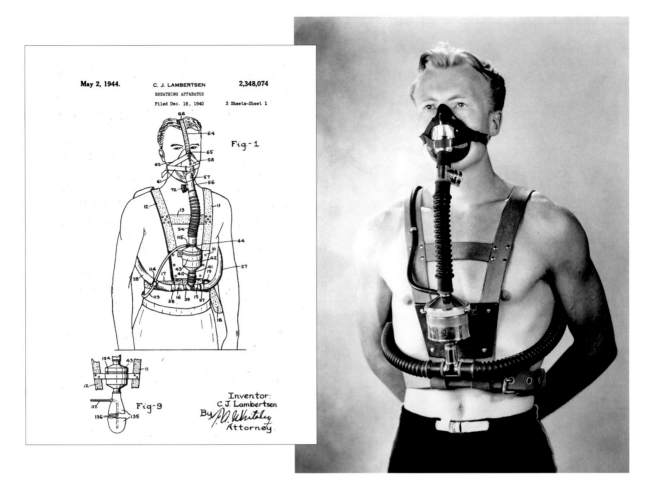

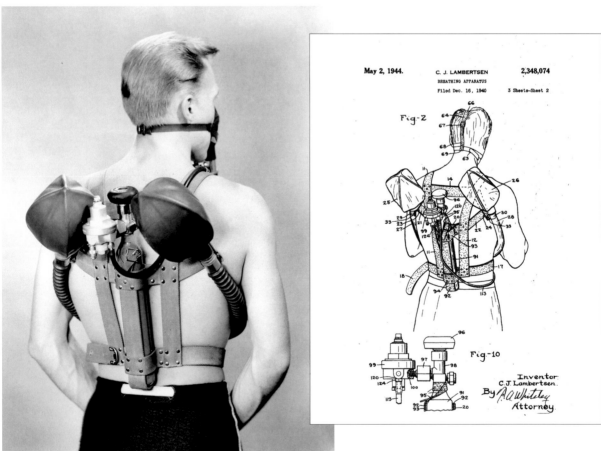

Christian Lambertsen (accompanied by U.S. Patent drawing) models his invention of the the Lambertsen Amphibious Respiratory Unit (LARU) Mark I in 1940. The first underwater rebreather device allowing a diver to move about without producing breathing bubbles. (Photo: USPTO / NSW Publications, LLC)

LEFT AND ABOVE: *An OSS motorized canoe on the beaches of an OSS Maritime Unit training site near San Diego, California. (Photo: National Archives / NSW Publications, LLC)*

LEFT: *An OSS motorized canoe being shown to a group of U.S. Marines at an OSS California training base not far from San Diego. (Photo: National Archives / NSW Publications, LLC)*

UNDERWATER DEMOLITION TEAMS IN THE PACIFIC

During the Tarawa landing at the Gilbert Islands on 22 November 1943, a submerged reef caused amphibious landing craft to founder far offshore, resulting in the loss of hundreds of U.S. Marines from enemy fire and drowning. After that experience, Adm. Kelley Turner, commander of the 5th Amphibious Force, directed that thirty officers and 150 enlisted men be moved to Waimanalo

ATB (on the "big island" of Hawaii) to form the nucleus of a reconnaissance and demolition-training program. It was there that the UDTs of the Pacific were born.

This first UDT group became UDT-1 and UDT-2, provisional UDTs with strengths of about fourteen officers and seventy enlisted men each. UDT-1 was commanded by Cdr. Edward D. Brewster and UDT-2 by Lt. Cdr. John T. Koehler. These first UDT men came from volunteers throughout the fleet: Navy and Marine Corps personnel, mainly Seabees, or demolition-trained engineers from the Army and Marine Corps. They saw their first action on 31 January 1944, in the attacks on Kwajalein and Roy-Namur during Operation Flintlock in the Marshall Islands. Because of the lesson of Tarawa, heavy emphasis was placed on pre-assault recon-

naissance and demolition of natural and man-made obstacles as necessary before Marine Corps landing craft came ashore.

Following Flintlock, the UDT men returned to Hawaii in February 1944, and moved to the island of Maui, where Lieutenant Commander Koehler was ordered to establish a naval combat demolition training and experimental base on a beach near the Kamaole ATB. The new UDT training base would substantially increase the emphasis on swimming. Army and Marine Corps personnel were returned to their parent organizations. With rare exception, all subsequent UDTs were formed from naval personnel, primarily Seabee men trained at the NCDU School at Fort Pierce.

It became clear during Operation Flintlock that each UDT should have its own ship to avoid delays that always seemed to happen when personnel were assembled for an assault operation. Destroyer-type ships were converted to amphibious

personnel destroyers (APDs) that carried UDTs to operations throughout the rest of the war. For UDT men the APD was their home away from home; many were on their assigned ships for months at a time.

UDT men could be seen wearing three common uniforms. Their primary uniform was Navy-issue blue dungarees, blue shirt, white hat, and black shoes or boots. Their green fatigues were Marine Corps–issue green working uniforms, with boots called "boondockers," and helmet liners. Their working uniform was simply swim trunks and specially designed coral boots to protect their feet. In the South Pacific, they wore swim trunks on board ship even when not needed for work in the water. Because of the damaging effects of the hot direct sunlight in the tropics, UDT men needed to maintain a protective tan, without which they might burn badly during actual operations. The men became known as Naked Warriors: they engaged in combat clad only in swim trunks because the only weapon they took into combat was a sharp knife. During actual reconnaissance operations the men wore only swim trunks, swim fins, face mask, and a web belt with K-Bar knife; they also carried a special pencil and Plexiglas slate on which to record information underwater.

During preparation for the Marianas operations the need for a centralized command focused on UDT activities became apparent. The Mariana Islands were key strongholds to be taken before any plans could be made to invade Japan. They are situated south of Japan, north of New Guinea, and immediately east of the Philippine Sea. The northern islands include Saipan and Tinian. The southern islands include Guam, which is now a U.S. territory. The UDT training program had been expanded to include one hundred–man teams, necessitating a higher echelon of operational command, standardization of tactical procedures, new equipment and training methods, coordination of information gained by UDTs, and dissemination to the assault forces.

In November 1944, the commander of the Navy's Pacific Fleet Amphibi-

"The Naked Warrior:" a classic picture of a UDT operator freediving to place a demolition charge on an underwater obstacle. (Photo: Courtesy of Tom Hawkins)

ous Force, named Capt. B. Hall Hanlon, USN, the first commander of UDTs (ComUDTs), Pacific Fleet Amphibious Force (known as "MudPac" by the men). Captain Hanlon was a Naval Academy graduate with no demolition experience, but he had rank and organizational skills, and that is what the UDT men needed at the time. Lieutenant Commander Kauffman, who had commanded UDT-5 for five months from April 1944, until the following August, became his chief of staff.

ComUDTs had three major responsibilities. The first was administrative oversight and training of the teams. This included coordinating NCDU training at Fort Pierce and at the advanced naval combat demolition training and experimental base at Maui. The staff also planned and assigned teams for particular combat operations, ensured their preparedness, and made arrangements for their rest and rehabilitation after operations. A second responsibility was planning and writing training orders and operational plans and briefing, rehearsing the teams, and conducting liaison with fire-support and assault forces for each operation. The final responsibility was tactical. During assault combat operations, ComUDTs had immediate operational control of all participating UDTs, APDs, and close fire support ships. The ComUDT's staff was made up of fourteen officers and twenty-one men, about half of them with demolition experience, divided into operations, demolition, communications, intelligence, and administrative departments.

Between December 1944, and August 1945, the UDT Naked Warriors saw action across the Pacific in every major amphibious landing, including Eniwetok, Saipan, Guam, Tinian, Angaur, Ulithi, Peleliu, Leyte, Lingayen Gulf, Zambales, Iwo Jima, Okinawa, Labuan, Brunei Bay, and Borneo. On 4 July 1945, at Balik-

ABOVE, TOP: *Typical dress of a UDT combat swimmer during the 1950s and early 1960s. Note dry suit, life vest, and face mask over a protective hood. (Photo: Courtesy of Tom Hawkins)*

ABOVE, BOTTOM: *Lt. Cdr. Francis Douglas Fane, USNR became legendary Commander of Underwater Demolition Unit TWO at NAB, Little Creek after World War II. He went on to command UDU ONE in Coronado during the Korean War. Fane is responsible for introducing OSS Maritime Unit diving capabilities to the UDTs in 1947, and was author of the definitive history of UDT in a book entitled* The Naked Warriors *published in 1956. (Photo Courtesy of Tom Hawkins)*

RIGHT: *UDT divers enter the escape trunk of a submarine to conduct lock-out/lock-in operations. Here they are seen wearing open-circuit SCUBA, which was routinely used for basic training. (Photo: Courtesy of Tom Hawkins)*

papan on Borneo, UDT-11 and UDT-18 spearheaded one of the last and least-recorded offensive actions of the war.

It is a little-known fact that UDT men were the most decorated Navy combat veterans of World War II. Cumulatively they were awarded 750 Bronze Stars, 150 Silver Stars, two Navy Crosses, and many Purple Hearts—quite remarkable for men who went into combat carrying no weapon other than a K-Bar knife. Given an average of one hundred officers and men in each team, there were about 2,800 active UDT personnel at the end of the war. A World War II battleship had a complement of three thousand men, and a present-day aircraft carrier has more than six thousand persons—figures that put the size of the heroic Pacific UDTs in perspective.

Thirty-one UDTs were organized during World War II. Since UDT-1, UDT-2, and Team Able (mentioned below), were disbanded almost as quickly as they were formed, there were at most twenty-eight teams at any one time. All teams were Fort Pierce trained except for UDT-1 and UDT-2 (the provisional teams), and UDT-14, UDT-16, and UDT-17, which were made up largely of fleet volunteers trained in Hawaii. The remaining teams, including Team Able, all completed training at Fort Pierce before leaving for Hawaii.

From June 1943 until September 1944, all of the men leaving Fort Pierce were organized into six-man NCDUs and formed into one hundred–man UDTs after they arrived for advanced training at Maui. In November 1944, however, ComUDTs began forming the numbered teams at Fort Pierce so that the men

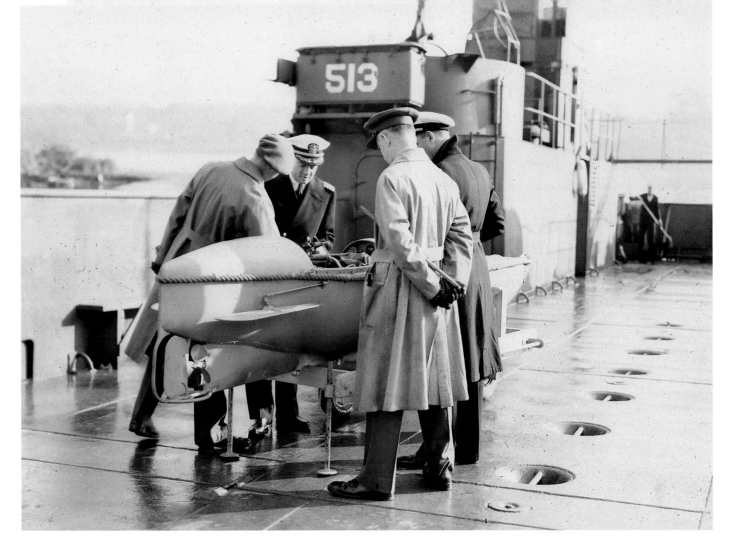

could work and train together before going to Maui. In November 1944, UDT-18 was the first numbered team to leave Fort Pierce.

Team Able was an anomaly and merits special recognition, because it was a makeshift team that is rarely recognized in UDT histories. It was made up of several NCDUs whose training began at Fort Pierce, but had not been completed on Maui. On the way to Hawaii, Team Able's transport ship was forced to return to San Fran-

Sailors examine the small submersible, the Sleeping Beauty, and other special swimmer delivery vehicles. (Photo: Courtesy of the Lambertsen Collection)

cisco because of a nonrepairable engineering casualty, causing the men and their equipment to be transferred to another ship. Instead of going directly to Maui, however, the second ship went to the Solomon Islands, where UDT-3, -4, -5, and -7 were preparing for operations at Saipan, Guam, and Tinian. The NCDU men were assigned temporary duty with these teams.

After these operations, the teams returned to Turner City near Tulagi in the Solomon Island chain. Here, and without a formal ceremony, the men were assembled on board USS *Noa* (APD-24) and designated Team Able, to participate in the Peleliu operation. En route to Peleliu on 12 November, the *Noa* was struck from behind by USS *Fullam* (DD-474) and slowly sank with all of Team Able's operational gear on board. The team saw no action at Peleliu and eventually made its way to Maui, where, again without ceremony, the men were assigned to other UDTs.

On 17 June 1945, Capt. Robert H. Rodgers, USN, became ComUDTs at Pearl Harbor. Arrangements were being made to send twenty-eight teams, on twenty-eight APDs, to ATB Oceanside, California, for a month of cold-water training, which was to begin on 15 August 1945. Additionally, a new command organization was authorized by the commander of Pacific Fleet Amphibious Forces.

The underwater demolition team collection at Oceanside was made a flotilla, with two subordinate squadrons. Captain Rodgers served in the dual capacity of commander, Underwater Demolition Flotilla; and commander, UDTs. Under him were Underwater Demolition Squadrons One and Two (UDS-1 and UDS-2), each with a command staff. USS *Hollis* (APD-66) served as command ship for the Underwater Demolition Flotilla, and USS *Blessman* (APD-48) and USS *Laning* (APD-55) were designated as squadron command ships. Even today, this remains the largest single NSW organization ever gathered under one commander for combat operations.

The planned training at Oceanside was abruptly curtailed after President Harry S. Truman ordered the use of nuclear weapons at Hiroshima, Japan, on 6 August, and at Nagasaki, Japan, on 9 August 1945. With a Japanese peace offer on 10 August, the UDTs and their APDs in training on the West Coast were alerted to proceed toward Japan, and with the Japanese surrender on 14 August, they were ordered to move to Japan without haste.

The ComUDT's staff was by this time in Manila and quickly wrote and distrib-

An OSS Maritime Unit diver using the Sleeping Beauty submersible canoe while penetrating submarine nets during a training operation in Cuba during World War II. (Photo: National Archives / NSW Publications, LLC)

ABOVE, TOP: *The small submersible, Sleeping Beauty, and its pilot making the first successful rendezvous and docking with a submerged and underway submarine off the coast of St. Thomas, Virgin Islands, Oct. 1948. (Photo: Courtesy of the Lambertsen Collection)*

ABOVE, CENTER: *Lieutenant Lillyman (Royal Marines, ISLD) or Sgt. Larry Tweedy USAAF, diving in the OSS submersible Sleeping Beauty. (Photo: Courtesy of Lambertsen Collection)*

ABOVE, BOTTOM: *The Toy II, most likely in November 1944, Solomons Island, Maryland. (Photo: Courtesy of the Lambertsen Collection)*

LEFT, TOP: *OSS Maritime Unit swimmer in a Sleeping Beauty cutting though a submarine net. (Photo: Courtesy of the Lambertsen Collection)*

LEFT, BOTTOM: *Sgt. Larry Tweedy, AUS in an OSS submersible Sleeping Beauty hooking up a SBUWT (underwater telephone). Johnny Campbell, USN (Maintenance) at his side. (Photo: Courtesy of the Lambertsen Collection)*

uted Operation Plan No. 8-45, which served as a general guide for the occupation period. Under this plan the flotilla was divided into three groups of six teams each, under 3rd, 5th, and 7th Amphibious Force commanders, respectively. The teams in each group performed several administrative reconnaissance missions, provided assistance in harbor clearances, and performed ship demilitarization.

All UDTs were subsequently withdrawn, and on 28 September, ComUDTs and staff embarked for ATB Coronado to establish the peacetime UDT organization. Rapid demobilization at the conclusion of the war left only four active-duty UDTs, each with a complement of seven officers and forty-five enlisted men. In 1946, postwar, UDT-1 and UDT-2, commanded by Lt. Cdr. Walter Cooper, were

After evacuation of the last troops and equipment, the USS Begor (APD-127) stands offshore of Korea as the Underwater Demolition Team detachment destroys the port facilities in what was described as the single largest non-nuclear explosion up to that time. (Photo: Courtesy of Tom Hawkins)

assigned to commander of the Pacific Fleet Amphibious Force, and based at Coronado. UDT-2 and UDT-4, commanded by Lt. Cdr. Francis Douglas "Red Dog" Fane, were assigned to the commander of the Atlantic Fleet Amphibious Force, and based at Little Creek. This small force had to prepare for possible future wars and make every effort to maintain combat readiness.

UNDERWATER DEMOLITION
TEAMS IN THE KOREAN WAR

A UDT platoon on deployment in the Mediterranean during the early 1960s. The picture is noteworthy and has historical interest because of how the men are outfitted. (Photo: Courtesy of Tom Hawkins)

The Korean War was a pivotal point for the UDTs and a prime example of their versatility and adaptability. When the war broke out on 25 June 1950, a ten-man UDT detachment led by Lt. (jg) George Atcheson was in Japan with Amphibious

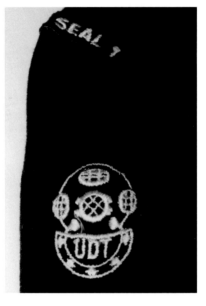

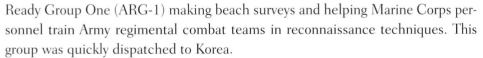

Ready Group One (ARG-1) making beach surveys and helping Marine Corps personnel train Army regimental combat teams in reconnaissance techniques. This group was quickly dispatched to Korea.

On the night of 5 August 1950, the detachment departed USS *Diachenko* (APD-123) with its inflatable boat to conduct a demolition raid against a train bridge-tunnel near Yosu. Lieutenant (junior grade) Atcheson and BM3 Warren "Fins" Foley, as the swimmer scouts, moved through five hundred yards of swift current, exiting the water just below their target. After patrolling up a twenty-foot embankment and making a hasty reconnaissance, they signaled the remaining men in their boat to land with the explosives. Without warning, ten North Korean soldiers on a handcar came out of the tunnel and opened fire. Foley was hit and fell over the seawall. Lieutenant (junior grade) Atcheson threw several hand grenades

ABOVE: *UDT-SEAL operators being snared during cast and recovery operations. Men would line up at 25-yard intervals to be snared out of the water by a man in the inflatable boat, which was being towed by the UDT reconnaissance craft. Men would be picked up to the seaward side of the boat to protect them from gunfire ashore. (Photo: Courtesy of Tom Hawkins)*

RIGHT, TOP: *UDT men retrieve a training version of the Special Atomic Demolitions Munition (SADM). A pressure-proof container was one of the initial items placed on the wish list of items on the start-up documents for the SEAL teams. The containers allowed use of SADMs in underwater environments. The SADM was a Navy project demonstrated as feasible in the mid-to-late 1960s, however, it was never used operationally. The project was designed to allow one individual to parachute from any type of aircraft carrying the weapon package, which could be placed in a harbor or other strategic location that could be accessed from the sea. Another parachutist without a weapon package would follow the first parachutist to provide support as needed. The two-man team would place the weapon package in an acceptable location, set the timer, and swim out into the ocean where they would be retrieved by a submarine or other high-speed watercraft. These types of weapons are no longer in the stockpile, as a result of the Strategic Arms Reduction Treaty (START) negotiations. (Photo: Courtesy of Tom Hawkins)*

RIGHT, BOTTOM: *UDT operators practice installing a flotation collar on a mock-up of an Apollo space capsule. During the early days of America's space flight program, UDT men assisted in the retrieval of Mercury and Apollo space capsules returning from space in the Atlantic and Pacific. (Photo: Courtesy of Tom Hawkins)*

that dispersed the enemy and allowed time for the UDT men to get clear and return to the *Diachenko*. Foley, who had a smashed kneecap and wounds in his hand and thigh, was the first U.S. Navy casualty of the Korean War.

During the month of August, additional UDT personnel began to arrive, under Lt. Cdr. D. F. "Kelley" Welch, commanding officer (CO) of UDT-1. They were committed to a somewhat new mission—night coastal demolition raids against railroad tunnels and bridges. The U.S. Navy and Marine Corps were being called on to conduct onshore reconnaissance and raiding operations, and the UDT men were given the task. In the words of UDT Lt. (jg) Ted Fielding, "We were ready to do what nobody else could do, and what nobody else wanted to do."

On 15 September 1950, UDT-1 and UDT-3 supported Operation Chromite, the amphibious landing at Inchon. UDT men went in ahead of the landing craft to scout mud flats, mark low points in the channels, and search for mines. UDT men served as wave-guides for landing craft loaded with Marines.

In October 1950, UDTs supported mine-clearing operations at Wonsan Harbor, in which the men would free swim and dive to locate and mark mines for minesweepers. On 12 October, two U.S. minesweepers, USS *Pirate* (AM-275) and USS *Pledge* (AM-277), hit mines and sank within miles of each other. UDT men rescued twenty-five Sailors. The following day UDT operator William Giannotti completed the first U.S. combat diving operation using an Aqua Lung when he dove on USS *Pledge* to mark its location for later exploitation and removal of its valuable minesweeping equipment.

In February 1952, UDT-5 was reestablished to relieve some of the burden placed on the deployment of UDT-1 and UDT-3 over the previous two years. The team continued supporting minesweeping operations until midsummer, when it conducted

Operation Fishnet in September 1952, aimed to disrupt North Korea's military economy, which was based on fish as much as on rice. This was the last extensive UDT operation in the Korean War; an armistice ended fighting on 27 July 1953.

The war substantially changed UDT operational doctrine, giving the men vastly expanded mission capabilities. In addition to their traditional roles of amphibious reconnaissance and mine and obstacle clearance, the UDTs saw that the scope of their mission was expanded to include stealthy infiltration from the sea to conduct raids and attack enemy shipping, port, and harbor facilities; clearance of ordnance from the high seas; infiltration and intelligence gathering; and the covering of the withdrawal of friendly forces.

During the Korean War UDT-2 and UDT-4 of the Atlantic Fleet were never committed to battle. These teams were involved in experimental programs involving the Aqua Lung development, lockout from submerged submarines, cold-weather diving operations, parachute training, and use of miniature submarines and submersibles.

On 8 February 1954, UDT-1, UDT-3, and UDT-5 on the West Coast were redesignated UDT-11, UDT-12, and UDT-13, respectively. UDT-2 and UDT-4 on the East Coast became UDT-21 and UDT-22. This renumbering was to conform to the use of odd numbers for Pacific Fleet units and even numbers for Atlantic Fleet units. Soon thereafter, UDT-13 was disestablished, leaving only four UDTs: two in Coronado (UDT-11 and UDT-12) and two in Little Creek (UDT-21 and UDT-22), none fully manned. They continued routine deployments to the Mediterranean and western Pacific, started attending jump school, and made several newsworthy deployments to the Arctic and Antarctic. In these units the officer ranks were almost entirely depleted of regular Navy officers in favor of reserve officers and "mustangs" (officers promoted from senior enlisted ranks). The reason was that regular officers had to go to sea (i.e., on board ship) to earn promotion. Many officers remained in the reserves and did not go anywhere in the service—except out of the Navy after their first tour of duty.

ABOVE: A rare photograph of the wet-deck shelter, a one-of-a-kind system built to carry SEAL Delivery Vehicles aboard diesel-powered submarines. The shelter provided protection for the SDV while the submarine was maneuvering at top speeds underwater and while on the surface. (Photo: Courtesy of Tom Hawkins)

LEFT: UDT Replacement Training Class 5 celebrated their graduation with a bang. (Photo: Courtesy of the Tom Hawkins)

BELOW: The Central Intelligence Agency 19.5-foot submersible, though never seen by the public, is a three-man submersible manufactured by the CIA Office of Technical Service during the Cold War. Although it carried no weapons, was cramped, had limited endurance, and required a mother ship for transport and recovery, it worked in a similar fashion to that of Navy SDVs. Its small size, ability to run semi-submerged, quietness, and wooden construction made sonar or radar detection an improbability. The vessel could be submerged without personnel in depths up to 30 feet and left on the bottom for a period of up to three or four weeks. Additionally, when it was running in the "deck wash" position with only the Plexiglas observation bubble above the surface, the submersible was almost impossible to see. (Photo: Greg E. Mathieson Sr. / NSW Publications, LLC)

CDR (SEAL) TOM HAWKINS,
USN (RET)

SEALs and Special Boat Teams
1960s–1987

CHAPTER 2

SEALs AND SPECIAL BOAT TEAMS (1960s–1987)

Cdr. (SEAL) Tom Hawkins, USN (Ret.)

SEAL TEAMS: THE BEGINNINGS

AFTER THE KOREAN WAR, PRESIDENT DWIGHT D. EISENHOWER ushered in what came to be known as the New Look in U.S. strategic affairs. The Korean War had resulted in a huge buildup in the armed forces, and President Eisenhower did not want to go back to the prewar status quo. What emerged was a deep dependence on nuclear weapons and long-range airpower to deter war. Between the end of the Korean War and the beginning of the Vietnam War buildup in 1965, U.S. military end-strength never fell below 2.5 million, averaging 2.8 million. In the late 1950s, however, there was a growing need for skills involving nonstrategic forces with special operations capabilities. The Army had the Green Berets Special Forces, the Navy had the UDTs, and the Marines had Force Reconnaissance units.

During the final years of his administration, President Eisenhower began to engage these specialized forces to address small conflicts involving U.S. interests.

PAGES 54–55: *SEALs board a ship during a training exercise aboard the USS Mount Whitney in the early 1990s. A ship-boarding assault technique known as VBSS or Visit, Board, Search, and Seizure is one way of dealing with piracy and ships transporting illegal arms. (Photo: Greg E. Mathieson Sr. / NSW Publications, LLC)*

Early members of a SEAL team platoon in preparation for a full-equipment parachute jump. (Photo: Courtesy of Tom Hawkins)

ABOVE: *Early members of the SEAL teams boarding a helicopter in preparation for a water jump, a technique that was perfected by UDT and SEAL team operators. (Photo: Courtesy of Tom Hawkins)*

LEFT, TOP: *Mk VII SDV crew seen testing a variety of equipment that included an experimental diving apparatus made by the Westinghouse Corporation, a Fenzy buoyancy compensator, and an underwater communication device. (Photo: Courtesy of Tom Hawkins)*

LEFT, BOTTOM: *President John F. Kennedy inspects UDT and SEAL team operators during a visit to Naval Amphibious Base, Little Creek, Virginia, early in his presidency. Actions initiated by President Kennedy are often credited with establishment of the U.S. Navy SEAL teams in January 1962. (Photo: National Archives / NSW Publications, LLC)*

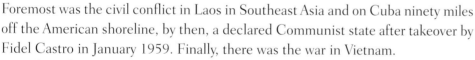

Foremost was the civil conflict in Laos in Southeast Asia and on Cuba ninety miles off the American shoreline, by then, a declared Communist state after takeover by Fidel Castro in January 1959. Finally, there was the war in Vietnam.

It has often been said that President John F. Kennedy directed establishment of the U.S. Navy's SEAL teams for activities in Vietnam. That is a good legend, but it is not quite true. History itself has demonstrated that formation of the SEAL teams was an evolutionary process, one that did not happen overnight or result from the efforts of an isolated few. The concept emerged largely because of the efforts of many individuals, as well as in response to developments surrounding UDT experiences in Korea, post-Korea, and later world events, especially in Laos and Cuba.

After the Korean War, the future of the UDTs was uncertain. Mission activity during that war had brought about a new range of operating concepts for the UDTs—behind-the-lines operations, inland raids, targeting of railroad tunnels, disruption of enemy movements, and the total destruction of Hungnam, Korea. The old premise that UDT responsibilities ended at the high-water mark was already

"The men with green faces," as the SEALs were called in Vietnam. The SEAL seen in the center of the picture works with Vietnamese navy SEALs known as Lien Doc Nguoi Nhia or LDNN. (Photo: Courtesy of Tom Hawkins)

LEFT: *Capt. Phil Bucklew, a member of the early Atlantic Scouts and Raiders as both an officer and chief petty officer. In the Pacific theater, Lieutenant Bucklew later served with the SACO to organize behind-the-line operations in China against Japanese invaders. He began a career in coaching after the war, but returned to the Navy during the Korean War as a member of the highly classified Beach Jumper Units. He remained in the Navy and during the Vietnam War became Commander, Naval Operations Support Group, Pacific, where he commanded all of the UDT, SEAL, Beach Jumper, and Special Boat Units in the Pacific. He is best known for the "Bucklew Report," a comprehensive look at U.S. Navy operations in Vietnam. (Photo: Courtesy of Tom Hawkins)*

RIGHT: *BM2 (later Master Chief) Bill Bruhmuller and others quietly left the Navy and the SEALs to be assigned to the CIA for missions involving Cuba. After the Cuban Missile Crisis they were returned back to active duty status with the Navy and the SEAL Teams. (Photo: Courtesy of Bill Bruhmuller)*

in the past. Much of the postwar analysis occurred within the CNO's staff (known as the Office of the Chief of Naval Operations, or OPNAV) at the Pentagon or at the Bureau of Naval Personnel, but the discussions also involved UDT officers.

As early as 1958, Adm. Arleigh A. Burke, as CNO, proposed initiation of covert measures designed to keep the Communist powers off balance. Understanding where President Eisenhower and later President Kennedy wanted to focus in the area of unconventional warfare, Admiral Burke directed OPNAV to organize new or existing Navy units for smaller conflicts.

After considerable study it was determined that expanding the UDT mission would hinder their traditional and now doctrinal responsibilities to the amphibious force. As a result, it was considered that new units should be established possessing the operational experience of the UDTs but incorporating the new warfare concepts learned during the Korean War.

Because the UDTs were doctrinally tied to the amphibious force, they had been denied opportunities to use Army and Marine Corps training schools or to add essential equipment to their material allowances for new mission capabilities. It was intended that any new unconventional warfare units would not be doctrinally hindered and that they would have the freedom to establish a broader and more flexible mission, establish separate personnel and material allowances, and work their own budgets.

SEALs in Southeast Asia

In early 1960, because of the crises in Laos and Cuba and the increasing insurgency in South Vietnam, Admiral Burke directed his staff to prepare options with respect to unconventional warfare. Among other recommendations, the staff suggested, "the Underwater Demolition Teams and Marine reconnaissance units were considered organized and capable of expansion into unconventional warfare."

More concrete steps were taken on 13 September 1960, when an OPNAV Unconventional Activities Working Group was formally established. This group reported to Adm. Wallace M. Beakley, Strategic Plans Division, assistant CNO for fleet operations and readiness; he directed the group to investigate "naval unconventional activity methods, techniques and concepts, which may be employed effectively against Sino-Soviet interests under conditions of cold war."

The concept for special operations units within the Navy, and even the name "SEAL," had already emerged in outline form by 10 March 1961, when Rear Adm. William E. Gentner Jr., director of the Strategic Plans Division, approved preliminary recommendations of the Unconventional Activities Committee (successor to the Unconventional Activities Working Group), and forwarded them to the CNO for review and concurrence. Included among these was a recommendation for a wide range of "additional unconventional warfare capabilities within, or as an extension of, our amphibious forces," and that operations conducted in "restricted waters" are to be emphasized.

SEAL Team ONE, Det Golf contingent in Nha Be, South Vietnam, circa 1966. The boat (LCM) in the background was being modified for SEAL team use. The man on the boat was not a SEAL, but helped crew the boat on numerous ops. Pictured (l-r) Standing: Mike Tomsho, Bill Pechacek, Roger Moscone, UID, Swazo, Smith, UID, Jimmy Pahia, UID, UID, Bob Henry, Carl Marriott, Leon Rauch, UID, UID. Kneeling: Maynard Weyers, Rascheck, Billy Machem, Shinners, Van Orden, Wilcox, Doc Cline, Ron Bell, Tom Truxell. (Photo: Courtesy of Tom Hawkins)

In April 1962 Lt. (j.g.) Philip P. Holts and AOIC Lt. (j.g.) Jon R. Stockholm of SEAL Team ONE (ST-1) led a combined ST-1 and SEAL Team TWO (ST-2) nine-man detachment to Vietnam. Their mission was to train selected Vietnamese Coastal Force personnel in reconnaissance, sabotage, and guerrilla warfare, and to prepare them to instruct succeeding classes of Biet Hai commandos. In the photo standing (l-r) are SF1 Robert F. Fisher (ST-1), FTG2 Carl D. Marriott (ST-1), SN Robert D. Paul (ST-1), SK2 William E. Burbank (ST-2). Kneeling: SM2 David A. Wilson (ST-1), DM2 Alwyn J. Smith Jr. (ST-1), DM1 Lenard A. Waugh (ST-2), EN2 Theodore E George (ST-1). (Photo was taken by BM1 Jack R. Perkins)

The committee also proposed establishment of one unit each, under the Pacific and Atlantic amphibious commanders that "would represent a center or focal point through which all elements of this specialized Navy capability (naval guerrilla warfare) would be channeled. An appropriate name for such units could be 'SEAL' units, SEAL being a contraction of SEA, AIR, LAND, and thereby, indicating an all-around, universal capability." Initial units would consist of twenty to twenty-five officers and fifty to seventy-five enlisted men.

On 3 May 1961, Admiral Burke signed a memorandum to his staff: "We should have a record of all Naval personnel, particularly officers, who have been especially trained in guerrilla warfare, UDT, psychological warfare, and what the Army calls 'Special Forces Training.' . . . I know this is going to be difficult, but we are going to have to take over such operations as river patrol in the Saigon Delta, in the Mekong River, and other areas. Our people will have to know thoroughly how to fight and live under guerrilla conditions."

Two months later, on 13 May 1961, Admiral Beakley addressed a memo to the CNO that proposed a concept of operations, a detailed mission and tasks statement for SEAL teams, and other background information—including UDT

special operations during the Korean War. He wrote, "If you agree in the foregoing proposals, I will take action to establish a Special Operations Team on each coast."

On 25 May 1961, President Kennedy delivered a special message entitled "Urgent National Needs" to Congress: "I am directing the Secretary of Defense to expand rapidly and substantially, in cooperation with our Allies, the orientation of existing forces for the conduct of non-nuclear war, paramilitary operations, and sub-limited or unconventional wars. In addition, our Special Forces and unconventional warfare units will be increased and reoriented. Throughout the services new emphasis must be placed on the special skills and languages which are required to work with local populations." President Kennedy's speech is the closest he came to actually directing formation of SEAL teams. Although they began organizing as early as November 1961, two SEAL teams were officially authorized by the CNO that December, and both units were formally established in January 1962. Their mis-

ABOVE: *Rows of boxes still remain classified SECRET and TOP SECRET within the Navy History and Heritage Command in Washington, D.C. For this project it took several years to finally declassify CNO Burke documents and others which show the origins of the U.S. Navy SEALs. (Photo: Greg E. Mathieson Sr. / NSW Publications, LLC)*

RIGHT: *This newly released CNO SECRET document from May 1961 displays the acronym SEAL and its intended use for the first time. It also shows that the first group of SEALs would be 20/25 officers per unit augmented by some 50/75 enlisted men. These 70/100 men would make up the "First SEALs" within the United States Navy. It also shows the coordination established between the CIA, Army, Marines, and Department of State. (Photo: Greg E. Mathieson Sr. / NSW Publications, LLC)*

SECRET

3. Functional lines of responsibility between CIA, Army, Marines and Navy are overlapping and there is a continuing requirement for cross-pollination, support, and liaison. These units would provide a working mechanism to effect coordination.

4. Upon achievement of a complete cycle of operations it should be self-perpetuating, inasmuch as it will generate its own inputs and thereby develop the ultimate magnitude of the program.

5. Of the 21 allied and neutral countries presently appraised as having an existing or potential insurgency threat and possibly needful of advice and assistance on short notice, only Bolivia is without a potential naval implication. The remaining countries are characterized by coast lines, harbors, rivers, island complexes and a substantial number of delta areas, and hence, potentially represent a need for naval assistance. Commercial lines of communications are particularly vulnerable to insurgency action and pose varying naval implications.

6. Approximately twenty to twenty-five officers per unit would be needed to initiate a flexible program. Elements of these officers would be involved in (1) training, (2) operations - deployed trouble shooters, (3) equipment development and (4) administration. Augmenting enlisted personnel, an estimated 50-75 men per unit, would include various ratings in support of the spectrum of activities which evolve.

7. This cadre of trained personnel would provide a capability in being for limited war situations as well as general war. Historically, some unique naval requirement in war, usually unforseen and unplanned, has arisen, which has required activities of this general nature. This in turn has necessitated hurried improvision and has leaned heavily on individual ingenuity and adaptability. Although we cannot eliminate such occurrences, we can minimize their frequency and enhance our flexibility. Further, the application of ingenuity is often time consuming, expensive, wasteful and overtaken by events.

8. An appropriate name for such units could be "SEAL" units SEAL being a contraction of SEA, AIR, LAND, and thereby, indicating an all-around, universal capability.

2

SECRET

4. Silent, small individual weapon.

5. Hand held micro-jet missile weapon.

6. Hand held air gun firing pellets or micro-missiles with lethal and paralyzing effects on human targets.

7. Improved, light weight, specialized weapons and mounts for small craft.

8. Improved, light weight body armor.

9. Explosive line charges for obstacle/mine clearance (ahead-thrown line demolition charge).

10. Small, quiet, high speed, shallow water craft, armored and mounting special armament, for offensive assault and harbor/river defense. (Could be manifested in form of hydrofoils, GEM's, catamarans, or planing hulls).

11. Waterjet propulsion for catamarans or planing hulls.

12. Midget submarines for harbor reconnaissance or delivery UDT personnel/agents close inshore.

13. Surface-to-surface anti-radiation missile which could home on radar or radio electronic emissions.

14. Shallow-draft LCU type craft for use as mobile hospital/aid station.

15. Anti-personnel munitions (booby traps).

16. Multiple capability amphibian for use in water, swamps, wooded areas, open ground.

17. Chemical plant defoliant to destroy natural cover/camouflage.

18. Improved capability by patrol and river craft to avoid submerged obstacles. Recent advances in Sonar, particularly of mine-hunting types, may lend themselves to adaptation to provide shallow water craft with relatively simple, inexpensive, light-weight equipment capable of detecting shoals, reefs, pinnacles, coral heads and submerged obstacles and of determining if they may be passed over or how to maneuver around them.

19. Swampboat, minimum draft, quiet, not affected by debris or weeds for transportation of personnel or cargo.

2

C. COMMUNICATIONS/ELECTRONICS EQUIPMENT

1. Lightweight, compact, rugged intercept equipment to cover appropriate frequency bands as intelligence indicates.

D. SUPPLY AND LOGISTICS

1. Aerial emplaced underwater supply caches with capability to surface on electronic command (for emergency/high priority items).

2. Improved means of aerial delivery of personnel, supplies and equipment.

E. MEDICAL SUPPLIES

1. Vaccines for following diseases:

Hepatitis	Japanese BE Encephalitis
Dengue	Rift-Valley Fever
Phlebotomus fever	Brucellosis
Scrub Typhus	

2. Antibiotics and Chemotherapeutic Drugs for:

Filariasis	Schistosomiasis
Leishmaniasis	Trypanosomiasis

3. Polyvalent antivenoms for poisonous snakes of foreign countries.

4. Geomedical studies on medical problems and diseases in Africa, and parts of South America and Asia.

3

TAB B

LIST OF ALLIED AND NEUTRAL FOREIGN COUNTRIES WHICH MIGHT REQUEST
THE UNITED STATES TO PROVIDE ADVICE AND ASSISTANCE ON SHORT NOTICE

AREA	COUNTRY
LATIN AMERICA	BOLIVIA
	COLOMBIA
	DOMINICAN REPUBLIC
	EL SALVADOR
	HAITI
	HONDURAS
	PANAMA
AFRICA	ANGOLA
	CONGO
	ETHIOPIA
	FEDERATION OF RHODESIA AND NYASALAND
	KENYA
	SUDAN
MIDDLE EAST	IRAN
	IRAQ
SOUTHEAST ASIA	BURMA
	CEYLON
	LAOS
	S. VIETNAM
FAR EAST	INDONESIA
	S. KOREA

TOP, LEFT: *Establishment document for the SEAL teams lists "Midget submarines for harbor reconnaissance or delivery UDT personnel/agents close inshore." (Photo: Greg E. Mathieson Sr. / NSW Publications, LLC)*

TOP, RIGHT: *Early supply list for the newly formed SEAL teams. (Photo: Greg E. Mathieson / NSW Publications, LLC)*

LEFT: *Documents, now declassified for the first time, show the countries where the newly formed SEAL teams might be expected to operate. (Photo: Greg E. Mathieson Sr. / NSW Publications, LLC)*

Op-07M/rls
Ser OO20P07M

(3) Mine Warfare Equipment

Demolition initiator used in shallow-water, moored mines fabricated from commercial oil drums (30 and 55 gallons). Mines are actuated by contact and are self destroying if the mooring parts or if swimmers attempt to remove them.

(4) Close air support weapons:

BULLPUP
MK 11 gun pod (20 mm a/c gun)
ZUNI
2.75 FFAR

(4) Landing Craft, Mechanized

(6) 10 ft. Rescue Boat

(7) 36 ft. Landing Craft, Personnel

(8) Inflatable Boats (7 and 10 person sizes)

(9) 20 mm, 40 mm guns, recoilless rifles (75 mm) for use on small craft

(10) Medical supplies

(a) Vaccines to immunize against most diseases endemic to foreign countries.

(b) Antibiotics and Chemotherapeutic drugs for prophylaxis and protection against many diseases prevalent in foreign countries.

(c) Items for chlorination and water purification.

(d) Impregnated clothing for protection against certain insects.

(e) Bed nets

(f) Repellants

(g) Insecticides

(h) Individual, precooked and survial rations

(i) Rodenticides, poisons, traps

DOWNGRADED AT 3-YEAR INTERVALS
DECLASSIFIED AFTER 12 YEARS
DOD DIR 5200.10

SECRET

Op-00/rar
Op-00 Memo 00242-61
3 May 1951

SECRET

MEMORANDUM FOR OP-01

Subj: Guerrilla warfare

1. We should have a record of all Naval personnel, particularly officers, who have been specially trained in guerrilla warfare, UDT, psychological warfare, and what the Army calls "Special Forces Training". We should get more people below the age of 35 trained in this field.

2. Training is of course one of the key factors in guerrilla warfare. We will need such things as training pamphlets on this subject. We should take a look at the Army pamphlets. We should send people through other Service schools as well as our own survival courses and probably set up courses at the amphibious schools.

3. I know this is going to be difficult, but we are going to have to take over such operations as river patrol in the Saigon Delta, in the Mekong River, and other areas. Our people will have to know thoroughly how to fight and live under guerrilla conditions.

4. Will you please give me a list of equipment which has been developed such as silent motors, etc., along with things that we might need now. It might be beneficial to look at the Army's list of equipment.

ARLEIGH BURKE

Copy to:
OP-09
OP-03
OP-04
OP-06

SECRET

MEMORANDUM FOR THE CHIEF OF NAVAL OPERATIONS

Via: Deputy Chief of Naval Operations (Plans and Policy)

Subj: JCS 1969/222 - Defense Resources for Specific Unconventional Operations (U)

SUMMARY

1. JCS 1969/222 would forward a memorandum for the Secretary of Defense with a revised working survey of Defense resources for specific unconventional operations (guerrilla, counterguerrilla and countersubversion). This survey is a corrected and revised paper based on the Assistant to the Secretary's (BGEN Lansdale) survey of "Defense Resources for Unconventional Warfare" (JCS 1969/220). The JCS consider the revised document to be an acceptable basis for discussion on the subject with other governmental agencies in connection with National Security Action Memorandum (NSAM) No. 56 (JCS 1969/215).

PROBLEM

2. To review the survey "Defense Resources in Unconventional Warfare" and assure it represents a realistic accounting of current Service capabilities in specific unconventional operations (guerrilla, counterguerrilla and counter-subversion).

BACKGROUND

3. In NSCAD #56 (JCS 1969/215) the President requests that the Secretary of Defense, in coordination with STATE and CIA, make an estimate of requirements in the field of unconventional warfare and paramilitary operations and recommend ways and means to meet these requirements. BGEN Lansdale's survey addresses only the Defense current assets in unconventional warfare. Unified commanders have been requested (JCS 999057) to provide estimates of future requirements of indigenous paramilitary forces on a country to country basis (by 15 August), from which an evaluation can be made of applicable Defense assets to paramilitary operations (due 29 August).

DISCUSSION

4. The information contained in BGEN Lansdale's survey is basically good, however, in some instances it is inaccurate and incomplete. Each Service has checked its portion and revised it accordingly. The revised survey is factual and provides an acceptable basis for further discussion. CIA has been requested to conduct a similar survey.

Navy capabilities pp 14 - 16

RECOMMENDATION

5. Recommend approve JCS 1969/222 as written by telephone vote. (INCL 1ST CORRIG)

COORDINATION

6. a. OPNAV: Op-343E, Op-922H4, Op-923T, Op-07M, Op-403E.

b. Other Services are expected to approve the paper as written by telephone vote.

Wm E Gentner, Jr

EXCLUDED FROM AUTOMATIC REGRADING

Op-605F/sy
Ser 00355P60

4. The Navy has a unique and inherent capability in its Underwater Demolition and Beach Jumper Units, together with submarine forces, to conduct clandestine or covert special missions in support of counterguerrilla operations. Submarine and underwater demolition tactics are be their basic nature weapons systems employing stealth. Beach Jumper Units are special forces with a primary mission of tactical deception. These forces can conduct and provide support to special operations specifically adapted to particular country insurgency situations.

5. The following steps are being taken in furtherance of an improved naval guerrilla/counterguerrilla capability:

a. Increased emphasis on shallow water or riverine operations, with particular stress on its application to guerrilla/counterguerrilla operations.

b. Increased emphasis on the training of selected MAAG/Mission Advisory personnel and other selected personnel in the naval aspects of counterguerrilla operations as applicable to the specific country or area assignment.

c. Development of a tactical manual which reflects naval aspects of guerrilla/counterguerrilla operations.

d. Feasibility study of small anti-amphibious mines to be coupled with a fast mine laying technique, to include shallow water devices and application to guerrilla/counterguerrilla operations.

e. Development of specialized armament for use aboard small, fast, general purpose ships/craft in guerrilla/counterguerrilla operations.

f. Plans for the establishment of specialized naval units having a mission designed to (1) develop a specialized naval capability in naval guerrilla/counterguerrilla operations, to include the training of selected personnel in a wide variety of skills, (2) develop doctrinal tactics and (3) develop support equipment.

2

OFFICIAL FILE COPY - OPNAV FORM 5000-1 (REV. 8-59)

SECRET

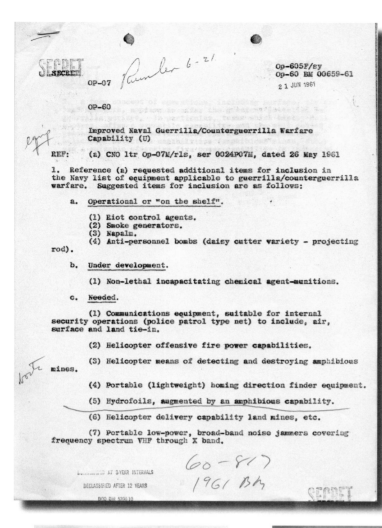

FACING PAGE

TOP, LEFT: *Early documents require teams to have everything for every possible contingency, including vaccines for various diseases and antibiotics. (Photo: Greg E. Mathieson / NSW Publications, LLC)*

TOP, RIGHT: *On 3 May 1961, Chief of Naval Operations (CNO) Adm. Arleigh Burke puts out a SECRET memo asking for a list of naval personnel, particularly officers below the age of 25 with special skills in guerrilla warfare, UDT, and psychological warfare. This list of men would make up the first candidates to be U.S. Navy SEALs. (Photo: Greg E. Mathieson Sr. / NSW Publications, LLC)*

BOTTOM, LEFT: *One 20 July 1961, Capt. William E. Genter Jr, Director, Strategic Plans Division, highlights in a briefing memo that President Kennedy wanted the Secretary of Defense to coordinate with the Department of State and the CIA to make an estimate of requirements in the field of "unconventional warfare." The Army's Green Berets were moving ahead; the SEALs would be shortly behind, but better equipped. (Photo: Greg E. Mathieson Sr. / NSW Publications, LLC)*

BOTTOM, RIGHT: *The new SEAL mission is beginning to take shape in documents from the Chief of Naval Operations Office in early 1961. (Photo: Greg E. Mathieson Sr. / NSW Publications, LLC)*

ABOVE

TOP, LEFT: *During the early planning for the SEAL teams, much of the equipment was "on the shelf," but they were also bringing in new items being developed by the U.S. Navy and others. The SEALs became a testing ground for many of the newest technologies, one of which was hydrofoil boat design. (Photo: Greg E. Mathieson Sr. / NSW Publications)*

TOP, RIGHT: *In April of 1961, things were not moving fast enough for Admiral Ulysses S. Grant Sharp Jr. in establishing the Navy SEALs. He criticized his boss CNO Areigh Burke in saying "that the CNO had done little, if anything, to increase the emphasis on counterguerrilla warfare." He strongly suggested "we had better get going." Anything that could be dreamed of, designed, or created would go to the newly formed SEAL teams. Many items, such as hydrofoils, were still under development at the time. (Photo: Greg E. Mathieson Sr. / NSW Publications, LLC)*

BOTTOM, LEFT: *Named "High Pockets," this small hydrofoil was built by a U.S. Navy contractor, Baker Manufacturing Company, in Evanville, Wisconsin. It had surface-piercing type V-foils. The Chief of Naval Operations and others listed prototype hydrofoils on the list of equipment they wanted to issue to the SEAL teams as they formed up. (Photo: Courtesy of the Naval History and Heritage Command)*

BOTTOM, CENTER: *This 9-foot hydrofoil called the "Hydrofin" was invented by Christopher Hook of England. It was the first successful submerged foil boat. Prototype hydrofoils were on the first equipment list put together for the first Navy SEAL teams in the early 1960s. (Photo: Courtesy of the Naval History and Heritage Command)*

BOTTOM, RIGHT: *In early 1962, the Navy was working with hydrofoils as seen here during a demonstration of the "Highlander" by Baker Hydrofoils on the Potomac River near the Pentagon. The 40-foot boat could travel in excess of 35 knots and was designed as an amphibious cargo/personnel carrier and also used as a swimmer-recovery craft. (Photo: Courtesy of the Naval History and Heritage Command)*

ITEMS AVAILABLE OR UNDER DEVELOPMENT FOR SUPPORT OF G/CG OPERATIONS
* Indicates items under development

A. AIRCRAFT, AIR ORDNANCE AND RELATED ITEMS

    1. Close Air Support Weapons:

        a. Low drag, General Purpose (GP) and Fragmentation Bombs and Bomb Clusters.

        b. Fire Bombs (Napalm) MK 77, 78, 79.

        c. Chemical Bombs M 70A1, AN-M78, AN-M79.

        d. Incendiary Bombs AN-M47A4, AN-M76.

        e. LAZY DOG Missile Strafing Dispenser, AERO 7D.

        f. LAZY DOG Missile Cluster Adapter, MK 44.

        g. Multiple Bomb Rack, A/A37B-1.

        h. Aero 14B Airborne Spray Tank w/non lethal, incapacitating agents.

        i. Helicopter Riot Control System using M4 Dispenser with CS or other incapacitating agents.

        j. BULLPUP.

        k. MK 11 Gun Pod (20mm A/C gun).

        l. 2.75 FFAR.

        m. HE Bombs.

        n. High Speed Air Delivery Container, M-4A. (Bomb type container; 500# capacity).

    2. Aircraft Flares, surface markers, signals and signal projectors, photoflash bombs and cartridges.

    *3. Emergency Landing Mat material.

    *4. Aerotriever, Air-ground pick-up system.

    *5. Air Delivery System for personnel, supplies and equipment.

    *6. Anti-personnel warhead for ZUNI.

DOWNGRADED AT 3-YEAR INTERVALS
DECLASSIFIED AFTER 12 YEARS

Enclosure (1) to Memo
Ser 0036P07M of   1

---

    *7. Air-to-surface weapons ROCKEYE, SADEYE, SNAKEYE, GLADEYE, WALLEYE.

B. SMALL CRAFT AND RELATED ITEMS

    1. Silent running outboard motors.

    2. Landing Craft, Mechanized.

    3. Landing Craft, Personnel.

    4. Landing Craft, Vehicle, Personnel.

    *5. Hydroskimmer LCVP (GEM type craft).

    6. Inflatable boats, outboard powered.

    7. Paddleboard, Inflatable.

    8. Rafts, Inflatable.

    9. Airboats, Navy Rescue and Commercial.

    10. Waterjet Boats, Commercial.

    11. Minesweeping Launch, 36'.

    12. Swimmer support boats, outboard powered.

    13. Landing Craft, Swimmer Recovery (LCSR).

    14. Portable hydrofoils for attachment to 16' commercial boat.

    15. Rubber covered kayaks (Foldable).

    16. Rescue Boat, 10'.

    17. Special equipment for small craft:

        a. Battlefield surveillance radar (MARCORPS equipment).

        b. Man pack and portable radios of various types for ship-shore-boat-aircraft communications.

        c. Portable Flame Thrower.

        d. Mortars, 81mm and 60mm.

        e. Howitzer, 75mm Pack.

Reading like an inventory of James Bond's closet, the first early wish list that got passed around for the establishment of the SEAL teams included pretty much anything that the founders wanted. If they made it, it got listed; if it didn't exist, they designed it; if it was being designed, they would be one of the first to get it. Whether that happened or not it is another subject, but the documents show that the Navy wanted to be the best and to have the best. (Photo: Greg E. Mathieson Sr. / NSW Publications, LLC)

        f. Small Arms (pistols, rifles, recoilless rifles, submachine guns, machine guns, grenades (AP, Smoke, Gas, Incendiary).

        g. 40mm grenade launcher and grenades.

        h. 20mm, 40mm guns.

        i. URN-14 (a device to assist in small boat navigation during darkness and poor visibility).

        j. Motorboat Booms.

        k. Smoke Generators, Smoke Pots, floating.

        l. Signals and signal projectors.

        m. Hand Fire starters.

        n. A chemical/radiological lighting device is available for markers, reading lights, guide and trail indicators; no batteries (Commercial).

    *18. Hydrofoil LCVP.

    *19. Landing Craft, Support Small (LCSS). (Armored version of WWII LCPL. Plans available).

    *20. LCM (Armored) (Plans available).

    *21. Landing Vehicle, wheeled, LVW.

    *22. Landing Vehicle, Hydrofoil, LVH.

    *23. IR ground surveillance device (MARCORPS development).

    *24. REDEYE S-A missile (AA).

C. UDT/UNDERWATER SWIMMER EQUIPMENT

    1. UDT equipment.

    2. SCUBA equipment.

    3. Tools, equipment, explosives and detonation devices.

    4. Underwater Locator AN/PQS-1.

    5. Ordnance Locator MK 9, Mod 0.

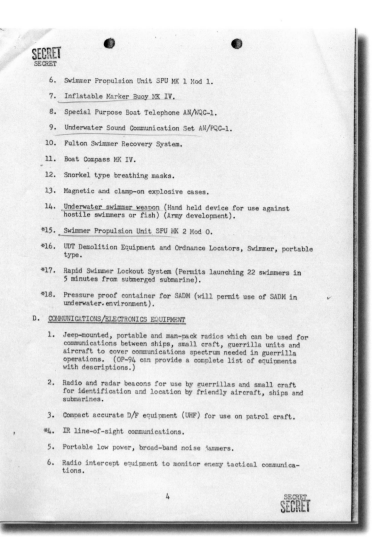

6. Swimmer Propulsion Unit SPU MK 1 Mod 1.

7. Inflatable Marker Buoy MK IV.

8. Special Purpose Boat Telephone AN/WQC-1.

9. Underwater Sound Communication Set AN/PQC-1.

10. Fulton Swimmer Recovery System.

11. Boat Compass MK IV.

12. Snorkel type breathing masks.

13. Magnetic and clamp-on explosive cases.

14. Underwater swimmer weapon (Hand held device for use against hostile swimmers or fish) (Army development).

*15. Swimmer Propulsion Unit SPU MK 2 Mod 0.

*16. UDT Demolition Equipment and Ordnance Locators, Swimmer, portable type.

*17. Rapid Swimmer Lockout System (Permits launching 22 swimmers in 5 minutes from submerged submarine).

*18. Pressure proof container for SADM (will permit use of SADM in underwater environment).

D. COMMUNICATIONS/ELECTRONICS EQUIPMENT

1. Jeep-mounted, portable and man-pack radios which can be used for communications between ships, small craft, guerrilla units and aircraft to cover communications spectrum needed in guerrilla operations. (OP-94 can provide a complete list of equipments with descriptions.)

2. Radio and radar beacons for use by guerrillas and small craft for identification and location by friendly aircraft, ships and submarines.

3. Compact accurate D/F equipment (UHF) for use on patrol craft.

*4. IR line-of-sight communications.

5. Portable low power, broad-band noise jammers.

6. Radio intercept equipment to monitor enemy tactical communications.

4

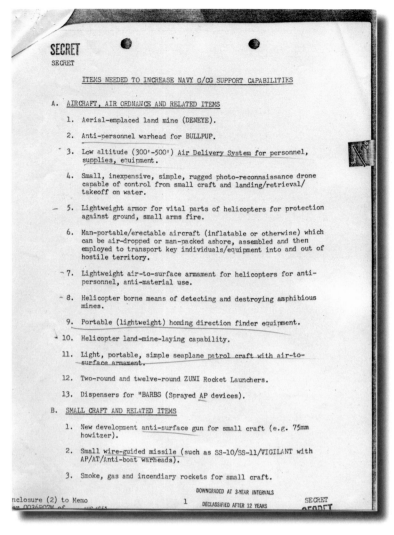

ITEMS NEEDED TO INCREASE NAVY G/CG SUPPORT CAPABILITIES

A. AIRCRAFT, AIR ORDNANCE AND RELATED ITEMS

1. Aerial-emplaced land mine (DENEYE).

2. Anti-personnel warhead for BULLPUP.

3. Low altitude (300'-500') Air Delivery System for personnel, supplies, equipment.

4. Small, inexpensive, simple, rugged photo-reconnaissance drone capable of control from small craft and landing/retrieval/takeoff on water.

5. Lightweight armor for vital parts of helicopters for protection against ground, small arms fire.

6. Man-portable/erectable aircraft (inflatable or otherwise) which can be air-dropped or man-packed ashore, assembled and then employed to transport key individuals/equipment into and out of hostile territory.

7. Lightweight air-to-surface armament for helicopters for anti-personnel, anti-material use.

8. Helicopter borne means of detecting and destroying amphibious mines.

9. Portable (lightweight) homing direction finder equipment.

10. Helicopter land-mine-laying capability.

11. Light, portable, simple seaplane patrol craft with air-to-surface armament.

12. Two-round and twelve-round ZUNI Rocket Launchers.

13. Dispensers for "BARBS (Sprayed AP devices).

B. SMALL CRAFT AND RELATED ITEMS

1. New development anti-surface gun for small craft (e.g. 75mm howitzer).

2. Small wire-guided missile (such as SS-10/SS-11/VIGILANT with AP/AT/Anti-boat warheads).

3. Smoke, gas and incendiary rockets for small craft.

DOWNGRADED AT 3-YEAR INTERVALS
DECLASSIFIED AFTER 12 YEARS

Enclosure (2) to Memo ... OO36ROZM of ... 1

sion: conduct unconventional warfare, counter-guerrilla warfare, and clandestine operations.

SEAL Team 1 was established at the naval amphibious base (NAB), Coronado and co-located with UDT-11 and UDT-12. SEAL Team 2 was established at the NAB, Little Creek and co-located with UDT-21. The UDTs supplied the manpower to establish the new SEAL teams; at the time of their formation and throughout much of the Vietnam conflict, the existence of these new units remained highly classified.

On 18 January 1962, a special group (counterinsurgency) comprising senior White House, State Department, Defense Department, Joint Chiefs of Staff (JCS), and Central Intelligence Agency (CIA) representatives lent support to covert operations in North Vietnam. The group would exploit opportunities for covert action in North Vietnam as envisioned by Adm. Harry D. Felt, commander in chief, U.S. Pacific Command. Felt believed that North Vietnam feared material losses and the establishment of an effective resistance; this belief would figure prominently in development of clandestine operations in the waters off North Vietnam.

In anticipation of these operations, in January 1962, SEAL Team 1 sent CPO Robert Sullivan and CPO Charles Raymond to take initial surveys and prepare for training indigenous South Vietnamese in the tactics, techniques, and procedures (TTPs) of maritime commandos.

In November 1963, less than one year after the SEAL teams had been established, the Navy formed planning and coordinating staffs called naval operation support groups (NOSGs), with one staff in the Pacific and one in the Atlantic. These were forerunners of today's Naval Special Warfare groups (NSWGs). They

LEFT: One of the more unique items on the the first SEAL team equipment list was one of the most powerful weapons known to man, atomic bombs. UDT and later SEAL Teams worked and trained with SADMs (Special Atomic Demolition Munition), also known as the "back-pack nuke," specially designed for the SEAL Teams in pressure-proof containers for undersea operations. (Photo: Greg E. Mathieson Sr. / NSW Publications, LLC)

RIGHT: The wish list for the first SEAL unit included aircraft and various other unique items such as the Folton Air Recovery system, which allowed for extraction capability but was later abandoned. To this day, SEAL teams still need to rely on others for air support and transport and do not have a dedicated unit assigned to WARCOM. (Photo: Greg E. Mathieson Sr. / NSW Publications, LLC)

were co-located near their subordinate units at Coronado and Little Creek, where they remain today.

During the same period, the Navy approved reestablishment of UDT-22 at Little Creek. Boat support units (BSUs) were established to provide dedicated maritime mobility for the UDT and SEAL teams, and existing Navy beach jumper units (BJUs) were reorganized for support of smaller worldwide conflicts. The BSUs were a new concept, but the BJUs originated during World War II and were established again for Korea. Their mission involved tactical cover and deception. UDTs, SEALs, BJUs, and BSUs were all organized as subordinate commands under the NOSGs. The BSUs are discussed extensively in Chapter 7.

SEALs and Cuba

The men of the newly formed SEAL teams began by adopting many of the same capabilities as their Army Special Forces and Marine Corps Reconnaissance Unit counterparts. They attended various Army and Marine Corps schools, but at the same time began equipping themselves to operate as commandos from the sea. Having come from the UDTs, the men had quite good water and seaborne infiltration skills, so they began concentrating on land, air, and language capabilities.

In addition to skills learned from Korea, it was probably UDT participation in highly classified Cuban operations that helped to accelerate formation of the SEAL teams—especially the ill-fated 1961, CIA-sponsored invasion of Cuba that took place in the Bay of Pigs (Bahía de Cochinos). Many details about UDT activities leading up to the Bay of Pigs remain classified because they were in support of guerrilla militia units covertly organized by the CIA. Even today many of the men involved believe that they cannot talk about what they actually accomplished. Their activities, however, involved advisory elements providing training assault swimmer and raiding skills to Cuban freedom fighters. No direct combat actions were to be undertaken by any UDT personnel, and none was planned.

Brigada de Asalto (Assault Brigade) 2506 was the self-designation of Cuban exiles who named their invasion force after the number assigned to their first training casualty. Each freedom fighter had been given a number, beginning with 2,500, to make the force seem larger than it really was—there were actually only 1,511 men in the ranks. Much of their training was accomplished at a clandestine bases located in south Florida and in the Central American country of Guatemala.

The invasion began on 17 April 1961, when Brigade 2506 landed at Giron Beach (Playa Girón) at the mouth of the Bay of Pigs. The invaders were quickly engaged and defeated by Cuban military elements.

Initially, the CIA denied having any connections with this CIA-planned operation, but the United States had supported an invasion that was a total failure, and the freedom fighters had been wiped out almost immediately by Fidel Castro's troops. President Kennedy took full responsibility for the debacle, even though the plans had been put in place during the Eisenhower administration; it was little more than a month later that President Kennedy addressed the joint session of the Congress previously discussed.

Early picture of a member of SEAL Team TWO in 1965 rigged for a full equipment jump with inflatable boat, paddles, backpack, and demolitions. Note the flotation bladder on top of his backpack. (Photo: Courtesy of Tom Hawkins)

SEALS IN SOUTH VIETNAM

During this same period, the U.S. government agreed to increase aid to South Vietnam in the fight against Viet Cong rebels. The agreement included paying for a larger Vietnamese army as well as for more U.S. advisors in the field.

Viet Cong (properly the Viet Nam Cong San, or Vietnamese Communists) was the term applied by the regime of the first president of South Vietnam, Ngo Dinh Diem, to refer to about 10,000 Communist troops that had been left in hideouts in

SEALs parachute jumping from an Albatross seaplane. (Photo: Courtesy of the National Navy UDT / SEAL Museum)

This photograph depicts the camouflage dress of a typical SEAL platoon during the mid-1960s. Note the use of the beret, which was a whim that did not endure.

South Vietnam after the Geneva Conference of 1954 ended the French Indochina War (1946–1954). Most Communist troops, according to the agreements, should have withdrawn to North Vietnam; these stay-behind troops were supported and later directed by North Vietnam.

The Viet Cong, or VC, as they were often known, first tried subversive tactics to overthrow the South Vietnamese regime and later resorted to open warfare. They were subsequently reinforced by huge numbers of North Vietnamese troops infiltrating south.

By the time the VC began fighting the Army of the Republic of Vietnam (ARVN; the Army of South Vietnam), the insurgency had set up a national infrastructure throughout South Vietnam. The People's Liberation Armed Forces (PLAF) was the armed wing of the National Liberation Front (NLF) that joined with the North Viet-

SEAL Team ONE Foxtrot Platoon, Republic of Vietnam (l-r) Standing: LDNN Tang, Tom "Ma" Hazelton, "Doc" Gillis," John "Mr. H." Hallow, Kid Carson Scout Guide, Julius "Sto" Stocinus. Kneeling: James "Marty" Martin and Danny "Midget" Horell. (Photo: Courtesy of Tom Hawkins)

SEALs on patrol in Vietnam with a POW. (Photo: Courtesy of Tom Hawkins)

namese army to fight against South Vietnamese and U.S. forces. The PLAF fighters were seeking to overthrow the South Vietnamese government and reunify Vietnam.

Rather than having to create liberated zones as in a classic insurgency, the NLF was already in control of such zones throughout the south at the start of the war. This group was known by the SEALs as COSVN (pronounced "Cosvin"), Central Office for South Vietnam, or Viet Cong infrastructure (VCI). COSVN was the senior headquarters used by the North Vietnamese Communist Party for political and military activities; it was set up throughout the country as a parallel government to that of South Vietnam. Officials of the VCI became primary targets for SEALs as the war progressed.

The U.S./ARVN response—conducting large-unit conventional campaigns and simultaneous counterinsurgency operations—was ineffective, largely because the VCI in many areas had been in place for almost twenty years and thus were well entrenched. One method to combat this was formation of U.S.-advised and

LEFT: *Navy SEALs as they interdict a sampan on the rivers of Vietnam. The sampan and individuals would be searched and perhaps detained for further questioning. (Photo: Courtesy of Tom Hawkins)*

RIGHT: *SEALs being transported aboard a PBR during infiltration operations in Vietnam. (Photo: Courtesy of Tom Hawkins)*

LEFT: *Mk VIII SDV being recovered from the water via lifting sling. (Photo: Courtesy of Tom Hawkins)*

RIGHT: *A Navy SEAL testing the experimental General Electric Mk 10, which was a closed-circuit, mixed-gas underwater breathing apparatus (UBA) tested as part of the Swimmer Support System development program in the early 1970s. The backpack contained diver communication and navigation capabilities. (Photo: Courtesy of Tom Hawkins)*

-trained provincial reconnaissance units, or PRUs, that had their origins in the CIA counterterror teams first organized in the mid-1960s with the aim of putting the VCI under pressure. Later called the Intelligence Collection and Exploitation program (ICEX), it evolved into the more elaborate Phung Hoang, or Phoenix program. The U.S. military took control of the program from the CIA in 1968.

The objective of the Phoenix program was neutralization of the VCI through the collection of data on them that could lead to their identification and subsequent neutralization. PRUs operated as the major enforcement arm of the Phoenix program and neutralized the targeted VCI. SEALs accomplished substantial work in the PRU program within their areas of responsibility.

When working with PRUs, SEALs often would wear the familiar VC black pajamas. Much effort was put into learning to walk, move, and think like VC, with

Originally called Fast Attack Vehicles (FAV), this Desert Attack Vehicle (DAV) was used by SEAL teams for missions involving airfield seizures and desert and mountain operations. FAVs employed a host of weapons including the .50-cal. seen in this photograph. (Photo: Courtesy of Tom Hawkins)

the main objective to become as invisible as possible by moving around the jungle and delta marshes like the VC.

U.S. Navy participation in the Vietnam War before 1964 involved primarily offshore blue-water operations that included a host of Navy ships. In 1964, the commander-in-chief of U.S. Pacific Command tasked Navy captain Phillip H. Bucklew to go to Vietnam to evaluate the overall situation and report his findings. Captain Bucklew was at that time the first commander, NOSG, Pacific, to whom the SEALs reported. He also was a former Scout and Raider from World War II, and one of the few senior officers in the Navy that truly understood unconventional warfare.

Captain Bucklew's Vietnam Delta Infiltration Study Group was tasked with conducting a comprehensive analysis of the problem of enemy infiltration of men and supplies into South Vietnam's Mekong Delta region and across the Cambodia and Laos borders.

The findings of the group were published in the "Bucklew Report," which concluded that the border infiltration problem was significant and needed to be stopped if there was to be success in the Vietnam War. Captain Bucklew's recommendations were for the United States to develop an extensive riverine operations capability that would assist the South Vietnamese military in conducting counterinsurgency operations to stop the infiltration problem.

A CH-47 helicopter lifts and transports a Special Operations Craft, Riverine (SOCR) during training operations along the Pearl River in Mississippi. Note the SOCR crew climbing a caving ladder into the helo as it returns to its rendezvous location. (Photo: Courtesy of Tom Hawkins)

NAVAL SPECIAL WARFARE GROUPS

As the war progressed, the NOSG staffs began to mature and in 1967 were renamed NSWG Atlantic and NSWG Pacific. NSW was quickly becoming a focused and professional Navy warfare specialty area, and began adapting to its growth and worldwide responsibilities. There were three NSWGs: those already established at Little Creek and Coronado, and NSWG, Vietnam (NAVSPECWARGRUV), a component of commander, Naval Forces, Vietnam staff in Saigon.

The Saigon staff coordinated all NSW activities ongoing in Vietnam, including SEAL platoon assignments and logistics and intelligence support, which by

LEFT: *A SEAL conducts CQB, Close Quarters Battle, as he enters a kill house wearing a gas mask and armed with an MP5. Much of SEALs training is done with live ammunition. (Photo: Greg E. Mathieson Sr. / NSW Publications, LLC)*

BELOW: *The experimental General Electric Mk 10, a closed-circuit, mixed-gas underwater breathing apparatus (UBA) tested as part of the Swimmer Support System development program in the early 1970s. The backpack contained diver communication and navigation capabilities. (Photo: Courtesy of Tom Hawkins)*

ABOVE: *Landing Craft, Swimmer Reconnaissance (LCSR). A total of 30 gas-turbine-powered LCSRs were built to support UDT and SEAL team operations for a brief period during the late 1960s. With a length of 52 feet, it was very roomy and had a cabin at the stern where the swimmers would ride during transit. During swimmer-launch operations, they would jump off the stern. For recovery, the craft would employ the Fulton recovery system by snagging two sleds while under way at high speed. The sleds can be seen mounted over the swimmer cabin in this photograph. The LCSR was versatile, but could not be deployed from a variety of Navy ships. It was also noisy because of the gas-turbine engines, and not well suited for clandestine operations near the beach. As a result, the boat's history in NSW was very short lived. (Photo: Courtesy of Tom Hawkins)*

TOP, RIGHT: *Mk IX SDV with Standoff Weapons Assembly (SWA) during sea trials in Newport, Rhode Island, circa 1978. The SWA was a modified Mk 37 torpedo designed for launch from the SDV using a periscope while just awash on the surface. The SWA was never placed into service, because the Mk IX SDV program was canceled for a variety of reasons. (Photo: Courtesy of Tom Hawkins)*

BOTTOM: *Sea-Float was a unique way of moving around a Special Operations Base. It allowed SEALs to maintain the additional security of being on the water while conducting land operations. Similar bases were used during Operation Desert Storm. (Photo: Courtesy of Tom Hawkins)*

this time had increased considerably. Commander, NAVSPECWARGRUV, represented the first theater-based command and control element established for NSW units (NSWUs) since the underwater demolition flotilla and underwater demolition squadrons during World War II.

SEAL platoons operated under two liaison elements: SEAL Detachment (Det) Alpha and SEAL Det Bravo. Det Alpha was the command-and-coordinating element for all SEAL platoons assigned from SEAL Team 2. Det Golf supported platoons from SEAL Team 1.

SEAL platoons were assigned to a specific operating area in Vietnam, and, for the most part, operated autonomously. Each SEAL platoon had a mobile sup-

port team (MST) boat element assigned. The MSTs were small groups of men that came from BSU-1 in Coronado, where they were specially trained to conduct SEAL operations. MSTs operated a variety of boats that included the light, medium, and heavy SEAL support craft (HSSC). These craft will be highlighted in Chapter 7.

The U.S. Navy Game Warden operations, conducted by Task Force 116, got under way in early 1966. The Navy wanted to secure vital water passages throughout the Rung Sat Special Zone (just south of Saigon) and establish presence patrols on the Mekong Delta rivers, where VC transported arms and supplies brought in from Cambodia, shifted guerrilla units, and taxed and harassed the population.

On 1 April 1967, the Navy activated Helicopter Attack (Light) Squadron Three, or HA(L)-3, at Vung Tau with responsibility for providing Task Force 116 with aerial fire support, observation, and medical evacuation. By September 1968,

ABOVE: *Instructors keep a close watch at various depths over the careful ascent of these Phase Two trainees from the bottom of the Training Center's deep dive tank. They are teaching the procedures for avoiding accidents during dives greater than one-atmosphere, and the tank provides clear water in which to conduct such training. U.S. Navy SEALs BUD/S Class 144 in March 1987. (Photo: Dave Gatley)*

RIGHT: *U.S. Navy SEALs, BUD/S Class 144 during their "Hell Week" training in March 1987. Surf Passage, an exercise in navigating the ever-present surf conditions off Coronado's beaches as a team. SEAL instructors use Surf Passage as a tool to teach teamwork, coordination, good communication skills, leadership, endurance, and other attributes. Failures usually result in repeating the task or enduring additional push-ups and running evolutions. They will learn that it will take the entire team, working together, to maintain proper handling of these heavy rubber crafts and to propel them through a surf line. That communication under tiring, difficult, dirty, and miserable conditions is essential to accomplishing their tasks. (Photo: Dave Gatley)*

this naval aviation squadron, known as the Seawolfs, was organized with detachments of two helicopters each at Nha Be, Binh Thuy, Dong Tom, Rach Gia, Vinh Long, and on board three landing ships tank (LSTs) stationed in the larger rivers of the Mekong Delta. They flew Bell UH-1B (Hueys) primarily as gunships. They were armed variously with 2.75-inch rockets, .50-caliber, 60-mm, and 7.62-mm machine guns, miniguns, grenades, and small arms.

While the majority of SEAL operations were conducted from boats, it was in Vietnam that SEALs first began developing air-assault tactics using

Army and Navy helicopters. Operations involved helicopters in "slick" configurations that carried passengers but were lightly armed with door guns. As the war progressed, SEALs and Seawolfs worked closely together in areas where they were co-located, and became a team like no others even into the modern day. Sadly, HA(L)-3 was eliminated after the Vietnam War ended. It represented really the first and last time that SEALs would have almost dedicated combat air support.

By mid-1968, SEAL Team 1 had fielded twelve twelve-man platoons, each comprising two squads of six men

TOP: *Having endured almost six full days of punishing Hell Week training and kept sandy, tired, wet, and disoriented, these BUD/S trainees are approaching the end of this infamous ordeal. Crawling through colored-smoke filled and barbed-wire lined paths BUD/S Class 172 moves toward the final rope crossing of a pit filled with muddy water and more noise and smoke. Over one-third of their starting class enrollment has dropped out or were injured enough to roll back to the next class. (Photo: Dave Gatley)*

CENTER: *Playing along California's beautiful beaches is considered a joyful experience by most visitors. Not so much for BUD/S Class 172. All during Hell Week these prospective SEALs will stay wet, cold, sandy, and sleep-deprived. They are ordered to lie in the surfline—an act that will be repeated dozens of times, day and night, throughout each sleepless day of Hell Week. Nearly two-thirds of their class are expected to drop out during the first month of their training. (Photo by Dave Gatley)*

BOTTOM, LEFT: *On the Naval Special Warfare Center beaches, just south of Coronado, California, SEAL trainees learn how to disarm and kill an opponent in CQT (Close Quarters Training) using a knife and body weight to control the attack. (Photo Dave Gatley)*

BOTTOM, RIGHT: *US Navy SEALs, BUD/S Class 172 is nearly 36 hours into their Hell Week and still no sleep. Each IBS (Inflatable Boat, Small) boat crew has dug a foxhole with their paddles and is now simulating defending these holes (with the same paddles) along the surf line of Coronado, CA. This physically punishing exercise in teamwork is part of the test to see if they have what it takes to become a SEAL. (Photo Dave Gatley)*

each. Most operations conducted in Vietnam by SEALs were squad-sized operations. Generally four or five platoons at any given time were deployed to South Vietnam. In early 1967, SEAL Team 2 from the Atlantic Fleet provided another three platoons. SEAL platoons launched operations largely in the central delta area IV Corps ("Four Corps") region. Although focused primarily on the areas to the south and west of Saigon, SEALs also mounted operations in the I Corps ("Eye Corps") and II Corps ("Two Corps") tactical zones.

SEAL platoons were never assigned permanently to Vietnam, but were sent on temporary duty assignments for periods of about six months at a time. Many of the men made several tours.

SEAL platoons carried out day and night ambushes (but much preferred night operations), hit-and-run raids, reconnaissance patrols, and special intelligence operations. Calling them the "men with green faces" for the face camouflage they used, the VC feared SEALs and often put a bounty on their heads. SEALs used a variety of craft, including self-developed SEAL Team Support Craft (STAB), river patrol boats (patrol boat, riverine, or PBRs), sampans, and helicopters for transportation to and from their target areas.

Although it had little impact on SEAL operations, in the beginning of 1968, the North Vietnamese and VC orchestrated a major offensive against South Vietnam. From a purely military standpoint the Tet Offensive was a major disaster to the Communists, but it revealed that the coastal Market Time and Game Warden patrol operations on major river systems were not decisively affecting the border infiltration problem.

The SEALORDS (Southeast Asia Lake, Ocean, River, and Delta Strategy) program was initiated as a determined effort by U.S. Navy, South Vietnamese navy, and

ABOVE: *A SEAL team operator prepares to board a helicopter aboard a Navy aircraft carrier. At one point groups of SEALs would remain at sea aboard carrier task forces. (Photo: Greg E. Mathieson Sr. / NSW Publications, LLC)*

BOTTOM, LEFT: *Navy SEALs coming in from the sea with their weapons in hand; using Drager rebreathers and carrying their fins. This has been the traditional photo most of the world has seen of SEALs over the years. Much has changed as a result of current world needs, technology, and training. (Photo: Greg E. Mathieson Sr. / NSW Publications LLC)*

BOTTOM, RIGHT: *Navy SEALs conduct shipboarding drills using caving ladders. This operational technique requires extreme upper-body strength and is accomplished from static and underway platforms during day and nighttime operations. (Photo: Courtesy of Tom Hawkins)*

ABOVE: SEALs armed with H&K MP5's and shotguns take down a crew member of a ship they boarded during a training exercise aboard the USS *Mount Whitney* in the early 1990s. VBSS, Visit, Board, Search, and Seizure, is one of a number of ways of dealing with piracy and ships transporting illegal arms. (Photo: Greg E. Mathieson Sr. / NSW Publications, LLC)

RIGHT: At times, training can get pretty real, as SEALs here take down a sailor on the steel deck of the USS *Mount Whitney* as he's playing the part of a group that has taken control of a ship. (Photo: Greg E. Mathieson Sr. / NSW Publications, LLC)

A UDT-SEAL operator executes a water recovery aboard a U.S. Navy CH-46 helicopter during training operations. (Photo: Courtesy of Tom Hawkins)

allied ground forces to stop the influx of men and supplies crossing the Cambodian border to sustain enemy forces operating in the Mekong delta and Saigon areas.

In June 1969, the U.S. Navy anchored a mobile pontoon base in the middle of the Ca Mau region's Cua Lon River. This base, called Sea Float, was strategically located, but in a difficult place because of heavy VC opposition, strong river currents, and the distance to logistic support facilities. SEAL and Seawolf detachments operated very successfully from this afloat operating base. Sea Float denied the VC a safe haven even in its isolated corner of the delta.

In the spring of 1969, President Richard M. Nixon initiated his new policy of Vietnamization. This had little impact on SEAL platoons, which continued to operate somewhat independently. Also, except for continued SEAL support by HA(L)-3 and aircraft of similar unit, the U.S. Navy's role in Vietnam pretty much ended in April 1971, when Solid Anchor (previously Sea Float) became a Vietnamese responsibility.

FINAL SEAL OPERATIONS IN VIETNAM

In about six years of heavy involvement in Vietnam, the relatively small group of SEALs accounted for six hundred confirmed VC killed and three hundred almost certainly killed. Numerous others were captured or detained. No statistical tally can be placed on the effects of the intelligence gathered by SEALs, but the SEALs made a contribution to the war out of all proportion to their numbers.

Navy SEALs train in the use of caving ladders. (Photo: Greg E. Mathieson Sr. / NSW Publications, LLC)

Early on Naval Special Warfare and the SEALs worked with marine mammals such as the dolphin seen here. Later the dolphins became part of a program now known as the Navy Marine Mammal Program within the Biosciences Division of the Space and Naval Warfare Systems Center Pacific located in San Diego, California (Photo: Greg E. Mathieson Sr. / NSW Publications, LLC)

In the psychological war, too, they were extraordinary, going some way toward evening up the unspoken balance of terror and gaining a reputation as fearsome and extraordinary warriors.

During the month of October 1965, UDT commander Robert J. Fay was hit by a mortar round and became the first NSW operator killed in Vietnam.

In February 1966, a SEAL Team 1 detachment arrived in Vietnam to conduct direct-action missions. Operating out of Nha Be in the Rung Sat Special Zone, the first SEAL operator killed while engaged in active combat was RD2 Billy Machen, killed in a firefight on 16 August 1966.

The last SEAL platoon departed Vietnam on 7 December 1971. The last SEAL advisors left Vietnam in March 1973. Between 1965 and 1972, there were forty-six SEALs killed in Vietnam. On 6 June 1972, Lt. Melvin S. Dry was killed when he jumped into the ocean from a helicopter. He was the last Navy SEAL killed in the Vietnam conflict.

INTO THE PRESENT

The U.S. Special Operations Command (USSOCOM) was activated on 16 April 1987, with approximately 47,000 active and reserve forces from the Army, Navy, and Air Force. The Naval Special Warfare Command (NSWC) was established with overall responsibility for all U.S.-based NSWGs and their overseas-based Naval Special Warfare Units (NSWUs) and component SEAL and Special Boat Teams (SBTs). The principal Special Operations Force (SOF) core tasks assigned SEAL teams include:

- Counter-proliferation (CP): Stem the growth of nuclear, biological, and chemical weapons.
- Counterterrorism (CT): Prevent and preempt terror activities across the full spectrum of potential terrorist activity. SEAL teams are the principal maritime CT force within USSOCOM.
- Foreign internal defense (FID): Organize, train, equip, and assist foreign

host-nation governments. This can range from civic action such as building schools to paramilitary training.

- Special reconnaissance (SR): Surveillance to collect intelligence. Familiarly referred to as "sneak and peek," SEALs have done SR in littoral regions to the mountains of Afghanistan.
- Direct action (DA): Short-duration attacks on enemy facilities, the old inland demolition raid type of operation. Targets range from buildings, bridges, to personnel capture; the meat-and-potatoes operation for SOF.
- Unconventional warfare (UW): Organizing and often leading indigenous forces in, perhaps, a counterinsurgency effort, for example, today in Iraq and Afghanistan.
- Civil affairs, psychological operations (PSYOPS), and information operations (IO): Of limited use, these are normally carried out by sister services, but SEALs and SBT members have participated in them over the years.

Other SOF collateral activities make up a "grab bag" of exercises covering coalition support, combat search and rescue (CSAR), counterdrug activities, humanitarian demining operations, humanitarian assistance (such as evacuating embassies), security assistance, and other special activities. This last is referred to by a USSOCOM manual as "subject to limitation imposed by Executive Order and in conjunction with a presidential finding and congressional oversight, plan and conduct actions abroad in support of national foreign policy objectives so that the role of the U.S. government is not apparent or acknowledged publicly." This would appear to relate to "covert operations," and it does. These normally remain within the purview of the CIA, but on occasion SEALs, working with interagency partners, can be tapped for collaborative special operations, actions, or activities.

SEALs with high-technology weapons and other equipment infiltrate from the sea in their combat rubber raiding craft (CRRC). (Photo: Greg E. Mathieson Sr. / NSW Publications, LLC)

COMMAND STRUCTURE

REAR ADM (SEAL) GEORGE WORTHINGTON
USN (RET)

BELOW: *Led by their instructor at the center of this group, the class goes through and practices each of the maneuvers that will be done while free-falling before opening their chutes after jumping from the jump plane: "You play the way you train" types of routines build automatic responses and procedures for each evolution they face in the training program. Over and over, each routine will be rehearsed by each student until it becomes automatic for them. Static Line, Free Fall, and HALO (High Altitude Low Opening) programs are all conducted for WARCOM at Tactical Air Operations, a professional skydiving school on the West Coast. (Photo: Dave Gatley)*

CHAPTER 3

COMMAND STRUCTURE

Rear Adm. (SEAL) George Worthington, USN (Ret.)

UNDERSTANDING HOW NSW FORCES ARE ORGANIZED WILL afford a clear view regarding their deployments and operations. NSW is organized around the NSWC, which is the maritime component of the USSOCOM. NSWC is located in Coronado, California, and is commanded by a two-star rear admiral. NSWC is further organized into NSWGs, NSWUs, and NSW teams. Each NSWG is commanded by a Navy captain, and has responsibility for subordinate overseas-based NSWUs and United States–based SEAL teams, SEAL delivery vehicle teams (SDVTs), and SBTs. These teams are the front-line operational units deployed forward on a rotational basis or as needed to accomplish specific mission tasking.

NSWC also has responsibility for the NSW Training Center and the NSW Development Group (DEVGRP), which are also commanded by Navy captains. In total, the number of military and civilian personnel serving in NSW on any given day is around 8,900 men and women, including 2,700 officers and enlisted SEALs and 750 enlisted SWCC operators, which is a very small fraction of the U.S. Navy.

Remaining personnel provide combat support (CS) and combat service support (CSS), or they perform a variety of staff functions that include operational planning, maintenance, intelligence collection and analysis, and budget preparation.

All U.S. Navy commands and units west of the Mississippi River are odd numbered, while units on the east are even numbered. Thus, commander, NSWG-1 (CNSWG-1), commands SEAL Teams 1, 3, 5, and 7; and Logistic Support Unit One (LOGSU-1), which are home ported at the Joint Expeditionary Base (JEB) Coronado, San Diego, California, NSWU-1 in Guam, and NSWU-3 in Bahrain. CNSWG-2 commands SEAL Teams 2, 4, 8, and 10, LOGSU-2, and NSWU-4, which are home ported at JEB Little Creek, Norfolk, Virginia, and NSWU-2 and NSWU-10 in Stuttgart, Germany. CNSWG-3 is headquartered at JEB, Coronado, and commands SDVT-1 in Pearl Harbor, Hawaii. CNSWG-4 is headquartered at JEB, Little Creek, and commands SBT-12, SBT-20, and SBT-22 located in Coronado, Little Creek, and the Stennis Space Flight Center, Mississippi, respectively. NSWG-10 was recently formed; it commands Support Activity One, Coronado, and Support Activity Two, Little Creek. CNSWG-11 was established to organize the NSW reserve force; it is located at Coronado. Its component commands are SEAL Teams 17 and 18, which are located at Coronado and Little Creek, respectively.

When deployed overseas, components of these commands can be combined to form a task-organized NSW squadron (NSWRON), which is composed of an entire SEAL team, and is commanded by the SEAL team's CO. Deployed NSWRONs can perform a full spectrum of core SOF tasks worldwide. NSWRONs adopt the number of the SEAL team commander being deployed (e.g., SEAL Team 8 would become NSWRON-8), and may include combat-enabling technical and administrative support functions and personnel provided from the various NSWGs.

The primary mission of the operational SEALs, SDVTs, and SBTs is to conduct maritime special operations in support of national security objectives.

NSWRONs deploy in support of a geographic combatant commander at a

LEFT, TOP: *The BUD/S quarterdeck, adjoining what is known as "The Grinder," a courtyard located in the center of the BUD/S training center. The Grinder is also used for each class's graduation exercises–they begin here and they finish here. Helmets lining the edge of the facility are from those trainees that chose to not continue, or dropped out of the incredibly tough training program. World renowned for degree of difficulty in the three primary phases of training, roughly two-thirds of each class will drop out before graduating. Those leaving will place their helmet here–having been "rung out" with the infamous brass bell in the foreground. (Photo: Dave Gatley)*

LEFT, CENTER: *SEAL and SWCC recruiting in the field. Special Warfare Boat Operator 2nd Class Ronnie Longoria, from Special Boat Team 20, talks with high school students attending the National High School Wrestling Championship at the Virginia Beach Convention Center. Longoria volunteered to work with the Navy SEAL Accelerator, which travels the country introducing careers that are available in the Navy special warfare community. (Photo: Mass Communication Specialist Seaman Apprentice Joshua Adam Nuzzo)*

LEFT, BOTTOM: *The Logistics Support Units (LOGSU) maintain inventories of nearly every part of every item the SEALs and SWCC units need, be it boats and engines, parachutes and uniforms, nuts and bolts, or uniform patches and flags. (Photo: Greg E. Mathieson Sr. / NSW Publications, LLC)*

BELOW: *Logo and patch for Detachment Kodiak, the cold weather training outpost located on the beautiful but very cold and remote island of Kodiak, Alaska. Known mostly for its fishing fleet and industry Kodiak Island allows the SEALs in training to experience real-world cold weather conditions and helps build their individual confidences and knowledge of handling these extreme conditions. (Photo by Dave Gatley)*

Jump School has moved from the U.S. Army command to a combat training program much closer to "home" for the SEALs training programs on the West Coast. Here Class 264 practices some of the maneuvers that will be performed while free-falling, just before opening their chutes. Tactical Air Operations is a professional sky diving school contracted for teaching SEALs and others. Static-Line, Free-fall, and HALO (High Altitude Low Opening) programs are all conducted at this school. (Photo: Dave Gatley)

theater-based NSWU, which is under the operational control of a Theater Special Operations Command (TSOC). Within the U.S. Central Command (CENT-COM, with an area of responsibility in Middle East–North Africa–Central Asia) and for tasking in Iraq and Afghanistan, Joint Special Operations Task Force (JSOTF) units comprising Army, Navy, Air Force, and Marine Corps SOF have been organized based on theater needs. Take a historical example: in the Vietnam era, SEAL team platoons reported in Vietnam to the commander, U.S. Naval Forces, Vietnam, which command reported to the U.S. Military Assistance Command, Vietnam (MACV), a four-star Army general. Operations in Vietnam were supported and coordinated by a deployed group, NSWG (Vietnam). This group advised the fledgling Vietnamese Sea Commando units and supported American SEALs and their combatant craft, which were operated and maintained by the BSU-1 MSTs—operationally and logistically.

During the Vietnam War, UDTs operated much like SEAL platoons in terms of reporting responsibilities. If, however, UDT platoons were part of the 7th Amphibious Force, they retained their afloat chain of command to the amphibious unit. When teams and elements report into a contested area, all command and control arrangements are solidified well in advance. This was true following 9/11 when SOF units, including NSW SEALs, moved into Afghanistan to destroy the Taliban terrorist network. The region fell under the operational control of CENTCOM, who serves as the geographic combatant commander for this region. The SOF units were further assigned to a JSOTF under the Special Operations Command, Central (SOCCENT), which was commanded by a Navy SEAL admiral, who divided the country for operations between his assigned Army Special Forces and Navy SEALs, Army north/Navy south. They had the support of conventional

forces and supported them in return. It was an exceptional SOF success!

SEALs train intimately with SBTs in the open ocean, surf zones, littoral regions, and rivers. Early SEAL and SBT team history was developed on the rivers of the Mekong Delta in South Vietnam, where SEALs worked with the BSU MSTs, the forerunners of today's SBTs. SBTs are manned by SWCC crewmen. Following SWCC training, combatant-craft Sailors are assigned to an SBT at Little Creek, Virginia; Coronado, California; or Stennis, Mississippi. Craft they will operate and maintain are varied and capable. The workhorse of the SEAL team is the Zodiac F-470; it does not require a SWCC crewman, but SBTs maintain an inventory for their own use. SWCC skills come into particular play on board the Mark V (Mk V) special operations craft (Mk V SOC), special operations craft, riverine (SOCR), and the 11-meter NSW Rigid Hull Inflatable Boat (RIB, pronounced "rib").

Life in a SEAL team, SDVT, or SBT is a challenging career from training and operational standpoints. Advanced training is arduous and time consuming; in recognition, SEALs and SWCCs were recently assigned a Navy rating code for their specialties. Heretofore, Sailors selected specific Navy "ratings" as electricians, machinists, boatswains, and so on. Today, with so much time required in actual NSW deployment and combat operations, it was time to "get serious" about warfare skills. The SEAL rating is called special warfare operator (SO), and the SWCC rating is called special warfare boat operator (SB).

NAVAL SPECIAL WARFARE-21

Initiated in the late 1990s, NSW-21 was COMNAVSPECWARCOM's (commander, NSWC; also CNSWC) overarching plan to modernize and restructure

Exhaustion sets in as the skydiving SEALs students grab some sleep anywhere they can, in this case on the floor of the classroom before their next evolution. (Photo: Dave Gatley)

BOTTOM, LEFT: *Every parachute jump is followed by the student repacking their chutes themselves. They do that under close supervision, as shown by a female jump instructor illustrating how to squeeze all the air out of the partially folded chute by laying on it. The Jump School has moved from the U.S. Army command to a combat training program much closer to "home" for the SEALs training programs. Tactical Air Operations is a professional skydiving school in East County San Diego. Static-line, Free-fall, and HALO programs are all conducted at this school. Here, Class 264 is undergoing such instruction. (Photo: Dave Gatley)*

BELOW: *Naval Special Warfare (NSW) Group Four – Little Creek, Virginia, which is comprised of Special Boat Team 12 – Coronado, CA, Special Boat Team 20 – Little Creek, VA, and Special Boat Team 22 – Stennis, Mississippi. (Photo: Dave Gatley)*

NSW for the future. It represented the most comprehensive NSW community reorganization since the UDTs were reorganized into SEAL teams in 1983. The goal was to increase relevance and effectiveness to reflect the maturity of theater SOF operations, while maintaining operational support and focus to the joint task force commanders. As one of many structural and operational changes, entire SEAL teams would deploy as task-organized NSWRONs into theater with combatant craft, swimmer delivery vehicles (now called SEAL delivery vehicles, or SDVs), explosive ordnance disposal (EOD), and operations, intelligence, and logistics enablers commanded by a SEAL team CO. The transition was difficult to implement because it had so many moving parts; the new organizational structure provided TSOC commanders with a more responsive NSW capability, however. Fortunately, it also set the stage for NSW to effectively deploy for sustained operations after 9/11 to meet the new tasking requirements.

Before NSW-21, SEAL teams would deploy forward with one or several platoons and SBT detachments with a mix of combatant craft. Training preparation normally began six months before a deployment with a readiness exercise in advance of the deployment date. The units were not tied together as a compact, discrete entity. The senior officer assigned the deployment might have been the team executive officer or the senior platoon commander. This system worked well

Once in the air and climbing to altitude in their jump plane, a SEAL skydiving student checks his altimeter to see how much farther he has to climb before his jump today at 10,000 feet. (Photo: Dave Gatley)

for years; with the surge in operational tasking for NSW forces, however, a more robust organization was deemed necessary—thus NSW-21.

The cornerstone of NSW-21 was that an entire SEAL team would deploy under the SEAL team CO, who would command a task-organized NSWRON. The squadron would be identified by the number of the deployed team (e.g., NSWRON-1 if SEAL Team 1 was assigned). The SEAL team CO, as NSWRON commander, commanded two or three SEAL Troops, which are strike force elements made up of combined SEAL platoons, SBT detachments, and all other logistics and engineering support personnel assigned, who would work up together beginning six months prior to deployment. The enhanced training is specific, detailed, and intense. The NSWRON moves out as an integrated unit and reports into the TSOC or JSOTF for follow-on operational assignments. This organizational change places many more responsibilities on the SEAL team COs. But the dramatically increased operational tempo (OPTEMPO) since 9/11 has required more NSW experience in theaters. In the "old days," SEAL team COs would only deploy to theaters a couple of times during their teams' deployment cycle. Today, SEAL team COs are full-time participants in their commands' employment. NSW-21 was an idea whose time had come and has proven effective since implementation. The first squadron was deployed under the CO, SEAL Team 7.

New students from BUD/S Class 264 practice all evolutions of a jump repeatedly. In this training session they are all rigged up exactly as they would be under a real chute. They rehearse each sequence of steps again and again under close supervision to make sure they understand the steps for a good jump scenario. When they actually make their jumps, this practice should kick in automatically. (Photo: Dave Gatley)

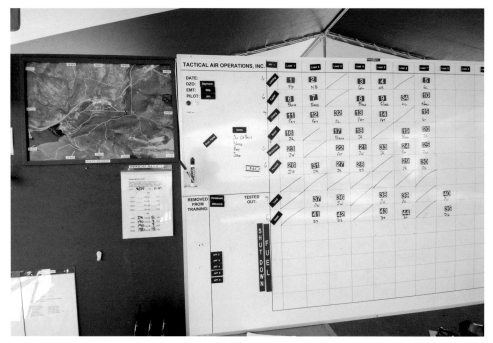

ABOVE: *Like so much of their other training programs, these students are practicing their maneuvers all the time. Their instructors go from one to another reviewing exactly what the SEAL-in-training will do immediately after leaving an airplane, skydiving from 10,000 feet in these early exercises. When they actually jump, they will know the steps by heart. (Photo: Dave Gatley)*

RIGHT, TOP: *Each jump is videotaped, usually by each student's instructor. All students on the flight review each others' tapes, noting what mistakes and what successes they performed during their fall through the air. The feedback while the experiences are fresh in their minds has proved a valuable part of each jump. (Photo: Dave Gatley)*

RIGHT, BOTTOM: *The Jump Board at Tactical Air Operations lists all the flights for the day, the instructors, the number of jumpers on each flight, and generally tracks all the classes' progress for each day. An aerial view and map on the left shows the layout of the jump zone. (Photo: Dave Gatley)*

SEAL TEAM OPERATIONAL CYCLE

NSW SEAL teams—and every other unit—participate in a two-year training/operational cycle. Six months are spent in professional development, six months in unit-level training (ULT), six months in squadron integration training (SIT), and six months on deployment. Squadrons are only formed up to prepare and deploy overseas.

Discussed earlier, NSW-21 became the cornerstone of NSW deployment. In years past, SEAL platoons deployed overseas singly, accompanied with whatever boat support the platoon might require. SDVT platoons would deploy in a similar way, and pick up any required boat support once in theater. Predeployment work-up stressed platoon maneuvers; what boat support required was scheduled by the team training cadre on a case-by-case basis. No more. Today, entire SEAL teams marry up with SBT counterparts—and other logistics elements, as required—and train together for six months prior to deployment. This combined unit is referred to as an NSWRON, headed up by the SEAL team CO; it takes the SEAL team number as its identifying handle—for example, NSWRON-1, NSWRON-3, NSWRON-5, and NSWRON-7 for West Coast teams; and NSWRON-2, NSWRON-4, NSWRON-8, and NSWRON-10 for East Coast teams.

Important in the interoperability training are the training detachments on each coast assigned to the group. These organizations focus on integration training, joint operations, complex command and control, and the validation exercise. During these training phases, SEALs participate in advanced courses offered by the NSW Center's (NSWCEN, or the Center) Advanced Training Command (ATC) and detachments located in Key West, Florida; Little Creek, Virginia; Hurlburt, Florida; Kodiak, Alaska; Panama City, Florida; Yuma, Arizona; and Pearl Harbor, Hawaii. The ATC provides more than forty individual courses. Representative samplings are sniper training, lead breaching, close quarter defense (CQD), maritime scout, photographic intelligence collection, SDV operations, and advanced special operations techniques.

NAVAL SPECIAL WARFARE SQUADRON MAKEUP

NSWRONs come together six months before going overseas. The NSWRON consists of a SEAL team, assigned SBT elements, SDVs, logistics, mobile communications team (MCT) elements, and any extra personnel required; they are assembled and put through all the predeployment training wickets. A SEAL team consists of a headquarters staff, logistical and technical personnel, and the operational platoons. Each platoon consists of two officers and twelve enlisted men—all are "shooters" or "operators." There are eight operational platoons in a SEAL team and, as discussed above, each team forms the nucleus of the deployable SEAL team. Exercises are conducted jointly with Army and Marine units. SEALs participate in many exercises at the Army's National Training Center at Fort Irwin, California, where Close Quarters Battle (CQB) and urban missions are jointly rehearsed. FID exercises are conducted, also, with military and civilian role players simulating enemy captives. At the end of the run-up period, the squadron completes a series of final battle problems (FTXs), after which certi-

Jump School for the SEALs, SWCC, and others has moved from the U.S. Army command to a combat training program much closer to WARCOM. Using a commercial contractor such as Tactical Air Operations, a professional skydiving school, saves valuable time and money while maintaining the quality of the programs' material. (Photo: Dave Gatley)

LEFT: *Three skydivers orbit as they approach the landing zone, remaining clear of each other while a new trainee SEAL skydiver approaches first (gray). These modern parachutes are self-inflating "ram-air" wings that control the speed and direction and are highly maneuverable, even when loaded with full military packs. (Photo: Dave Gatley)*

BELOW: *The Tactical Air Operations (San Diego, California) Military Freefall School coin representing their certified SEAL Jump School on the West Coast. (Photo by Dave Gatley)*

ABOVE: *Members of Leap Frog demo team on SEAL beach – watching as the remaining jumpers descend to the beach during the annual UDT-SEAL Association East Coast reunion. (Photo: Greg E. Mathieson Sr. / NSW Publications, LLC)*

BELOW: *The U.S. Navy Parachute Team known as the Leap Frogs debrief following their demonstration before the NSW Foundation annual gathering in Little Creek, Virginia. The team, made up of active-duty Navy SEALs and SWCC travels around the county to help promote recruiting for SEAL candidates. (Photo: Greg E. Mathieson Sr. ./ NSW Publications, LLC)*

fication to deploy is given by the NSWG commander. This deployment mode has been in effect for several years, and has met with complete approval by the geographic commanders.

With the inception of NSW-21, teams were reorganized into six platoons. The 2006 quadrennial defense review (QDR) resulted in a shift toward the speed, agility, and precision required for irregular warfare operations, including wars of long duration such as the global war on terror (GWOT). As a result of the QDR, the FY 2007 budget substantially increased the size and capabilities of SOF, including the addition of additional SEAL and SBT operators and support technicians. This resulted in a fast-paced recruiting effort for volunteers for SEAL training.

Several other stand-alone organizations are part of the NSWC structure. Let's look at three important elements: Leap Frogs, MCTs, and LOGSUs.

Navy Parachute Team: Leap Frogs

The U.S. Navy parachute team Leap Frogs is considered to be one of the most accomplished parachute demonstration teams in the country. Its inauspicious beginning in 1963 can be attributed to retired Navy SEAL Capt. Norman H. Olson, who at the time was CO, UDT-11. The following year the team was officially recognized by its parent command, NOSG Pacific, and became known as the UDT Para-Team. It retained that name until 1969, when it took on a more recognizable identity that reflected the team's origins—the Leap Frogs.

Prior to the establishment of the UDT Para-Team, and in commemoration of the fiftieth anniversary of naval aviation in 1961, the U.S. Navy parachute exhibition team, the Chuting Stars, was formed from selected test jumpers at the Navy Test Parachute Unit, Naval Air Facility, El Centro, California. Two years later, however, they were the victim of budget cuts and their operation discontinued.

The U.S. Navy Parachute Team Leap Frogs perform a drag-plane maneuver during a demonstration at SEAL Beach in Little Creek, Virginia. Linked together by their legs, these three members illustrate the degree of agility and confidence that these skydivers are capable of during this daring maneuver. A typical Leap Frogs performance consists of fourteen jumpers leaping out of an aircraft at an altitude of 12,500 feet. During free fall, jumpers reach speeds of 120 mph and can accelerate up to 180 mph by pulling their arms to their sides and straightening their legs into what is called a "track." (Photo: Greg E. Mathieson Sr. / NSW Publications, LLC)

Subsequently, Naval Air Technical Training Center, Lakehurst, New Jersey, picked up the mantle of the Chuting Stars but they too met the same fate of budget cuts and were grounded by the Navy.

The patch of the U.S. Navy Parachute Team Leap Frogs demonstration team. (Photo: Dave Gatley)

With little or no knowledge of the aforementioned efforts by the naval aviation community, the formation of today's Navy parachute team—Leap Frogs is a story of "boot straps." The original five members from UDT-11 and UDT–12 paid for all their own equipment—Bell helmets, pioneer jump suits, French jump boots, altimeters, and paracommander parachutes—the most radical change in parachute design in thirty-five years. Its activities were conducted on a "not-to-interfere" basis with other military duties and at no cost to the government, other than utilizing normally scheduled aircraft. The Para-Team's initial purpose was to visually enhance the many local UDTSEAL demonstrations, both on base and off. These demonstrations met with immediate success in helping to tell not only the UDTSEAL story, but also the Navy story. As time went on, the UDT Para-Team gained popularity, and requests for locally sponsored weekend demonstrations spread throughout California and Arizona.

In 1969, when the Para-Team's professionalism became nationally recognized,

the name Leap Frogs was adopted. Concurrently, under the leadership of Lt. "Scotty" Lyon, the team was officially designated by the Navy Recruiting Command as the Navy Parachute Team (NPT).

The West Coast was on the leading edge of military demonstration jumping, but the East Coast had not progressed significantly in this regard. In 1968, however, when retired Captain Olson was reassigned as chief staff officer, NSWG Atlantic, he convinced the group commander to establish a demonstration team similar to the one in the Pacific. For the next several years, the UDT-SEAL Para-Team Atlantic put on demonstrations throughout the East Coast; their big break came in 1973 during the Annual Azalea Day Festival Air Show at the Naval Air Station, Norfolk. Historically, this had been a Blue Angels/Golden Knights show; that year, however, the Army had a scheduling conflict and had to renege. As a result, the Para-Team filled the gap and put on a superb demonstration.

Fortuitously, commander Navy Recruiting Command was in attendance and expressed his pleasure to the Para-Team's immediate superior, commander Naval Inshore Warfare Command, Atlantic. Several weeks later, Captain Olson had a personal audience with commander Navy Recruiting Command, who signed off on combining and supporting both demonstration teams under the NPT umbrella.

The NPT (West) continued to retain Leap Frogs as their name, and the NPT (East) adopted Chuting Stars as theirs. For the next dozen years, the Mississippi served as the dividing line for demonstrations scheduled by Navy Recruiting Command. As time progressed, annual joint training evolved, all-Navy and all-military free-fall records were jointly established, and selected personnel from both teams participated in military and national competitions.

Since the team's inception in 1964, its members were on temporary additional duty orders from their respective parent commands, and thus were subject to recall

if dictated by operational requirements. This had a significant impact on continuity, both in terms of retaining sufficient team members and in the proper balance of expertise to maintain the professionalism expected by the public. Also, each member had to maintain his proficiency and qualifications as a combat swimmer, demolitionaire, and tactical parachutist, as well as keeping current in special areas of expertise mandated by fleet and joint operational commanders.

In the mid 1980s, due to funding constraints and OPTEMPO, the Chuting Stars were disbanded and the Leap Frogs assumed responsibility for all official parachute demonstrations within the Navy.

Until 1994, this thirty-year history of NSW's involvement with the NPT had been a series of ups and downs, primarily due to the temporary nature of personnel assignments. When the CNO assigned the Leap Frogs the mission of demonstrating Navy excellence throughout the United States by supporting Navy recruiting efforts and promoting the NSW community to the American public, however, the NPT was institutionalized as a permanent organization within NSW.

Today's U.S. NPT comprises fifteen Navy SEAL commando and SWCC boat warrior billets. Personnel receive permanent change-of-station orders and are drawn from the NSWGs located on the East and West Coasts. Upon completion of their three-year tour, members return to operational SEAL teams or special boat squadrons (SPECBOATRON).

That notwithstanding, over the past decade the operational demands of the GWOT have taken center stage, and the size of the NPT has been reduced and reorganized to include one officer in charge (OIC), seven SEALs or SWCCs, one public affairs specialist, one hospital corpsman, two parachute riggers, and one civilian contractor as team safety officer.

During winter training between January and March, each jumper will make close to two hundred jumps, demonstrating the full spectrum of required skills. When the season begins, the NPT will conduct more than 140 demonstration jumps into high schools, colleges, professional sporting events, and air shows throughout the country. Many of the shows are jumps into Major League Baseball

ABOVE, LEFT: *Here a member of Class 264 is undergoing instruction with heavy military equipment and jump attire at the Tactical Air Operations professional skydiving school. Having released the gear pack from under him, this jumper concentrates upon his final few feet of approach to the ground without fear of tripping over the lower pack. (Photo: Dave Gatley)*

ABOVE, RIGHT: *Class 264 is undergoing instruction with full military equipment and jump attire during their skydiving exercises. They have already dropped their front equipment pack so that they will be clear of that load when their feet hit the ground at high speed. These modern parachutes are self-inflating "ram-air" wings that control the speed and direction and are highly maneuverable, even when loaded with full military packs. (Photo: Dave Gatley)*

BELOW: *Gathering and collapsing his chute following the landing – this Class 264 student will have to repack his own gear after clearing the landing zone. There will then be a full video review of his and other team members' jumps. Errors and good points will be stressed to help reinforce the value of each jump's lesson. (Photo: Dave Gatley)*

and National Football League season openers, and always include a cold weather jump into December's Army–Navy game.

A typical Leap Frog performance consists of jumpers exiting an aircraft at an altitude of 12,500 feet. During free fall, jumpers reach speeds of 120 miles per hour and can accelerate up to 180 miles per hour by pulling their arms to their sides and straightening their legs into a "track." The jumpers typically open their parachutes at around 5,000 feet by releasing a smaller pilot chute that deploys their main blue-and-gold canopy. After deploying their chutes, the Leap Frogs fly their canopies together to build dramatic canopy-relative work formations.

The Leap Frogs are renowned for exciting and complex formations, such as downplanes, sideplanes, dragplanes, diamonds, big stacks, tri-by-sides, and "T" formations. Following each performance, the Leap Frogs make themselves avail-

able to the public to answer questions about the Navy and the NSW community, as well as to sign autographs.

Since the NPT's earliest days, one area is often overlooked by those who think the NPT is an end in itself, and that is the jumping expertise that NPT members bring back to their operational commands when their tour is over. This expertise complements and enhances the operator's tactical proficiency, particularly in areas relating to High Altitude Low Opening (HALO) and High Altitude High Opening (HAHO) parachute jumps.

The initial static line and free-fall parachute training that all SEALs and SWCCs undergo makes them basically qualified, but the free-fall expertise that is introduced to the operational teams by former NPT members enhances the level of their tactical proficiency in terms of quality and the time it takes to instill an effective capability. This has been proven since the earliest days in the mid-1960s, and more so today, when the capability to effectively insert SEALs by air into terrain heretofore thought impossible to reach has been perfected. This presents a capability they were not expected to have, in areas they were not expected to be in.

Today, parachuting is an essential qualification for all SEALs. It was not always so, but the Leap Frogs have contributed significantly toward that end. The air

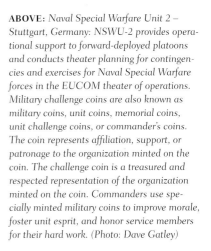

ABOVE: *Naval Special Warfare Unit 2 – Stuttgart, Germany: NSWU-2 provides operational support to forward-deployed platoons and conducts theater planning for contingencies and exercises for Naval Special Warfare forces in the EUCOM theater of operations. Military challenge coins are also known as military coins, unit coins, memorial coins, unit challenge coins, or commander's coins. The coin represents affiliation, support, or patronage to the organization minted on the coin. The challenge coin is a treasured and respected representation of the organization minted on the coin. Commanders use specially minted military coins to improve morale, foster unit esprit, and honor service members for their hard work. (Photo: Dave Gatley)*

LEFT, TOP: *Static Line, Free Fall, and HALO programs are all conducted at this Tactical Air Operations school for both SEALs and SWCC. The class shown here is undergoing such instruction with oxygen equipment in preparation for HALO jumps. The jump boss checks each student for a thumbs-up before leaving the plane. (Photo: Dave Gatley)*

LEFT: *At 20,000 feet, high above the clouds in a HALO jump exercise, this student gets ready to make the leap while the instructor supervises. By this stage of their training, these relatively new jumpers are really quite advanced. (Photo: Dave Gatley)*

capability represented by the out-spanned wings of the eagle on the SEAL breast insignia defines strength, courage, and the ability to operate from the air. SEALs carry out this mission with ingenuity, secrecy, and daring.

Mobile Communications Teams

In 1977, a rudimentary MCT was formed in cooperation with the Navy's Inshore Undersea Warfare Group One (IUWG-1) in Coronado to provide generic communications support for NSWG-1. During this period many older U.S. Navy ships were being decommissioned, and their radios were available for "recycling." IUWG-1, although not a part of NSW, was primarily staffed with radiomen and electronics technicians who understood the capabilities of these radios. At the time, NSWG-1 had no organic communications capabilities, and all communications services had to be provided by "over-the-counter" facilities maintained by either the NAB or other commands. Development of an organic communications capability for NSW made sense. Moreover, the Navy's battle area surveillance system vans were available and already lead lined and electrically wired for radios. Stripping out their sensor gear and substituting communications equipment was a simple matter. Finding the appropri-

BOTTOM, LEFT: *LOGSU (Logistical Support) technicians are "loading-in" communications equipment, LAN servers, antennae arrays, etc., for the CERTEX exercises that begin in several weeks with SEAL teams preparing to be deployed. Here the communications technicians unpack and help each other set up the SDN-H (Heavy) satellite antennae to be used during this FTX exercise simulating "real combat" situations. This antenna is one of the largest suitcase-deployable broadband satellite antennas for support of SOF operations. (Photo: Dave Gatley / NSW Publications, LLC)*

BOTTOM, RIGHT: *Logistics Support Units (LOGSU) purchase, maintain, and account for the issue of everything from pants and body armor to boats and weapons and everything in between. (Photo: Greg E. Mathieson Sr. / NSW Publications, LLC)*

ate radios took some thinking, but the communications systems were available and being acquired from retiring ships up and down the West Coast.

The radios were installed in the battle area surveillance system vans and experimental trials were conducted. Later, Naval Communications Security engineers tested the newly configured vans for errant signal emissions; they never even got a needle to move on their sensing equipment owing to the lead lining already present in the vans. Thus, the MCT was born. It eventually was organized under the NSWG-1, where staff began exercising in local training operations; later they deployed to Hawaii for mid-Pacific exercises. The MCT traveled all over southern California providing services for NSWG-1, SEALs, and their assigned support craft. The MCT had the capability to communicate with fleet ships and units as well. Later, a satellite capability was added. The MCT, now more mature, deployed to South Korea for annual unconventional warfare exercises. During Operation Desert Storm the West Coast MCT deployed to Kuwait and was able to facilitate logistics support for the deployed group.

Today, MCTs are in service on both coasts. The electronics configuration is standardized and monitored by the NSWC. The teams have proven themselves invaluable in numerous deployments, including combat. MCTs "are responsible for providing rapid, reliable, robust and deployed strategy and tactical communications in support of NSWG forces capabilities and Command and Control readiness." This capability does not come cheap. It takes up to $125,000 to train an MCT operator—including formal schools, equipment familiarization, on-the-job training, and associated travel. A Sailor is normally assigned to an MCT for three years, with an option to extend a year. MCT operators participate in the same predeployment training cycles as their SEAL and SWCC counterparts. They deploy with them as part of the NSWRON. Deployment mount-out equipment is configured for ground mobility and flyaway load configurations of up to fifty tons.

The MCTs number upward of a hundred officer and enlisted communicators. They train in abbreviated small-unit tactics, attend small-arms training, and are required to maintain tight physical standards. MCT detachments are deployed in support of NSWRONs in the Middle East and the Philippines. They also participate in every NSW exercise while at home and deployed. In the words of one OIC, "Effective command and control equates to the speed of command." When SEALs can communicate, their mission has a greater chance of success.

One of the problems the MCTs face is retention of trained operators. Unlike the SEALs and SWCCs whose members are "closed-looped" detailed—that is, they remain in the teams for full careers—MCT operators rotate in and out during their three- or four-year tours. Again, it costs a lot of money to get an MCT operator up to snuff. In addition to the dollars cited above, it takes six months to

ABOVE, TOP: *Lt. Cdr. Daniel Link serves the spirtual needs of the SEALs and the members of WARCOM both at home and in war zones. (Photo: Greg E. Mathieson Sr. / NSW Publications, LLC)*

ABOVE, BOTTOM: *The Armor of God Chaplain's Coin: The Armor of God is based on a scripture found in the New Testament. The Apostle Paul states in Ephesians 6:12–13, "For we wrestle not against flesh and blood, but against principalities, against powers, against the rulers of the darkness of this world, against spiritual wickedness in high places. Wherefore take unto you the whole armor of God, that ye may be able to withstand in the evil day, and having done all, to stand." On the front side of the coin are two shields bearing the letters "RWH," which stand for "Return With Honor." This reminds us of the importance of not just serving, but serving honorably. (Photo: Dave Gatley)*

BUD/S trainees eat as they move quickly down the service line, sice time is critical during training. (Photo: Greg E. Mathieson Sr. / NSW Publications, LLC)

ABOVE: *Surfboards line the back of the WARCOM Headquarters building. Its proximity the beaches of Coronado, CA, affords the staff one the nicest work places in the US Navy to do their daily PT. (Photo: Greg E. Mathieson Sr. / NSW Publications, LLC)*

RIGHT: *Never sitting still, always moving. BUD/S trainees move from one training evolution to the next, running in formation. (Photo: Greg E. Mathieson Sr. / NSW Publications, LLC)*

BELOW: *Callenge coin of the Commander, Naval Special Warfare Command, which is one of the most coveted and highly sought after in the SEALs. The coins, uniquely shaped as a traditional SEAL diver's fin, carry the Admirals' flag on the rear side and a golden trident on the front side. (Photo by Dave Gatley)*

train a proficient MCT operator. The MCTs would like to keep people longer, but whether or not they achieve "closed-loop" status remains to be determined.

Logistics Support Units

Times have changed! Before the formation of USSOCOM in 1987, SEAL teams maintained much of their own operational equipment. They still keep up personal operating gear; the sophistication of newer technology equipment, however, precludes individual SEAL members simply "scrubbing and blow drying" intricate electronic equipment. Today, nearly 60 percent of the personnel assigned to NSW serve in CS or CSS roles. The LOGSU is NSW's CSS organization. Before USSOCOM, NSWUs operated independently or as part of the fleet logistics structures, where many CSS needs were met. Through progressive reorganization, NSW is now deployed in an expeditionary posture, separate from the fleet fixed-shore

Group Four, Special Boats personnel participate in water polo during weekly training in the area training pool. (Photo: Greg E. Mathieson Sr. / NSW Publications, LLC)

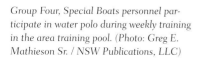

installations, driving the need to properly define, resource, and implement an appropriate CSS and expeditionary logistics paradigm.

Mentioned earlier was the QDR and budget initiatives to revitalize SOF, which included personnel, facilities, operating equipment, communications-electronics gear, and, most importantly, the logistics support infrastructure needed to support the operational teams at home and abroad.

NSW depends on the LOGSUs to provide the critical, non-SOF assistance necessary for them to defeat the enemy. LOGSUs are manned and organized to properly support both garrison and the greatly expanded expeditionary operations of NSW. Two LOGSUs were commissioned under CNSWG-1 and CNSWG-2 during the NSW-21 initiative. Their mission is to ensure maximum logistics support and enable NSW to remain a viable, relevant force for many decades to come. LOGSUs are tasked to plan, integrate, synchronize, and provide logistics support for its NSWG and subordinate units and SEAL teams, and to directly support NSW operations and training during times of peace, crisis, and war.

The LOGSUs' expeditionary mission involves a fully manned, trained, and equipped CSS "troop" assigned to each SEAL team. The CSS troop's mission is to provide comprehensive logistics support to include supply, ordnance, weapons, first lieutenant (surface craft and motors), dive, air, Seabee support, and tactical/nontactical mobility to SEAL teams. LOGSU commanders are responsible to man, train, and equip the CSS troop deploying with each NSWRON. The CSS troop will likely comprise 80 percent of the men and women making up the NSWRON.

The LOGSU's garrison mission is to provide administrative, supply, medical, combat services (base camp and vehicles), combat systems support (dive, air, and surface craft), and weapons systems support (small- and large-caliber firearms, visual augmentation systems, and ordnance). This includes supporting nondeployed forces throughout their predeployment training cycle. In addition to the SEAL teams, the LOGSUs support their respective NSWG headquarters staff, training detachment, support activity, and overseas NSWUs and detachments.

For SEALs this meant changing to the German Draeger closed-circuit self-

ABOVE: *A comical calisthenics poster hanging in one of the BUD/S instructors training rooms making fun of the numerous types of exercises trainees go through each day. (Photo: Courtesy of Tom Hawkins)*

BOTTOM, LEFT: *As throughout the Navy, the Chiefs make things run on time and run right. This Senior Chief is pulling together his fellow SEALs for a training demonstration of SEAL capabilities for a group of VIPs. (Photo: Greg E. Mathieson Sr / NSW Publications, LLC)*

BELOW, TOP: *NSW Group 2 techs train at the Blackwater training facility in Moyock, NC. Training consisted of vehicle convoy and protection under attack as well as machine-gun training. (Photo: Greg E. Mathieson Sr. / NSW Publications, LLC)*

BELOW, BOTTOM: *NSW Group 4 medics and medical gear stand ready during SWCC fast rope training on the Osprey aircraft at Hurlburt Field, FL. (Photo: Greg E. Mathieson Sr. / NSW Publications, LLC)*

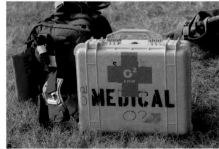

The Logistics Support Unit (LOGSU) is responsible for everything from boots and belts to armored vehicles and boats. Here, Reliability Enhanced High Mobility Multipurpose Wheeled Vehicle (HMMWV) await departure to a forward operating area. (Photo: Greg E. Mathieson Sr. / NSW Publications, LLC)

contained underwater breathing apparatus (SCUBA). It meant a new communications plan covering manpack radios and position locators. It meant new small arms and new parachutes with distinctive automatic opening devices. It included night visual augmentation equipment allowing the operators to "see" in pitch-black surroundings. For boats, it meant new silent outboard engines. New boats, in fact—the Seafox, a thirty-five-foot spitfire capable of thirty-five knots, new for the SEAL ship-to-shore transition—later replaced by RHIBs. Maintaining all this new equipment required full-time attention. There was not enough time or expertise in a SEAL platoon to maintain all the new items coming into the teams. The Department of Defense (DoD) budget compensated for this by permitting NSW to plan modest growth of technical support.

Today's LOGSUs work for the group commanders and are indispensable to day-to-day operations, especially since establishment of the SEAL and SWCC ratings. The LOGSUs are headed by Navy supply corps commanders and staffed with many standard Navy ratings, none of them SEALs. The LOGSU mission is this: "Provide Naval Special Warfare Group components with doctrinal logistics support to enable successful garrison training and deployed operations." This is a simple, straightforward mission, but it requires more than four hundred personnel

A WARCOM mass communications cameraman (L) prepares to follow in a SEAL breaching team during CQB (Close Quarters Battle) training. In the war zones an MC would be doing much the same function in filming similar activites. Support staff are in harm's way as much as the SEALs during missions where they are working closely together. Navy Mass Communications Specialist 1st Class Robert Richard McRill and Cryptologic Technician 1st Class Steven Phillip Daugherty were killed in one such mission alongside of Navy SEAL Jason Dale Lewis in Baghdad in 2007. (Photo: Greg E. Mathieson Sr. / NSW Publications, LLC)

to carry out. For example, each LOGSU has twenty-one officers of varying designators, three hundred enlisted personnel, forty-five chief petty officers in nineteen rates, and forty-nine civil servants and contractors. Fifty percent of the LOGSU personnel are deployed at any one time.

The "tooth to tail" ratio has been altered to such a degree that none of the operational SEAL teams could perform without the support of these highly technical units. They are indispensable to effective maritime special operations; they are the unsung heroes.

Military Construction—The Infrastructure

Accompanying photographs highlight specific buildings that offer more than just roofs. The SDVT-1 facility in Pearl Harbor, Hawaii, is one such. This facility houses a state-of-the-art underwater operations capability. SDVT operations are arguably among the toughest and most complex jobs that SEALs do, and engineering maintenance for them has to be of the highest quality. The underwater diving operational profiles for SDV operations are the most precise the community undertakes. This facility is central to combat readiness.

Other interesting buildings are the mission support centers attached to each NSWG. These facilities are beefed-up operations centers crammed with electronics, intelligence and status board displays, and cryptographic and communications equipment. They are manned 24/7 by experienced Navy operations specialists and communicators. Their reach is worldwide. These buildings are operational marvels.

Another building worthy of inclusion here is the NSWC headquarters in Coronado. This headquarters is staffed with military and civilian personnel responsible to

The SEAL Mission Support Center at Naval Special Warfare Group ONE (NSWG-1) has developed a Mission Support Center (MSC) to provide mission planning as well as intelligence, logistics, and administrative support to deployed SEAL units. This is a special operations command and control element facility that establishes critical and secure communication with the theater special operations command, allied forces, and theater command system. These include connectivity for the SEAL mission support center (shown here) and other intelligence feeds, either directly or through JFSOCC (Joint Force Special Operations Component Commander). (Photo: Dave Gatley)

ABOVE: *The new SDVT-1 facility at Pearl Harbor, Hawaii, with its state-of-the-art underwater operations capability allows for year-round training and maintenance. (Photo: Greg E. Mathieson Sr. / NSW Publications, LLC)*

BOTTOM, RIGHT: *BUD/S training during their second phase is spent mostly in the combat pool. In this evolution, one trainee tries to rescue another. That rescued swimmer offers physical resistance that the rescuer must overcome in order to complete the mission and rescue his party. This is an underwater view of that conflict, while swim gear floats or sinks all around them — thrown in by one of the instructors at poolside. (Photo: Dave Gatley)*

BELOW: *The Commodore's Coin NSW Group Three: Comprised of SDV (SEAL Dive Vehicle) Team 1 & Detachment 2 — Pearl City, HI. (Photo: Dave Gatley)*

USSOCOM for all NSW training, equipment, and selected operations (on a case-by-case basis). The building was dedicated in 1991 to honor Capt. Frank Kaine, USNR, a World War II veteran and member of the first naval combat demolition unit class in Fort Pierce, Florida, in June 1943. Captain Kaine served throughout World War II and became known as "MacArthur's frogman." He remained in the Navy after the war and went on to serve at every level of responsibility in NSW. The NSWC headquarters with its communication facilities is able to respond in real time to arising logistics requirements.

A note on general military construction: when the West Coast UDTs came out of World War II and later Korea, their beach site abodes were Quonset huts—with volleyball nets. Their facilities were upgraded to a set of blockhouses just behind the beach in Coronado. East Coast frogmen crammed into a variety of leftover World War II buildings at the NAB, Little Creek. It was not until the mid-1980s that military construction was attacked with serious intent. The deputy secretary of defense signed a memorandum dated 3 October 1983, directing all services to

revitalize their SOF. To do this the force had to grow. This meant enlarging training and operational unit facilities. In Coronado, the BUD/S command had to grow with a second floor, and a new combat training tank was constructed with a fifty-meter world-class swimming pool.

A year or two later, an enclosed, deep-water fifty-meter pool was built at Little Creek. Other California military construction followed with new training facilities in Niland and San Clemente Island, California. Because of a robust and focused military construction program, NSWC teams and staffs are no longer required to share office spaces. All commands are linked with local area networks, internal communications, and secure phone lines. The reach is worldwide.

USSOCOM has published a *Military Construction Master Plan* to support future growth. The overall USSOCOM plan extends for five years and is reviewed and updated annually to coincide with the DoD budget preparation process.

The NSW organization continues to change with increased requirements imposed by the operational environment, primarily the GWOT. Contributions of NSW are growing daily. The community is receiving support from all levels within the DoD, Navy included. The CNO has placed SEAL team recruitment as his top priority. While financial support comes primarily from USSOCOM, the Navy has stepped up with a guarantee of total support of NSW as well. Times, indeed, have changed, but the teams are earning their keep.

Doing flutter kicks and push-ups on the "Grinder" in the BUD/S center area is an almost daily event. Getting sprayed down with a hose can at times be a welcome thing given the sand, sun, and heat. (Photo: Greg E. Mathieson Sr. / NSW Publications, LLC)

TRAINING AT THE NAVAL SPECIAL WARFARE CENTER

REAR ADM (SEAL) GEORGE WORTHINGTON
USN (RET)

CHAPTER 4

Training at the Naval Special Warfare Center

Rear Adm. (SEAL) George Worthington, USN (Ret.)

PAGES 106–107: *Coronado beaches serve as the morning physical training course, where running-conditioning is done from one end of the beach to the other on the sand, and it's just the beginning of the day for this class in BUD/S (Basic Underwater Demolition/ SEAL) training. This grouping leads the large pack much farther behind them, but sharing in the grinding run are their instructors, who have nothing to prove except they can do the routine too. These First Phase students will do various grueling IBS (Inflatable Boat, Small), Pool, and Log-PT exercises, and are kept wet and sandy all day—every day. (Photo: Dave Gatley)*

RIGHT, TOP: *"The Only Easy Day Was Yesterday," the unofficial motto of the UDT, U.S. Navy SEALs posted on the wall of the BUD/S Grinder area. This plaque was presented by the BUD/S class of 1989. (Photo: Greg E. Mathieson Sr. / NSW Publications, LLC)*

BOTTOM, LEFT: *Students during BUD/S who at anytime decide that the SEALs are not for them can simply ring the bell in the Grinder area of the center and leave. The helmets along the way leading up to the bell signify the members of that BUDs class that left for one reason or another. (Photo: Greg E. Mathieson Sr. / NSW Publications, LL)C*

BOTTOM, RIGHT: *SQT (the SEAL qualification training phase) places these two trainees into unknown territory on Kodiak Island, AK. They must utilize all their navigational and survival skills, along with practicing their SEAL training to locate a "meet" point where they will join up with other two-man teams, and from there spend three days traversing the remote areas of the island's mountains to reach a predetermined destination point—all part of their SQT training in the coldest of conditions. Detachment Kodiak is a small training command that specializes in training SEAL platoons and Special Boat Unit Detachments in maritime and land cold-weather operations. Units train in long-range maritime and land navigation, across-the-beach operations, and other cold weather operations. The 28-day SEAL cold-weather maritime course has a staff of 18 and also supports the 12-day maritime operations course during the SEAL qualification training phase. (Photo: Dave Gatley)*

"So, You Wanna Be a Frogman?"

THUS ASKS THE SIGN ON A LIFE-SIZED STATUE OF A HALF-MAN/ half-aqua monster inside the physical training "Grinder" of the NSWCEN in Coronado, directing itself at BUD/S candidates. The Center, established in 1986, is responsible for basic and advanced training of SEAL team candidates ("trainees"), SWCC, and other personnel in special operations. Before that time, the training had been carried out by a department of the naval amphibious school. The best in-depth examination of a BUD/S class was written by retired Navy SEAL captain Dick Couch: *The Warrior Elite* (2001). Couch followed Class 228 through its basic training, and you can almost feel the pain!

The Center is without doubt the cornerstone of NSW careers. It is the basis of every single Navy SEAL and combat crewman, all of whom will return at various points throughout their time in NSW for refresher and advanced courses. NSWCEN was dedicated to a famed Scout and Raider Capt. Phillip H. Bucklew, USNR, whose history was mentioned above. In 1965, all that existed of NSW training were two basic courses: one in Coronado and one in Little Creek. Advanced training was either conducted in house, taught by others that had extensive operational experience, or offered at other service schools.

Training, training, training—it's what NSW is all about. Whether as a basic student, operational team leader, or experienced old-timer on instructor duty, SEALs and SWCCs train year in, year out for their entire careers. From classroom to field exercise, from continental United States, joint training with U.S. counterparts, or combined training with foreign allies overseas, NSW teams and units are

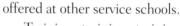

continually in some form of training regimen. More discussion on specific training opportunities will follow with descriptions of deployments.

As of this writing, recruiting SEALs is the Navy Recruiting Command's number one priority. The Navy is looking for athletic candidates who will be committed to excellence, mission completion, and a dynamic Navy career. Unwavering determination is the primary characteristic sought. The right mind-set can often outperform a more physically capable athlete. Singleness of purpose is the driving motive that will ensure success in BUD/S. This is the thrust of recruiting new candidates—to make sure the candidate knows what he is in for. Still, only one-third of any class will complete the BUD/S training program.

BASIC UNDERWATER DEMOLITION/ SEAL TRAINING

BUD/S is a twenty-seven-month training program. It is broken down into three distinct phases, each discussed in detail later in this chapter. Essentially, First Phase is oriented on physical toughening of trainees and lasts seven weeks. The most infamous component of this phase has become known as Hell Week, arguably the toughest five days in any service training program. Hell Week is viewed as a rite of passage that assists in preparing trainees for the next two phases, but successful completion of Hell Week does not ensure a trainee will complete First Phase.

Second Phase, the diving phase, is an intense course that sets BUD/S apart from other services. Open-ocean deep dives, underwater compass course swims in San Diego Bay with open-circuit (compressed air) and closed-circuit (pure oxygen), and mock ship attacks round out this intense in-water training. Not everyone passes this demanding phase. Trainees receive diving pay beginning with this phase.

Third Phase comprises land warfare, small-unit tactics, and demolitions and weapons training. It is very demanding, requiring trainees to achieve satisfactory goals on the rifle and pistol ranges, demonstrate above-average knowledge of military explosives and other ordnance (grenades, shaped charges), and perform in a series of small-unit tactical problems. Training is conducted on the Coronado

TOP: *These future warriors have just finished six days of punishing and brutal endurance evolutions, kept wet, sandy, cold and tired. These boat teams are working as a team, even though they are exhausted beyond belief. They are the survivors of the BUD/S (Basic Underwater Demolition/SEAL) Hell Week, where most of the starting class has dropped out, voluntarily or by injury. The 185-pound rubber boats that are carried on their heads during these punishing first few weeks are just part of the next thirty weeks of SEAL training, considered the foundation and soul of the SEAL operator's community. This class is headed for a few days off for rest and recuperation. (Photo: Dave Gatley)*

BOTTOM, LEFT: *Sandy, wet, tired, and miserable from only a few hours sleep in six days of the notorious Hell Week, the crews stand at attention after having rolled around in the sand. This class (270) of BUD/S trainees has just returned from a two-mile round-trip run carrying their ever present IBS (Inflatable Boats–Small) with them. During each day of this First Phase of training, the 185-pound rubber boats are usually carried either on their heads at their sides wherever they go. (Photo: Dave Gatley)*

BOTTOM, RIGHT: *Hell Week for Class 270. These wet BUD/S trainees aren't allowed to walk, but must crawl from their team IBS boats (background), to the feet of their instructor, bunching up as close as they can until ordered to stop. Wet, cold, sandy, and very tired—all part of the design built into every class training routine to see if these apprentice warriors have the heart and character to perform their missions under these trying conditions, day after day.... the same conditions that often exist on real SEAL operators' combat missions. (Photo: Dave Gatley)*

strand and at the offshore channel island, San Clemente Island, an inhospitable, rocky, windswept island outcropping some eighty miles off the southern California coast. A new training facility was constructed there in the early 1990s, which was a huge improvement over the previous site. Even with the improved facilities, the arduousness of San Clemente Island training has not changed.

BASIC UNDERWATER DEMOLITION/SEAL CULTURE

Before discussing individual training phases, some thoughts about the BUD/S "culture" might be enlightening. BUD/S is relentless. A 24/7 mind-set is required—total commitment, in other words. Trainees are required to compose their own class marching songs. The senior officer in the training class is held responsible for the class. He is assisted by other officers and the senior enlisted trainees. (His authority does not exceed that of the instructor cadre except in extreme circumstances, and then only in accordance with U.S. Navy procedures.) All participants in BUD/S—instructors and trainees—are subject to the Uniform Code of Military Justice; rank retains its responsibilities. Altercations of any kind in BUD/S are extremely rare, even among trainees. The senior instructor on a training evolution arbitrates in case of misunderstanding concerning training objectives.

One cultural hallmark unique to BUD/S is the frogman refrain, "Hoo Yah!" Trainees greet each instructor daily with a hearty "Hoo Yah!" and the instructor's name, officer or enlisted. Every order is responded to with "Hoo Yah!" Inanimate things are greeted with "Hoo Yahs": "Hoo Yah mountain!" "Hoo Yah surf zone!" "Hoo Yah beach!" "Hoo Yah rocks!" It is the response suitable for any situation. Army Airborne and Marine Reconnaissance have similar howls; back in the "real Navy," orders are habitually responded to with "Aye, aye, sir!" Not in BUD/S—there, "Hoo Yah!" covers it all.

Another cultural idea drilled into the trainees' minds from Day One is never to leave your swim buddy. During rubber boat dumping drills, if your buddy goes overboard, you follow him and stay with him in the water. The concept of being your brother's keeper takes on new significance in BUD/S.

A word about the class proctor is in order. This worthy duty takes on an extremely important leadership role, since the proctor becomes the first interface official between the class and the instructor cadre. He meets throughout the day with the class senior officer to chastise class performance, spirit, motivation—and offer suggestions when needed, often to help the class with forthcoming evolutions,

ABOVE: *Class 261 has placed its haversack high explosives on marine obstacles just off shore, returned to the beach, and blown them up from a safe distance. Collected together, the teams watch the results of their exercise—a demolition and beach clearing of the concrete and steel obstacles that once lined that beach front. The blasts rose water spouts 100 feet high and were loud enough to startle anyone in the vicinity. (Photo: Dave Gatley)*

RIGHT (LEFT): *SEAL Class 261 trainee teams back their way into the surf, carrying their individually prepared heavy haversack high explosives. Working as a team, they will place these Mk 138 satchel charges of high explosives. The satchels have an air bladder that allows the bags to float to where they will be sunk by the trainees by knifing the bladder. (Photo: Dave Gatley)*

RIGHT (RIGHT): *Standing at attention and ready for an instructor's equipment check of their rebreather gear and all other associated diving gear, this Phase Two trainee is preparing for his evening swim of underwater navigation in San Diego Bay. (Photo: Dave Gatley)*

Center expectations, and the like. The proctor is always an experienced enlisted SEAL operator with years of SEAL team service. The relationship is never familiar, always professional. Interestingly, the class proctor will someday serve with members of the class. A normal tour of duty for BUD/S personnel is three years, so Sailors assigned to the BUD/S cadre will always find their way back into operational teams. These instructors are personally committed to ensuring that only the best survive. This does not mean they eliminate aspirant trainees on a whim: criteria are in place and developed over many decades of training men to become SEALs. The official standards are on paper and must be met, but they do change periodically with events learned from ongoing operations. Standards are never static but also never arbitrary or quixotic. Let's look at the three BUD/S phases a little more closely.

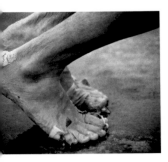

BOTTOM (LEFT): *BUD/S Class 172 during Hell Week training, where hours of grueling training in wet and sandy conditions has taken a toll that each trainee knows about—their body. These waterlogged, bandaged, sore feet tell volumes as this trainee gets ready to reenter the pool yet again. Most SEALs remember this image which hangs in the BUDs Quarterdeck for every trainee and visitor to see. They identify closely with what it depicts about the rigorous training that they all have had to go through to attain their Trident. (© 2001 DAVE GATLEY)*

BOTTOM (RIGHT): *After losing an evolution during their Combat Swimming Pool exercise, this group, a portion of BUD/S Class 172, undergoes a cold hell during Hell Week training by taking a cold shower. They attempt to keep each other warmer by huddling close. This cold shower is considered the "penalty box" (called such by the instructors) for their having lost during a water exercise. (Photo: © 2001 Dave Gatley)*

First Phase: Physical Training

First Phase is aimed at improving the physical stamina of the trainee. Extreme calisthenics, beachfront distance runs, bay and ocean swims, and surf passage with rubber boats form the basis of this phase. It is unrelenting, and previous sports injuries tend to announce themselves. Part of the grueling training is in rubber boats. Seven men are organized into boat crews. The crew gets the boat to the surf zone by carrying it on their heads, often over a few miles. Part of the drill includes rock portage over the rock jetty fronting the Del Coronado Hotel on Coronado Beach. This drill is first learned during daylight hours and is repeated at night.

Most training days during this phase start with early morning calisthenics—warm-up jumping jacks, torso twisting and stretching, hundreds of push-ups, leg levers (called flutter kicks), sit-ups, and more stretching. This is followed by a euphemistically named "conditioning hike"—basically a long-distance run in formation in soft sand, rarely on hard-pack sand. The longest conditioning hike is sixteen miles. Runs are normally conducted three times a week—Mondays, Wednesdays, and Fridays. There is a timed, four-mile run once a week. If you do not make it to the end of First Phase, you are dropped from training—another immutable standard.

One of the challenging aspects of BUD/S is having a uniform inspection every day—with shined boots, too! The tough part is getting the sand out of "greens" and boots spit-shined. Woe to the trainee who fails daily inspection: "Hit the surf!" is a line everyone gets used to. Often, when one trainee gets ordered into the surf, the rest of the class will join him. ("Never leave your swim buddy" is a rule all Navy divers adhere to.) Of course, this inspection rule is waived during Hell Week.

Every Thursday, trainees are invited to negotiate the Center's obstacle course (O-course), a challenging body-breaker that tends to ensure a lot of sand gets in

ABOVE: *Gathered for early morning review and equipment checks, these trainees will practice in the daylight for their coming over-the-beach exercise at night, where they will be emerging from the Pacific Ocean and navigating in the dark to their mock target sites. "Train as you play": each trainee is equipped much as they would be in the real world of battle. (Photo: Dave Gatley)*

LEFT (TOP, LEFT): *Class 261, like preceding classes, goes through rigorous physical exercises every day. Yet even after a full day of training programs, there is still the "Frog Hill" run to make—to touch the head of the bronze frog monument at the top. Competition to be the first each day is also part of the routine. They still wear their tactical assault vests which offer many quick access pouches/pockets for ammo, radio, and other mission gear. These vests can be custom-fitted with a broad assortment of adjustable pouches. (Photo: Dave Gatley)*

LEFT (TOP, RIGHT): *Although the supervisors are always present, by this phase of their training the men are feeling much more comfortable working together as a team. Although the training has elevated in risk, they are working much quicker, and requiring less intensity of supervision—they are very close to becoming SEAL team members. (Photo: Dave Gatley)*

LEFT (CENTER, LEFT): *Third Phase Class 261 trainees are gathered for an early morning review and equipment checks prior to beginning the new day's exercises and missions. Trainees are learning to become far more familiar with their hardware.(Photo: Dave Gatley)*

LEFT (CENTER, RIGHT): *A SEAL's weapon is built for getting wet, for the dirt and sand. A SEAL uses his drinking water to flush the sand out of the breach of his weapon. (Photo: Dave Gatley)*

LEFT (BOTTOM): *Taking up mock defensive positions amidst the shoreline rocks, just off the beach, these trainees will practice in the daylight for their coming over-the-beach exercise at night with each trainee equipped much as they would be in the real world of battle. Note: The padding on their rifles helps protect the trainee coming through the heavy surf. (Photo: Dave Gatley)*

SEAL trainees move through the surf during a
daylight over-the-beach exercise. (Photo: Dave
Gatley)

your uniform. Climbing, rappelling, swinging, bouncing through snake obstacles,
and hard breathing sum up the course. Rare is the trainee who does not lose some
hand skin his first run through the O-course. It is relentless in reaching inside every
trainee. Most trainees try to psych the O-course. Forget it: instructors know all the
tricks, like starting Week 1, slow and gradually speeding up as the phase continues.
It really hurts to have to run the course twice! Each man is expected to better his
O-course time every week.

Swimming starts out in First Phase in the amphibious base combat training tank.
This tank, built in 1985, has three graduated depths for diving training. It is here that
trainees learn the underwater recovery strokes SEAL use in combat. Longer bay and
ocean swims follow when the school is comfortable with trainees' water capabilities.
It is said that the swimming separates the men from the boys, but this is, admittedly,
simplistic. Still, the water performance of SEALs creates a confidence level that is
applicable throughout other areas of training. In the littoral regions where SEALs
operate, it is reassuring to have the ocean at your back. SEALs operate with the Navy
and can be inserted and extracted by surface craft, ship, or submarine.

The other physical training—push-ups, chin-ups, tricep dips, stomach crunches,
flutter kicks, and stretching—is developed throughout Second Phase. The only
weight involved is your own body, and of course the muscle to lift the rubber boats—
where you are normally one of seven. All the land physical training translates to the
water: flutter kicks develop the strength to push the fins. The runs develop wind
for long surface swims and, later, underwater compass attacks using SCUBA. All
the upper body strength improvement exhibits itself almost immediately on the
O-course.

"Hell Week"

Forget the quotation marks: Hell Week is real, and it hurts! Hell Week begins Sunday evening of the fourth week of First Phase training. The stunned trainees are "rousted out" with light, fire, noise, water hoses, shock, and awe—lots of blank submachine-gun firing, flares, hosing down, yelling orders and commands—basic harassment. Some are intimidated, others are energized, and all have to perform. No trainee is dry. It is, in fact, a frogman training program.

Hell Week concludes on noon Friday. It used to terminate on noon Saturday, but experience showed that the extra twenty-four hours required disproportionately more time for the men to recover. By about Wednesday, the class has lost its largest percentage of drops. By Thursday, the trainee is pretty much physically and mentally flat-lined, on automatic, feeling no pain but still having to perform.

Evolutions during Hell Week include a lot of rubber boat work, capsizing outside the surf zone, boat races—on land and water—and rock portage (again!); and treasure hunts, following clues all over the amphibious base, in the bay, in the ocean, down the strand beach, back and forth with seemingly no purpose other than to separate boat crews. Part of Hell Week is a trip to the demo pit that accomplishes the same demanding end: challenge trainees with more water, mud, chills, explosions, and smoke.

It is like this all through Hell Week: what's around the corner? The first Sunday night is a no-sleep night. After that, trainees might get a total of five hours of sleep the entire week. The week is designed that way to instruct the potential SEAL

LEFT: *"Battle Rattle," fully geared up and ready to do battle, and wet from their insertion OTB (over-the-beach) approach, this trainee leads his team in practice during daylight. This is but one of the many times they have gone through this similar evolution, they continue to practice their "Over the Beach" techniques before having to accomplish the same task in the total darkness of night. (Photo: Dave Gatley)*

CENTER: *The "O" Course looms during Third Phase training; even after completion of all running, long swims, smoke grenades, explosives, and obstacles- like the hand-over-hand rope crossing seen. If he drops, he'll have to start the course over again. All part of the continuing grind toward training and conditioning that never seems to end. (Photo: Dave Gatley)*

RIGHT: *A BUD/S trainee, burdened with his weapon and full combat dress, attempts another obstacle on the very demanding "O" Course while surrounded with a cloud of red smoke. (Photo: Dave Gatley)*

ABOVE: *Trainees have to learn to become an expert with all weapons. Here, under the close observation and supervision of an instructor, this trainee has to score well, even after his long swims and running evolutions up and down hills. The instructor helps him hone his shooting skills with subtle suggestions and corrections. (Photo: Dave Gatley)*

RIGHT, TOP: *Live fire training on a shooting range at Camp Pendleton, where the trainees also practice a "carry" of their wounded comrade (simulation) as they pull back running. Then they'll drop and shoot targets again at the next set of targets. (Photo: Dave Gatley)*

RIGHT, CENTER (LEFT): *Kodiak Island, AK, where cold weather training, including hardware, clothing, weapons, survival, and navigation takes place. This class has been issued a small fortune (over $10,000 worth) in camping supplies, hiking gear, and hardware, not unlike a weapon system in itself. These Advanced Training students are sorting it all out (in their quarters) for the next day's mission— three days of hiking, camping, and navigation over the snow-covered mountains, valleys, and rivers. (Backgrounder: Cold weather garment issue is a clothing system officially known as the "protective combat uniform" [PCU]. Made up of multiple layers of special hi-tech fabric and shell materials that protect the SEAL operator in temperatures that range to fifty degrees below zero Fahrenheit. There are seven layers in the system that enable each operator to match his needs in any given condition and weather. To that is added PEPSE [Personal Environmental Protection and Survival Equipment]—all the other hi-tech accessories, like sleeping bag, shelter, boots, snowshoes, folding ski poles, skis, crampons, pads, shovel, gloves (6 pairs & types), water filtration system, folding saw, and much more. Then he also has the MAS (Military Assault Suit), which is a specially designed lightweight dry suit—for surface swimming, keeping the operator dry. (Photo: Dave Gatley)*

RIGHT, CENTER (RIGHT): *A class in mountaineering and cliff climbing as well as in rappelling equipment, tools, ropes, knots and skills. The instructor goes over some of the techniques with each tool. Not your traditional class, this is being conducted at Detachment Kodiak located in Kodiak, Alaska, which is a small training command that specializes in training SEAL platoons and Special Boat Unit Detachments in maritime and land cold weather operations. Units train in long-range maritime and land navigation, over-the-beach operations, and other cold weather operations. The 28-day cold weather maritime course has a staff of 18 and also supports the 12-day maritime operations course during the SEAL qualification training phase. (Photo: Dave Gatley)*

ABOVE, BOTTOM (LEFT): *A student takes a break to study his courses on his Apple laptop during the SEAL Qualification Training (SQT) cold weather training at Kodiak Island. On the bed, he has topographical maps that cover the next three days' mission hike so that he can help plot out their course. (Photo: Dave Gatley)*

ABOVE, BOTTOM (RIGHT): *Each paired team goes over the separate route instructions, setting way-* points in navigation aids like this GPS unit prior to leaving the parking lot. They will navigate their way in the extremely cold temperatures of Kodiak Island to meet up with other pairs, hike some more, and then set up a camping spot. Two nights of camping, advanced navigation, mountain trails in heavy snow, valleys, and rivers to cross. All make up a major exercise that will test their survival, navigation, and endurance—all taught extensively over the many months of their training. (Photo: Dave Gatley)*

operator that he can function beyond what he thought was possible. Sometimes it is necessary in combat.

Dropping on request (DOR) is available to trainees throughout training. The trainee who for whatever reason of his own feels inadequate or not up to the challenge consults his boat coxswain, normally a student officer. He next interviews with his class proctor, then with the senior instructor, and possibly with the Center CO. After the trainee's decision has been made—normally in the face of strong encouragement to stick it out—the individual reports to Center Grinder, where hangs a ship's bell. The trainee rings the bell three times, and then places

TOP, LEFT: *To build their confidence again in their skills and abilities, all SQT (SEAL Qualification Training) trainees go for a swim in the freezing waters off Kodiak Island—lowering their core temperatures. This "rewarming exercise" is where they'll learn a true appreciation for their equipment. They strip to the first layer and skivvies, wading into the freezing water in late winter, remaining neck deep for ten minutes. A corpsman, onshore, checks to make sure they are cold but not reaching hypothermic conditions. Leaving the freezing water, they return to get their gear, head for the tree line and brush, out of the cold winds, working in pairs—their aim is to get dry and warm—quickly. (Photo: Dave Gatley)*

TOP, RIGHT: *While one half the class is practicing on tactical cliff climbing on Kodiak Island, the other half is practicing river crossing while still remaining "tactical" and providing security and protection for the team as they would in a real combat situation.*

Techniques in crossing a river by rope tactically with all the gear they are handling takes incredible teamwork—a fundamental tool they have been taught from the beginning of their training. Here, the last team member to cross the river pulls several backpacks fully loaded trailing behind him. (Photo: Dave Gatley)

RIGHT: *Using the Buddy System to ford these fast currents in the very cold waters of this crossing point provides twice the traction and stability needed to accomplish this task. Again, teamwork provides the solution in their training, and a means for the individual along with roughly 65 pounds of gear to move where others might not be able to. Part of their MAS (Military Assault Suit) clothing—the lightweight dry suit allows them to remain comfortable even in these freezing waters. All this cold weather training is being done at Detachment Kodiak. (Photo: Dave Gatley)*

BOTTOM, LEFT: *Having crossed the clearing and stream ahead of the main group, this SEAL trainee sets up a lookout post to guard the river crossing point in this freezing environment. These SQT (SEAL Qualification Training) exercises help build a confidence in all that they have been taught to date, in all the expensive gear they've been issued for survival and protection, giving them an exercise that will test all they know, and be a test of all their conditioning. "You play the way you train." (Photo: Dave Gatley)*

BOTTOM, RIGHT: *The main group of SQT (SEAL Qualification Training) warriors to be are finding their way through the shallows of this stream, after having camped and hiked for several days across the mountains and valleys to get to their assigned destination. Normally this large a detachment would not be grouped this tightly for security reasons. (Photo: Dave Gatley)*

his helmet on the ground near the bell. Every class ends up with a long row of helmets—a reminder that in every BUD/S that attrition rates are high, often around 75 percent, a breathtaking number for any other training.

Trainees that DOR are provided in-depth counseling regarding their next assignment and encouraged to get on with their naval career—and life. It is definitely not the desire of NSWCEN or instructor staff to leave former trainees permanently scarred psychologically. Some are called to try BUD/S, few make it. Following Hell Week, the survivors have a rest-and-recovery week with light physical training and more emphatic classroom work, and then are eligible to continue to Second Phase.

ABOVE: *The class in mountaineering and cliff climbing as well as rappelling equipment, tools, ropes, knots, and skills—all get a field tryout as each trainee faces rappelling down a sheer cliff face, as well as climbing back up. This is straight down, not a sloping face. Further complicating the training is that this is all being done off the cliffs in Alaska in freezing weather. (Photo: Dave Gatley)*

RIGHT: *In less than ten minutes after their freezing swim, they will team to erect their tent, start their cooking stove, heat a drink like cocoa, dry and dress themselves and slip into their sleeping bags—huddling for warmth until the water heats. Some will dragg the stove into the tent to aid the warming process. The whole warming exercise is a teaching tool, allowing them to trust what they can do under the most severe conditions to regain control over their environmental conditions, and build trust in the training and gear they've been issued. (Photo: Dave Gatley)*

Despite the very watchful eyes of the BUD/S instructors, students find ways to lighten the moments in training. (Photo: Greg E. Mathieson Sr. / NSW Publications, LLC)

Second Phase: Diving

Second Phase, eight weeks, encompasses the diving instruction of BUD/S and differentiates SEALs from other SOFs. Whether in the open-ocean or riverine environments, competency in the water is a positive confidence builder within the aspiring commando. Picking up extra pay for diving is a plus, too. BUD/S students learn open-circuit (compressed-air, or CO_2) and closed-circuit (pure-oxygen, or O_2) SCUBA. Open-circuit SCUBA is commonly understood by the civilian community—lots of bubbles expended into the surrounding waters by the diver's exhalation. Closed-circuit SCUBA, on the other hand, emits no telltale bubbles, because divers' exhaled breath is recycled through chemical scrubbers that eliminate it. This is important when making approaches on enemy ships at anchor; bubbles give away a diver's presence. The training is very comprehensive and demanding. It is tough, but swimmers are given every chance to make up failed swims. Instructors spend extra time with trainees who exhibit weakness in some area of diving.

Underwater competence starts out in the combat training tank. Successful completion of pool work qualifies the trainee to advance to more demanding compass swims conducted in San Diego Bay. Normally, a target is selected on the beach, and trainees are put together in diver pairs and released at varying distances. Later, they are scored on their accuracy in relation to the target. Diving compass swims start with daylight approaches using open-circuit SCUBA. Later, they perform night dives. After successful completion of the open-circuit phase, trainees advance to closed-circuit SCUBA, which involves a more complex and complicated process. The closed-circuit rig is set up with a detailed checklist. Once the closed-circuit rig is ready, the diver dons the rig and "purges" it of any residual nitrogen (N_2), so that he is breathing only pure oxygen. Once divers display no adverse affects from the pure oxygen, they are released in pairs to complete the compass swimming training evolution.

Third Phase: Land Warfare and Demolitions

After the dive phase, the much-reduced (by now) class moves into Third Phase, land warfare: small-unit tactics, patrolling, demolitions, and small arms. The preponder-

ance of this training is conducted at San Clemente Island. Home to goats, sea birds, and great lobsters, San Clemente Island is where SEAL trainees learn underwater demolition technology, and the basics of demolition preparation and handling, underwater obstacle location and destruction, small arms, and introduction to small-unit tactics. The trainees also conduct weapons training while at San Clemente Island and at the Marine Corps Base, Camp Pendleton.

One piece of BUD/S lore that is reemphasized in Phase Three is that training gets harder, not easier, as a trainee progresses. Although not as arduous as Hell Week per se, Third Phase is grueling. Second Phase is tough, too, but owing to the inherent danger associated with diving, trainees are somewhat more rested during this phase. The culture shock returns during Third Phase. At San Clemente Island, trainees practice overland combat demolition raids, most of them at night. The trainees brief the mission, depart camp after sundown, conduct the training

operation, and often are only back after midnight when gear cleaning is performed before hitting the racks—for maybe four hours of sleep.

Reveille is followed by calisthenics and breakfast prior to classroom instruction. After the brief classroom session, trainees hit the ranges for small-arms or demolition instruction. Much the same schedule is followed at the mainland camps. Third Phase rushes to a close with final graduation field exercises, during which the trainees get a mission, plan it, and execute it.

Third Phase completes BUD/S proper. Students are not yet SEALs; the class will not receive its SEAL tridents (uniform insignia) until completion of SEAL Qualification Training (SQT). The class, dressed in utilities, gets an "atta' boy" from the Center CO. Then the men assemble to draw equipment for SQT and look forward to another nineteen weeks of in-depth, specific NSW instruction that will make them all "full-up" SEALs ready to join their teams.

Attrition

A quick statistical note about BUD/S attrition will answer some questions that the reader might have. A Center presentation reports that 7.2 percent of trainees DOR during the pretraining and indoctrination phases, informal periods intended to get

The beginning and the end of the famous O-course (Obstacle Course) at the Basic Underwater Demolition/ SEAL training area, which students master after many weeks of repeated passes though the course. (Photo: Greg E. Mathieson Sr. / NSW Publications, LLC)

students up to snuff physically. These dropouts are for varying reasons, some physical, some attitude adjustments—in other words, the realization sinks in that maybe this training is not what an individual thought it would be. The three weeks of First Phase preceding Hell Week account for a whopping 27.3 percent of drops. This "truth in advertising" really centers the trainee's attention on what BUD/S is all about. The culture shock is bone-chilling for people unused to discipline and extreme physical exertion. It is a wake-up call for many of the high school athletes who thought they have what it takes to become a Navy SEAL. During Hell Week itself, 20.7 percent quit— no sleep and cold water pretty much account

PREVIOUS PAGE

TOP, LEFT: *During the First Phase of BUD/S (Basic Underwater Demolition/SEAL) Training, Hell Week trainees (Class 268) must carry their IBS (185 pounds of Inflatable Boat) with them everywhere. They will run with the boat on their heads wherever they go: chow, the O-course, combat pool, beach—everywhere. They have to lift and hold the boats high above their heads, and it hurts; it burns the triceps, neck muscles, hands, and backs. The design is to build their conditioning and test their wills, their "mettle," not to punish. (Photo: Dave Gatley)*

RIGHT, TOP: *BUD/S surf passage in the CRRC (Combat Rubber Reconnaissance Craft or Zodiac), an early exercise in working as a team in the ever-present surf conditions off Coronado's beaches. SEAL instructors stress the importance of teamwork, coordination, good communication skills, leadership, endurance, and other attributes. (Photo: Dave Gatley)*

RIGHT, CENTER: *BUD/S trainees, under the view of Coronado Island's condominiums, work at lifting and keeping the heavy CRRC above their heads. (Photo: Dave Gatley)*

RIGHT, BOTTOM: *Hell Week for Class 270 continues with yet another exercise. BUD/S trainees, who have returned from a two-mile run carrying their IBS, now do push-ups off their boats. The 185-pound rubber boats are usually carried either on their heads or at their sides, but they are also used in this manner. (Photo: Dave Gatley)*

BOTTOM: *Along the beaches of Coronado Island, IBS team leaders meet with the instructor to get a set of instructions while their crews support the boats on their heads. How they execute this mission may well determine both the outcome of the objective and whether they will be pulling extra duties, push-ups, boat drills, rolling in the sand, Log-PT, running conditioning—or just resting while another boat crew is paying the price for having made mistakes. (Photo: Dave Gatley)*

BUD/S Surf Passage, an exercise in working as a team by navigating their CRRC through the surf. (Photo: Dave Gatley)

for these losses. After Hell Week, an average of 5 percent DOR for a variety of reasons: failure in dive training; inability to grasp the essentials of dive tables, explosives technology, or small-unit tactics; or other substandard performance. Interestingly, only 0.6 percent DOR during Third Phase.

To the end of trying to get as many trainees through as possible, the Center has a counter-attrition program that specifically addresses curricula revisions such as rollback procedures in certain cases, overhaul of the indoctrination phase, selection reviews, instructor development (with psychological screening), critique reviews, student qualification, preparation, and performance. There is a psychologist and exercise physiologist on the Center staff. Psychological profiling efforts have been aimed at identifying the factors leading to success at BUD/S, but nothing has been 100 percent accurate in predicting who will make it.

SEAL Qualification Training

Completion of BUD/S once culminated with a graduation ceremony at the Center with families, a speaker (usually a successful senior SEAL commander), and a highly energized atmosphere. Awards were given, "Hoo Yahs" were exchanged with the BUD/S class just beginning training, and finally the senior trainee requested permission to "ring out the class." Permission obtained, he ran to the bell and rang it three loud times; the final stroke was greeted with a loud chorus of "*Hoo Yah!*" from the class. All has changed, however, with the addition of SQT. Graduating from SEAL basic training is a mere formality today—although momentous enough. Today, it is a significant stepping-stone to more detailed NSW training. Another nineteen weeks of specific SEAL subjects await the newly graduated BUD/S Sailors. SQT includes but is not limited to the following formal subjects: medical, communications, land navigation, weapons/demolitions, small-unit tactics, combat swimmer tactics (ship attacks), and maritime operations.

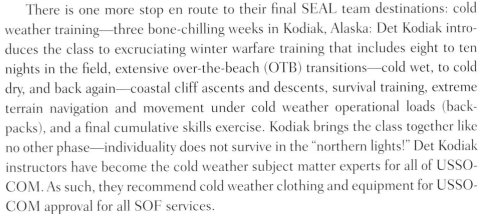

There is one more stop en route to their final SEAL team destinations: cold weather training—three bone-chilling weeks in Kodiak, Alaska: Det Kodiak introduces the class to excruciating winter warfare training that includes eight to ten nights in the field, extensive over-the-beach (OTB) transitions—cold wet, to cold dry, and back again—coastal cliff ascents and descents, survival training, extreme terrain navigation and movement under cold weather operational loads (backpacks), and a final cumulative skills exercise. Kodiak brings the class together like no other phase—individuality does not survive in the "northern lights!" Det Kodiak instructors have become the cold weather subject matter experts for all of USSO-COM. As such, they recommend cold weather clothing and equipment for USSO-COM approval for all SOF services.

Airborne Training

Upon completion of BUD/S, new graduates line up to go to the Army Airborne School at Fort Benning, Georgia, where they undergo the Army's three-week basic static-line jump course. One significant change in the training involves parachute training. BUD/S graduates normally attend Fort Benning for three weeks to achieve their basic parachutist silver jump wings. The Center and NSWC have outsourced this training to a contractor in San Diego. The plan is for the just-graduated BUD/S class to report the Monday following BUD/S to the Lake Otay Tactical Air Operations site outside San Diego. The static-line course takes only five days, owing to the small size of the class, the superb physical condition of the students, and the

PREVIOUS PAGE

BOTTOM, LEFT: *Rows of seven-man teams march around the O-course with telephone poles during this Log-PT, one of a series of physically challenging teamwork evolutions. These students will grind through this and the other tests to get past pain and discomfort. They'll be continually on the move for sixty hours during Hell Week before they'll get even two or three hours of sleep. One evolution follows another, and they are kept wet, sandy, cold, and tired—often falling asleep while taking their first bite of food. (Photo: Dave Gatley)*

BOTTOM, CENTER: *Grimacing from the effort required to support and lift these telephone pole segments during BUD/S Log-PT, the other members of this boat team try to support one of their team who is having trouble with muscles cramping. He is their weakest link now, yet they still want to support him, but can't, except verbally, because the whole log is in segments, further pressuring this team to improve and find a way to overcome any weaknesses. Ultimately, this trainee had to have his overly stressed muscles looked at by an instructor. (Photo: Dave Gatley)*

BOTTOM, RIGHT: *After only two days of Hell Week, and countless lifting exercises, BUD/S Class 270 trainees are grimacing from the physical effort required to support and lift this telephone pole over their heads during a Log-PT. (Photo: Dave Gatley)*

BELOW: *Yet another target in a strategic spot in the men's room at BUD/S. Training is a way of life. (Photo: Greg E. Mathieson Sr. / NSW Publications, LLC)*

RIGHT (TOP): *The BUD/S obstacle course, known as the O-course, is one of the most challenging in the world. It includes ropes, nets, climbs, walls, crawls, jumps and runs, which the students must complete more quickly in each successive phase. (Photo: Greg E. Mathieson Sr. / NSW Publications, LLC)*

RIGHT (CENTER): *BUD/S training is very taxing, and the intense lifting, carrying, and curling can lead to muscle strain and cramps. This young man is getting painfully stretched back out by one of his instructors after he couldn't control his arm's cramping during all the vigorous evolutions with the heavy telephone pole logs (Log-PT). Each participant is closely watched by their instructors, who are trying to test all their abilities without actually "breaking" their bodies. (Photo: Dave Gatley)*

RIGHT (BOTTOM): *A trainee from Hell Week during the first phase of the BUD/S program is having his blood pressure checked after exhibiting signs of extreme exhaustion. (Photo: Dave Gatley)*

fact that they are well screened for hazardous duty. Following static-line training, the class undergoes the three-week military free-fall course. Airborne training, then, will be one month with no cross-country travel required—and basically at half the time. Students get five static-line jumps and upward of twenty-five free-fall jumps, including night jumps with full combat equipment. Following this, they enter the SQT course. Successful completion of SQT wins the coveted SEAL trident. At that time, they are fully qualified SEALs ready to take their place in an active SEAL team or SDVT.

Special Warfare Combatant Craft Crewman

Before we move into advanced SEAL team training, capabilities, operational environments, and overseas deployment, we need to take a look at the Center training that the SWCC volunteers undergo in order to serve in an SBT.

As noted in Chapter 3, the SWCC volunteers U.S. Navy rating is special warfare boat operator (SB) and the SEAL rating is special warfare operator (SO). SEAL and SWCC designations are given once the men earn their distinguishing breast device—gold Trident for SEALs and silver combatant-craft device for SWCCs. Both ratings and designations are exclusive to NSW operations, but their

training is substantially different. SEALs operate on the water and below it and thus are divers. They also use parachuting and helicopters to conduct land warfare and train in small-unit tactics using small arms and demolitions, among other tools of the trade. SWCCs operate and maintain the family of combatant craft assigned to the SBTs. SBT-12 and SBT-20 operate primarily on the ocean surface, generally in the littorals, using the Mk V SOC and eleven-meter (thirty-six-foot) NSW Rigid Hull Inflatable Boat (RIB). SBT-22 operates almost exclusively in a riverine environment using the SOCR. SWCCs may be parachute qualified to tactically jump with certain combatant craft.

Sailors may rotate among the SBTs and remain a SWCC for their entire careers. This "closed-loop" detailing process was introduced in 1997, and has ensured a high-quality Sailor being assigned to the SBTs. Before that time, Sailors would be assigned to a boat team for merely two or three years, after which they would rotate back to the surface Navy. More specifically, prior to 1990, boat operators were sourced from fleet ratings and enjoyed no formal screening or training before reporting to their boat team. Quality suffered. It was an inefficient system owing to the amount of time it took to bring a man up to operational standards to operate the combatant craft in the nearshore regions where the SEALs work. In 1991, an eight-week introductory course was established, when the closed-loop assignment

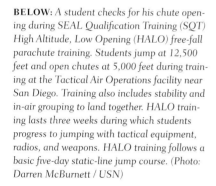

system was implemented. The SWCC warfare specialty was approved in 2001. SWCC training is more difficult and challenging than any other enlisted warfare-area qualification program in the Navy except BUD/S. It is divided into three distinct phases: indoctrination, basic crewman training, and crewman qualification training. Here's what the SWCC candidate learns:

- The two-week *indoctrination* phase is broken down into skills instruction and physical training, to include SWCC history, Navy core values, SWCC ethos, sports medicine, hygiene, and nutrition. Physical training centers on conditioning swims, calisthenics, basic water survival and rescue, and the O-course.

- The *basic crewman training* period is five weeks and continues physical training with conditioning swims, O-course, formation hikes, and water survival testing and rescue, including first aid and cardiopulmonary resuscitation (CPR). Basic coxswain skills are introduced, along with basic piloting, beach landing, hull inspection, and towing lash-ups. To illustrate the seriousness of this training, here is the basic water survival test: Jump ten feet into a pool in duty utilities and boots. Swim twenty-five meters demonstrating three surface breaks. Float prone three minutes. Remove uniform, inflate pants, and float for a minute. Finally, demonstrate swimming strokes—back, breast, side, and crawl—fifty meters each.

- The *crewman qualification training* portion of SWCC training lasts fourteen weeks. Physical training is continued. Instruction includes personal equipment, team skills, mission planning, engineering and damage control, combat medicine, material maintenance, and advanced crewman skills. Specific courses are held on small-boat operations, communications (all gear), sea-

ABOVE: *A BUD/S student takes a break on one of many hot days in training on the beaches of Coronado, CA. (Photo: Greg E. Mathieson Sr. / NSW Publications, LLC)*

RIGHT: *As the morning sun rises over the O-course at BUD/S, a student starts his day crawling under a row of logs before heading to the climbing ropes. The only easy day was yesterday ... is very real at BUD/S. (Photo: Greg E. Mathieson Sr. / NSW Publications, LLC)*

manship, weapons and optics (lasers and thermal equipment), and practical mission planning. In addition to this in-depth instruction, field exercises are held emphasizing weapons firing, land and long-range navigation, unconventional warfare, and night training events. All this is aimed at imparting theoretical and practical warfighting skills and at stressing the team concept. A final special boat physical test includes completing one hundred sit-ups in three minutes, one hundred push-ups in three minutes, ten pull-ups, a three-mile run in less than twenty-seven minutes, and a one-mile swim in sixty minutes with fins; and lifting a .50-caliber machine gun overhead three times. There are short rest periods between each test, but all candidates end up panting, guaranteed.

Advanced Training Command

The NSW ATC was formally established on 6 December 2006 as a component of the NSWCEN. Located on the former Imperial Beach Naval Communication

The members of the BUD/S Class 250 leave this lingering mystery for new students, "The Secret to BUD/S is under this rock." Do you know the answer? The rock is too big to be picked up by one person. Medal of Honor recipient Michael Monsoor was a member of Class 250. He gave his life to fellow team members by throwing his body on an enemy grenade. (Photo: Greg E. Mathieson Sr. / NSW Publications, LLC)

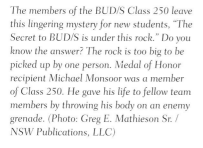

Station, the new command is five miles south of the NSWCEN, but still within Coronado city limits. It includes 540 acres sited on the ocean and offers thirty advanced training courses. It also supports seven detachments and fifteen training sites around the country, including detachments in Hawaii; Little Creek, Virginia; Kodiak, Alaska; Yuma, Arizona; Hurlburt Field, Panama City; and Key West, Florida. The official mission statement is to: "Provide standardized, accredited, and approved curriculum and training in support of NSW METLs [mission-essential task lists] to NSW forces and selected allies."

Today, it is hard to imagine that in the mid-1960s SEALs were trained by peers, other SEALs who had been in the teams awhile and had several overseas deployments under their belts. Later, during Vietnam operations, lessons learned from recent combat were incorporated into the advanced training syllabus. The ATC's focus is professional development of the NSW SEAL and SWCC operator and enabling of NSW support personnel.

A sampling of courses offered include reconnaissance skill encompassing photography (photographic image capture), special reconnaissance scout, NSW sniper, static-line jumpmaster, basic CQD (applying only requisite force and prisoner control techniques), NSW communications, diving equipment maintenance (used by other agencies, too), diving supervisor (responsible for safe SCUBA evolutions, training, and combat), firing-range operations safety, and special operations technician.

In 2006, the ATC graduated 1,218 students with a staff established at 199: 14 officers, 169 senior enlisted, and 16 civilian specialists. The ATC also supports SEAL trainees undergoing SQT and other SEALs requiring refresher training as necessary to maintain their operational skills. The ATC, like the NSWCEN, represents the only real Navy shore duty available to SEAL and SWCC enlisted personnel. Normal tours of duty last three years.

SEAL TEAMS AND WHAT THEY DO

REAR ADM (SEAL) GEORGE WORTHINGTON
USN (RET)

CHAPTER 5

SEAL TEAMS AND WHAT THEY DO

Rear Adm. (SEAL) George Worthington, USN (Ret.)

PERATION IRAQI FREEDOM (OIF) HAS BEEN COMPLETED, AND Operation Enduring Freedom (OEF) in Afghanistan and the Philippines may continue beyond the publication date of this book. They define the deployment aspects of all SEAL teams. Presumably, teams will one day return to routine deployments, but not anytime soon—not as long as the GWOT defines defense posture. In this war, SEALs have proven indispensable on many levels. Most of their activities remain classified, restricting the scope of this book to routine capabilities and training exercises, with only opaque allusions to ongoing combat operations.

The operational characteristics of SEAL teams derive from the acronym—*sea, air,* and *land.* In the past the SEAL teams consisted of ten platoons that were foremost and uniquely small-unit tactical organizations operating in eight-man squads and sixteen-man platoon-sized formations. Today, however, each SEAL team has nine platoons of twenty men each that have consistently morphed to meet the operational challenges and missions. Today, SEAL teams deploy as an NSWRON

PAGES 130–131: *Day and night training takes place all year-around at the Imperial Valley (California) Camp Billy Machen, which is the Navy SEAL desert warfare training facility located on the edge of the Chocolate Mountains Aerial Gunnery Range. This SEAL unit stands surveilling their operating area from a bluff as night falls. (Photo: Dave Gatley)*

RIGHT: *CQD (Close Quarter Defense) being taught at in the special Hood Room at the NSW SQT (SEAL Qualification Training) facilities, where scenarios are set up to test and train for quick and proper reaction to suddenly changing situations that may be life threatening. The hood is used until the scenario is set up, then pulled up to reveal the situation—all set in very low lighting. (Photos: Dave Gatley)*

BELOW: *The student here (R) reacts defensively to an attack by the man in black (L) at the special CQD (Close Quarter Defense) Hood Room. (Photo: Dave Gatley)*

132

that includes three troops, where three SEAL platoons make up each "troop." Once deployed, the troop can be task organized to perform designated missions, which may require from two to fifty SEALs and supporting elements.

Historically, the SEALs have consistently adapted to their combat needs. In 1983, the existing UDTs were reorganized into SEAL teams. Historically, the UDT doctrinal mission of beach reconnaissance and obstacle demolition continued during the Korean War. A Marine Corps division crossed two thousand yards of beach. To reconnoiter this area from a twenty-one-foot offshore depth to the high-water mark required soundings (and bottom searches) every twenty-five yards. The UDT was constructed to perform this task; it originally numbered twenty officers and one hundred combat swimmers. Brigade or smaller Marine Corps landings consequently needed fewer frogmen.

In World War II and later in Korea, the focus was a UDT doctrinal mission of beach reconnaissance and obstacle clearance; during the Korean War the UDTs added the inland demolition raid to their repertoire. The UDTs developed land tactics as a secondary capability to beach reconnaissance. It was this mission that separated a 1962 SEAL team from a UDT. During the Vietnam conflict SEALs became more involved with small-unit tactics and land warfare. Few SEAL platoons even mounted out SCUBA gear for their six-month in-country tours. Today, OEF and OIF once again have taken SEALs from the water and placed their combat swimmer capabilities on the back burner. Significant in-water preparation is still accomplished by all SEAL teams during their predeployment training periods, while the SDVTs focus completely on clandestine maritime special operations. In fact, for three years SEALs were almost completely tied up protecting high-level Iraqi officials, although of course they were also doing

ABOVE: *With the sun setting in the west, these SEALs practice OTB (over-the-beach) exercises off Coronado's Gator Beach. One SEAL is carrying the M240 machine gun (L), and the other (R) is carrying the new SOF combat assault rifle, or SCAR, which is a modular rifle made by FN Herstal (FNH) for the U.S. Special Operations Command (SOCOM). (Photo: Dave Gatley)*

RIGHT: *"Cover and Run" exercises are carried out in terrain that is very close to that found in the Persian Gulf. This at Niland's Camp Billy Machen, a Navy SEAL desert warfare training facility located on the edge of the Chocolate Mountains. The SEAL on the left carries the new SOF combat assault rifle, or SCAR. On the right is the Colt M4A1 carbine, which is the primary weapon used by SEAL operators. It is a shorter, more compact version of the M16A2 rifle. (Photo: Dave Gatley / NSW Publications, LLC)*

much more. If history is any guide, this will change, although the overall OEF mission remains steady for the long term.

Another example of mission focus is the use of SEALs in Africa. NSWG-2, Little Creek, deploys personnel in North Africa in its Trans-Sahara tasking to, as an NSWG-2 briefing slide puts it, "deny the Sahara and Sahel as sanctuary for terrorists, their networks, and the criminal activities that directly or indirectly support terrorist activities." The North African mission demonstrates the adaptability

of SEALs, and their growing range of capabilities to work in small units alongside indigenous forces. Historically, technological advances change the conduct of warfare, special operations included. Hence, when "UDT" transitioned to "SEAL" in 1983, much was needed in the way of new personnel, training, and equipment. This amounted to more than a simple name change. It was a significant plus-up in terms of capability and mission involvement.

ABOVE: *Illuminated only by munition explosions, this group of trainees raise their live-ammo-loaded weapons in a safe direction as they move through total darkness during this FTX (the final battle problem). All images done with proprietary ITT NV (Night Vision) intensifier equipment on digital cameras. (Photos: Dave Gatley)*

RIGHT: *This is a simulated attack from insurgents upon the ECJSOTF (Exercise Combined Joint SPEC OPS Task Force) while in a populated village in Southwest Asia. Here an insurgent actor takes aim while hiding behind a wall in the mock scenario and village. (Photo: Dave Gatley)*

SEAL TEAM OPERATIONAL CAPABILITIES

How do SEAL teams actually "play" within the overall operational constellation formed by joint SOFs? One way to explain it is to examine the operational capabilities SEALs train to. Let's start with the water, swimming and diving.

Diving Operations

Among all SEAL skills the underwater environment remains the most taxing . . . and dangerous. "Cross-tell" conferences among the East and West Coast NSWGs were scheduled annually after Vietnam, since the NSW community needed direction. The East and West Coast commands were not always in harmony about the way ahead, and these conferences were the mechanism to achieve agreeable and focused direction. During a 1972, or 1973, information exchange in Little Creek, Cdr. (later Rear Adm.) Chuck Le Moyne, USN, announced in an early plenary session that the thing that set SEALs apart from other SOF was that we did our thing underwater. These were true words that reminded us all that we were not in the business of challenging the Army for primacy in unconventional warfare—training and leading indigenous forces. The primary SEAL mission was essentially direct action and its underwater application—reconnoitering and destroying underwater obstacles and approaching landward targets from the sea.

Following some seven years in the Vietnam conflict, the small-unit tactics element was front and center in the minds of most. The West Coast group commander, Capt. David Schaible, USN, was exhorting his teams to get back in the water, and Le Moyne, as his chief staff officer, clearly and dramatically made this case at the cross-tell conference. It was during this period that the Naval Sea Systems Command (NAVSEA) was developing the submarine Dry Deck Shelters (DDSs) to transport SDVs. So, "back to maritime basics" ended up being the theme of the 1970s.

Open-ocean swims are not inherently difficult, but negotiating an agitated surf zone is. SCUBA diving is always challenging; doing it under a target ship has its own unique apprehensions that are only overcome through practice, practice, and more practice. We will show examples of each.

When a SEAL arrives at his operational team, he is ready in all respects to operate in the team. He has to meet new teammates, learn local customs, participate in team standard operating procedures, and learn his trade at first hand. Diving is a skill that improves with time. The more time a person spends diving, the better he gets. This theory is in financial practice in the French navy, where the French frogmen are paid extra money for diving. U.S. Navy SEALs receive extra hazardous duty pay for diving. The French navy pays by the dive, which encourages

LEFT: *SEAL Qualification Training (SQT) is a 15-week course designed to bridge the gap between BUD/S and the operational components. SQT teaches the full spectrum of basic SEAL skills/tactics with the goal of seamless integration into operational SEAL/SDV platoons. Students spend four weeks here at the naval remote training facility in Niland, CA, concentrating on tactics, weapons familiarization, and demolition. The SEAL Warfare Designator (Trident) is awarded following successful completion of SQT. Navy SEALs are maritime special operations forces who strike from the SEa, Air and Land. They operate in small numbers, infiltrating their objective areas by fixed-wing aircraft, helicopters, navy surface ships, combatant craft and submarines. SEALs have the ability to conduct a variety of high-risk missions—unconventional warfare, direct action, special reconnaissance, combat search and rescue, diversionary attacks and precision strikes—all in a clandestine fashion. (Photo: Eric S. Logsdon, USN)*

RIGHT: *In this final battle problem, a CERTEX (Certification Exercise), this unit approaches their mission target, a suspected insurgent village on an intelligence-gathering probe, yet ready to do battle if necessary. The exercise is taking place at a vast desert facility, now known as the NTC, National Training Center. (Photo: Dave Gatley)*

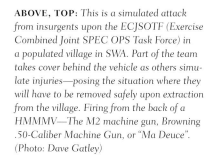

ABOVE, TOP: *This is a simulated attack from insurgents upon the ECJSOTF (Exercise Combined Joint SPEC OPS Task Force) in a populated village in SWA. Part of the team takes cover behind the vehicle as others simulate injuries—posing the situation where they will have to be removed safely upon extraction from the village. Firing from the back of a HMMMV—The M2 machine gun, Browning .50-Caliber Machine Gun, or "Ma Deuce". (Photo: Dave Gatley)*

ABOVE, BOTTOM: *Here, a realistic explosion (controlled) is set off near a SEALs exercise at Fort Irwin to simulate the real-life distractions and disturbances that might occur in the field. NSW is conducting a final training session called CERTEX (Certification Exercise) that measures and tests a SEAL team's performance in realistic combat situations. (Photo: Dave Gatley)*

ABOVE, RIGHT: *In this final battle problem, a CERTEX (Certification Exercise), this unit approaches their mission target, a suspected insurgent village on an intelligence-gathering probe, ready to do battle if necessary. (Photo: Dave Gatley)*

their divers to spend more time underwater. They become very good at it. In fact, during the early 1980s there was a navy-to-navy personnel exchange program with the French frogmen. The French divers taught U.S. Navy SEALs their method of attacking targets underwater—they were much more refined than we were at the time. The executions learned from the French have become the standard in our teams today. One can certainly learn special operations techniques from a myriad of sources, which is what exchange programs are supposed to do.

The SEAL teams routinely perform open-circuit SCUBA dives for administrative purposes, such as overt obstacle clearance when an element of secrecy is not required. Routine diving requalification dives by administrative staff personnel are usually performed using open-circuit rigs. The setup is simpler—charge the bottles, check emergency procedures, rig individual dive gear, and hit the water.

For operational SEALs, most requalification dives are performed using their tactical Draeger pure oxygen, closed-circuit diving apparatus, which emits no telltale bubbles. These diving units are technically more complicated and time consuming to operate and maintain; they represent an excellent example of modern technology, however, and provide a significant tactical underwater capability.

Navy SEALs operate from U.S. Navy submarines. In addition to the SDVTs, SEAL teams routinely requalify in submarine lock-out/lock-in (leave and return to) exercises. These exercises can occur off San Diego and Little Creek, as required. The SDVT is headquartered in Pearl Harbor, Hawaii—much warmer water. Submersible operations are time consuming—as are all diving evolutions—and inherently risky. In the "old days," UDT frogmen and SEALs would operate from diesel submarines and swim up and down the conning tower to the forward lock-out hatch. They would release Zodiac rubber rafts—today called Combat Rubber Raiding Craft (CRRC)—from afterdeck compartments on the submarine, swim up to them, and proceed on their assigned mission. Some old diesel boats were configured to "bottom"—that is, to settle down on the ocean bottom near a beach with about thirty feet (one atmosphere) of water above the deck. The submarine captain could raise his periscope and pan the beach for enemy activity. SEALs nor-

mally lock out, proceed on the mission, and, when complete, paddle or motor back out to the submarine and lock back in.

Several methods of conducting a clandestine beach reconnaissance have been developed over the years, permitting a SEAL element to check out a prospective beach landing site while remaining totally under water.

Requalification dives usually require a compass course of a mile or a tactical evolution conducted against a ship at anchor. Most of the time these training evolutions are scheduled after dark and the "target ship" never knows the SEALs were there. Special safety precautions have to be exercised during the time the SEALs are underneath the ship, such as securing the seawater intakes and tagging any engineering that could interfere with the evolution. Safety is always paramount.

Dressed in his forest camouflage outfit, this SEAL team member provides cover while his partner checks the brush for a "drop" communication during a CERTEX mission. SDV-T1, Charlie Platoon training on an island in the Puget Sound/Admiralty Inlet and Strait of Juan de Fuca area. They conduct a mock surveillance and reporting scenario from their "hides" mission. (Photo: Dave Gatley)

Back to the submarines: the Navy has developed a piggyback shell called the DDS, or Dry Deck Shelter. This is essentially a deployable diving chamber capable of housing a single SDV or multiple dive pairs. (Swimmers always operate in pairs.) The DDSs became operational in the early 1980s. Later, a dual configuration—two DDSs—was developed. Operational diving procedures call for the embarked SEALs to brief their operation to the ship's company (CO, executive officer, operations officer, diving officer, and significant enlisted watch standers). Lock-out/lock-in navigational specifications are agreed upon, and the SEALs prepare to launch on their mission. Other tactical specifications are mapped out, as well, such as communications procedures, emergency recovery procedures, and so on.

At H-hour, the SEALs are launched from the DDS, which can release far more swimmers than an air-lock chamber. CRRC and men can be prepositioned inside the DDS; it is filled with water until the inside pressure exceeds the outside sea pressure, and the after-steel door is swung open to the sea. SEALs emerge, inflate the CRRC on deck, and ascend to their craft to head off to the OTB insertion point. They conduct their mission, return to the camouflaged CRRC, safely launch back out through the surf, and motor back out to the submarine pickup point. Underwater electronic pingers allow the submarine to track the withdrawing SEALs. The CRRC hooks on to the submarine periscope and begins the deflation evolution to recover the craft. Meanwhile, designated SEALs free-dive to the submarine deck astern of the DDS and begin breathing on hookah rigs before reentering the DDS where an air bubble is maintained just above the hatch. If this bubble is not available, the swimmers continue breathing on hookah rigs until all swimmers and CRRC are recovered. A hot shower is next, but only after securing all the operational equipment. "Take care of your gear first" is a time-proven axiom of SEAL team operations. Following personnel cleanup, the element is assembled to debrief the operation. When all personnel are safely recovered and the DDS outer door secured, the submarine seeks a deeper and more secure depth. Any intelligence to be sent to higher headquarters is assembled, formatted, and sent forward. Mission accomplished.

Air Operations

Air operations, especially those involving free-fall parachuting, are immensely popular with SEALs, but there is an exacting trail to get to that graduation jump. Following graduation with the Army basic parachutist badge, the historic Silver Wings, the SEAL returns to his command and completes five more team jumps to win the gold Navy–Marine Corps Gold Wings. These jumps are all static-line jumps whereby the static line deploys a modified, steerable parachute.

Formerly, BUD/S graduates lined up to get to the Army basic parachute course at Fort Benning, Georgia. Today, instead of going all the way back to Fort Benning, the Navy has contracted static-line and free-fall training for SEALs and EOD personnel. The school, near San Diego's Otay Lake reservoir, has operated since 2004, and has trained more than 1,500 SEAL and EOD free-fall jumpers, including Air Force combat medics. The civilian instructors come from military backgrounds; some come from Great Britain. The modified course is based on the United States Parachute Association advanced free-fall program. Jumpers are accompanied "out the door" by seasoned skydivers. Each initial jump is pho-

BOTTOM: *Coronado Bay—CRRC (Combat Rubber Raiding Craft), and "Battle Rattle" SEALS readying for an OTB. Fully "jocked up," these SEALs simulate an over-the-beach maneuver covering all compass directions defensively. The CRRC is also known as an IBS (Inflatable Boat, Small), or Zodiac. (Photo: Dave Gatley)*

BELOW: *SEALs deployed and recovered from this rubber boat (IBS) are tied up to a moving RIB (Rigid Hull Inflatable Boat). This is the recovery phase of the cast and recovery mission, designed to speed up the retrieval of a SEAL team from over-the-beach or other missions that involve water transfers. At Little Creek, Virginia. (Photo: Dave Gatley)*

ABOVE: *New to the problem of underwater navigation is the Mk 107 Mod 0 Hydrographic Mapping Unit (HMU). The U.S. Navy SEALs now use this as their standalone navigation aid instead of the familiar tactical board. Wearing the LAR-V MK 25 provides this SEAL with enough oxygen to stay underwater for three to four hours. This is a closed-circuit oxygen rebreather, which is a specialized type of underwater breathing apparatus that keeps all exhaled gases within the rig. This design is unlike SCUBA tanks, which expel gases leaving telltale bubbles on the surface. (Photo: Dave Gatley)*

RIGHT: *The Mk 107 Mod 0 HMU is reflected off the diver's face mask—showing navigation points and routes underwater. (Photo: Dave Gatley)*

BELOW: *SEAL Team Close Quarter Combat (CQC) practice can be done at the NSWG-1Advanced Training Course facility in Imperial Beach. The "Shoot House" is where realistic non-lethal ammo is used in the continuing training exercises designed to introduce SEALs to CQC situations involving urban room-to-room clearing. (Photo: Dave Gatley)*

tographed by a videographer; after the jump the jumper is debriefed individually. For civilians, training to initial qualification requires seven increasing-level skydives. SEALs will make about twenty-five jumps, including night jumps with equipment—rucksack and weapon.

Another method of parachuting involves HAHO (High Altitude High Opening). Jumpers exit a fixed-wing aircraft at 30,000 feet or more, open immediately, and steer their canopies long distances cross-country to the insertion point. These operations are extremely dangerous and normally only practiced by special units.

SEALs accomplish tactical insertions using parachutes and helicopters. During the Vietnam era, daylight helicopter insertions made up the majority of SEAL missions in the delta. The choppers have improved since the old Hueys, although a few Hueys remain in service. SEALs now use the HH-60 Black Hawk, the Navy version. These are formed into reserve squadrons on both coasts; they provide support to NSW. Helicopter Sea Combat Squadron 84 (HSC-84) Red Wolves and Firehawks of HSC-85 are Naval Reserve helicopter squadrons, and the only two squadrons in the U.S. Navy dedicated to supporting Navy SEALs and SBTs, and tasked to perform CSAR. They can deploy anywhere in the world within seventy-two hours of notice; the helicopter sea combat squadrons (HSCs) currently support SEALs and SWCCs only during training in the United States. Several have suggested that these squadrons be tactically assigned full time to the NSWGs, but as of this writing this assignment has not been made. The SEALs also use the tactical lift of Army and Air Force aviation on selected, joint training exercises and, of course, in combat as the local situation demands. SEALs have deployed from Army helicopters in Afghanistan and Iraq on several joint operations.

One method of inserting SEALs by helicopter involves fast roping, a technique whereby the SEAL slides down a thick hawser using insulated gloves and his legs. It is a fast technique and can be used in a variety of insertion modes. The chopper hovers above the ground (or rooftop), SEALs quickly slip down, and the chopper

SEAL students conducting a HALO jump, also known as Military Free Fall (MFF). These jumps require special training, along with close attention to details and equipment. In typical HALO/HAHO insertions, the SEALs are dispatched from altitudes between 20,000 feet and 35,000 feet. (HAHO - High Altitude High Opening).

is out of there. Speed is the secret of making the most of this insertion. The fast-rope capability, once classified, was developed by English SOFs and adopted by the SEALs. The insertion technique involves a low-level helicopter approach to the target, where a specially designed fifty- or ninety-foot rope secured to the helicopter is tossed out. SEALs slide down the rope. Using this procedure, an entire sixteen-man platoon can be on the ground in less than twenty seconds. SEALs also have developed the capability to rappel from helicopters in the same fashion as they do in mountaineering operations.

Insertion onto decks of ships is rehearsed routinely, inasmuch as NSW has the maritime charter under USSOCOM. "Ship take-down" is the nominal term for these operations. A SEAL element—normally a seven-man squad—will insert by fast rope onto a suspected merchant ship in order to check for contraband—weapons, armaments, illegal commodities, drugs, and so on. Called VBSS (Visit, Board, Search, and Seizure) these operations were introduced during the first Persian Gulf War in 1990, with great success. SEALs practice these evolutions during ULT periods.

A future development SEALs can expect is operating from the new V-22 Osprey, a vertical, fixed-wing aircraft that can travel farther into a hostile region to extract teams of SOF. A normal fixed-wing aircraft can deliver a team by parachute,

BOTTOM, LEFT: Challenge coin from the NSW SEAL Team Eight - front (variant 1), SEAL Team EIGHT based at Little Creek, VA. (Photo: Dave Gatley)

BOTTOM, RIGHT: Challenge coin of SEAL Team 10, which is based at Little Creek, Virginia. (Photo: Dave Gatley)

SEALs moving across a ship during a Visit, Board, Search, and Seizure (VBSS). Using small caving ladders, this technique requires extreme upper-body strength and is accomplished from static and underway platforms during day and nighttime operations in coordination with SWCC operators from the Special Boat Teams. (Photo: Greg E. Mathieson Sr. / NSW Publications, LLC)

but a longer-reach aircraft is required to extract them, hence, the Osprey. Helicopters will remain functional for shorter distances. During the opening phases of OIF choppers operated from U.S. Navy carriers.

Extraction from an area also can be accomplished by the special procedure insertion and extraction system rig whereby up to seven SEALs are tethered to a line dropped to them from a hovering helicopter. They are quickly flown to a safe area and recovered on board the chopper for transit back to their command or forward operating base (FOB). SEALs may also be administratively extracted by helicopters once they have landed on the ship's deck.

SOF air operations are supported by all services assigned to USSOCOM. Army aviation has the 160th Special Operations Aviation Regiment (Airborne) stationed at Fort Campbell, Kentucky. SOAR (A), or the Night Stalkers, provide a variety of rotary wing aircraft. The Air Force Special Operations Command in Hurlburt Field, Florida, fields several types of aircraft, rotary and fixed wing—all available for joint use with all SOF elements.

Future UAS capabilities that USSOCOM intends to field for SOF will include higher-resolution video sensors, electronic warfare sensors, and integration of weapons delivery systems. The NSWC is coordinating with USSOCOM,

the Office of Naval Research (ONR), the Naval Research Laboratory, and the Air Force Research Laboratory to deliver the most advanced UAS technologies to support NSW in the GWOT.

Land Operations

Call it patrolling. SEALs can hike for extended periods, even in difficult conditions. For instance, the Afghanistan mountainous terrain has been a severe challenge at 10,000 feet altitude. Suffice it to say that SEALs spend months perfecting a patrolling capability suitable to the terrain they find themselves in—from the swamps of the Vietnamese Rung Sat Special Zone, to the deserts of Iraq, to the mountains of Afghanistan, to the snow-covered mountains of Kodiak, Alaska. SEALs patrol in it all.

The important point about the "land" element in "SEAL" is that much of NSW combat takes place on land. Small-unit tactics comprise the cornerstone of SEAL team land warfare training. SEALs routinely train in deserts, jungles, and, most recently, on mountains. On the West Coast, sites around California provide various topographies ranging from desert to mountain. East Coast training areas include

geography similar to that found in Europe. In addition, SEALs use several sites in the Caribbean for tropics training. Small-unit training scenarios are routinely practiced both in the United States and overseas.

SEAL Qualification Training

After completing BUD/S training, all graduates immediately attend SQT, which is the training that actually trains and qualifies them to become a SEAL. SQT is an arduous twenty-six-week program of basic and advanced sequential courses of instruction consisting of survival, escape, resistance, and evasion; tactical air operations (static-line and free-fall); tactical combat medicine; communications; advanced special operations; cold weather mountaineering; maritime operations; combat swimming; tactical ground mobility, land warfare (small-unit tactics, light and heavy weapons, demolitions), armed CQD, and close quarters combat. SQT emphasis involves building and developing the individual operator (officer and petty officer) capable of joining an NSW troop with minimal deviation in operational capability. Students are broken into twenty-man platoons with two ten-man squads. Each platoon is assigned a mentor or chief to evaluate performance throughout the training period. SQT teaches standardized TTPs as they relate to current lessons learned.

Upon completion of SQT, each man is awarded the Navy enlisted classifica-

tion code (NEC 5326) or naval officer billet code or (NOBC 1135), and is authorized to wear the gold Navy SEAL Trident breast insignia. From SQT the men are assigned to an operational SEAL team and can immediately begin predeployment with the team or NSWRON.

UNIT-LEVEL TRAINING

The majority of SEAL team training is performed during ULT. This is training performed inside the SEAL team using own team cadre and other courses provided by the NSWCEN and ATC. In addition, individuals returning to the team from other duties may be sent individually to various courses offered by the training commands before joining a platoon. Routine ULT follows team standard operating procedures and the mission-essential task list (METL) approved by higher headquarters. SQT and METLs ensure all SEAL teams are training to an approved standard. Before establishment of SQT, the SEAL teams were not homogeneous in their approach to training. During the Vietnam era lessons learned in the field were directly applied to predeployment training curricula, which was only oriented toward missions being performed in Vietnam. Once all SEALs had been withdrawn from Vietnam, training became more or less a grab bag of exercises. The most pronounced training ideology was expounded by Capt. Dave Schaible calling his group back to basics . . . and into the water. At the SEAL team level, a lot of training depended on the orientation of the CO: If the CO was an avid diver, diving operations were stressed. If the commander was a land guy, that was the emphasis. Still, minimum requalification dives had to be maintained, as did quarterly parachute jumps and demolition requalifications, but the team emphasis was not standard. Today, with SQT and METLs, ULT, and later SIT, group commanders can be confident in the continuity of the SEAL teams' training and skills.

SEAL Delivery Vehicles and Submarines

CDR (SEAL) Tom Hawkins, USN (Ret)

CHAPTER 6

SEAL DELIVERY VEHICLES AND SUBMARINES

Cdr. (SEAL) Tom Hawkins, USN (Ret.)

IN 1952, A THEN-CLASSIFIED REPORT, "UNDERWATER SWIMMERS," prepared for the ONR Panel on Underwater Swimmers, Committee on Amphibious Operations of the National Research Council, described the basic task of SDVs. These prescient words are just as relevant today as they were more than fifty years ago:

Whenever it is necessary to operate near an enemy held shore in as complete secrecy as possible, the approach to the objective must be made under water. The first part of the approach can be made in a fleet-type submarine, but these 1500-ton vessels cannot operate submerged in water shallower than 60 feet, and depths less than 150 feet are considered hazardous. The final submerged approach must

be made by swimming or in a small submersible. On many coasts throughout the world, depths less than 60 feet extend out several miles from shore. In these areas even men equipped with SCUBA would not have enough breathing gas to swim the distance and return. Moreover, they would be seriously fatigued when they reached their objective after their swim of several hours. To supplement their swimming, they must have a small, powered submersible.

EARLY DEVELOPMENT

Modern swimmer propulsion vehicles were first used at the beginning of World War II by the Italians against the British in the Mediterranean; the Italians pioneered use of small submersibles for stealthy attacks on shipping. These small submersibles were "wet" in design: during their use, divers would be totally exposed to the water. The British used this type of vehicle only during an interim period preceding the launching of their small "dry" miniature submarines, called the X Craft.

As a naval "have-not" nation prior to and during World War II, Italy pioneered the use of the underwater swimmer as a military weapon; the capability was inexpensive relative to its cost. Concurrently, they developed underwater vehicles and operating procedures to transport divers and their explosive payloads to targets. The targets were to be enemy warships and Allied merchantmen in their own harbors.

The first Italian vehicle for swimmer use was designated the Siluro a Lenta Corsa, nicknamed "Pig." This was the now famous two-man human torpedo configuration that carried an explosive payload as one or two detachable nose sections. The two crewmembers, wearing closed-circuit underwater breathing gear, sat astride the vehicle. The operator was provided with basic navigation and control instruments such as a magnetic compass, a clock, and a depth gauge.

The first Italian operation using Pigs occurred in August 1940. These vehicles became most famous for their exploits at Alexandria, Egypt; and at Gibraltar. Within two years, the efforts of the Italian 10th Light Flotilla resulted in 265,352 tons of shipping sunk or severely damaged, for a total of thirty-one ships. This included use of underwater swimmers and motor torpedo boats (MTBs) in addition to the Pigs. It is significant to note that fifteen of the thirty-one ships sunk or damaged were the result of attacks using Pigs. The most spectacular attacks resulted in sinking or damaging the battleships *Queen Elizabeth* and *Valiant* in the harbor of Alexandria in December 1941.

One of the Italian Pigs was salvaged after an unsuccessful Italian attack on Gibraltar, so the British navy was not blind to what the Italians were doing. They were

TOP: *Navy divers and SEAL operators from SEAL Delivery Vehicle Team Two (SDVT-2) stand within the Dry Deck Shelter (DDS) which holds the SDV that is deployed via a sledlike platform off the nuclear-powered guided missile submarine USS Florida (SSGN-728). (Photo: Andrew McKaskie / USN)*

BOTTOM, LEFT: *A member of SEAL Delivery Vehicle Team Two (SDVT-2) prepares to launch one of the team's SEAL Delivery Vehicles (SDV) from the Los Angeles–class attack submarine USS Philadelphia (SSN-690) on a training exercise. The SDVs are used to carry SEALs from a submerged submarine to enemy targets while staying underwater and undetected. (Photo: Andrew McKaskle / USN)*

BOTTOM, RIGHT: *A Navy diver and special operator from SEAL Delivery Vehicle Team Two (SDVT-2) performs SDV operations with the nuclear-powered guided missile submarine USS Florida (SSGN-728). (Photo: Andrew McKaskie / USN)*

already in the process of producing their midget submarine called the X Craft, to be manned by three or four men. British versions of the Pig, however, were developed as an interim measure, while awaiting completion of the first X-class submarines.

The two British submersible systems, one wet and one dry, were entirely different, although they were designed to achieve similar objectives. The X Craft was a complete submarine in miniature with internal working space for its reduced crew. The British submersible, called Chariot, was manned by a crew of two, who, like the Italian operators, wore SCUBA equipment and diving suits and sat astride the vehicle.

In October 1942, the British undertook an operation using two Chariots to attack the German battleship *Tirpitz,* lying in hiding at Håkøy, near Tromsø, Norway. The operation was not successful: both Chariots were lost en route while being towed to the target.

On 15 March 1943, the first X Craft was launched after being under construction for the better part of three years. X Craft were designed with wet and dry compartments, commonly called the W and D by the men, which were used by the underwater swimmers to lock in and lock out of the craft. Swimmers from the X Craft could be used to place charges underneath target ships, or the craft could penetrate a defended harbor and drop side-loaded demolition charges. One charge could be carried on each side of the pressure hull, and each charge contained four thousand pounds of high explosives. Timers to explode the charges were set

from within the submarine before they were released.

British exploits are best known because of their operation against the German battleship *Tirpitz*, when two X Craft successfully planted four of the two-ton side charges beneath the mighty combatant as it lay in a Norwegian fjord. X Craft were used in Europe, the Mediterranean, and in the Far East.

The operations of the Italian and British submersibles are significant: these were the only combatant submersible vehicles operated under combat conditions. Not all operations were successful, and they were accompanied by a period of learning through extremely trying conditions. In the sinking of battleships *Queen Elizabeth*, *Valiant*, and *Tirpitz*, the strategic importance of the capability could not be questioned. Fortunately for the Allies, the gallantry and courage of the Italian Pig operators went for naught, since the Italians never exploited the advantage gained by their navy.

In the United States, the only combat swimmer capability that attempted to duplicate what had been done by the Italians and British was accomplished by the OSS MU. This unit was formed for the purpose of maritime sabotage, and adopted much of the training and many of the tactics of the British. In the autumn of 1942, OSS attempted to exploit a submersible they called the Toy. It was not a successful project; the significance of the Toy was that the MU divers recognized the limitations of their breathing apparatus and the need for assisted propulsion. During World War II, OSS MU embraced the British-developed submersible canoe, which they called Sleeping Beauty; this one-man submersible was eventually acquired for training. It was later deployed with OSS to the Pacific theater of operations, where the men used the submersible to train for operations against the main island of Japan, but it was never used operationally.

On the last day of the war, the OSS was disbanded, and this included the MU. Fortunately,

Pier side with the USS Ohio, the first SSGN. Boomer class submarine modified to handle SOF (Special Operations Forces) and serve as a host for Navy SEALs, their SDV (SEAL Delivery Vehicle), and a considerable amount of SOF gear along with its normal complement of the ship's Tomahawk missiles. Rolled up on the deck (foreground and left) are the F470 Combat Rubber Raiding Craft (CRRC), also known as the Combat Rubber Reconnaissance Craft, a specially fabricated rubber inflatable boat often used by SEALs and Marines, among others. Though the Zodiac Group produces a large range of both inflatables and rigid-hulled boats, the name "Zodiac" has become synonymous with the CRRC. These will all be loaded along with their outboard engines below deck to be launched from underwater. (Photos: Dave Gatley)

Dr. Christian J. Lambertsen (mentioned in Chapter 1), who was an Army medical officer assigned to OSS MU, collected and saved all of the combat swimmer equipment. He had been MU's swimmer trainer and developer of their diving apparatus, the LARU. Had it not been for Dr. Lambertsen, the skills developed by OSS MU during the war would have been lost. During the postwar period, he began a one-man campaign to introduce his diving capability to the U.S. Coast Guard, Army Engineers, and the Navy's UDTs. The LARU, a closed-circuit pure-oxygen rebreather that left no telltale bubbles, was optimum for use by the UDTs.

POSTWAR SUBMERSIBLES

In 1947 and 1948, the UDTs adopted the OSS MU equipment and tactics, including the LARU and the submersible canoe Sleeping Beauty. While not the ideal

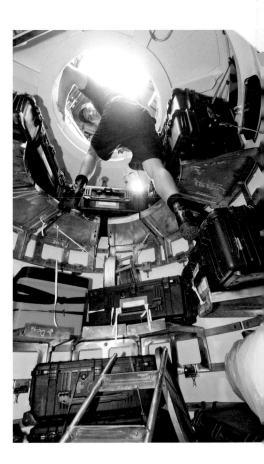

The X-1 was the U.S. Navy's only midget submarine. It was built by the Fairchild Engine and Airplane Corporation. It was originally conceived and designed to support Underwater Demolition Team operations; however, its capabilities to support the UDTs were extremely limited. Instead the X-1 was used for research and testing to assist the Navy in evaluating its ability to defend harbors against other small submarines. The X-1 was originally powered by a hydrogen peroxide/diesel engine and battery system; however, an explosion of its fuel supply in May 1957 resulted in its conversion to diesel-electric drive. This photograph was taken while X-1 was performing experimental trials in the Chesapeake Bay in 1966. (Photo: Courtesy of Tom Hawkins)

Navy SEALs utilizing a new storage concept aboard the USS Ohio SSGN-726 (Submersible Ship Guided missile—Nuclear) where the ship replaces the Tomahawk missile tubes with a SOF Canister tube containing specialized gear for deployment and mission. This procedure saves valuable time by getting the sub turned around in port faster and back out to sea with a fresh crew. (Photos: Dave Gatley)

vessel, Sleeping Beauty demonstrated the value of a swimmer-assisted propulsion vehicle to the UDTs, and set the stage for a flurry of activity throughout the ensuing decade to acquire expanded capabilities.

Little occurred surrounding combatant submersible development during the Korean War period. In 1952, there was increased interest within the submarine force surrounding development of an X Craft–type miniature submersible for UDT use. During this period, too, the UDTs worked with the British navy to evaluate their X Craft submarine in the Chesapeake Bay. Subsequently, plans were drawn up for development of the U.S. Navy X-1 submarine.

The USS X-1 was a dry submersible, originally conceived in 1953, for tactically transporting swimmers. It was diesel powered on the surface and used hydrogen peroxide in the diesel engine for submerged operation. Batteries and a DC motor provided emergency submerged propulsion.

Construction of the X-1 was started in 1954, by the Fairchild Engine and Airplane Corporation under the cognizance of the ONR for ultimate assignment to the amphibious forces. Early in the construction phase, however, the Navy transferred the project to the Bureau of Ships (BuShips, since renamed NAVSEA), and the craft was delivered to the submarine forces instead. With this change the X-1 became more of a submarine-force submarine and less of an amphibious-force swimmer delivery vehicle.

The USS X-1 had a maximum range of 1,800 miles at four knots on the sur-

TOP, LEFT: *Pearl Harbor, Hawaii—Pier side with the USS Ohio, the first SSGN 726 former Boomer-class submarine modified to handle SOF (Special Operations Forces). Storage hatches, prior Trident ICBM missile launch tubes, are opened to load up gear for a mission. Also pictured is the hatch to the DDS (Dry Dock Shelter), used for carrying a minisub, the SDV (SEAL Delivery Vehicle). (Photo: Dave Gatley / NSW Publications, LLC)*

TOP, RIGHT: *SDV seen being loaded into a Dry Dock Shelter (DDS) topside at Pearl Harbor, Hawaii—Pier side with the USS Ohio, the first SSGN 726 former Boomer-class submarine modified to handle SOF (Special Operations Forces) and serve as a host for the SEALs and their SDV (SEAL Delivery Vehicle). Pictured here is the SEAL Delivery Vehicle Mk VIII, a wet submersible designed to carry combat swimmers and their cargo in compartments that are flooded with water. The former (ICBM) missile launch tube hatch (foreground (R)) is now used for storage of SEAL equipment. (Photo: Dave Gatley/ NSW Publications, LLC)*

CENTER: *Side view of an SDV being loaded into a DDS topside of the USS Ohio. (Photo: Dave Gatley / NSW Publicatons, LLC)*

BOTTOM, LEFT: *An SDV performing its first maneuvers off the deck of the USS Ohio. Docking and locking out of the DDS on the ship's deck. (Photo: Dave Gatley)*

BOTTOM, RIGHT: *Pearl Harbor, Hawaii— Pier side with the USS Ohio. The Dry Dock Shelter (DDS), an underwater housing for the minisubmarine SEAL Dive Vehicle (SDV) looms above the deck and the old launch tube. Some of the former Trident ICBM tubes have been converted into storage lockers for Special Operations hardware and SDV/ASDS, HSDV/ ASDS batteries and weapons, while others carry Tomahawk missile canisters. (Photo: Dave Gatley)*

face, under diesel power. On the hydrogen peroxide system, its submerged range varied from 180 miles at two knots to 140 miles at ten knots. On battery power (emergency only) its submerged range varied from twelve miles at two knots to six miles at five knots. When the hydrogen peroxide system was removed and replaced by increased battery capacity, the submerged range was reduced considerably from eleven-and-a-half miles at two knots to seven miles at six knots.

As late as February and March 1964, the X-1 operated for four weeks with UDT and SEAL personnel at the UDT training facility, St. Thomas, Virgin Islands. As a result of these operations, the UDT commands reaffirmed the requirement for a dry combatant submersible for use by underwater swimmers.

From 1952 to 1955, at least sixteen free-flooding or wet SDVs were proposed or built in the United States. Of those, four were built under Navy contract or at a Navy research and development (R&D) laboratory, and ten were built by civilian contractors. Eight of those ten were built by the Aerojet General Corporation, which became very active in the design and construction of SDVs, also called swimmer propulsion units (SPUs) at the time.

Aerojet became the undisputed leader in developing SPUs throughout the 1950s. Their first was an experimental pedal-powered craft designed and built in 1952. With its design, a single underwater swimmer lay prone on the vehicle and by means of pedals drove counterrotating propellers at about one hundred revolutions per minute for a three-knot velocity.

In 1953, Aerojet designed the miniature submarine Mark III (Mk III), the first of their submersible vehicles where the swimmer actually sat inside a free-flooding hull. This vehicle was available with pedal power, carbon dioxide power, or battery power. Battery power was considered most efficient for speed and duration.

In 1954, Aerojet produced the miniature submarine Mk VI. This was a two-man wet submersible with a free-flooding hull with divers sitting within the vehicle hull. It, too, was both pedal powered and battery powered. Maximum speed under battery power was five knots.

Aerojet produced the Mk VII in 1955. It incorporated a free-flooding fiberglass hull for two men lying prone side by side, with head and shoulders housed in large transparent Plexiglas windows integrated as part of the hull. Visibility downward, ahead, and to either side was unrestricted. The vehicle was built with both

pedal and battery power available, and was the first Aerojet vehicle to have breathing air cylinders installed for use by the crews. A speed of four knots for a one-mile sprint was claimed for two men pedaling. With battery power a two-horsepower motor provided the vehicle with a maximum speed of five knots and a cruise speed of three knots. Range on battery power was about seven nautical miles.

During the 1950s, several other SDVs were built by industry or under Navy contract. Examples of these submersible vehicles were the Sea Sled, Aquabat, Drut, Trass and Sea Horse, Mk I Mod 1, Modified X-1, PR-77, and Convair Model 14.

Sea Sled

Sea Sled was the first venture by a Navy laboratory to design and construct an SDV. It was the accomplishment of the Navy Underwater Sound Laboratory, New London, Connecticut, at the request of East Coast UDT personnel and was a cumshaw development. ("Cumshaw" is a Navy term for something obtained through unofficial means, whether deviously or simply ingeniously.) A diver rode prone on the Sea Sled, which was funded in part by money allocated for electronics development and thus was shown on the books as an electronics carrier. One vehicle was built for test and evaluation to acquire information and data for construction of improved vehicles.

Although evaluated by UDT personnel, no additional Sea Sleds were constructed. The primary advantage of a prone-ridden vehicle was its capability to operate in very shallow water, a capability particularly useful for the clandestine reconnaissance of a prospective landing beach. The Sea Sled had one speed forward (three knots) and a range of about twenty nautical miles.

Aquabat

In 1957 the Underwater Sound Laboratory produced a second SDV design called the Aquabat, which was a two-man wet submersible designed for mine recon-

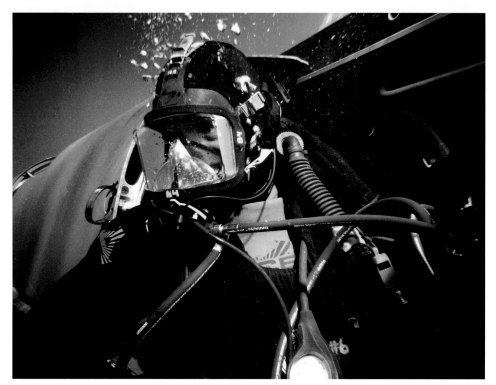

naissance, location, and classification in shallow waters. It was equipped with object-locating sonar, with the operator in a rear seat having full control of the sonar equipment. Aquabat was designed and built as a two-man vehicle, where both operators sat upright in the free-flooding hull. Propulsion was provided by a three-and-a-half-horsepower twenty-four-volt DC motor. Speed control was accomplished through a combination mechanical-hydraulic system. This system provided variable speed control both ahead and astern. Aquabat was operated by UDT personnel in the waters off New London, Connecticut, and St. Thomas, Virgin Islands. The vehicle had a number of shortcomings, although it incorporated some very sophisticated subsystems. It was a most significant development in advancing SDV capabilities; it is probably safe to say, however, that its primary shortcoming was that it was way ahead of its time.

Drut

In 1960, the UDTs were still looking for a satisfactory and reliable SDV. In that year a two-man wet submersible called the Drut was conceived, designed, and

built by personnel of UDT-1 at the NAB, Coronado, California. Two SCUBA-equipped operators rode astride and semiprone on the body of the vehicle, which looked strangely like the expendable external fuel tanks carried by jet aircraft. The hull was constructed, in fact, from drop-tanks used on the Chance Vought F7U Cutlass aircraft. Four tank sections made up the vehicle body. The complete craft was built from scrap parts taken mostly from the salvage yard of the Naval Air Station at North Island in San Diego. It was not a sophisticated vehicle and represented no great technological breakthrough but was mute testimony to the passion for SDVs in the UDTs.

Trass and Sea Horse

The Navy had long been interested in the work of the Italians in the area of submersibles. In the late 1950s, a private concern, Costruzione Motoscafe Sottomarini Industries of Livorno, Italy, was offering custom-built or off-the-shelf SDVs to individuals, commercial companies, and foreign governments. In 1960, the Navy purchased four Trass III vehicles, and in 1962 it purchased four Sea Horse II vehicles for evaluation. The Trass was a four-man wet vehicle, and the Sea Horse a two-man wet vehicle. Both vehicle types were tested and evaluated by East Coast and West Coast UDTs and found wanting in a number of respects. Nonetheless, eight Trass and eight Sea Horse vehicles were acquired and extensively modified by the Navy Mine Defense Laboratory (MDL), Panama City, Florida, in 1964. Major modifications included relocation of the operator controls to the forward crew stations, installation of a Plexiglas windshield and a one-piece sliding Plexiglas canopy, installation of an improved battery with an increased capacity, increase in the rudder and stern plane surface areas, relocation of these control surfaces behind the screw for increased control surface effectiveness, and redesign of vehicle instrumentation.

Mark 1, Model 1

In the 1960s, several attempts were made commercially to build SDVs for the UDT and SEAL teams. Aerojet built three SDVs under contract to BuShips. The

foremost of these were the Mk 1 Mod 1 SPUs delivered in 1962, which actually towed a diver when under way. Its primary disadvantage was that the swimmer required body English and swim fins to control the vehicle. In practice, swimmers found this to be very difficult to do; accurate course and depth keeping required considerable effort. The SPU also allowed little or no provision for payload.

Modified X-1

In November 1963 the Republic Aircraft Corporation submitted a proposal to BuShips to modify the X-1 again for UDT-SEAL use. The proposed modification would permit the transport of twelve fully equipped swimmers, increase the battery capacity, improve the steering and diving-control system, and modify the diesel-exhaust system to allow higher-power output from the diesel

engine. BuShips approved the proposed design, but the modifications were never funded.

PR-77

In 1964 the MDL exploited a French-built two-man SDV called the PR-77, an innovative teardrop design where the operators rode sitting upright side by side. In 1965, the MDL designed and built a two-man submersible that borrowed heavily from the design of the PR-77. Although this vehicle experienced significant experimental growing pains, it became a test bed for development of a contract specification for the Class I and Class II SDVs outlined in the Swimmer (later SEAL) Support System, the Navy's technical development plan (TDP) 38-02.

Convair Model 14

In December 1966, General Dynamics Corporation's Convair Division in San Diego delivered five new-design four-man SDVs built under contract to NAVSEA (formerly BuShips), with operational and technical guidance provided by commander, NOSG, Pacific (today's NSWG-1). This vehicle was often referred to as a modified Trass, but was designated the Convair Model 14. It was capable of a sustained five-knot cruising speed for eight hours; the four divers sat upright in a free-flooding hull constructed of 0.08-inch thick fiberglass. Two crew compartments fore and aft were separated by a main ballast tank, and these compartments were enclosed by sliding clear-plastic canopies intended to reduce drag.

The Convair Model 14 represented the latest thinking in the design and construction of SDVs in the United States at the time. It was considered an interim capability because the longer-range Class I and Class II SDVs to be acquired under the TDP 38-02 program were being prepared for design and construction by industry. The Convair 14 was a very basic design and had none of the sophisticated subsystems considered necessary for a truly advanced SDV design such as mapping sonar, obstacle-avoidance sonar, total-depth recording equipment, and other

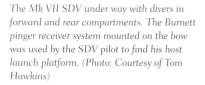

equipment that would be incorporated in the advanced-technology TDP 38-02 Class I and Class II vehicles.

In the early 1970s, the Convair Model 14 was designated the Mk VII SDV and, because of substantial delays in building the TDP 38-02 vehicles, would be substantially improved through progressive alteration and modification with advanced sonar and other capabilities. The Mk VII SDV was the first production SDV accepted by the U.S. Navy and the first truly reliable submersible designated for combat use by the UDT and SEAL teams. It would also be the first SDV used in a real-world combat deployment.

The SEAL Support System would revolutionize the underwater combat capabilities of the UDT and SEAL teams. Originally conceived in the early 1960s, the plan called for development of Class I and Class II UBAs, Class I and Class II SDVs, and conversion of USS *Grayback* (SSG-574) and sister ship USS *Growler* (SSG-577), former Regulus-missile submarines, as host platforms for transport, launch, and recovery of SDVs and crews.

Specifications for the new UBAs and SDVs were completed in 1967. A contract was awarded to the Scott Aviation Corporation for development of a closed-circuit pure-oxygen rebreather (Class I), and closed-circuit mixed-gas rebreather (Class II) to replace the Emerson and Mk VI UBAs in the current inventory. The Class II UBA was intended to operate for six hours at a time to complement the capabilities of the Class I SDV, which would have extended range, depth controls, and navigational operating capabilities.

A contract was awarded to the Aerojet Corporation for development of the six-man Class I SDV and two-man Class II SDV. The Class I SDV's primary mission was infiltration and exfiltration of UDTs and SEALs on shore, and delivery of special weapons. The primary design mission of the Class II SDV was amphibious reconnaissance, but later it also included weapons delivery.

The Aerojet SDV development program was very technical and very complex, and after several years' time ran into extreme performance difficulty. The single vehicle delivered under the contract was very heavy, and it was next to impossible for it to attain the neutral buoyancy necessary to trim out the vehicle for speed, range, and safety. The Aerojet program was eventually terminated and placed under government control at a special project office set up for this purpose at the Naval Weapons Center, China Lake, California.

Because of the Aerojet contract delays, a separate and robust program was established to improve the Mk VII design and outfit it with advanced capabilities. Correcting the Mk VII SDV deficiencies became a matter of priority, and an aggressive program was directed from the highest levels of the Navy staff to mod-

LEFT: *The SDV Mk VII, Mod 2 seen being launched into the water from its towing trailer during training operations at the U.S. Naval Station, Roosevelt Roads, Puerto Rico. Observe the SDV being sling-lifted and see an inflated buoy on top of the craft. For safety during training, this buoy would be towed behind the SDV so that a surface support boat could track the crew's underwater movement. (Photo: Courtesy of Tom Hawkins)*

RIGHT: *A rare historical photograph of the Mk VII SEAL Delivery Vehicle (SDV) seen alongside a modified Italian manufactured Trass III submersible (foreground), which was extensively modified by the U.S. Navy to accommodate UDT needs. The Mk VII SDV was made by the Convair Division of the General Dynamics Corporation under the direction of Commander, Naval Operations Support Group, Pacific (forerunner of Naval Special Warfare Group ONE). (Photo: Courtesy of Tom Hawkins)*

The Mk IX SDV changing crews on the surface. This was a low-profile SDV, where the divers were transported in a prone position. The aft section contained a large cargo compartment for weapons and other items. The Mk IX was built as a weapons delivery platform. (Photo: Courtesy of Tom Hawkins)

Mk IX SDV in its Little Bo Peep configuration. The weapon seen mounted on the starboard side of the SDV was known by the acronym LAM (Limpet Assembly, Modular), hence the capability designation adopted by the men. (Photo: Courtesy of Tom Hawkins)

ernize and improve this SDV. This was vitally important because the long-range Class I and Class II SDV development had been essentially stalled, giving the Mk VII improvements substantial urgency. These improvements included ahead- and bottom-looking navigation sonars, internal and external communications systems, and improved control and propulsion systems, among other capabilities. Some of the Mk VII's accelerated modernization was driven by the fact that the USS *Grayback* had completed its hangar modifications and was returning to fleet service, and a more reliable SDV was needed by the Pacific Fleet commander to conduct clandestine operations.

THE VIETNAM ERA

The Navy's Regulus missile program ended in 1964, when *Grayback* was withdrawn from active service. Along with its sister ship, *Growler*, it became the designated candidate for conversion as a troop and SDV transport ship specifically for UDT and SEAL team use. As a result, *Grayback*'s second conversion began in November 1967 at the Mare Island Naval Shipyard, California. The conversion was originally estimated at $15.2 million, but actually was $30 million, absorbing the funds programmed for *Growler*'s conversion. *Grayback* was reclassified from Regulus missile–launching submarines (SSG) to amphibious personnel submarines (LPSSs) on 30 August 1968, and once again entered active service. During this period she was deployed to the western Pacific and considered for unconventional warfare operations against VC and North Vietnamese forces.

Early in 1972, *Grayback* and the SDVs got their first call to combat duty. Their highly classified operation surrounded the escape and recovery of two U.S. airmen being held as prisoners of war at the infamous North Vietnamese prison known to American prisoners of war as the "Hanoi Hilton." Armed with fresh intelligence that the prisoners were planning to steal a boat and travel down the Red River to the Gulf of Tonkin, Adm. Thomas H. Moorer, chairman of the JCS, authorized Pacific Command (PACOM) to execute Operation Thunderhead, a rescue plan proposed by the Pacific Fleet. Full details of the operation were known to only a handful of officers individually cleared by Adm. John S. McCain Jr., the PACOM commander.

The escape plan was set in motion and involved two Mk VII SDVs and members of SEAL Team 1 and UDT-11, who were led by SEAL Lt. Melvin "Spence" Dry. An SDV was to be launched at night from the submerged submarine in an SDV crewed by two UDT-11 operators, who would deliver the team to a small island off the mouth of the Red River. There two SEALs would establish a hiding place to watch for any sign of the escapees. Should they be sighted, the SEALs would intercept them and coordinate their rescue with the waiting ships of the Seventh Fleet.

Grayback arrived on station on 3 June 1972, and the SEALs decided to conduct a clandestine SDV reconnaissance mission that night. One of the two SDVs on board was launched from *Grayback* shortly after midnight, but a combination of navigational errors and strong currents took them off course. After searching for more than an hour without sighting the island, the SDV crew aborted the mission, but was unable to find their way back to the *Grayback*. A decision was made to abandon the SDV after its battery power was exhausted.

Back on board *Grayback*, after the first SDV departed the ship for the tactical reconnaissance mission, the second SDV was launched for near-ship training and rehearsals that involved practice launch-and-recovery operations. This SDV was to remain within range of the ship's acoustic homing beacon so that it could easily return to the *Grayback*'s hangar on call or when planned. Upon launch, however, the SDV foundered in approximately sixty feet of water. Its four-man crew abandoned the boat and came to the surface, where they were subsequently recovered.

The tactical SDV crew was rescued early the next morning by a Navy HH-3A combat search-and-rescue helicopter; to preserve operational security, the helicopter's door gunner sank the SDV, which was too heavy to be retrieved. The four SDV crewmembers were flown to the nuclear-powered guided-missile cruiser USS *Long Beach* (CGN-9), where they were debriefed. Planning began for their return to *Grayback*.

The decision was made to transport the four men by helicopter from the *Long Beach* for a night water cast adjacent to *Grayback*. (Note: Casting is a technique used by SEALs to jump into the water from helicopters at low altitude and slow speed without parachutes.) Unfortunately, during the cast procedure, which occurred on the night of 5 June at 2300, Lieutenant Dry was killed. He was the last SEAL lost during the Vietnam War.

THE SEAL DELIVERY VEHICLE TEAMS

The Mk VII SDV was vastly improved after this failed mission, which remained highly classified for many years. The improved Mk VII became the workhorse of the 1970s, through several capability modifications, and they were largely responsible for establishing the need for SDV teams on both coasts. When the teams were organized, they included a mix of SEAL operators and fleet Sailors with various technical ratings to maintain the SDVs and DDSs.

During a deployment with the ARG in the Mediterranean Sea, an SDVT-2 platoon conducted clandestine reconnaissance off the beaches of a target country to acquire hydrographic information for a contingency amphibious landing. This was the first real-world use of an SDV in the Mediterranean or Atlantic by U.S. combat swimmers. Although this operation and Operation Thunderhead can now be discussed in general terms, many SDV missions have been planned that cannot be outlined; they will remain classified for many years to come.

In the Navy Training Plan for the TDP 38-02 program, it had been envisioned that each UDT and SEAL team would be outfitted with SDV capabilities. In practice, however, it was quickly learned that the SDVs were maintenance intensive and that the skills necessary to pilot and navigate these sophisticated platforms were not just unique, but were extraordinary. For several years the Mk VII SDV had been issued to all of the UDT and SEAL teams, but some simply let them sit idle because they did not have the time or personnel to establish their capabilities.

With the planned reestablishment of UDT-22 at NAB, Little Creek, in 1979, however, it was decided to organize it as the first team dedicated solely to the operation and maintenance of the SDVs, and this was done very effectively. This closely coincided with fleet introduction of the Mk VIII and Mk IX SDVs, which at long last represented materialization of the Class I and Class II SDVs envisioned under TDP 38-02.

The SDV program was managed out of the NSW program office (Code SEA O6Z) at NAVSEA in Washington, DC. It would take several years for the Mk VIII and Mk IXs SDVs to phase-replace the Mk VIIs because the new SDVs were assembled one at a time at the Navy laboratory in Panama City, Florida, and were not mass-produced. The focused SDV build program at Panama City was unique, and a full-blown SDV support organization was established, without which the SDV program might have foundered. The organization in Panama City resulted from a relocation of the original group that had been established at China Lake in the early 1970s. This dedicated Panama City staff also created the opportunity to continually upgrade the SDVs' operating capabilities through a continuous experimentation and modernization program. In addition to Panama City, many of the electronic subsystems designed and built for the SDVs were accomplished at the Applied Research Laboratory, Austin, Texas.

MATURATION OF THE SEAL DELIVERY VEHICLE

When the UDTs were transformed into SEAL teams in 1983, UDT-12 and UDT-22 were officially established as SDVT-1 and SDVT-2 respectively. Within a year of their establishment, they began deploying SDVs operationally. SDVT-1 had the advantage of USS *Grayback* to provide tactical mobility. USS *Cavalla* (SSN-684), a 637-class (long-hull) fast attack submarine, was being modified to replace the *Grayback*.

The SDV team on the East Coast had considerable difficulty finding tactical mobility platforms, and was largely relegated to deployments on amphibious ships. This created the opportunity for creativity and innovation. SDV towing sleds had been fabricated, and they could be used to assist launching and recovering SDVs from the high freeboard of amphibious ships. These sleds were quite ingenious: at idling speed they would sink on floats that would allow them to remain just below the surface of the water. The SDV could easily maneuver in and out of the sled and, when secured to the sled, could be towed by a high-speed support craft. The forward speed of the boat would cause the sled and the SDV to drain residual water and allow the sled to get up on its planing hull for high-speed transits. The sled could actually increase the tactical range of the SDV mission by getting it closer to the shoreline without using valuable battery power.

Because *Growler* had not been converted for use on the East Coast, the men fashioned the concept of a wet deck shelter to be used on conventional submarines in the Atlantic. One shelter was fabricated and delivered. It was designed to accommodate either an Mk VII or Mk VIII SDV (with bow planes removed). This shelter was used several times for training, but was never deployed operationally.

Because submarine services were difficult to obtain for underway training, a

LEFT: *Line drawings that depict the various models of the Mk VII SEAL Delivery Vehicles over time. (Photo: Courtesy of Tom Hawkins)*

RIGHT: *Mk VIII SDV being loaded aboard its host submarine and Dry Deck Shelter (DDS) in preparation for underway operations. (Photo: Courtesy of Tom Hawkins)*

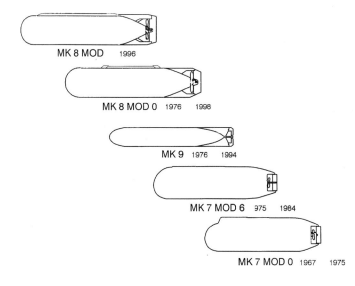

 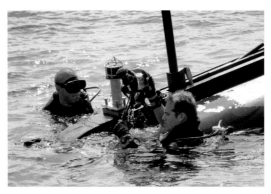 

submersible training platform (SUBTRAP) was fabricated. With a variable ballast system, the SUBTRAP was towed by a surface vessel; it was designed to represent the deck of an underway submarine. The training device was operated and maintained by the SDVTs. Although quite innovative, they were very maintenance intensive and not often used because they took SDV operators and technicians away from their primary jobs.

The Mk VIII SDV was designed for personnel and weapons delivery. It could carry six fully equipped divers or two or three divers and weapons. These weapons included the Mk 4 and Mk 5 limpet mines, and the Mk 36 charge, which was also a limpet. The Mk IX SDV, which was a low-profile design intended primarily for reconnaissance missions, also had a cargo compartment that could carry the same weapons.

Under the swimmer (later SEAL) weapons system, the TDP 30-01 development program, a special weapon was designed exclusively for the Mk IX SDV. It was called the Standoff Weapons Assembly (SWA), and was a modified Navy Mk 37 torpedo. For a long time the Mk 37 was the primary U.S. submarine-launched antisubmarine warfare torpedo. It was replaced by the Mk 48 torpedo in 1972. As a result, many of the torpedoes remained in the Navy inventory and were available for use. The technical challenge in modifying the Mk 37 torpedo for the Mk IX SDV was its unique swing-arm assembly or launcher rail. The SDV and weapon were required to fit inside the submarine DDS; the only way to do this was to hard-mount them inside the DDS (for submarine safety), then place them on the swing-arms once the shelter was flooded, which made the torpedoes neutral in buoyancy. Once outside the DDS, the torpedoes would be swung down and locked into position for SDV transit and launch.

The SWA was aimed using a periscope, and, once prepared for launch, could be fired after its gyrocompass had stabilized. Safety was built into the SWA, since it could not arm itself until it had traveled a distance of 750 yards. The SWA capability completed successful operational evaluation and was being prepared for fleet service; because of cost considerations, however, the Mk IX SDVs were removed from the Navy inventory before the weapons could be delivered. They were not compatible with the Mk VIII SDV, so the weapon system never entered SDVT service.

Before the Mk IX SDVs were eliminated, the men at SDVT-2 developed what they called the Bo Peep weapons delivery configuration. This involved carrying the Mk V limpet-mine assembly on the SWA swing arms. The Bo Peep allowed the Mk IX to carry an even heavier payload of weapons than nominally could be used on one SDV combat sortie.

The Mk VIII SDV remained the workhorse submersible throughout the 1980s and into the early 1990s, at which time a complete modernization program was initiated. This was called the Mod 1 program, and resulted in a new SDV with pro-

pulsion, navigation, sonar, and electronic subsystems that were substantially more capable and efficient.

The Advanced SEAL Delivery System

In the mid-1980s, the Navy initiated a requirement for the Advanced SEAL Delivery System (ASDS). Early on it was decided that the ASDS would be a one-atmosphere environment miniature submarine that would be large enough to clandestinely deliver a SEAL squad to the near shore area, where they would lock out for movement on shore. The Navy staff conceived early on that the ASDS would be operationally and tactically transported by the Navy's submarine force. In 2003 the ASDS and its host submarines became a reality. The single ASDS was assigned to SDVT-1 at its homeport location at Pearl Harbor, Hawaii. The ASDS completed its first deployment on board USS *Greeneville* to the Indian Ocean and Persian Gulf, after which the commander, NSWC, remarked, "It has been used operationally to great advantage and has proven successful . . . The capability is greater than we ever expected. . . . There is no substitute for this capability; it is both covert and persistent."

Even with such glowing remarks, the ASDS has not been without its difficul-

USS Greenville (SSN 772) transporting the Advanced SEAL Delivery System ONE (ASDS-1) Piranha while conducting ASDS sea testing off the coast of Pearl Harbor. The ASDS is a 65-foot minisubmarine, which connects and rides on the top of the much larger Los Angles Class submarines. (Photo: Courtesy of the U.S. Navy)

ties. It experienced significant growth problems, as outlined in a 2003 Congressional Budget Office study that cited two major technical problems: noisy propellers and silver-zinc batteries that depleted more quickly than planned. A new propeller made of composite material was developed to rectify noise problems, and development of lithium-ion batteries was undertaken to replace the original silver-zinc batteries. The cost of the ASDS continued to spiral, and Congress withdrew funding for additional platforms until technical difficulties could be overcome. Unfortunately, in November 2008, the ASDS caught on fire during battery charging pier side, and it was completely destroyed; the follow-on submersibles were never built.

The operating characteristics of the SDVs and ASDS and their TTPs remain highly classified and cannot be discussed in detail. All of the men who operate these submersibles are Navy SEALs, and they go through a special SDV training and qualification course of instruction before arriving at an SDVT. The SDV training school is located at the Navy R&D laboratory in Panama City, Florida, and is uniquely co-located with the laboratory's SDV technical support personnel, where all modernization features can quickly be incorporated.

The men who choose to become SDV pilots and navigators represent a special breed, even among their counterpart SEALs. The complexity of the SDV electronic communication, navigation, and rendezvous and docking systems requires extensive basic and requalification training to achieve the efficiency required to undertake multifaceted operations that occur underwater, and often through unknown ocean conditions in hostile or nonpermissive waters. These operations are compounded substantially in complexity when conducted from an underway submarine at night.

The length of SDV missions extends for several hours, with the men all the while exposed to the environmental extremes of water depth and temperature. The men are clad in thermal-protective dress, the Mk 16 UBA with full face mask, life preserver, compass, depth gauge, and other electronic devices with which to

The Central Intelligence Agency's 19.5-foot submersible, though never seen by the public, is a three-man submersible manufactured by the CIA Office of Technical Service for the CIA during the Cold War. Although it carried no weapons, was cramped, had limited endurance, and required a "mother ship" for transport and recovery, it worked in a similar fashion to that of Navy SDVs. Its small size, ability to run semi-submerged, quietness, and wooden construction made sonar or radar detection improbable. The vessel could be sunk in depths up to 30 feet and left on the bottom for a period of up to three or four weeks. When it was running in the deck wash position with only the Plexiglas observation bubble above the surface, the submersible was almost impossible to detect. (Photo: Greg E. Mathieson Sr. / NSW Publications, LLC.)

perform their mission. This makes the SDV very tight when six operators, or two or three operators and weapons systems, are on board. Moreover, the men conduct essentially nonworking dives as they sit in the SDV during transit, making the dive somewhat boring and providing plenty of time for them to think about how cold they are getting.

While never considered by the United States in World War II, the SDV has evolved as a fully developed capability of strategic importance within the national command structure. As current SDV capabilities continue to improve, the next-generation combatant submersibles are already being considered and, together with the Navy's submarine force, will

continue to ensure a fully clandestine capability for SEALs to be on time and on target when needed.

SUBMARINES

Submarines are also very special boats to the SEAL teams and especially to today's SDVTs. The UDT-SEAL-submarine relationship has evolved, beginning with a failed UDT operation during World War II when six UDT operators—PO Bob Black, PO John MacMahon, PO William Moore, PO Leonard Barnhill, PO Warren Christensen, and CPO Howard Roeder—were members of a special-mission group in August 1944 that accomplished the only UDT submarine-launched operation during the war.

The men left the surfaced submarine USS *Burrfish* (SS-312) in rubber boats for reconnaissance operations at the strategic islands of Peleliu and Gap, in the Palau Islands. Two operations were launched on consecutive nights; Petty Officers Black and MacMahon and Chief Petty Officer Roeder never returned from the second operation. It was later learned that they were captured and executed by the Japanese. Their remains have never been recovered, and they remain the only NSW warriors never to have been returned from battle. Submarines were never considered a worthy host ship for the UDTs during World War II: because so many men had to get to the beach, submarines simply were not practical. Surface ships and specifically the APDs were ideal. UDTs would not seriously see submarines until the postwar period at the island of Vieques, Puerto Rico, when in February 1947, UDT men began practice operations launching and recovering rubber boats from USS *Grouper* (SS-214).

On 20 and 21 February 1947, with *Grouper* sitting on the bottom of Lindberg Bay at St. Thomas, Virgin Islands, UDT-2 and UDT-4 men, using the LARU, began for the first time practicing lock-out and lock-in operations through the ship's escape trunk. This was the same diving apparatus adopted by the OSS MU during World War II.

On 22 February, with USS *Grouper* under way at a dead-slow speed, Lieutenant Commander Fane, the UDT commander, and Dr. Christian Lambertsen, inventor of the LARU and trainer of the OSS swimmers during World War II, were the first ever to lock out and lock in to an underway submarine. The feasibility of launching and recovering UDT

ABOVE: *Challenge coin from the NSW SDV Team One. The SDV team operates and maintains submersible systems that deliver and recover SEALs in hostile areas and conduct reconnaissance and DA missions.*

A Navy senior chief briefs an SDV team aboard a support ship before deploying on an exercise in which the SEALs and SDV will rendezvous with an Ohio-class submarine somewhere in the Pacific. (Photos: Greg E. Mathieson Sr. / NSW Publications, LLC)

divers from a submerged and underway submarine thus had been operationally demonstrated.

On 14 October 1948, at St. Thomas and on board USS *Quillback* (SS-424), the UDT men launched and recovered the British-made Sleeping Beauty submersible canoe for the first time from the deck of a submerged submarine. This operation was accomplished with men from both East and West Coast UDTs; when the men returned to their home bases at Little Creek and Coronado, the concept for the submersible operations platoon had been established. UDTs had transformed themselves from reconnaissance combat swimmers to clandestine combat divers with a host of new underwater infiltration and sabotage capabilities.

From 1948, through the outbreak of the Korean War, UDT-1 and UDT-3 continued training operations with a host of submarines that included USS *Redfish* (SS-395), USS *Seafox* (SS-402), USS *Ronquil* (SS-396), and USS *Perch* (SSP-313).

On 31 January 1950, *Perch* was reclassified an amphibious personnel transport submarine (APSS) and was to some extent dedicated for Marine Corps and UDT training. She operated up and down the West Coast with UDT and Marine Corps reconnaissance personnel and conducted numerous operations in the western Pacific with the UDTs.

Perch saw distinguished service during the Korean War, conducting a host of combat patrols, and launching and recovering the British Royal Marines 41 Commando and Korean special forces working with the UDTs and U.S. Marines. After the war, *Perch* continued to support UDT training operations along the coast of southern California and when on patrol in the Pacific.

In October 1962, *Perch* was re-homeported to Subic Bay, the Philippines, where the West Coast UDTs had their western Pacific base of operations. From there she began a series of operations with the UDTs off the coast of Vietnam.

In March 1953, USS *Tunny* (SSG-282) became the first Regulus missile–launching submarine in the U.S. Navy; she served in this capacity for nearly twelve years. In 1966, her missile hanger was converted into a troop berthing compartment, and she was redesignated an APSS. *Tunny* was uniquely and specifically modified to support waterborne unconventional warfare. One of the many modifications was to the sea suction piping (water inlet to cool the equipment), which was customized to allow either a bottom or top inlet, depending on the tactical

An SDV is lifted from darkness of the Pacific by a Navy support ship during late night training exercise with an Ohio-class submarine. (Photo: Greg E. Mathieson Sr. / NSW Publications, LLC)

situation. Switching to upper inlet allowed the ship to be bottomed before lockouts commenced, thus allowing a stationary platform and safe haven for the UDT and SEAL swimmers. *Tunny* relieved *Perch* in August 1966 at Subic Bay, and spent much of the next two years operating in South China Sea and elsewhere conducting unconventional warfare operations. *Tunny* carried UDT, SEALs, Army Special Forces, British and Taiwanese special forces, Marine Corps Force Recon, and others on a variety of special missions, including reconnaissance in preparation for amphibious assault operations off the coast of Vietnam, where she gathered navigational and oceanographic information.

The East Coast UDTs continued to refine their underwater skills with *Grouper*, *Quillback*, and most frequently with USS *Sealion* (APSS-315), which had been on service in the Pacific during World War II. Along with *Perch*, she had been designated for conversion as a troop carrier. During conversion in April 1948, her torpedo tubes and forward engines were removed and her forward engine room and forward- and after-torpedo rooms were converted to berth troops. The forward engine room and after-torpedo room were designed for alternative use as cargo space. The wardroom was redesigned for use as an embarked detachment operations center, the beam aft of the conning tower was extended, and a large watertight cylindrical chamber was installed aft of the conning tower to store equipment.

In the spring of 1949, *Sealion* was ordered to the Atlantic and homeported at various times in New London, Connecticut and Norfolk, Virginia, for duty. Throughout the 1950s, and 1960s, she conducted numerous training operations

LEFT: *Navy SEALs recover an SDV to a support ship during a rendezvous exercise with an Ohio-class submarine in the Pacific at night. (Photo: Greg E. Mathieson Sr. / NSW Publications, LLC)*

RIGHT: *Each SDV Team ONE operator is assigned a cage, where diving and other equipment is secured. Wet clothing and equipment can be dried here after an SDV training mission. (Photo: Greg E. Mathieson Sr. / NSW Publications, LLC)*

A member of SEAL Delivery Vehicle Team Two (SDVT-2) prepares to launch one of the team's SEAL Delivery Vehicles (SDV) from the back of the Los Angeles–class attack submarine USS Philadelphia (SSN 690) on a training exercise. (Photo: Andrew McKaskle / USN)

with Marines, UDTs, BJUs, and on occasion with Army Special Forces units off the Virginia and Carolina coasts and in the Caribbean. On 15 September 1967, she was moved to Key West, Florida, for her last two years of active service.

During the early 1950s, the East Coast UDTs were experimenting with the British X Craft miniature submarine in the Chesapeake Bay. At the same time, the U.S. Navy had embarked on construction of the X-1, a similar design concept, which was intended for UDT use. The British used X Craft submarines extensively during World War II, and the U.S. had nothing comparable until 1952, when plans for the X-1 were drawn up. Its keel was laid on 8 June 1954, and it was accepted into the U.S. Navy on 7 September 1955 as the USS X-1. It always retained its X designation, which indicated that it was experimental. Although UDT men did accomplish limited training with the X-1, it was never accepted for operational use, and never completed any kind of combat patrol.

During many years of active service, *Perch, Tunny*, and *Sealion* represented an era when submarines would be dedicated for UDT and SEAL team training. These submarines were very old and always in line to be retired. Fortunately, the need for their replacements was considered by the NSW leadership. Working with the Navy on a long-range development plan called the Swimmer (later SEAL) Support System, the program was established to accommodate conversion of USS *Grayback* (SSG-574) and USS *Growler* (SSG-577) for UDT and SEAL team use. Like *Tunny,* these submarines had been purpose built to launch sea-to-surface Regulus missiles. Two chambers had been constructed into the bow of these submarines to provide them this capability. As more modern Polaris nuclear submarines entered service, *Grayback* and *Growler* became obsolete for missiles, but ideal candidates to be used as troop transports, and specifically to conduct mass-swimmer lock-outs and to transport SDVs.

Changes to *Grayback* during conversion included these: her sail was extended ten feet, auxiliary tanks were added to the forward position of the engine room, her missile chambers were converted to carry sixty-seven embarked troops and SDVs, and a diver's decompression chamber was constructed in the starboard hangar. By adding the auxiliary tanks to the engine room, her length was extended 12 feet to an overall length of 334 feet.

On 30 August 1968, *Grayback* entered Pacific Fleet service and was given the designation LPSS. *Growler* was intended for service in the Atlantic Fleet, but because of cost increases during conversion of *Grayback, Growler* was never converted. Many operational lessons were learned during operations with *Grayback*; because of age, however, she was decommissioned January 1984.

A member of SEAL Delivery Vehicle Team Two (SDVT-2) climbs aboard one of the team's SEAL Delivery Vehicles (SDV) before launching from the back of the Los Angeles-class attack submarine USS Philadelphia (SSN 690) on a training exercise. (Photo: Andrew McKaskle / USN)

DRY DECK SHELTERS

During the period of *Grayback*'s service, the Navy was in the process of converting several of its 637-class long-hull submarines to accommodate a new DDS, which was built under the TDP 38-02 follow-on development program. The DDS was a specially built external chamber that could be bolted on and bolted off a submarine; when installed, it could transport one SDV or be used for mass-swimmer lock-out operations. The original plan was to modify all but one of the 637-class submarines, with the concept of flying a DDS to meet a submarine deployed anywhere in the world.

Six DDSs were constructed; each was 11.6 meters (thirty-eight feet) long by 2.7 meters (nine feet) diameters (external). Each adds about thirty tons to its host submarine's submerged displacement. The DDS can be highway transported on specially built transporters or on special transporters by C-17 aircraft. Once at the port of embarkation, one to three days are required for installation and testing. Each has three HY-80 steel sections covered with a glass-reinforced plastic fairing: a spherical hyperbaric chamber at the forward end to treat injured divers, a smaller spherical transfer trunk (entry point into the submarine), and a cylindrical hangar with elliptical ends to house one Mk VIII SDV or twenty SEALs with four CRRCs. Each host submarine was specially modified to accommodate the DDS, with the appropriate mating hatch configuration, electrical connections, and piping for ventilation, divers' air, and draining water.

The first DDS was built by the General Dynamics Electric Boat Corporation and designated DDS-01S (S for starboard, or the side to which the outer hangar outer door opens). It was completed in 1982. The remaining five—DDS-02P

(P for port-side opening), DDS-03P, DDS-04S, DDS-05S, and DDS-06P—were built between 1987 and 1991 by the Newport News Shipbuilding Company. The DDSs need port and starboard swinging doors because host submarines with the capability to carry two DDSs side by side required the doors to swing in opposite directions. Each DDS is expected to have a useful life of about forty years.

The follow-on replacement for *Grayback* was the 637-class submarines. The longer-hull ships were considered the only fast attack submarines in the fleet that had the necessary ballast to carry a DDS, which was very large and extremely heavy with flooded seawater to launch the SDVs. The first ship modified to accept the DDS was the Pacific Fleet's USS *Cavalla* (SSN-684), and it was the first to successfully perform DDS operations in 1983. Five other ships in the class would eventually complete modifications to carry the DDS: USS *Archerfish* (SSN-678), USS *Silversides* (SSN-679), USS *William H. Bates* (SSN-680), USS *Tunny* (SSN-682), and USS *L. Mendel Rivers* (SSN-686).

These submarines were used extensively for training and often for long-duration patrols in the Mediterranean Sea and Pacific Ocean with the DDS and SDVT personnel embarked. The original concept was to have every DDS capable of being transported by every modified submarine in the class; it was discovered during testing, however, that each submarine was slightly different and required its own set of piping to accommodate a particular shelter. Consequently, DDSs in the Atlantic only fit submarines assigned to the Atlantic, and vice versa for those in the Pacific.

The next submarines designated for modification were two Ethan Allen–class

ballistic missile submarines, USS *Sam Houston* (SSBN/SSN-609) and USS *John Marshall* (SSBN/SSN-611). These were the first former ballistic-missile submarines converted as nuclear-powered attack submarines (SSNs) for SEAL and SDVT use; these would become the first submarines to have the capability to carry two DDSs simultaneously. They became available only because of the Strategic Arms Limitation Treaty between the United States and the Soviet Union which required the United States to eliminate numerous missile silos, including those on submarines.

On 15 December 1986, the *John Marshall*, in conjunction with SDVT-2, began transit for deployment with its DDS crew embarked as a part of the ship's company to the Mediterranean Sea. When a DDS is not attached to a submarine, it is stored and maintained by SDVT members and can be used for shore-based training by actually flooding it with water. In an arrangement worked out with the submarine force, it was agreed that when the DDS is embarked on board a host submarine it becomes a department of the ship and directly responsible to the ship's CO. The SDV and SEAL operators remained an embarked (supported) detachment.

On 1 May 1989, after conducting a variety of exercises with carrier battle groups and other submarines, the *John Marshall* departed again for a Mediterranean deployment. This was the first time a submarine had deployed anywhere in the world with two DDSs on board, adding a unique flexibility and endurance to the fleet commander for special warfare operations. On 26 January 1991, the ship again departed Norfolk for what would be its final deployment to the Mediterranean. Equipped with two DDSs, the ship operated in direct support of Operation Desert Storm and provided significant capability options to the Sixth Fleet commander. Finally, in September 1991, and just before her retirement, the *John Marshall* served as flagship in the Caribbean Sea for the largest submarine-special warfare exercise since World War II. On board were more than 191 personnel, including three flag officers and SEAL and Army SOFs embarked to conduct joint special operations during a training exercise called Phantom Shadow. USS *Sam Houston*, sister ship to *John Marshall*, performed the same exceptional service with

Navy SEALs prepare to submerge in their SDV on their way toward a naval warship harbor to conduct underwater training operations of placing limpet mines to the bottoms of ships. (Photo: Greg E. Mathieson Sr. / NSW Publications, LLC)

An SDV is lowered into the bay for nighttime training by SEALs at the former SDV Team Two. (Photo: Greg E. Mathieson Sr. / NSW Publications, LLC)

Submersible Training Platform (SUBTRAP) seen pierside after operations with the Mk IX SDV. The SUBTRAP is towed underwater by a surface craft and operated by a SEAL team diver, who maintiains depth and ballast control. (Photo: Courtesy of Tom Hawkins)

the SEALs in the Pacific, supporting many SDV and dual-DDS operations and deployments.

In late 1991, the relationship between the SEAL and submarine community became solidified, and the Navy began long-range planning to convert additional submarines for special operations use. This included long-range planning for the new ASDS, which was becoming a reality and also in need of a host operational platform.

The next ships to be modified would not be needed to carry the ASDS, and came from the Benjamin Franklin–class ballistic submarine. They were USS *James K. Polk* (SSBN/SSN-645) for service in the Atlantic, and USS *Kamehameha* (SSBN/SSN-642) for service in the Pacific. Both of these former ballistic-missile submarines had the capability to carry the DDS in a single or dual side-by-side configuration. Decommissioning of these ships in 2002 was offset by modification of the improved Los Angeles–class submarines, which were the first host ships to have the capability to carry the DDS and the new ASDS.

Today, Los Angeles–class ships supporting the SDVT include the USS *Los Angeles* (SSN-688), USS *Charlotte* (SSN-766), and USS *La Jolla* (SSN-701) in the Pacific; and USS *Dallas* (SSN-700), USS *Philadelphia* (SSN-690), and USS *Buffalo* (SSN-715) in the Atlantic. These were the first submarines modified to transport the DDS and ASDS, and can carry one or both simultaneously.

With the end of the Cold War, the Navy realized that it no longer needed all eighteen of its Ohio-class fleet ballistic missile submarines (SSBN) to fulfill the nation's strategic deterrence. Rather than scrapping submarines with decades of additional service left in them, however, the U.S. Navy began converting them to nuclear-powered guided-missile submarines (SSGNs), and working with the

SEAL teams to begin transforming four of the submarines into multi-mission ships equipped in part for NSW missions.

The USS *Jimmy Carter* (SSN-23) was the third and last Seawolf-class submarine to be built, and one of the few ships in the U.S. Navy to have been named for a person who was alive at the time of the ship's naming. The *Jimmy Carter* is roughly one hundred feet longer than the other two ships of her class. This is due to the insertion of a section known as the multi-mission platform, a modification that was necessary to allow installation of the DDS and ASDS and to permit the ship to perform other classified missions. Despite these modifications the ship retained all warfighting capabilities, and now supports the fleet commander as an attack submarine in conducting undersea warfare, surveillance and reconnaissance, covert special operations, mine warfare, and strike operations. The ship also incorporates a new, specially designed combat swimmer silo or internal lock-out chamber that permits up to eight combat swimmers and their equipment to lock out/lock in at one time. This is a significant capability when the DDS is not embarked. The *Jimmy Carter*'s inherent stealth enables surreptitious insertion of the SDVs, ASDSs, and combat swimmers into previously denied areas.

In December 2006, the General Dynamics Electric Boat Corporation completed its conversion of USS *Ohio* (SSGN-726) from a ballistic-missile platform to a guided-missile submarine capable of carrying 154 Tomahawk cruise missiles and more than sixty SOFs for extended periods. USS *Michigan* (SSGN-727), USS *Florida* (SSGN-728), and USS *Georgia* (SSGN-729) have also completed conversion and been returned to service.

On 12 October 2004, the USS *Virginia* (SSN-774) was accepted by the Navy as the lead ship in a new class of submarines that will host SEAL, SDV, and other SOF capabilities. Virginia-class USS *Texas* (SSN-775), USS *Hawaii* (SSN-776), USS *North Carolina* (SSN-777), USS *New Hampshire* (SSN-778), USS *New Mexico* (SSN-779), and USS *Missouri* (SSN-780) have now entered service. SSN-781 through SSN-785 are under construction or authorized for construction and not yet commissioned: *California*, *Mississippi*, *Minnesota*, *North Dakota*, and *John Warner*, respectively. Virginia-class submarines SSN-786 through SSN-791 have been authorized, but not yet named.

Challenge coin from the SDV Team Two, issued in commemoration of SDV Team Two upon its Disestablishment Ceremony held on 8 August 2008 marking its 25 years of service from May 1983- August 2008. (Photos: Dave Gatley / NSW Publications, LLC)

Submersible Training Platform (SUBTRAP) seen under way for training with an Mk VIII approaching for recovery from the stern. The SUBTRAP was towed by a surface vessel and operated by SEAL divers, who control depth and ballast. (Photo: Courtesy of Tom Hawkins)

Special Boat Teams

CDR (Seal) Tom Hawkins, USN (Ret)

CHAPTER 7

Special Boat Teams

Cdr. (SEAL) Tom Hawkins, USN (Ret.)

Origins of Special Boats in Naval Special Warfare

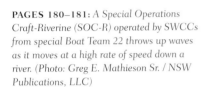

PAGES 180–181: *A Special Operations Craft-Riverine (SOC-R) operated by SWCCs from special Boat Team 22 throws up waves as it moves at a high rate of speed down a river. (Photo: Greg E. Mathieson Sr. / NSW Publications, LLC)*

BELOW, LEFT: *Making training runs in San Diego Bay is the coxswain of SBT-12 of the Mk V who sits centerline in the wheelhouse, manning the powerful 4500 hp twin diesel engines and the 54-ton, 75-foot aluminum hull. Designed to be transportable by C-5 aircraft, the craft can be delivered to waters around the globe. (Photo: Dave Gatley / NSW Publications, LLC)*

BELOW, RIGHT: *Members of Special Boat Team-12 (SBT-12) conduct training runs in San Diego Bay, California. (Photo: Dave Gatley / NSW Publications, LLC)*

SINCE ALL COMBAT OPERATIONS THAT ORIGINATE FROM THE SEA are naval in character, special boat capabilities can be described as those that generally fall into the category of maritime special operations. Such operations tend to be more commando, or more out of the norm and less doctrinal than conventional naval operations. They might also require voluntary service or specialized training, or be considered extreme hazardous duty.

The story of special boats actually begins during World War II and covers four very different and very distinct dimensions: ships, submarines, combatant-craft systems, and small surface combatant craft.

Small boats have played a significant role in the evolution of NSW. Until the modern day, they were used exclusively for the ship-to-shore movement of men assigned to special maritime units, who would perform a task of some tactical significance. Generally, these special units were tasked to perform some kind of intelligence collection, demolition, or sabotage operation on shore and, in the case of the UDTs and later SEALs, to react to their own reconnaissance and intelligence collection.

The chronology of these special units can be somewhat opaque. The first men

focused and trained for special boat capabilities during World War II were the U.S. Navy's Amphibious Scouts and Raiders (Joint) and OSS MU in the Atlantic, Mediterranean, and Southeast Asia theaters of operation.

In May 1942, a group of Navy volunteers was sent to Solomons ATB near Patuxent River, Maryland, where they were trained in landing-craft operations. The following August, these men were sent to ATB Little Creek, where they were combined with men from the Army to form a unit called Amphibious Scouts and Raiders (Joint). This new unit was commanded by 1st Lt. Lloyd E. Peddcord Jr. (Army) with Ens. John Bell (Navy) as his executive officer.

The Scouts and Raiders began intense preparation for a critical mission in Operation Torch, the amphibious assault of North Africa and the first Allied invasion of World War II. The assault operation was conducted in November 1942.

These amphibious commandos were trained to operate at night and tasked to identify and reconnoiter prospective landing beaches, and, using lights or other means, to accurately guide Allied assault waves to those beaches.

Navy men assigned to the first Scouts and Raiders group were not given duties on shore, but rather left those duties to Army Raider personnel who had trained for them. The Navy men were strictly boat operators for special kinds of missions.

Because they were so new, Scouts and Raiders did not have boats assigned to their units and relied on craft assigned to the ships on which they were being transported. In some instances, they actually fabricated their own boats.

Scouts and Raiders went on to support landings in Sicily, Salerno, Anzio, Normandy, and southern France using everything from kayaks to the ship's family of landing craft. Operations performed by the Scouts and Raiders are very much resident in the SEAL and SBTs of the modern day, although their capabilities have been greatly expanded.

While not under the domain of the U.S. Navy during World War II, special boat capabilities were a primary focus of the OSS, which formed a special operations branch called the Maritime Unit (MU) to focus on such capabilities. In 1943, OSS MU personnel were assigned to British 14th Army in the Southeast Asia Command (SEAC). Two OSS detachments were assigned to SEAC—Det 101 for the India-Burma theater and Det 102 for China.

MU Far East operations were conducted under the direction of Det 101 located in Kandy, Ceylon. It was often reported that General MacArthur did not understand or did not like OSS and refused to use them. This somewhat explains why the OSS was assigned for operations with the British.

OSS forces in the SEAC were responsible for operations in Burma, Malaya, Thailand, and Sumatra, and organized into a subelement called Det 404. British MTBs were used by the OSS MU personnel to conduct extensive coastal operations during the Arakan operation in Burma. The MU was organized to carry out sabotage against enemy shipping and for stealthy forays into enemy harbors.

Due to a slower start and the nature of the overall strategic picture in SEAC, and owing to vast water distance problems, the task of Det 404 was much more difficult than the tasks of most OSS organizations overseas. MU's largest contribution involved the conduct of clandestine operations for the infiltration and exfiltration of agents and underground groups.

In Europe, MU personnel did much the same thing when they carried out extensive and highly successful clandestine ferrying operations in the Aegean Sea. OSS personnel and supplies were clandestinely transported to Greece in support of resistance groups and guerrilla forces. A fleet of caïques operated by indigenous crews plied the waters between Cyprus and secret bases in Turkey. From these bases smaller craft took over, making pinpoint landings at night on the Greek coast. In addition to landing agents and keeping them supplied, this clandestine special boat operation evacuated many refugees and rescued numerous downed pilots.

OSS MU activities were highly classified during the war, and remained so until the mid-1990s. In retrospect, their lessons and exploits remain valid in the modern age, and today's SBTs possess all of the capabilities used by OSS MU, although the methods and equipment are vastly improved.

There was nothing special about the boats used to transport the NCDUs at

Normandy and in southern France. They were taken ashore by ship's company, where they operated out of inflatable rubber boats laden with explosives. They were taken near shore in a variety of naval craft and from a variety of Navy ships.

In the Pacific, the UDTs operated their own boats for training and during combat operations. They used LCPRs (landing craft personnel, ramp) carried by specially configured high-speed transports, or APDs. The inflatable boats were used to transport the men closer to the beach, and were launched from the LCPRs. They were usually propelled by paddles; in some instances, though, swimmers would simply push them to the blasting area. The rubber boat was also used in combination with the LCPRs to drop and pick up swimmers at high speeds.

The Pacific UDTs wrote a remarkable page in the history of special boats and indeed special ships, APDs that were specially configured to support UDT personnel and their support craft. APDs were destroyer escort–class ships converted as high-speed transports by increasing troop berthing and equipment storage amidships, and adding four LCPRs and a boom crane aft. Because of the kamikaze threat, APDs were relatively well armed: three-inch .50-caliber guns replacing her original five-inch .50-caliber single 40-mm guns aft along with five 20-mm antiaircraft guns. To offset these additions, four depth charge throwers and a single depth charge stern rack were removed.

LCPRs were the boats used to transport UDT personnel from their APDs to the beach or to the swimmer or demolition drop-off area. These were high-speed boats, used to intercept small attack boats, and could handle a maximum of about twenty swimmers. Each LCPR carried two .50-caliber machine guns that were used both for answering enemy fire from the beach and as a weak antiaircraft response.

The LCPRs were manned by trained UDT operators. The crew consisted of a coxswain, a radioman, a machinist mate, two gunner's mates, and the boat officer.

ABOVE: *The RIB (Rigid Hull Inflatable Boat) from SBT-12 on a speed run in San Diego Bay, with the skyline in the background. The NSW RIB performs short-range insertion and extraction of SOF, limited coastal patrol and interdiction and reconnaissance. It can also be airdropped by parachute from a C-130 or larger aircraft. Each craft is manned by a crew of three SWCCs and can carry eight SOF or other personnel. (Photo: Dave Gatley / NSW Publications, LLC)*

LEFT: *An F470 Combat Rubber Raiding Craft (CRRC), also known as the Combat Rubber Reconnaissance Craft, is a specially fabricated rubber inflatable boat used by SEALs and Marines, among others. (Photo: Dave Gatley / NSW Publications, LLC)*

LCPRs also were used administratively to carry explosives and other supplies into the beach for demolition operations.

During the war in the Pacific, the APDs and UDTs were almost inseparable, each becoming somewhat of a family unit. This was the first and only time in the history of NSW that ships were totally dedicated for combat use. APDs were used by the UDTs in the Korean War also, but they were never dedicated platforms, and were never again available in the same numbers as during World War II.

Four UDTs were formed after World War II, and they maintained what had become a doctrinal custom of owning and operating their own boats. The postwar UDTs continued to use the LCPRs, but modernized to the newer LCPL (Landing Craft Personnel, Large), which was designed as its replacement. When the UDTs began overseas deployment as part of an ARG, they took their own boats on board the amphibious ships for tactical use.

The UDT and SEAL teams also maintained warm weather training areas and strategic FOBs at Subic Bay in the Philippine Islands; St. Thomas in the U.S. Virgin Islands; and later at the Naval Station, Roosevelt Roads, Puerto Rico, where boats were kept and maintained for training. The tradition of UDTs using their own boats was maintained until formation of BSUs in 1963, when Sailors from the fleet were specially trained to support UDT and SEAL operations.

Some still believe that the origins of special boats in NSW began with the BSUs, while others believe that the story began with the MTBs or patrol torpedo (PT) boats that operated throughout the Pacific during World War II. The genesis of special boats, however, is much deeper rooted, stretching back to the early days of World War II.

PT boats were small, fast vessels used by the British and American navies to attack larger surface ships. MTBs were formed into squadrons nicknamed "the mosquito fleet." The mission of the American PT boats was to battle destroyers; many questioned the military effectiveness of these boats in this role, however. Their psychological impact in deterring Japanese attacks was equally important, especially

after Pearl Harbor, when the Navy was short on larger ships and just beginning to build its massive naval fleet that would become more effective later in the war.

Though often said to be made of plywood, PT boats were actually made of two-inch-thick planks of mahogany. And, as storied as their history might be, PT boats never played more than a minor role in supporting special units such as the Amphibious Scouts and Raiders or the UDTs. They were used on occasion by the special group of NCDUs that remained together throughout the war working in and around the Philippine Islands. British MTBs were used extensively by the OSS MUs assigned to Det 401 during operations in Burma.

VIETNAM AND OPERATIONAL PLAN 34-A

There was no boat development for the UDTs during the 1950s and into the early 1960s, a period of prolonged peace. The U.S. Navy's Mk 4 aluminum LCPLs had been supplemented by the newer Mk 11 LCPLs, which were made of fiberglass, but the UDTs continued to operate with the ARGs and launch and recover their own boats from amphibious ships.

When SEALs began deploying to Vietnam, they had no boat support at all. Moreover, with little U.S. Navy presence, they could only rely on their own creativity.

RIGHT: Instructors watch a Basic Crewman Training (BCT) student demonstrate knot-tying skills during water proficiency training at Naval Amphibious Base, Coronado. BCT is the first phase of the Special Warfare Combatant-Craft Crewman (SWCC) training program. SWCCs operate and maintain USSSCOM's inventory of state-of-the-art, high-performance boats used to support SEALs in special operations missions worldwide. (Photo: MC 2nd Class Christopher Menzie / US Navy)

BELOW: Basic Crewman Training (BCT) students watch an instructor demonstrate knot tying skills during water proficiency training at Naval Amphibious Base, Coronado. (Photo: Christopher Menzie / US Navy)

Intended or not, the Vietnam conflict was another epoch where special boats became almost essential to the operational capability of the SEAL teams and their MSTs. A lesser-known part of the special boat story involves operations conducted in support of the CIA and later the Military Assistance Command, Vietnam—Special Operations Group (MACV-SOG).

In 1958, the South Vietnamese government created a secret special service directly under their president. That branch, supported and financed by the CIA, conducted special operations. In April 1964, the government created the Special Exploitation Service to take over these operations; MACV-SOG was established at the same time to assume the CIA's job of assisting, advising, and supporting the new organization in the conduct of highly classified sabotage and psychological and special operations in North and South Vietnam, Laos, Cambodia, and southern China. MACV-SOG was a joint service unconventional warfare task force engaged in highly classified clandestine operations throughout Southeast Asia. It was given the title Studies and Observation Group as a cover.

MACV-SOG's primary responsibilities included conducting cross-border operations regularly to disrupt the VC in their own territories, tracking imprisoned and missing Americans and conducting raids to free them, training and dispatching agents into North Vietnam to run resistance movement operations, and conducting psychological operations.

MACV-SOG's Maritime Studies Branch and Maritime Studies Group were organized in response to Operational Plan 34-A (OP 34-A), and included U.S. Navy SEAL advisors, Vietnamese Naval Sea Commandos, and PTF (patrol torpedo, fast) boats provided by the U.S. Navy. The PTFs were assigned to MST-1 (the deployed name for BSU-1 assets). OP 34-A assets were based at Camp Tien Sha (China

ABOVE: *Members of Special Boat Unit 12 operate Fountain High Speed Boat as part of protecting the fleet in Ras Al Mishab, Saudi Arabia in 1991 during Desert Shield and Desert Storm operations. (Photo: Courtesy of Tom Hawkins)*

BOTTOM: *SWCC operators line up their RHIBs in preparation for a MCADS training drop in which they will stand by for safety and parachute recovery. (Photo: Greg E. Mathieson Sr. / NSW Publications, LLC)*

Beach), Da Nang, and included seven "Nasty"-class PTFs, three fifty-foot Swift boats, one LCM-6 (one of the Navy's family of landing craft, medium-class boats), two Vietnamese wooden fishing junks (a sixty-ton and a one-hundred-ton), and one Skimmer boat. From 1964 through 1972, the PTFs conducted a secret and deadly war with North Vietnamese forces around and above the demilitarized zone.

As the Navy's coastal patrol and interdiction resources grew, gas turbine–powered hydrofoils—USS *Flagstaff* (patrol gunboat hydrofoil [PGH]-1) and USS *Tucumcari* (PGH-2)—from BSU-1 joined the effort. PGH-1 and PGH-2 operated out of the Da Nang base. The complex nature of the PGH and lack of logistics support saw them phased out of the coastal interdiction role after a six-month trial, and both were returned stateside in early 1970: *Flagstaff* was sent to the NAB, Coronado, and *Tucumcari* was transferred to the NAB, Little Creek.

The MACV-SOG story is important: it established a foundation for many future NSW operations, and especially the future of special boats.

During the mid- to late 1960s and early in 1970, SEALs were operating

throughout Vietnam, mainly concentrated in the delta region, known as IV Corps ("Four Corps"). The delta is a mass of large rivers, estuaries, and small canals where the largest movement of commerce and people occur.

Early in the war, the SEALs had no dedicated boat support and were substantially hampered by what little Navy support did exist. They used Mk 4 LCPLs modified extensively with gun mounts, radar, and protective sun shields; and Navy PBRs that were continuously improved as the war progressed. The LCPLs were propeller-driven craft that tended to be slow-moving targets and could not maneuver well in the small shallow-water canals where the SEALs frequently operated. The PBRs were built with water-jet propulsion systems to overcome this limitation.

Members of SEAL Team 2 began adaptation of commercial fiberglass craft with outboard motors that produced much higher speeds, and equipped them with gun mounts. Several boats were acquired and sent to Vietnam. They were called STABs by the men (for SEAL team assault boat). The boat was never adopted by the Navy because improved platforms like the PBR were coming into service.

A Navy LCM-6, nicknamed the "Mighty Mo," also had been modified to support the SEALs. The LCM was eventually called the HSSC, or Heavy SEAL Support Craft. The HSSC was equipped with a 106-mm recoilless rifle mounted on the top of the well deck, which the men enclosed with aircraft revetment and sandbags. The craft also had an Mk 18 40-mm automatic grenade launcher, two to three M2 heavy machine guns, and an 81-mm mortar in the well deck. Three Claymore mines each were attached to the armor plating on the port and starboard sides of the boat for close-in ambushes. In practice the HSSC proved to be too slow and noisy for most operations, but was an excellent fire-support platform for SEALs on shore.

Ultimately, in the late 1960s, a hasty boat development program was established in Washington to procure specially designed boats to support SEAL opera-

TOP, LEFT AND RIGHT: *SEALs are inserted into the shorelines of Vietnam using a PBR (Patrol Boat Riverine). (Photos: Courtesy of Tom Hawkins)*

BOTTOM, LEFT: *An HSSC (Heavy SEAL Support Craft) being used by SEALs in Vietnam. (Photo: Courtesy of Tom Hawkins)*

BOTTOM, RIGHT: *A UDT Mk IV LCPL with the Fulton Recovery System. (Photo: Courtesy of Tom Hawkins)*

SWCC basic training students complete a run down the beaches of Coronado and form up with their gear of life jackets and CRRC paddles. (Photos: Greg E. Mathieson Sr. / NSW Publications, LLC)

tions. These were the Light SEAL Support Craft (LSSC) and Medium SEAL Support Craft (MSSC).

The LSSC was a squad-sized boat with water-jet propulsion and a very small draft that could get into shallow water regions. The boats had M-60 machine guns mounted at both port and starboard locations and a 60-mm grenade launcher aft. It was propelled by two 427-horsepower gasoline engines driving Jacuzzi water-jet pumps. The boat was twenty-four feet long, with ceramic armor strips and self-sealing fuel tanks. It was easily distinguished by its low profile and Raytheon radar mounted just below the driver's seat.

The MSSC was a platoon-sized boat that also was propelled by water jets with a shallow draft; it had a top speed of about thirty-five knots. The MSSC was designed with Pintel mounts, allowing heavier weapons such as the 7.62-mm minigun that could fire six thousand rounds per minute, and the Mk 18 automatic grenade launchers.

None of the LSSC, MSSC, or HSSC craft was returned to the United States after the Vietnam War. The LSSC and MSSC were eventually replaced with better designed craft.

In 1968, the MSTs were authorized to develop the concept of tactically transporting SEAL-MST craft with CH-47 Chinook helicopters. The idea was to extend the range of the boats by inserting and extracting SEALs and MST crews into areas where they were not expected and to expand rescue and escape and evasion capabilities.

The concept came about in 1966, after SEAL Team 2's attempt to use helicopters and lifting slings to transport their STABs. Unfortunately, a boat was dropped in the NAB, Little Creek commissary parking lot, and further testing was terminated. In 1968, however, the mission capability received renewed interest, wherein two attempts at lifting an LSSC with the Army's CH-47 helicopter were successful, because the procedure had been somewhat refined. A third test for distance and altitude was not successful, and the boat was dropped from the underway

LEFT: SWCC utilize the same O-course that the SEALs use during their initial training in Coronado. Upper-body strength is paramount for working on the special boats. (Photo: Greg E. Mathieson Sr. / NSW Publications, LLC)

RIGHT: SWCC and SEALs hold the book of instructions for their instructor in the early morning hours. (Photo: Greg E. Mathieson Sr. . NSW Publication, LLC)

helicopter from several thousand feet and destroyed. The helicopter delivery concept was terminated and not revived again until some years later.

Through a somewhat complex postwar organizational structure, the NSWGs and their BSUs ended up becoming the repository of the brown-water Navy, much of it organized into the naval reserve components. It is this postwar period when the NSW combatant-craft community began truly to distinguish itself. It was also a period of dynamic change for the NSW community.

POST-VIETNAM

After the Vietnam War the BSUs were reorganized as coastal river squadrons (COS-RIVRON) with subordinate coastal river divisions (COSRIVDIV). The COSRIV-

RON was a senior planning staff that reported to the NSWG commander, Atlantic, and the COSRIVDIVs, who reported to the COSRIVRON commander, were made up of a combination of active and naval reserve personnel, largely with Vietnam veterans. The units continued to operate the LCPLs and PBRs that had been made famous in Vietnam. Additional craft were eventually added and included the landing craft, swimmer reconnaissance (LCSR); the patrol boat (PB) Mk 3, or Sea Specter; the Seafox, also known as the special warfare craft, light (SWCL); and the mini-armored troop carrier (MATC), called "Mini" by the men.

The LCSR and PB Mk 3 were new to the inventory, and represented the first craft in the NSW inventory that could not be taken on board ship because of their

large size. Ship-to-shore movement would be accomplished by the Seafox, which replaced the LCPLs in the inventory in 1979. (The U.S. Navy stopped purchasing the LCPLs and required NSW to design and acquire its own ship-to-shore craft.)

The fifty-two-foot LCSRs were short lived in the NSW inventory and really only experimental, because they were powered by very noisy gas-turbine engines that were difficult to maintain. Uniquely, however, the boat was configured with the Fulton recovery system, a personnel-recovery system adapted from a similar concept developed for fixed-wing aircraft. In the Fulton system, swimmers would launch from the LCSR by simply jumping from the stern of the boat at very high speed. For recovery, the LCSR would make a high-speed pass around the swimmers and drop off two sleds that were attached by a line. The swimmers would mount the sleds and paddle out the distance of the line. The LCSR would return at high speed and capture the line, which would reel the swimmers back to the fast-moving boat. Little information exists about the LCSR today, except in the memory of those that had the opportunity to operate with it.

The MATC was a thirty-six-foot all-aluminum-hull craft designed for high-speed patrol, interdiction, and clandestine missions in rivers, harbors, and protected coastal areas. The Mini was almost a twin of the MSSC built for SEALs in Vietnam, but with a much-improved design. The Mini had a large well area for transporting combat-equipped SEALs or cargo, or for gunnery personnel operating its seven organic weapons stations. It was equipped with a hydraulic bow ramp and water-jet engines to give it the capability to move closer to the beach for infiltration and exfiltration operations. The Mini had a somewhat low silhouette that made it difficult to detect, and it was extremely quiet at idle speeds. Its high-resolution radar and multiple communication suites provided a good all-weather surveillance and command and control presence for interdiction and counterdrug operations. The boat had an overhead canopy that could be removed and stowed below. The crew size was normally four, but could be modified depending on the mission and mission duration.

SEALs drop a CRRC into the ocean from a support Black Hawk from the US Army's 160th Special Operations Aviation Regiment (The Night Stalkers). (Photo: Greg E. Mathieson Sr. / NSW Publications, LLC)

SEALs in a CRCC await pickup by Special Warfare Combatant-Craft crewmen (SWCC) from SBT-20 in a Mark V. (Photo: Greg E. Mathieson Sr. / NSW Publications, LLC)

An SBT RIB outfitted with heavy weapons makes its way though rough seas. (Photo: Greg E. Mathieson Sr. / NSW Publications, LLC)

Surrounded by heavy weapons, SWCC operators prep and test radio gear aboard a Special Operations Craft-Riverine (SOC-R) before moving down a river. (Photo: Greg E. Mathieson Sr. / NSW Publications, LLC)

The Seafox was designed to be a multi-mission craft, but its primary mission was over-the-horizon insertion and extraction of SEAL elements. The SEALs rode in the after-end of the boat, which was separated from the crew compartment by the boat's engines. Seafox was designed to operate at speeds in excess of forty knots in Sea State 4, and was powered by twin diesel engines. With its water-jet propulsion, Seafox had the capability to operate in water as shallow as three-feet, and, for planning, could travel about three hundred miles round-trip in the open ocean. To expand its tactical capabilities, the boat could be moved by a trailer on highways or transported on its trailer by C-130 aircraft. Most importantly, however, the Seafox could be deployed from naval amphibious ships. Her armament consisted of two M-60 7.62-mm machine guns on the forward structure and two .50-caliber machine guns aft, which were interchangeable with M-19 grenade launchers.

Other than the MSSC and LSSC in Vietnam, Seafox was the first boat in the inventory built exclusively to accommodate SEAL capabilities. As a result, it was designed with what today would be considered primitive stealth technology. Its paint was nonmetallic, it incorporated infrared reduction features, the interior of the engine compartment was shielded against radar, the radar and communication mast was covered with radar-absorbent material, and the exhaust was muffled and discharged underwater.

In 1979, the COSRIVRONs and COSRIVDIVs were reorganized as special boat squadrons and units (SPECBOATRON and SBUs). SPECBOATRON-1 was located at the NAB, Coronado, and SPECBOATRON-2 was located at the NAB, Little Creek. SBU-12 was located at the NAB, Coronado; SBU-13 at Mare Island, California; SBU-20 at the NAB, Little Creek; and SBU-22 at New Orleans. SBU-24 was later established at the Panama Canal Zone, but was disestablished when the canal was turned over to Panama in 1999.

SBU-12 and SBU-20 were largely active-duty commands that used all but riverine craft, whereas SBU-13 and SBU-22 were largely reserve commands that used largely riverine craft. SBU-13 was eventually decommissioned and, in August

BELOW, LEFT: Challenge coin from Special Boat Team-12, which was established in Oct. 2002 as a result of NSW restructure force changes. The unit is located at the Naval Amphibious Base, Coronado, CA. SBT-12 deploys primarily to North East Asia, South East Asia, and the Middle East. (Photos: Dave Gatley / NSW Publications, LLC)

BOTTOM, RIGHT: Challenge coin from Special Boat Team 20, which was established in October 2002. SBT-20 is homeported at the Naval Amphibious Base, Little Creek, VA and deploys primarily to Europe, Africa, and the Middle East. (Photo: Dave Gatley / NSW Publications, LLC)

2002, SBU-22 was moved to its present home at Stennis Space Center, Mississippi, where it operates the SOCR, which will be discussed subsequently.

The USSOCOM was established in Tampa, Florida, in 1987, and since its formation assisted in the procurement of NSW's inventory of operational craft. These craft included the Mk V SOC, eleven-meter (thirty-six-foot) NSW RIB, SOCR, and the Cyclone-class patrol, coastal (PC) ships.

The Mk V SOC is a medium-range insertion and extraction platform for SEAL and other SOFs in a low-medium threat environment. Its secondary mission involves limited capabilities to conduct intelligence collection and reconnaissance missions.

The Mk V SOC usually operates in a two-craft detachment, and is fully interoperable with the eleven-meter NSW RIB. With a beam of seventeen and a half feet, the craft has enough room to carry four CRRCs with six outboard motors (including two spares) and fuel. A ramp on the stern of the boat allows SEALs to maneuver their CRRCs up and onto the stern while the Mk V is under way for fast recovery. The typical Mk V SOC mission duration is twelve hours; in the Persian Gulf, however, the men conducted many missions of seventy-two hours duration.

The Mk V has the capacity to carry sixteen fully equipped SEALs over a range of five hundred miles. Its twin maximum transmission unit (MTU) twelve-cylinder task element (TE)-94 diesel engines give it power and reliability and, coupled with its two water-jet outdrives, provides fast acceleration for operations near shore or in shallow waters. The boat is equipped with seats designed for maximum comfort and shock mitigation in high seas or heavy maneuvering, and allows passengers to either stand or sit. Even with these seats, the ride is very rough on the men, and without good training can result in serious injury.

Mk Vs are outfitted with five gun mounts for small-caliber weapons supporting any combination of M-2 .50-caliber heavy machine guns, M-240 or M-60 7.62-mm machine guns, or Mk 19 40-mm automatic grenade launchers. Together these provide 360 degrees of firing coverage. To defend against aircraft the craft have a station for firing the Stinger man-portable air defense system. Later improvements included mounting stations for GAU-17 miniguns, Mk 95 twin 50-caliber machine guns, Mk 38 chain guns, and Mk 48 25-mm guns.

Mk Vs deploy in two-boat detachments. A detachment is deployable on board two U.S. Air Force C-5 aircraft, can be under way within forty-eight hours of notification, and can be ready for operations within twenty-four hours of arrival at an

TOP, LEFT: *Blending in to their environment, SWCC operators prepare to push off to a mission down river in their SOC-R. (Photo: Greg E. Mathieson Sr. / NSW Publications, LLC)*

TOP, RIGHT: *A fully laden SOC-R throws up waves of water as it moves at a high rate of speed down a river. (Photo: Greg E. Mathieson Sr. / NSW Publications, LLC)*

BELOW: *SWCC operators load up in a Special Operations Craft—Riverine (SOC-R), preparing to push off for a mission downriver. (Photo: Greg E. Mathieson Sr. / NSW Publications, LLC)*

RIGHT: *The six barrels of the GAU-17/A glow from the intense heat as an SWCC operator fires the eletronically operated Gatling-type gun, which fires a 7.62-mm round at the rate of 6,000 per minute into an enemy shoreline. (Photo: Greg E. Mathieson Sr. / NSW Publications, LLC)*

BOTTOM, RIGHT: *A SWCC operator shown here aboard a SOC-R craft fires a GAU-17 along a river shoreline at night. (Photo: Greg E. Matihieson Sr. / NSW Publications, LLC)*

BELOW: *A Chinook tandem rotor heavy-lift helicopter inserts a Special Boat Team into a river. (Photo: US Navy)*

FACING PAGE

BOTTOM, LEFT AND RIGHT: *An SOC-R moves at a high rate of speed down a narrow waterway as SWCC operators man their weapons. (Photo: Greg E. Mathieson Sr. / NSW Publications, LLC)*

FOB. They can operate from shore facilities, from well deck–equipped ships, or from ships with appropriate crane and deck space capabilities. The Mk V SOC has its own transporter and prime mover and also can be moved overland on improved highways. Studies have been accomplished and planning is under way to replace the aging Mk V SOC with a new and more capable vessel called the combatant craft, large (CCL). The CCL will be a somewhat larger platoon-sized boat with advanced technology capabilities to conduct intelligence collection, surveillance, and reconnaissance missions.

The NSW RIB is a high-speed, high-buoyancy, and extreme-weather craft assigned the primary mission of insertion and extraction of SEAL tactical elements conducting over-the-beat (OTB) operations. The NSW RIB replaced three

previously manufactured RIBs used by NSW forces: the seven-meter (twenty-four-foot), nine-meter (thirty-foot), and ten-meter (thirty-two-foot) RIBs. The eleven-meter NSW RIBs remain the workhorse of today's NSW forces. The first detachments were delivered in November 1997. Unlike previous RIB configurations, the NSW RIB is quieter, faster, has a longer range, and can transport an entire SEAL squad. A major design improvement minimized the amount of water sprayed into the boats, and modifications to the engine compartment make repairs faster and easier. The NSW RIB's hull is a deep "V" fiberglass design with Kevlar-reinforced Vinylester resin with a rigid inflatable sponson manufactured from two-piece nylon-reinforced neoprene.

NSW RIB capabilities are substantially enhanced by its capability for no-notice deployments using the maritime craft aerial deployment system, whose capability

SWCC operators from Special Boat Team 20 conduct a Maritime Craft Aerial Deployment System (MCADS) where they push out an 11-meter Rigid Hull Inflatable Boat (RIB) from a C-130 and then parachute with it into the open sea, climb aboard, and move off to the mission. (Photos: Greg E. Mathieson Sr. / NSW Publications, LLC)

enables SEALs and SWCCs to rapidly deploy anywhere in the world with less than twenty-four hours notice.

The maritime craft aerial deployment system is deployed with the NSW RIB rigged on a platform with four large parachutes from the back of a C-130 or C-17 aircraft at an altitude of approximately 3,500 feet. Four special boat operators and a SEAL squad immediately follow the boat out of the plane and into the water. Within twenty minutes the SWCCs have the boat unpacked and rigged to get under way to deliver the SEALs, or to conduct their own mission.

Plans are now under way to replace the eleven-meter NSW RIB with an advanced technology boat called the Mk I Combatant Craft, Medium (CCM).

During the early 1990s, SBT-22 began operating with a boat called the coastal assault craft. This boat was soon replaced with the SOCR beginning in October 2000. It is the newest craft in NSW's combatant-craft inventory as of this writing. SOCR is designed to be fast and to operate with exceptional capability on inland waterways. SOCR is thirty-three feet long, with a nine-foot beam, and draws only eight inches of water at speed. Twin 440-horsepower diesel engines give it quick acceleration up to its rated top speed of forty-two knots. Weapons that can be mounted include the M-2 .50-caliber heavy machine gun, Mk 19 automatic grenade launcher, and 7.62-mm miniguns. Its aluminum hull makes it light and strong and capable of carrying up to 20,500 pounds in personnel and combat gear. SOCR can be transportable by U.S. Air Force cargo aircraft and slung beneath medium-lift helicopters such as the H-47 Chinook and H-53 Stallion/Pave Low.

THE PATROL, COASTAL

Any discussion about boats in NSW needs to include the now defunct Cyclone-class PC ships that graced the special operations inventory for about ten years.

Originally designated as patrol boat, coastal, the name was changed to PC when the U.S. Navy decided that they would become commissioned ships rather than having a combatant-craft status. The PCs were built by Bollinger Machine Shop and Shipyard of Lockport, Louisiana, and were assigned to the USSOCOM and NSWC and the SPECBOATRONs specifically. The primary mission of the Cyclone was to serve as a platform for conducting maritime special operations, including interdiction, escort, noncombatant evacuation, reconnaissance, operational deception, intelligence collection, and tactical swimmer operations. Her small size, stealthy construction, and high speed were tailored to performing long-range special operations insertion and extraction as well as other SOF support duties as needed. The ship's operational capabilities were designed to meet the unique requirements of its special warfare missions. Operationally, the Cyclone was capable of accelerating from a stop to thirty-five knots in less than three minutes, then decelerating from full ahead to fifteen knots astern in sixty seconds. In high-speed, hard-over turns, the ship barely heeled as the automatic stabilizers engaged. There were eventually fourteen ships constructed for NSW Navy use; they were very unpopular at USSOCOM because their operating costs were high and often prohibitive enough to keep the boats at the piers rather than under way or forward deployed. The PCs had a crew of four officers and twenty-four enlisted men and armament consisting of one Mk 96 and one Mk 38 25-mm machine gun; five .50-caliber machine guns; two Mk 19 40-mm automatic grenade launchers; and two M-60 machine guns. Sailors manning the PCs were made up of regular Navy ratings, and did not qualify for the SWCC warfare-area rating.

SWCCs operate and maintain the inventory of specialized boats described in this chapter, which are used to support SEALs and other SOFs. Individually, SEALs and SWCCs go through separate, but similar, specialized training programs that emphasize special operations in the maritime environment. SWCCs are trained extensively in craft and weapons Tactics, Techniques, and Procedures (TTPs.) SWCC operators must be physically fit, highly motivated, combat focused, and responsive in high-stress situations. Focusing on clandestine infiltration and exfiltration of SEALs, SWCC provide dedicated, rapid mobility in shallow-water areas where larger ships cannot operate.

ABOVE: *Because of the nature of the work environment, everything needs to be waterproofed and tethered, such as the 9-mm Sig Sauer 226 pistol here, so that it doesn't fall into the sea. (Photo: Greg E. Mathieson Sr. / NSW Publications, LLC)*

BOTTOM, LEFT: *A high speed Fountain Boat from Special Boats Unit 12 is seen operating in San Diego Bay. These boats were used during Desert Shield and Desert Storm to intercept enemy boats filled with explosives trying to attack U.S. Navy ships. (Photo: Greg E. Mathieson Sr. / NSW Publications, LLC)*

BOTTOM, RIGHT: *The USS Whirlwind, PC-11 was a Cyclone-class coastal patrol ship used by Naval Special Warfare in the early 90s. Designed for littoral operation, this ship was assigned to Special Boat Squadron Two. (Photo: Greg E. Mathieson Sr. / NSW Publications, LLC)*

COMBAT SUPPORT

CHAPTER 8

STAFFS AND TECHNICAL ORGANIZATIONS

Rear Adm. (SEAL) George Worthington, USN (Ret.)

WHY A CHAPTER ON NON-SEAL TECHNICIANS? GOOD QUEStion. Not so long ago the "technicians" in NSW were qualified frogmen and SEALs. Team Sailors did duties in platoons and departments. UDT and SEAL team departments kept the specialized equipment ready for checkout to the operational platoons as needed for exercises—and for overseas operations. While the enlisted ticket to quick advancement was to be found primarily inside the platoon structure, once a solid level of expertise was achieved, senior operators were detailed to manage the headquarters departments—diving, electronics, armory, "first lieutenant" and engineering, air operations, and administrative duties that involved inventory control and operation and maintenance of the command's operational equipment.

The discussion about technicians was opened in Chapter 2, which discussed

the organization of NSW. Here we will get into more detail, show photos of NSW technicians in action doing all the tasks they do: maintenance, supply, automotive, administrative, logistics, communications, diving, matériel, electronics, night vision support, and intelligence. At the risk of repeating some of that information, we will examine many facets of the contributions administrative technicians make to the entire NSW community.

Apart from the SEALs and SWCCs, the unsung heroes of NSW are the extraordinary Navy "enabling" technicians that support SEAL, SDV, and SBT operations—those other U.S. Navy ratings (skill sets) that allow the NSW operators to do their jobs. In 1983, the DoD issued a memorandum to the services to revitalize their SOFs. NSW began identifying the Navy technical ratings required to support the overall SOF expansion. Headquarters staffs were expanded with fleet technicians during the Navy's program objective memorandum process wherein needs are identified and funded three years out. Technical responsibilities have burgeoned since 1945! Fleet technicians are an integral part of NSW team structure today. We will investigate more-integrated specialties and how they contribute to the effectiveness of command, among them NSWC staffs and MCT and group supply support units.

LEFT: *Rigid Hull Inflatable Boats (RIB) (also knows as RHIB) are lined up ready for service at the NSWG-1 SWCC RIB garage at Coronado's Naval Amphibious Base (NAB). (Photos by Dave Gatley)*

RIGHT: *Navy Chaplains promote and serve the spiritual, religious, moral, and personnel well-being of SEALs, SWCCs, and other NSW members around the world—in war zones, during training, and at homeport locations. Photo: Greg E. Mathieson Sr. / NSW Publications, LLC*

NAVAL SPECIAL WARFARE COMMAND

The NSWC is the immediate commander in charge of all NSWGs in the United States. Commanded by a two-star rear admiral, this organization was formed in

1987, and has grown steadily since. Originally legislated by Congress—along with USSOCOM and other service components—NSWC has integrated training, management of resources, personnel assignment (in cooperation with the chief of naval personnel), and setting the training standards for each subordinate command and their component SEAL, SDV, SBT, NSW, and logistics units. The NSW community gets a great deal of help, most of it from non-SEAL personnel: technicians, civilian staff, and the occasional contractor.

A quick word of encouragement to the reader: it may appear "unsexy" to peruse exposition about essentially administrative organs, but these technicians are the unsung heroes of NSW. They make the SEALs effective. They ensure the equipment is there—SCUBA, ammunition, guns, radios, computers, parts, and other expendables. They fix the gear in the field when it breaks, and they replace it when it "dies." There is so much these support people do for the operators that words can only brush the surface of their many contributions—they are too numerous to count in the short space allotted here.

A large hunk of NSWC responsibilities involves finance—fiscal program planning for operations and matériel; annual budgets, including out-year planning targets; management of all NSWC's fiscal accounts: research, development, test, and evaluation; procurement; military construction; operations and maintenance, and manpower among them. Running a staff the size of NSWC requires administrative specialists. Major NSWC staff divisions are Personnel (N1); Intelligence (N2);

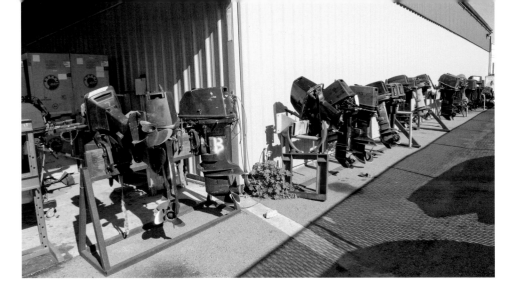

Operations and Plans (N3/N5); Logistics and Maintenance (N4/N9); Command, Control, Communications, Computers, and Automated Information Systems (N6); and Resources, Requirements, and Strategic Assessments (N8). In addition, staff positions are identified for a command inspector general, judge advocate general, public affairs, force medical, staff chaplain, safety and occupational health, and a command historian. Don't let the numbers confuse you; they are simply standard nomenclature for all Navy staffs. (Army numbers them S1, S2, etc., and joint staffs numbers them J1, J2, etc.)

It is important to note that during World War II and through the Korean War and early in the Vietnam era this kind of staff support was nonexistent. NSWGs Atlantic and Pacific staffs were established in 1963; however, they remained small staffs and did not really get adequate funding or manpower until the mid-1980s when the secretary of defense ordered a revitalization of all service SOFs. This highly technical support is now essential to NSW for the current conflict and will remain so into the future. In fact, today two-thirds of deployed NSW personnel are non-SEAL technicians—but essential to the operational success of the engaged SEAL and SBTs. NSWC technical support personnel deploy with the NSWRON, and are smaller mirror images of the NSWC divisions in which they work.

Personnel Division (N1)

The Personnel Division (N1) is staffed with naval officers, Sailors, and civilians. As expected, administrative ratings make up the lion's share of N1. The staff includes Navy yeomen and personnel specialists, human resource specialists, management analysts, and social services personnel. The N1 division is led by a Navy captain, who is "responsible for direction and supervision of Force and staff administration and personnel, to include all aspects of administrative assistance and training, decorations and awards, retention, equal opportunity and personnel distribution."

ABOVE: *A maintenance technician lowering a recently serviced outboard engine into a test tank to verify its operability. Keeping the outboards operational is very important for both training exercises and combat operations. These techs are a small example of the support the SEAL operators require wherever they are deployed. (Photo: Dave Gatley / NSW Publications, LLC)*

LEFT, TOP: *Rows of outboard engines line up behind the Logistic Support Unit One maintenance building; all awaiting servicing. (Photo: Dave Gatley / NSW Publications, LLC)*

LEFT, BOTTOM: *Maintenance technicians from Logistic Support Unit One are seen repairing one of the many outboard engines used by NSW operators. (Photo: Dave Gatley / NSW Publications, LLC)*

N1 personnel track NSWC and subordinate command manning levels, generic health issues, assignments, and internal personnel issues.

Intelligence Division (N2)

The Intelligence Division (N2) coordinates all intelligence requirements, reporting, and equipment issues. N2 technicians operate at classified levels in special access spaces. They assist deployed and home-based component commands with coordination of their operational intelligence needs. Division responsibilities are far ranging and increasing as NSW commitments expand worldwide. The assistant chief of staff for Intelligence is a special duty Navy captain–intelligence officer. As the staff organization manual directs, the Intelligence Division is responsible "for advising the Commander on current force intelligence capabilities and activities, potentially hostile forces, and foreign politico-military developments which could require commitment of NAVSPECWARCOM resources . . . [and] serving as [U.S.] SOCOM and Navy focal point for all aspects of intelligence support to NSW." N2's mission is "to build, maintain, and deploy the most capable, flexible, mission-focused intelligence cadre in the world and to represent the gold standard of continuous self-assessment and improvement."

NSWG-10 was recently established with subordinate NSW Support Activity One and Two, and mission support centers to organize, train, educate, equip, deploy, and sustain specialized intelligence, surveillance, and reconnaissance and preparation of the environment capabilities through existing NSWCs in direct support of SEAL, SBTs, NSWUs, and NSWRONs.

Operations and Plans Division (N3/N5)

The Operations and Plans Division (N3/N5) coordinates all operational plans and orders, ongoing operational activities, future operations, equipment requirements, mobility issues, air lift, deployment schedules, combat rules of engagement (originating at higher headquarters), manning imperatives (in coordination with N1), and other day-to-day activities. Future exercises and training environments, training areas, and required facilities planning are part of N3/N5 duties. Headed by a Navy SEAL captain, the division "is responsible for the assignment and supervision of all NSW forces involved in Joint and Fleet Unconventional Warfare (UW), Direct Action (DA), Special Reconnaissance (SR), Foreign Internal Defense (FID), Counterterrorism (CT) exercises, Riverine and Coastal Patrol and Interdic-

BELOW, TOP: *Teamwork is the basis of all that SEALs do. Here they are seen flushing out a Zodiac after training in Hawaii. (Photo: Greg E. Mathieson Sr. / NSW Publications, LLC)*

BELOW, BOTTOM: *HMMWVs (High Mobility Multipurpose Wheeled Vehicles) await shipment to SEALs. These vehicles have been specifically designed to withstand the harsh environment of Southwest Asia under increased payload demands. (Photo: Dave Gatley / NSW Publications, LLC)*

tion (CPI) operations and counter-drug (CD) activities. The N3/N5 is responsible for ensuring all plans affecting deployment and employment of assigned forces are refined and maintained." The N3/5 also provides direction and oversight to all NSW training and monitors Force readiness, and identifies, develops, and coordinates all NSW operational requirements. Of all the demanding duties, developing formal requirements is perhaps the most important.

Significant and demanding duties are involved in developing formal requirements. CNSWC (or COMNAVSPECWARCOM) has established a Requirements Review Board process within the N3/5 that allows new, emerging, or improved capabilities to be vetted at the NSWGs and NSWC for approval and funding as appropriate. Requirements are reviewed quarterly and involve actions and activities from the battlefield, training, or technical application. New requirements can drive long-range planning and perhaps considerable R&D efforts with significant impact on budget preparation.

Logistics and Maintenance Division (N4/N9)

The Logistics and Maintenance staff (N4/N9), headed by a Navy supply corps captain, and with a staff consisting of three other supply corps officers, thirty-three civilians, several Navy storekeeper ratings, and SEAL enlisted operators, facilitate specialized equipment management responsibilities. This staff works closely with the NSWG-1 and NSWG-2 LOGSUs to ensure that the operational teams have the equipment and resources necessary to conduct sustained combat operations. The N4/N9 is the largest NSWC division and is "responsible for all facilities, supply, and ordnance related matters." Assigned personnel supervise and direct facilities operations, civil engineering support equipment management, supply operations, plans, procedures, expediting integrated logistics support, theater logistics support, supply management assistance and inspections, configuration control, and all ordnance management operations. The N4/N9 division also assists with supervising and directing "maintenance operations, plans, procedures, logistics support, budget, and configuration control." Specific functions include military construction, contract administration, contractor relations, force supply-support guidance, policy development for supply support, and management of matériel. Personnel oversee all published logistics plans and operations. The division coordinates all logistics requirements for the subordi-

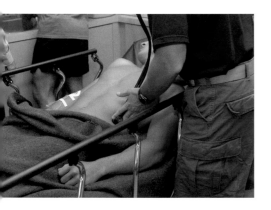

nate NSWGs, NSWCEN, and DEVGRP, and their subordinate SEALs, SDVs, SBTs, NSWUs, and sundry units.

Command, Control, Communications, Computers, and Automated Information Systems Division (N6)

The N6 division controls command, control, communication, computers (C4) and automated information systems. The functional statement for N6 addresses itself to "communications operations and interoperability issues, advising the Commander of current programs and acquisitions for C4 [command, control, communications, computers] programs . . . and general communications program management." Everyone is familiar with the contribution that computers have made to military matters. It is the same in NSW, where increasing electronic activities in intelligence and operations are driving forces for make-up and readiness posture. Subordinate commands have to communicate in the joint arena, so equipment has to be compatible. Too often, in the past, deployed teams have not been able to communicate—this as recently as during operations in Afghani-

A communications technician loads classified hard drives into portable comms servers that will be used in an upcoming training exercise. These nested boxes of communications gear are an essential part of a large deployment of SEALs; the servers handle all satellite and other Tactical Operations Center (TOC) communications. (Photo: Dave Gatley / NSW Publications, LLC)

stan. This staff agent liaises with the group MCTs and supports ongoing deployed operations as required. Routine staff functions include, briefly, evaluation of C4 requirements, maintenance of all communications plans and associated personnel training, evaluation of all joint communications systems supporting special operations, development of emergency action procedures, coordination of cryptographic phone systems, and support of all automated information systems—a big job that continues to grow day by day. We are in the computer age, and the N6 division ensures that the NSWC stays on the leading edge.

Force Financial Management Division (N7)

Force Financial Management (N7) personnel are often referred to as "bean counters." N7 "is responsible for the financial management processes, programs, and policies of COMNAVSPECWARCOM." Pretty simple, you think, but not so fast. This division is all civilian financial account analysts. They review every financial transaction carried out by the NSWC and subordinate command. The division advises the commander and all divisions on the formulation of financial plans and fiscal execution thereof. This includes claimancy issues, budgets, technical guidance regarding fiscal information, and effective management of NSWC resources. It is in overall charge of NSWC budget justification and mid-year review of cur-

LEFT: A Naval Special Warfare support member installs added ballistic protection to an up armored HMMWV used by Navy SEALs in the field. (Photo: Greg E. Mathieson Sr. / NSW Publications, LLC)

BELOW: A Navy mechanic works on the specialize up armored HMMWVs that the SEALs will use in the field. (Photo: Greg E. Mathieson Sr. / NSW Publications, LLC)

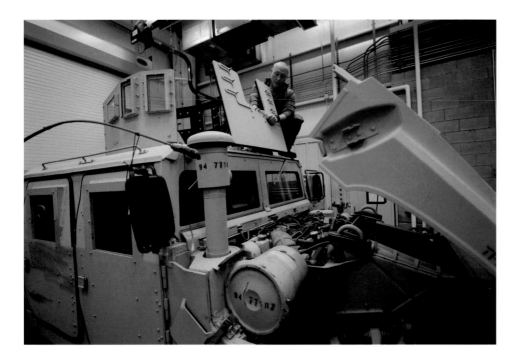

WARCOM Public Affairs Office, Lt. Tommy Crosby, working by the light of his laptop in a remote SEAL location in Iraq. All support staff, be they lawyers, medics, techs, public affairs and others, travel into the field in support of SEALs and SWCC around the globe. (Photo: Greg E. Mathieson Sr. / NSW Publications, LLC)

rent expenditures. This is unglamorous but extremely important work. The NSWC could not function without this foremost division.

Resources, Requirements, and Assessments Division (N8)

The Resources, Requirements, and Assessments Division (Staff code N8) develops, submits, and defends COMNAVSPECWARCOM material and funding requirements to USSOCOM for POM (Program Objective Memorandum—Department of Defense budgeting procedures) development and MFP-11 (Major Force Program) funding. Simply stated, this division develops the list of needs that go forward (up the chain of command) for funding. The list is detailed, definitive, and direct. It states the commander's assessment of his fiscal requirements to execute his mission. Like everywhere, no one gets everything he wants—except in the GWOT. NSW has received most of that requested. The 2008 Quadrennial Defense Review (QDR) last year ordered all SOF to grow 15 percent. Recognizing it takes years to train and develop SOFs, this will not be accomplished in the near term but is a multiyear commitment. As discussed in Chapter 3, it takes more than a year to "make" a SEAL operator. Staff, however, can requisition new technicians relatively quickly. In this regard, staff requirements can be assessed and positions filled with relative ease. Getting the shooters on line is obviously more difficult. So, with respect to this division, putting together a cogent list of requirements is a major undertaking, the sine qua non of ultimate operational success. It cannot be understated.

Legal, Public Affairs, and Medical Elements

In addition to the foregoing staff divisions, NSWC has three staff elements of growing importance: legal, public affairs, and medical. The staff judge advocate advises the commander on all things relative to rules of engagement, military justice, investigations, charges, and execution of legal matters affecting NSWC and all subordinate commands. Often, issues arise about legalities that need fundamental, judicial review. This Navy lawyer performs this increasingly sensitive task.

Public affairs conducts interface with other services and with the civilian community. Responsible for the public face of NSW, this officer is supported by a staff that continues to grow. Mass communications is the cornerstone of this section. Addressing the media is a primary responsibility, and public affairs personnel make sure the media reports on the right information.

An NSW Mass Communications Specialist (MC) videotapes a SEAL team during live fire training. Often MC personnel accompany SEAL teams into the field to document their activites. (Photo: Greg E. Mathieson Sr. / NSW Publications, LLC)

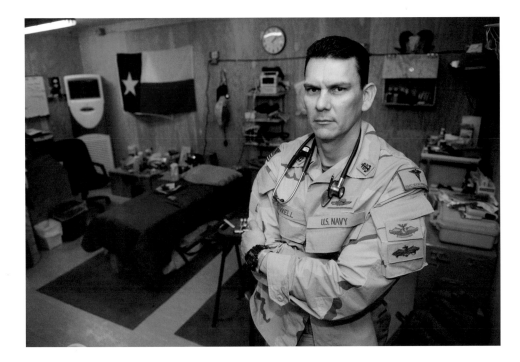

The force medical officer, a Navy doctor with a medical service corps assistant, oversees all aspects of NSW health, medical training and staffing, and preparation for overseas health matters. During Foreign Internal Defense (FID) operations SEAL medical specialists can get involved advising and treating local populations. The training of these individuals is reviewed by the force medical officer. The section is trained in diving medicine and oversees medical training of diving corpsmen.

Technical support personnel are essential to the overall functioning of NSWC, service, civilian, and contractor support. It is a far cry from the 1960s when one SEAL team per coast "did it all" with bare-bones support staffs called Naval Operations Support Groups (NOSGs).

THE MOBILE COMMUNICATIONS TEAMS

As we learned in Chapter 3, MCTs provide integrated communications for deploying units, SEALs, SDVs, and SBTs. They live by the same training cycle the other teams do. Briefly, they participate in professional developments, move into Unit

LEFT: *NSW Support staff pack parachutes which will deliver the weight of a Mk V boat from a C130 aircraft, safely to the open sea. (Photo: Greg E. Mathieson Sr. / NSW Publications, LLC)*

RIGHT: *Some of the unique skills of support staff of Naval Special Warfare extend to that of sewing and and making custom modifications to suit the needs of SWCC and SEAL operations. Here technicians are working on rigging that will support the weight of a Mark V Special Operations Craft when parachuted from a C-5 aircraft. (Photo: Greg E. Mathieson Sr. / NSW Publications, LLC)*

Naval Special Warfare support techs configure, service, and support the secure computer systems of SEALs and WARCOM commands. Here a tech is changing out hard drives on laptop computers. (Photo: Greg E. Mathieson Sr. / NSW Publications, LLC)

Level Training (ULT), then into squadron training in preparation for deployment, after which they deploy. An MCT mount-out package can weigh as much as fifty tons and normally requires a C-17 to transport. They remain deployed for six months, longer if required. We have discussed the individual training challenge to bring a fleet communicator to MCT operational levels; following is discussion of some of the requirements-based support provided to NSW organizations.

An NSW task group has 120 users of data, phones, and satellite radios. Cryptographic capabilities are inherent in NSW communications as well as in data burst equipment. Example circuits are one high frequency (HF), two very high frequency (VHF), two ultra high frequency (UHF), and three ultra high satellite frequency (UHF SATCOM). An NSW task unit (NSWTU), a step down, has sixty to one hundred users and requires one each of the foregoing frequency bands. A smaller element is a NSW task element (NSWTE), five to ten users, with concomitantly reduced frequency needs. NSW task groups (NSWTGs), NSTUs, and NSWTEs rely on the same technical expertise, varying from twelve at the group level down to seven at the element level.

The MCT provides detachments to every NSW-deployed location. There is an NSWSTG in Iraq, and deployed NSWTUs at several other locations including Zamboanga, Philippines. They are present at all static, overseas NSWTUs: Guam, Bahrain, Germany, and Spain. In addition to these, MCTs provide communications support to two mission support centers co-located with the NSWG locations, Coronado and Little Creek. To support individual SEAL teams, the MCTs provide two communications operators to each team, for a total of sixteen. MCT success depends on providing expert communications support to all users. They deploy in company with the overseas NSWRON—to Europe, Latin America, Central (Middle East–North Africa–Central Asia), and the Pacific. These regions are served by Theater Special Operations Commands that report to their geographic commanders. These include EUCOM, SOUTHCOM, CENTCOM, and PACOM, respectively. All the MCTs are chockablock with training, deployments, and an exceedingly high OPTEMPO. Today the stress and pressure is every bit as intense as it was during the Vietnam era. And, for all we know, there is no letup on the horizon. An example of deployed squadron support comes from the NSWG-1 MCT: one chief petty officer, nine tactical communicators (six to CENTCOM, three to

PACOM), six tactical communicators to NSWTG support, and two tactical communicators, each, to the deployed SEAL teams. These Sailors leave behind families, too, just as the SEALs do.

Group Logistics Support Units

The next organizations we will look at are the LOGSUs. It is worthwhile to repeat the mission of LOGSUs: "Provide Naval Special Warfare Group components doctrinal logistics support to enable successful garrison training and deployed operations." The group LOGSUs support every SEAL, SDV, and SBT. In this regard it is necessary to note a subtle element in the function the LOGSUs provide: "doctrinal logistics." This phrase means more than simple supply support of equipment and reordering of inventories. It includes supply support, of course—but it encompasses far more than paperclips and toilet paper. The LOGSUs service vehicles—they procure them, distribute them, maintain them—manage facilities,

ABOVE AND RIGHT: *Techs load Simunitions FX (R), a specialized nonlethal training cartridge similar to that of a paintball ballistic, but which allows techs and operators to fire them using their specialized weapons during training. (Photo: Greg E. Mathieson Sr. / NSW Publications, LLC)*

and provide technicians (e.g., parachute riggers, medical facilities). Following are their support functions, to wit:

- Supply: contract purchasing, finance
- Facilities: handle maintenance, renovation, upgrades
- Ranges: provide infrastructure to support training
- Medical: provide rehab, physical therapy, and mental health services
- Training: establish individual training for technicians assigned to teams

In terms of equipment maintenance and accountability, LOGSUs run what is called the "first lieutenant" department, responsible for hands-on maintenance of all assigned rolling stock and hardware. In air operations, that includes riggers and parachute packers; weapons and armorers; ordnance, stowage supervision, and allocation; diving, diving supervisors, and maintenance of individual SCUBA gear; transportation; all maintenance functions; and issue, repair, and recycling functions.

The Navy supply corps commanders in charge of the LOGSUs wear two hats. They are department heads within the NSWGs, and they are COs of the two LOGSUs. In this regard they have Echelon III and IV responsibilities. Echelon III describes the NSWG; Echelon IV includes the deploying SEAL teams. His troops are a combination of sea and shore duties—Navy terms surrounding personnel assignment and management. The LOGSUs can have upward of four hundred personnel assigned. As pointed out in Chapter 2, the LOGSUs are at all times more than 50 percent deployed or on temporary additional duty.

In their NSWG staff roles, the LOGSU officer, the logistics department head, runs shooting ranges, hazardous material management, safety programs, explosive safety, all facilities, and official contracting for various services. Overall, LOGSUs focus on both homeport (garrison) and deployed (expeditionary) logistics support. It is worth pointing out that, unlike previous eras, theater logistics nowadays is a joint function. During the Vietnam conflict, for example, deployed SEALs had to get their supplies from prepositioned U.S. Navy facilities, many in Subic Bay, the Philippines, or from home—with days lost in transit. Today, in the GWOT, NSW-deployed elements rely on U.S. Army and Marine Corps conventional forces' logistics structures. This is a far more streamlined process and obviously contributes to

ABOVE: *Contrary to the opinion of many, women have a place working alongside SEAL teams, though not in direct conflict operations. Here a tech, covered in machine gun ammo, awaits her turn on the firing range. Techs need to be prepared and capable of handling any situation that may develop in the field while working on the front lines in support of SEAL and SWCC operators. (Photo: Greg E. Mathieson Sr. / NSW Publications, LLC)*

operational efficiency. Specifically, a deployed NSWU reports to a JSOTF. In this organization a J4 logistician coordinates all SOFs in-theater logistics requirements. This sounds simple, but it has taken approximately twenty years to develop this lash-up! Let's now look at a standard LOGSU training cycle.

LEFT, TOP: *An NSW support technician fires an FN Minimi Special Purpose Weapon, also known as the M239 SAW (Squad Automatic Weapon) and Mk46, as adopted by U.S. SOCOM. (Photo: Greg E. Mathieson Sr. / NSW Publications, LLC)*

Professional Development Phase

First up is the six-month professional development phase. During this phase individual Sailors attend service schools, take leave, complete in-house training courses, and prepare for the upcoming Unit Level Training (ULT) phase. During

LEFT, BOTTOM: *A female tech with Naval Special Warfare loads an Mk 48, Mod O, lightweight machine gun (LWMG) during training on the firing range. (Photo: Greg E. Mathieson Sr. / NSW Publciatoins, LLC)*

A LOGSU support technician works on the engine of a Mine Resistant Ambush Protected (MRAP) vehicle. (Photo: Greg E. Mathieson Sr. / NSW Publications, LLC)

ULT, LOGSU elements support SEAL and SDVT training evolutions as required. These can be out-of-area (away from home) exercises. Specific tailoring of SEAL team needs is identified during this six-month phase. It is during this phase, too, that personal relationships are established between SEALs and LOGSU supporters. All will soon be together in a declared war zone for an extended period; they have to get along. If personality clashes are evident, they need be addressed before moving into the squadron training phase.

Squadron Integration Training Phase

The Squadron Integration Training brings together all the NSW disparate elements: SEAL teams, SDVT, SBT, MCT, LOGSU, and other administrative support. These elements rehearse together for six months before deploying to their assigned areas in Europe, the Middle East, Latin America, and the Pacific Far East (today, primarily operating out of Guam into the Philippines). Much of this phase can be out of area, for example, the Army Training Center, Fort Irwin, California or other off-site NSW training facilities—Marine Corps Camp Pendleton, La Posta, and Niland, California.

Finally, a quick look at the LOGSU personnel assigned to an individual SEAL team will give a concise idea of the level of effort available today. Eighteen technicians are assigned, made up of the following ratings: intelligence specialists, information technicians, storekeepers, personnel specialists, operations specialists, a builder, gunner's mate, hospitalman, culinary specialists, Navy diver, parachute rigger, construction mechanic, and utilityman. These terms may appear esoteric to the untrained eye, but they are family to the deploying SEAL team. In addition to the other administrative technicians already assigned to SEAL teams, the LOGSU deployers are integral to the teams' functioning overseas.

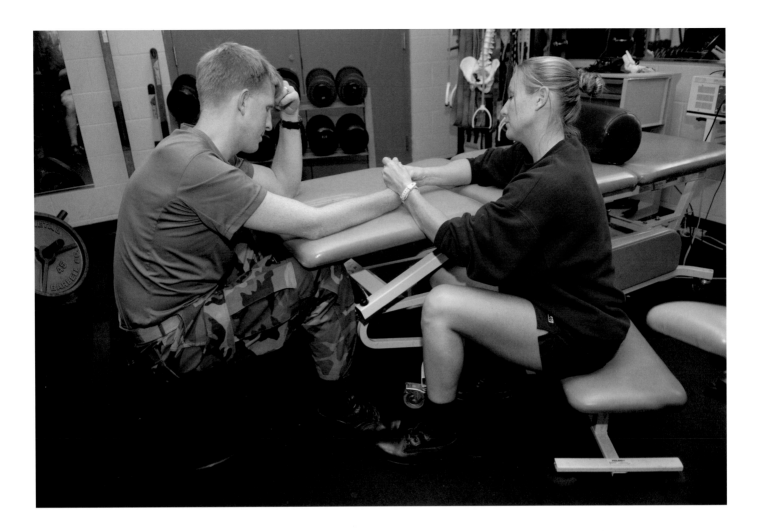

SUPPORT FROM NON–NAVAL SPECIAL WARFARE STAFFS

There are few shore-duty billets for enlisted SEALs; most are found at the NSW Center. As a result, the fleet technicians and other civilians present on a number of staffs are vital.

While the Vietnam conflict put SEAL teams on the map, 9/11 has reinforced the need for all SOFs, and NSW is in the forefront of U.S. Navy participation in the GWOT. But individual SEAL and SDVTs cannot do it alone. The technicians assigned to the teams and staffs are an integral part in the struggle. Next on our list are the technicians assigned to the NSWGs—beyond the MCT and LOGSU. Group technical support is required in all staff divisions, from personnel to operations to R&D. The largest administrative impact is in the N3/N5 Operations and Plans Division. That division follows operations and other events. Central to group operations are the mission monitoring centers, where manpower assigned is significantly heavy in non-SEAL ratings. These centers monitor all ongoing training missions and events. They also keep watch on international operations. Central to this task are operations specialists, electronics technicians (ET), and radiomen.

Finally, a nod to the technicians at the NSW training commands is necessary. Inasmuch as these two organizations represent the only significant opportunity for SEAL team operators to have shore duty, most of the authorized billets are coded for them. Nevertheless, the highly technical courses have to be staffed with subject matter experts. We acknowledge, again, their service and contribution to the overall mission of NSW.

Special Equipment

REAR ADM (SEAL) GEORGE WORTHINGTON
USN (RET)

CHAPTER 9

SPECIAL EQUIPMENT

Rear Adm. (SEAL) George Worthington, USN (Ret.)

NSW EQUIPMENT HAS EVOLVED SINCE 1943. THE FIRST NCDU did not hit the beaches of Normandy and the Pacific with the same load-out as modern-day SEAL operators in Afghanistan, Iraq, or the Philippines. Everything has changed over the years—men, training, and equipment. That NSW operational gear has become so technical has been, in fact, a determining element in the organization of NSWGs, NSWUs, SEAL and SBT teams, and supporting elements. Yesterday's logistical support departments pale in comparison to today's technical cadre throughout all NSWCs. As technology is introduced into the operational organization, the means to maintain it becomes critical to mission success. It is not reasonable to expect a SEAL or SWCC operator to be technologically trained to maintain, test, and perform line-level repairs on sensitive electronic firing devices and communications devices—not to mention computers. Technical expertise is in great demand in today's teams; the logistics functions of tracking, ordering, and maintaining inventories boggles the imagination. Specialists are the lifeblood behind successful NSW missions and are truly appreciated by the operators.

GEAR OVER THE YEARS

Before advancing into the table of organizational equipment for today's NSW, it is worth noting that previous SEAL capabilities involved varying outcomes, some more successful than others. One such procedure was the Fulton Skyhook recovery system, which incorporated a weather balloon tethered to a man on the ground or in the water. A specially rigged airplane that engaged the tether line with a V-shaped yoke snatched up the man, after which he was reeled into the aircraft. SEALs participated in the occasional testing, but the system was never formally accepted into the teams, largely because it was very complex for combat use. One SEAL was killed after he fell into the Chesapeake Bay when the tether line snapped as he was being hoisted into the aircraft.

More success was achieved by SEAL involvement with the Navy's Marine Mammal Program, which trained marine mammals to perform specific tasks. California sea lions were trained to attach recovery collars on practice ordnance canisters. The sea lions could dive to depths of more than one hundred feet to attach a specially built retrieval collar. Highly adaptable to human interface, sea lions proved to be capable and reliable for the very limited task assigned them. The sea lion program was called Quick Find.

Another marine mammal program handled by SEALs was use of Atlantic bot-

ABOVE: *This photo of a SEAL with a chain saw strapped to his back pretty much says "unconventional warfare." In fact it is part of the breaching equipment a SEAL might carry to cut through walls or doors when explosives are not a option. (Photo: Greg E. Mathieson Sr. / NSW Publications, LLC)*

LEFT, TOP: *Mechanic's gloves seem to be a favorite with a number of operators, given the contact with sharp objects, climbing, and items that can damage your hands. (Photo: Greg E. Mathieson Sr. / NSW Publications, LLC)*

LEFT, BOTTOM: *Inside the SEAL team equipment room are the various tools for missions for breaching access ways, such as crowbars, chain saws, or chisels. (Photo: Greg E. Mathieson Sr. / NSW Publications, LLC)*

BELOW: *SEALs over time seem to find the best, most durable, dependable, and lightweight equipment to suit their missions. Shown here is a mountaineering/caving ladder with a cable strength of 1,980 pounds and rung strength of 300 pounds each. This could easily hold several SEALs climbing a wall, ship, or other structure and yet roll up into a backpack. (Photo: Greg E. Mathieson Sr. / NSW Publications, LLC)*

tlenose dolphins to protect high-value, waterfront assets. A tagging device was mounted on a trained dolphin's rostrums. On command, and using their own internal sonar, the dolphins would seek a swimming intruder (surface or underwater) and tag him. This program was designated the Mine Detection and Neutralization System (Mk 18 Mod 0). It achieved approval for service use in March 1977, and full operational capability in 1979.

ABOVE: *K-Dog, a bottle nose dolphin from COMMANDER TASK UNIT (CTU-55.4.3), leaps out of the water in front of Sergeant (SGT) Andrew Garrett while training near the USS Gunston Hall (LDS 44) operating in the Arabian Gulf. (Photo: PH1 Brien Aho / USN)*

RIGHT, TOP (LEFT): *A sea lion trainer from Space and Naval Warfare Systems Center (SPAWAR), San Diego works on hand signals with Zak, a 375-pound California sea lion, during a patrol taking place in the Central Command Area of Responsibility. These highly trained animals are one of the best tools for swimmer detection. Here, Zak waits patiently for a snack during a patrol. (Photo: PH2 Bob Houlihan / USN)*

RIGHT, TOP (RIGHT): *A sea lion moves through the water carrying a device during one of the training patrols in the Central Command AOR. The mammal program was once under WARCOM and SEALs command, but it has been moved to another department.*

RIGHT, CENTER: *A LOGSU-1 technician moves vast amounts of equipment intended for SEALs and other NSW operators. (Photo: Dave Gatley)*

RIGHT, BOTTOM: *A drawer in the SEAL Team armory contains many gun-sight attachments developed by the U.S. Special Operations Command. (Photo: Dave Gatley)*

TOP, LEFT: *A lineup of Sig Sauer P226 pistols in the armory outnumbers most other weapons. It is the primary sidearm currently carried by Navy SEALs in combat operations. (Photo: Dave Gatley)*

TOP, RIGHT: *M79 grenade launchers line the wall of a SEAL Team Weapons Armory. The M79 is a single shot, break-open, shoulder-fired weapon that fires a high-explosive 40mm fragmentation grenade. (Photo: Dave Gatley)*

BOTTOM, LEFT: *Racks of the AT4 Rocket Launcher seen in a SEAL team armory. The AT4 munition can be fired from a confined space in an urban area. The AT4 CS consists of a shock-resistant, fiberglass-reinforced launching tube fitted with a firing mechanism, pop-up sights, a carrying sling, protective covers, and bumpers. The recoilless design is superior to that of rocket-type weapons for confined space applications. (Photo: Dave Gatley)*

BOTTOM, RIGHT: *An assortment of the MP5N sub-machine gun seen in a SEAL team gun locker. The MP5N Navy Model, developed by H&K especially for the U.S. Navy SEALs, fires from a closed and locked bolt in either the semi-automatic or automatic modes. This provides superior accuracy, especially critical on the first shot, which can mean the difference between life and death. The MP5 fires a 9-mm parabellum round in single shot fire, three-round bursts, or full automatic at 800 rounds per minute. It has a retractable buttstock, a removable suppressor, and illuminating flashlight operated by a pressure switch that is custom-fitted to the pistol grip. The SEALs primarily use the MP5 for counterterror-ism, close quarters combat, hostage rescue, and personal protection operations. It is compact, concealable, durable, maneuverable, and hard-hitting. It is easily controllable and the recoil is extremely smooth, allowing the shooter to obtain highly accurate shot placement. Depending on the mission, the MP5 may be operationally used in conjunction with the M4A1 for increased fire-power. H&K has an MP5SD model for missions where stealth and secrecy require fully integrated sound suppression. It also makes a version called the MP5K Machine Pistol, which weighs only 4.4 pounds, is less than 13 inches in length, and can be fired from inside a specially designed briefcase. This variant has three firing modes: semi, three-round burst, and full automatic. (Photo: Dave Gatley)*

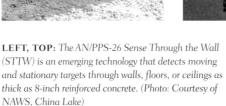

LEFT, TOP: *The AN/PPS-26 Sense Through the Wall (STTW) is an emerging technology that detects moving and stationary targets through walls, floors, or ceilings as thick as 8-inch reinforced concrete. (Photo: Courtesy of NAWS, China Lake)*

LEFT, BOTTOM: *The submersible anti-swimmer grenade can be set for depths of 10 to 100 feet. The grenade is armed after a sequence of events have occurred including reaching a desired depth and a desired passage of time. Failure of any of the events to occur will cause the grenade to be rendered safe, at which point it can be retrieved. (Photo: Courtesy of NAWS, China Lake.)*

ABOVE, CENTER: *Continued training of students in SEAL Qualification Training, seen here at the Imperial County NSW Desert Training Facility, Camp Billy*

Machen, east of the small community of Niland, California. Training at Niland includes live firing exercises with hand grenades and Claymore mines. Future training will include nighttime exercises using night vision equipment. (Photo: Dave Gatley)

ABOVE, RIGHT: *Naval special warfare members test the capabilities of a new night vision target system on a .50 caliber machine gun using tracer ammunition. (Photo: Photographer's Mate 2nd Class Eric S. Logsdon / US Navy)*

This Gen III twin-tube goggles is a ruggedized Navy qualified system that offers dual-channel depth perception. It can be handheld or helmet mounted, and it has improved flash response to maintain sharp image detail even through flares or lights. A 25-mm eye relief allows use with masks or goggles. (Photo: Greg E. Mathieson Sr. / NSW Publications, LLC)

Both mammal programs began in 1974, under the command and control of IUWG-1, at NAB, Coronado, where mammal pens were constructed. SEAL operators were assigned to IUWG-1 as trainers and handlers; most were Vietnam veterans. Although the SEAL operators were required to maintain basic diving and parachuting skills, they were essentially excused from classic SEAL missions. It represented shore duty for the men, although they could be sent on temporary duty out of the area. The sea lions were used on several missile tests, the dolphins on fewer. Transporting the dolphins was a logistical nightmare.

The marine mammal capability was transferred to the U.S. Navy's EOD program in 1981. There were two basic reasons for this transfer: SEALs were accepting increasing worldwide deployments, and EOD was a more reasoned mission for the program, considering the EOD mine exploitation role.

On the level of developing equipment for SEALs—and formerly UDT frogmen—the time line was laboriously slow. During World War II, slates and lead lines were considered modern tools for measuring depth and beach gradients. UDT men would swim through a prospective landing beach taking depth soundings every twenty-five yards. Each UDT was organized to support a Marine Corps division. The swimmers would plot a chart showing sloping gradients and potential obstacles, natural and artificial. It is done electronically today. Today, as in World War II, obstacles are identified—and swimmers plan how to blow them up or, if amenable with the overall amphibious plan, outflank them.

Prior to Vietnam, SEALs and their predecessors always paddled their tactical IBSs (Inflatable Boat, Small). During Vietnam the teams adapted to outboard motors and, during the 1970s, they acquired modernized versions of the IBS and began a program to silence the motors. The French company Zodiac had a worldwide reputation for producing inflatable boats—SEALs call them CRRCs, for

Layout of the training kit, which is similar to the SOTVS Kit issued to Scouts and Snipers when they finish their advanced training. PIC Course - 2 wks; Scout Course - 4 wks; Sniper - 6 wks. Kit: 1- DSLR; Lenses - 1/400mm IS tele; 28-135mm; 2 - 2X tele-extenders; Thales MBITR - std radio (UHF, VHF, SAT, Data); Kowa Spotting Scope - TSN #664 ED w/20-60 zoom eyepiece; WATEC Adapter + Low-Light, and Color Camera; SOC-HD (Spec OP CamCorder) - ruggedized; Steiner Binocs; Remote Shutter; GEMS NV (Integrity Data) (MicroSoft) MVM001 (PVS-18 similar); Rail/ Universal mount; Manifroto Tripods; USB Reader & multi/SD & CF; Filters -primarily Polarized. (Photo: Dave Gatley)

Combat Rubber Raiding Crafts. The Zodiac CRRC was adopted by the SEALs and has become the standard throughout the special operations community.

Wet suits to protect against cold water came after World War II. Today's wet suits are technical marvels. Face masks have come a long way, too; SDV operators use a full-face diving mask that permits communications between pilot and navigator. Even swim fins have evolved into energy-saving devices of many designs. SEAL operators pick their preference—except in BUD/S when all swimmers have identical models. Underwater compass boards have evolved; in 1965, and for a few years following, compass boards had a luminous compass and depth gauge. Today's models are electronic. Night vision was rudimentary in the Vietnam era; helicopter

CENTER, LEFT: This handheld, CNVD-Tor Clip-on Night Vision Device Thermal allows the operator to see clearly anything that is generating heat—like humans that may be hiding in brush or other confusing surroundings that ordinary night vision infrared devices might not reveal. These are a huge advantage for the operator entering an area that offers no starlight, moonlight, or other distant light sources. (Photo: Dave Gatley)

CENTER, RIGHT: With the introduction of the AN/PSQ-20 Enhanced Night Vision Device (ENVG) developed by ITT Industries, Northrop Grumman, and Insight Technology, the SEAL operator and SWCC crewman can now see in all light levels, adverse weather, and battlefield abscurant conditions. The ENVG combines traditional night vision technology, called image intensification, with thermal sensors. A thermal, or infrared, imager senses the temperature differences and warmer items appear brighter on a display. The fusion of both technologies results in night vision goggles that merge the strengths of image intensification—a clear, sharp green-tinted picture with the advantages of thermal infrared to see practically under any environmental condition. (Photo: Courtesy of NVESD.)

BOTTOM: The view as seen through one of the newest night vision devices—the AN/PSQ-20 Enhanced Night Vision Goggle (ENVG). The device incorporates both infrared and thermal imaging technologies. This technology enables the operator to distinguish human and other targets in near or total darkness. (Photo: Courtesy of NVESD.)

ABOVE: *At times SEALs wear helmet mounted cameras, which can record or be transmitted real time back to a command center or others with a need to watch the operation unfold, such as in the operation take down of Osama Bin Laden. It's also used as a training aid for the operators to review the mission or exercise to make corrections as need be. It also provides legal evidence in the event of lawsuits against the US Navy. (Photo: Greg E. Mathieson Sr. / NSW Publications, LLC)*

ABOVE, CENTER: *This SEAL is seen wearing the Colt M4A1 Close Quarter Battle Receiver (CQBR) with the Trijcoon Advanced Combat Optical Gunsight (ACOG), which is a fixed rifle-scope with an illuminated reticle pattern that marks a target. The weapons system was tested by the Naval Surface Warfare Center, Crane Division for USSOCOM. The M4A1 has a 14.5 inch barrel length, weighs 5.95 pounds, and fires the NATO 5.56 x 45 mm round. (Photo: Greg E. Mathieson Sr. / NSW Publications, LLC)*

ABOVE, RIGHT: *Unlike other military units in the United States military, SEAL operators have great latitude regarding uniform outfitting during operating and training exercises. Most outfitting decision involve combat loading and comfort. Cover and concealment are always considerations. The operator in this picture is seen wearing three separate and distinct uniform configurations. (Photo: Greg E. Mathieson Sr. / NSW PUblications, LLC)*

A U.S. Navy SEAL Combat Assault Dog (CAD) ready for combat. Like their human colleagues, CADs may also be equipped with a self-inflating lifejacket in the event that they wind up in water. The weight of their gear could otherwise pull them downward, but these dogs are highly trained to handle almost any threat that comes their way. (Photo: Greg E. Mathieson Sr. / NSW Publications, LLC)

pilots fly with it today, and SEALs use it on missions. Sniper rifles are state-of-the-art, as are the attached scopes.

SCUBA has improved the most. SEALs once used basic open-circuit compressed-air rigs, but today they use oxygen rebreathers. The German Draeger company closed-circuit SCUBA is the NSW gear of choice, capable of up to three hours underwater. Other mixed-gas rigs are available for selected operations.

Throughout NSW history, teams have co-opted gear from other services, primarily the Army and Marine Corps. This is not unusual, because services are assigned lead positions by the secretary of defense. We are going to present a range of operational equipment unique to NSW. Most of it "gets wet," unlike the other USSOCOM services. NSW is oriented to the maritime environment even though of late it has been oriented to the GWOT in Afghanistan mountains and Iraq deserts. We will look at the gear through the SEAL prism of sea, air, and land. Where an operator can enhance the presentation, we have sought models, all actual SEALs with identities obscured. For convenience of reference, some equipment discussed in other chapters is included here.

Finally, presenting the entire NSW table of organizational equipment would outstretch the limits of a single chapter in words and photography. We will present the major systems here and show some of the more esoteric communications–electronics technologies, avoiding in-depth technical data that would not contribute to the overall story.

SEA

The distinguishing attributes SEALs bring to USSOCOM is the capability to clandestinely infiltrate from the sea using a variety of diving apparatus, SDVs, submarines, and DDSs, and the significant surface mobility capabilities accomplished by the SWCCs with their combatant craft. Maritime special operations include major SEAL-SWCC capabilities not matched in other SOF units; SWCCs operate all surface combatant craft providing all SEAL mobility except the CRRC, which remains a stable craft still employed by the SEAL teams.

Mark V Special Operations Craft

The Mk V special operations craft (SOC) was the workhorse of the SBTs, but was removed from the active inventory in 2012. The eighty-foot Mk V draws five feet, has a top speed of forty-five knots, and can transport a sixteen-man SEAL platoon with four CRRCs or an SDV detachment. The craft cruises in Sea State 3 between twenty-five and thirty-five knots. It has a cruise range of 550 nautical miles and a payload of 6,500 pounds. It is outfitted with specially designed ergonomic seats for the crew of four and passengers. The Mk V is not a deep "V" hull craft, so it can be air-lifted; the at-sea ride is rough. (G forces exceeding thirteen have been recorded.) Still, the medium-range craft is central to the maritime missions of NSW. Onboard weapons include two .50-caliber machine guns and 40-mm grenade launchers. SOC deploy in two boat detachments with an MST for maintenance support.

Eleven-Meter Naval Special Warfare Rigid Hull Inflatable Boat

The eleven-meter (thirty-six-foot) RIB is a high-speed, high-buoyancy, extreme weather craft with the primary mission of insertion and extraction of SEALs and other SOFs. The NSW RIB's hull is made of glass-reinforced plastic, which is surrounded by inflatable tubes around the sides to protect operators and assist in sea-keeping. The NSW RIB is capable of forty-five knots and a range of two hundred nautical miles. It is equipped with two 470-horsepower twin Caterpillar 3126 diesels and two Kamewa water jets. It has gun mounts for M-60, M-2, or Mk 19 weapons. The NSW RIB hosts a crew of three and can transport a SEAL squad. Designed for littoral insertion, the NSW RIB can be parachuted into a denied coastal area. The RIB was basically designed to fulfill ship-to-shore transport of SOFs, normally SEALs.

Special Operations Craft, Riverine

The thirty-three-foot aluminum SOCR has a nine-foot beam and two-foot draft. Powered by twin diesels and water jets, its top speed is forty-two knots. It is heli-

The Semi-Autonomous Hydrographic Reconnaissance Vehicle (SAHRV) system used by Naval Special Warfare (NSW) forces in the conduct of mine countermeasures (MCM) and hydrographic reconnaissance operations in the very shallow water (VSW) regime. The SAHRV is a semi-autonomous (un-tethered) underwater vehicle and auxiliary equipment. The SAHRV was developed from the Woods Hole Oceanographic Institute (WHOI), based on the technology of another oceanographic research vehicle known as the Remote Environmental Monitoring Unit (REMUS). (Photo: Dave Gatley)

copter deployable and can operate with 7.62 medium machine guns and .50-caliber heavy machine guns. A SWCC crew of five normally operates the craft. It can transport SEAL elements in restricted inland waters.

Combat Rubber Raiding Craft

The CRRC is the real backbone of SEAL over the beach (OTB) operations. The standard model is the Zodiac F-470, a fifteen-foot inflatable with a six-foot beam capable of transporting eight SEALs (or other SOFs) at a speed of eighteen knots. The CRRC can be launched from a submerged or surfaced submarine or from the deck of any ship with crane capabilities. The Mk V SOC is designed to launch and recover the CRRC using a ramp system. The CRRC displaces (weighs) 265 pounds without engine—thirty-five or fifty-five horsepower—and fuel. The CRRC has attachable fuel bladders. Each team gets twenty craft before deployment. The NSW LOGSU detachments maintain the CRRCs.

TOP, LEFT AND RIGHT: *The LAR V Draeger rebreather is a closed-circuit underwater breathing apparatus. Running on 100 percent oxygen, all expelled breath is recycled into the closed circuit where it is filtered for carbon dioxide. The result is a complete elimination of expelled bubbles, which makes the Draeger ideal for clandestine amphibious operations. With a maximum depth of 30 feet, the LAR V Draeger rebreather cannot operate as deep as SCUBA systems. The unit's relatively small size and front-worn configuration makes it suitable for shallow water operation. Dive duration is affected by depth, water temperature, and oxygen consumption rate. (Photo: Greg E. Mathieson Sr. / NSW Publications, LLC)*

RIGHT, CENTER: *The TAC-100 Underwater Navigation Board is the original navigation platform used by professional divers around the world, and the basic navigation board that all SEALs*

training is conducted with. The TAC-100 integrates the TAC100-2 Underwater Compass onto a rugged and lightweight high-impact plastic console with easy-to-grip handles. Internal lubber lines keep the diver on course. A built-in adjustable chem-light holder on the console illuminates the compass for night operations and is usually customized to give off the least amount of light that might reveal the operator to anyone above water. (Photo: Greg E. Mathieson Sr. / NSW Publications, LLC)

RIGHT, BOTTOM: *The Aqua Lung Atlantis Diving Bouyancy Jacket is inflatable from two emergency cylinders, by mouth or optional MP inflator. This compensator allows the ability to adjust and control the overall buoyancy of the diver and the diver's heavy equipment; allowing the diver to achieve neutral buoyancy, remain at constant depth, or descend or ascend in a controlled way. (Photo: Greg E. Mathieson Sr. / NSW Publications, LLC)*

SEAL Delivery Vehicles, Dry Deck Shelters, Advanced SEAL Delivery System

Although first introduced into UDTs in 1947, the first truly operational SDVs were not available until the early 1960s. The SDVs are free-flooding submersibles capable of holding six men—pilot, navigator, and four SEALs. SDV operational parameters are classified, but the craft can navigate and maneuver completely submerged from a host submarine outfitted with a DDS. SDV training profiles routinely include harbor and port penetration as well as insertion of SEAL reconnaissance teams into denied areas.

Submarine DDS operations are by far the most complex underwater missions conducted by NSW, with success relying on synchronized efforts between the host submarine crew and NSW operators—SEALs operating the SDVs and Navy divers operating the DDSs. The DDS capability was introduced into the fleet in the mid-1980s. It is a forty-foot-long appendage that weighs 65,000 pounds and is fitted to a host submarine behind the sail. Depending on the host submarine, one or two DDSs may be embarked. The DDS can be used to transport and launch an SDV or to lock out combat swimmers. The DDS comprises three compartments: a transfer trunk that allows passage between the submarine and DDS, a hyperbaric chamber, and an elongated chamber that acts as an open-ocean interface to house either one SDV or a complement of CRRC and swimmers.

The ASDS is attached to a host submarine in the same fashion as the DDS. It is a one-atmosphere dry submersible or minisubmarine. A single ASDS vehicle was to have been the first of six submersibles, intended to clandestinely carry SEALs in a dry environment from the submarine to the infiltration areas, where a transport compartment would be flooded to allow the SEALs to lock out and conduct a mission. On 9 November 2008, however, the ASDS lithium-ion batteries were being charged when a fire erupted and burned for more than six hours. Firefighters sealed the ASDS to put out the fire and continued to hose it down to cool hot spots. It remained sealed for more than two weeks before the hatch was opened. As a result of the fire, the ASDS program was terminated, and USSOCOM and the Navy are exploring future program options. Four submarines and the new Virginia class have been converted to accommodate the DDS and ASDS.

Underwater Breathing Apparatus

SEALs first learn underwater diving with open-circuit compressed-air SCUBA. These rigs are essentially the same ones that civilian sport and commercial divers use. NSW uses open circuit for most administrative duties. Set-up is a relatively simple matter of checking attachments and ensuring the flask is recharged properly. On the operational side, SEALs use exclusively the German design Draeger LAR V, a self-contained pure-

LEFT: *Schematic drawings for the LAR V Draeger rebreather. The unit's relatively small size and front-worn configuration makes it suitable for shallow water operation. Dive duration is affected by depth, water temperature, and oxygen consumption rate. (Photo: Courtesy of Draeger)*

RIGHT: *Twin SCUBA tanks are lined up on special rolling racks, ready for diving exercises at the BUD/S training facility. Maintaining, testing, and refilling are daily affairs that are meticulously addressed for safety. Each rack is mounted on wheels to enable the transfer from one area to another without having to individually transport each. (Photo: Greg E. Mathieson Sr. / NSW Publications, LLC)*

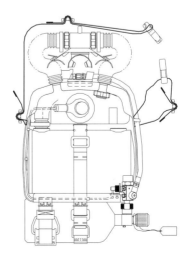

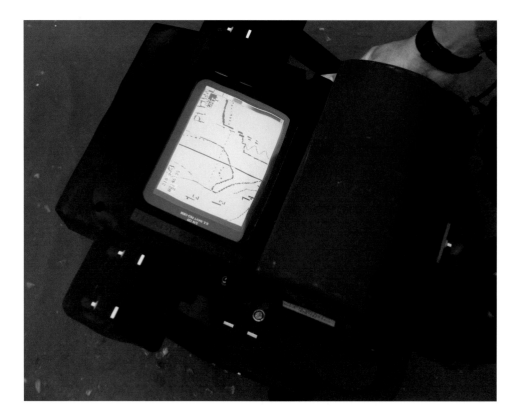

oxygen rebreather that emits no telltale bubbles. The Draeger is the mainstay of SEAL underwater insertion missions. The diver's exhaled breath is chemically scrubbed (cleansed of carbon dioxide) and recirculated to the diver with on-demand oxygen from the compressed canister. It provides a three-hour mission duration, but is limited to a depth of twenty-five feet owing to the potential for oxygen toxicity to humans under pressure. (Short excursions below this depth can be made, but with caution.) On a typical SDV insertion mission, SEALs and passengers will often be equipped with the Mk 16 UBA that provides a closed-circuit, mixed-gas capability, allowing SEALs to work and operate at deeper depths for extended hours. While in the SDV, the divers will routinely breathe boat-compressed air until departing to go on a mission. Dive pro-files on SDV missions are exacting and are backed up with electronic sensors.

Underwater Accessories

No SEAL diver descends without a solid list of operational accessories. SEALs outfit with buoy compensators, life jackets, diver's knife, emergency flares, wet suit, face mask, and swim fins. Many photographs have displayed Navy SEALs emerging from the sea bristling with weapons and other sundry gear, but in fact the diver takes only the equipment he needs to accomplish his mission. An important accoutrement is the underwater compass board that includes a waterproof compass and depth gauge. Neoprene wet suits protect the SDV divers from prolonged missions in coldwater environments. They vary according to personal preference and available options offered by the vendor. SDV operators have specially designed suits, inasmuch as these SEALs spend the most time training underwater. SDV operators wear full-face diving masks capable of compartment communication.

AIR

Air operations include transport to the target area, then insertion by parachute jumping, fast roping, or casting into water. Parachuting includes static line, HALO, and HAHO. Frogmen started jumping in earnest in the late 1950s, when selected operators were detailed to Fort Benning for Army Jump School. In the mid-1960s, SEALs became free-fall qualified, some attending Army HALO courses. All SEALs are required to be static line and HALO qualified. The new training courses have already been discussed, but it is yet another mark of how all NSW training has matured. In addition to parachuting, SEALs fast rope into target areas, using padded gloves to slide down long hawsers. HALO involves jumping, free falling to a lower altitude before deploying the main canopy. HAHO has the jumper deploying his canopy soon after leaving the aircraft at extreme altitudes and gliding a great distance over the ground before landing at a predetermined drop zone.

Aircraft

SEALs use all available airframes used by SOF. The Air Force provides specially configured aircraft that can insert SEALs with parachutes. Foremost is the C-130 airframe. USAF MH-53M Pave Low helicopters are electronically oriented to avoid enemy sensing systems; Army MH-60 Black Hawk helicopters also are available to SEALs. The Army MH-47 Chinook has been a standard insertion helicopter available to SOF: for many years SEALs jumped from Navy CH-46 airframes, similar to the MH-47, but smaller. These Chinooks are being phased out in favor of the upgraded Navy MH-60S Knighthawk; the Knighthawk has been in service since 2003, and participated in OIF. Knighthawks are multi-mission airframes tasked with special operations support, CSAR, and airborne mine countermeasures. Knighthawk incorporates design features from the Army Black Hawk and Navy Seahawk. It has a crew of four and transports thirteen SEALs with combat gear. Weight trade-offs are necessary depending on the mission; a demolition raid

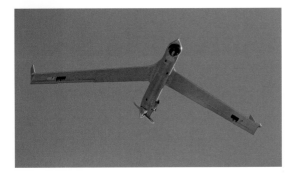

TOP AND BOTTOM, CENTER: *SWC SBT-12 launch of Scan Eagle off San Clemente Island. Navy SEAL SWCC operators launch a Scan Eagle UAV (Unmanned Aerial Vehicle) from a SWCC Mk V SOC for the first time, testing the capability and the new launching hardware employed to do it. This is seconds after the launch with the UAV in the air. (Photo: Dave Gatley)*

BOTTOM, LEFT: *Retrieval of the Scan Eagle from the pitching and rolling deck of the Mk V SOC is a matter of guiding/flying the UAV toward a stretched wire and snagging the line with one of the wing tips. Once captured, the deck crew can retrieve the UAV and prepare it for its next flight. (Photo: Dave Gatley)*

BOTTOM, RIGHT: *The Scan Eagle is seen here doing a fly-over the Mk V SOC, where the on board camera can be seen on its nose. (Photo: Dave Gatley)*

ABOVE, LEFT TO RIGHT: *Somewhere in Afghanistan, this General Atomics MQ-9 Reaper, an unmanned aerial vehicle (UAV) developed by General Atomics Aeronautical Systems, is ready for action. The MQ-9 is the first hunter-killer UAV designed for long-endurance, high-altitude surveillance. It is loaded with four AGM-114 Hellfire II air-to-ground missiles, and two GBU-38 JDAM (Joint Direct Attack Munition) bombs that are guided by its synthetic apeture radar. (Photo: Dave Gatley)*

will allow fewer passengers to accommodate the bulk munitions.

Parachutes

SEALs rely on Army parachutes or static-line operations. The standard T-10D (parabolic-shape main parachute) is being replaced by the T-11 (nonmaneuverable canopy personnel parachute system). Army basic training has students jumping from 1,250 feet; the SEAL course likes it a little higher, jumping from 2,000 to 2,500 feet above ground level. SEAL requalification likes it even higher, up around 3,500 feet, to afford the jumper time to try turns, stalls, and so on. A real-world operation, of course, would dictate the opening altitude. (Army Rangers often go out of the plane at five hundred feet, time for two swings in the harness before they're on the ground!)

Free-fall parachuting, or HALO, is required of all SEALs today. The parachutist exits the plane at a high altitude, up to 25,000 feet above ground level, and free falls to an opening altitude anywhere between 2,500 and 4,000 feet. (For comparison, civilian skydivers normally exit the plane at 13,000 feet and open between 2,000 and 5,000 feet, depending on training and United States Parachute Association license status—students obviously open higher.) SEALs train—and teams use—the MT-2XX military free-fall parachute manufactured by Para-Flite, Inc. It is a 370-square-foot canopy capable of a suspended weight of 360 pounds. These self-inflating "ram-air" airfoils known as para-foils provide control of speed and

HALO/HAHO gear, which are acronyms that describe methods of delivering personnel, equipment, and supplies from a transport aircraft at a high altitude via free-fall parachute insertion. HALO (High Altitude Low Opening) and HAHO (High Altitude High Opening) are also known as Military Free Fall (MFF). In the HALO technique, the parachutist opens his parachute at a low altitude after free-falling for a period of time, while in the HAHO technique, the parachutist opens his parachute at a high altitude just a few seconds after jumping from the aircraft. Added to this collection of jump gear is the full military pack, an almost hidden weapon under the SEAL's left arm. (Photos: Dave Gatley)

direction. These parachutes have built-in forward speeds upward of twenty-five miles per hour; it is important that the jumper land into the wind, like an aircraft. All this is complicated by the HAHO discipline that involves gliding longer from high altitude—requiring specialized survival gear because of low oxygen levels and cold temperatures.

Fast Roping and Rappelling Techniques

These techniques are accomplished from helicopters. Fast roping was developed by SEALs to get a squad down into the restricted area of a ship without having to land the chopper. A two-inch diameter nylon line is extended to the deck (or surface). The inserting SEALs use fast-rope gloves to protect their hands while they slide down the line. SEALs used to use mountaineering rappelling techniques, but have moved to the fast-rope method almost exclusively.

Special Procedure Insertion and Extraction System

Developed during the Vietnam era, the special procedure insertion and extraction system is usually used to extract a squad from a restricted area. SEALs on the

TOP: *SEALs of NSW Group II conduct extraction using a Special Patrol Insertion/ Extraction (SPIE) system. Here four SEALs are lifted out, wearing the SPIE rig from a hovering helicopter of the Army's 160th Special Operations Aviation Regiment (SOAR-A) "The Night Stalkers." (Photo: Greg E. Mathieson Sr. / NSW Publications, LLC)*

CENTER: *Predator MQ-1 based in Afghanistan. The General Atomics MQ-1 Predator is an unmanned aerial vehicle (UAV) which the Air Force describes as a MALE (medium-altitude, long-endurance) UAV system. It can serve in a reconnaissance role and also fire two AGM-114 Hellfire missiles. The aircraft, in use since 1995, has seen combat over Afghanistan, Pakistan, Bosnia, Serbia, Iraq, and Yemen. In addition, since 2005, U.S. Customs and Border Protection uses the aircraft (unarmed) for border patrol within the U.S. The MQ-1 Predator's fully operational system consists of four air vehicles (with sensors), a ground control station (GCS), and a Predator primary satellite link communication suite. (Photo: Dave Gatley)*

BOTTOM: *The MQ-9 Reaper at Bagram Air Base, Afghanistan. The airplane is the size of a jet fighter, powered by a turboprop engine, and is one-third larger than its cousin the Predator. It is able to fly at 300 mph and reach 50,000 feet. It is outfitted with infrared, laser and radar targeting, and a ton and a half of guided bombs and missiles. Its pilot, as it bombs targets in Iraq, will sit at a video console 7,000 miles away in Nevada. (Photo by Senior Airman Larry E. Reid Jr./ USAF)*

The WASP III Small Unmanned Aircraft System developed by AeroViroment is a handheld unmanned aerial vehicle (UAV) ideal for SEAL use in providing beyond-line-of-sight situational awareness. The unit has two onboard cameras that provide real-time intelligence to the operators in the field. Also equipped with a GPS, it can operate autonomously from takeoff to recovery. (Photo: Courtesy of AeroViroment Inc.)

ground attach themselves to an extended hook-up line attached from the helicopter. Snap links attach the man to the line—all great fun, especially if you're being hoisted out of a hot area!

LAND

Land operations usually make up the bulk of SEAL operations, such as small-unit tactics. SEALs use small arms and crew-served weapons, knives, demolitions, lensatic compasses, communications gear, global positioning systems (GPSs), cold-weather clothing, skis, snowshoes, tents, rappelling gear, and sundry other gear commonly associated with camping.

Desert Patrol Vehicle

The NSW desert patrol vehicle (DPV) is essentially a converted dune buggy, and would be at home on the Baja road race. DPVs are powered by two-hundred-horsepower VW engines. They have a payload of 1,500 pounds, can hit eighty miles per hour, and have a range of 210 miles. Optimal fuel bladders are available to extend the range. The vehicles mount a .50-caliber machine gun and a rocket launcher.

BELOW: The SEALs side-by-side vehicle: SEAL operators have chosen a beefed-up version of the Kawasaki Teryx RUV (Recreational Utility Vehicle). The vehicle replaces the DPV (Desert Patrol Vehicle) type dune buggy, which was much larger. Carrying two SEALs and their gear, the Teryx pulls, pushes, climbs, carries, and does just about anything SEALs need. It features a wider track for a safe ride while still keeping it narrow enough for tight trails or a pickup truck bed in the type country terrain and roads they travel on (IRAQ & certainly Afghanistan). The side-by-side can travel trails that no HMMWV, MRAP, or other combat vehicle can even begin to traverse. Its 90-degree 749cc V-Twin engine is the largest and most powerful in its class. (Photo: Dave Gatley)

RIGHT: The Logistical Support Unit (LOGSU) maintains a fleet of a variety of configured High Mobility Multipurpose Wheeled Vehicles (HMMWV) and shipping containers for equipment depending on the missions of the Naval Special Warfare operators and support teams. (Photo: Greg E. Mathieson Sr. / NSW Publications, LLC)

SEAL operators drive though the streets of Fallujah, Iraq, in a couple of Mine Resistant Ambush Protected (MRAP) vehicles outfitted with CROWS weapon systems and numerous communications systems. These armored fighting vehicles were designed for surviving improvised explosive device (IED) attacks and ambushes. The CROWS system allows for defeating the enemy with heavy firepower without exiting the vehicle. (Photo: Greg E. Mathieson Sr. / NSW Publications, LLC)

Desert patrol vehicles being used in Afghanistan allow for fast movement where most heavy armored Humvees can't go. Carrying three SEALs, a .50-caliber machine gun and satellite communications and GPS, these vehicles allow the operators to quickly move into a position and leave just as fast. (Photo: DoD)

The DPV has a three-man crew. Missions include fast attack and deep strike; surveillance and targeting; target-acquisition missions; reconnaissance and scouting; command and control; and peacekeeping. During Operation Desert Storm an NSWG-1 DPV detachment led American forces into Kuwait City. The OIC was an Army Special Forces major on exchange with the group. The detachment's primary mission was to be prepared to rescue downed Allied pilots.

After operations in Kuwait, DPV operations and training were suspended and the vehicles were placed in storage. They were brought out during Operation Desert Storm with the mission of rescuing downed pilots. They have again been eliminated from the active inventory of combatant vehicles.

High-Mobility Multipurpose Wheeled Vehicle

The SEALs suddenly thrust into Afghanistan needed armed mobility. The high-mobility multipurpose wheeled vehicle (HMMWV, or Humvee) was the solution; the SEALs had none in their inventory, however. They quickly acquired four, and broke all records modifying the vehicles to host a machine-gun mount and some small-arms protection. SEALs now have a robust inventory and variety of tactical ground mobility vehicles available and supported by the LOGSUs for training and combat use.

ABOVE: The CROWS or XM153 Common Remotely Operated Weapons Station system is designed for the SEAL operator to sit inside the MRAP vehicle and not be exposed to the enemy. Capable of operation under day and night conditions, the CROWS sensor suite includes both video and thermal cameras, as well as a laser rangefinder. Its sensor suite and fire control software permit on-the-move target acquisition and first-burst target engagement. (Photo: Greg E. Mathieson Sr. / NSW Publications, LLC)

RIGHT, TOP: Sometimes the terrain calls for dirt bikes or all-terrain vehicles to get around. LOGSU supplies what the SEALs need and what works for the mission. (Photo: Greg E. Mathieson Sr. / NSW Publications, LLC)

RIGHT, CENTER: LOGSU staff loading up a SEAL team truck with a pallet of ammo and other items. (Photo: Greg E. Mathieson Sr. / NSW Publications, LLC)

BELOW: A member of the WARCOM Naval Special Development Group tests the SOCOM MK23 Heckler and Koch pistol on the range. The match grade pistol was developed as a offensive handgun for USSOCOM SOF units.(Photo: Greg E. Mathieson Sr. / NSW Publications, LLC)

WEAPONS

Shoulder-Fired Weapons

An entire chapter could be written on NSW weapons; indeed, entire books *have* been written on the subject. Here is a tip-of-the-iceberg approach that will highlight the primary weapons in use in the teams. USSOCOM development continues with Army in the lead. A new combat assault rifle is under development—for example, Mk 13, Mk 16, and Mk 17 variants. Today, the M-4A1 carbine is standard; it is descended from the Vietnam-era CAR 15, which had a spotty reputation. During operations in Vietnam, SEALs used the Stoner light machine gun, which fired a 5.56-mm round, same as the Mk 15. They then used the Mk 14, interim replacement for the M-1. It is still in service with the teams. SEALs also used cut-down M-60 machine guns in Vietnam. In the mid-1980s, a couple of things happened. The lightweight M-60 was developed and tested by the East Coast SEALs. As soon as the weapon was approved for service use, the Marine Corps bought them. This M-60 version has a forward handgrip and a lighter weight.

Also during the 1980s, complaints came in from fleet SEALs that an entire new weapons suite was needed. A service-sponsored requirement and competitive contract was advertised to industry, and Germany's Heckler & Koch won the competition with its MP5 series, which is still in service.

We need not delve deeper into technological discussion except to indicate that magazine capacity varies as needed. The system is in use throughout the special operations community. Other rifles are at hand: the sniper series and several models of tactical shotguns, which will be addressed photographically.

Pistols

At one time SEAL pistol preferences depended on which coast an operator served: the East Coast liked the Smith & Wesson .357 Magnum, the West Coast liked the

TOP: *One of a number of unique weapons manufactured by China Lake for the U.S. Navy SEALs during the 1960s was this pump-action, 40-mm grenade launcher, serial #002, which operated like a conventional pump shotgun. Normally an M79 grenade launcher is loaded with one round, fired and reloaded. This specialized model works like a pump-action shotgun, holding numerous rounds of grenades in the tube below. (Photo: Greg E. Mathieson Sr. / NSW Publications, LLC)*

CENTER: *The Mk 1 Underwater Defense Gun, shown here closed and ready to fire, was first introduced in the 1970s—the forefather for today's P11. The Mk 1, a double-action pepper-box weapon, contains a removable cylinder magazine that contains six Mark 59 Mod O projectiles, 4.25-inch-long tungsten darts. With a muzzle velocity of 740f/s, it has an effective underwater range of 30 feet. (Photo: Greg E. Mathieson Sr. / NSW Publications, LLC)*

BOTTOM: *The .50-caliber Springfield sniper rifle was developed in 1968 for the SEALs by China Lake for use in Vietnam. It was never adopted because its large size and weight made it an impractical weapon to carry through jungles. (Photo: Greg E. Mathieson Sr. / NSW Publications, LLC)*

TOP, LEFT: *The prototype of the SOCOM MK23 Heckler and Koch pistol .45-caliber silenced pistol X23 Mod 034B. The match grade pistol was developed as an offensive handgun for USSOCOM SOF units. It was the first to incorporate a .45-caliber pistol with a suppressor, laser aiming module (LAM), and light. (Photo: Greg E. Mathieson Sr. / NSW Publications, LLC)*

TOP, RIGHT: *One of the workhorse weapons of the SEAL teams in Vietnam was the Stoner machine gun, designed by Eugene Stoner in the early 1960s. Coming out at the time of the M-16, the Stoner was a 5.56-caliber weapon known also as the M63A1. This one is serial #00320. In the 1980s the Stoner was phased out and replaced by newer M249 SAW. (Photo: Greg E. Mathieson Sr. / NSW Publications, LLC)*

BOTTOM, LEFT: *One of the first Smith and Wesson 9-mm model 39s, known to the Navy as the Mk Mod 0, 22 Hush Puppy, a silenced pistol designed for the SEAL teams during Vietnam. The name came about in that it was used primarily to silence enemy watchdogs that might give away an operation. (Photo: Greg E. Mathieson Sr. / NSW Publications, LLC)*

BOTTOM, CENTER: *The Sig Sauer P226-9-NAVY is produced to the exact specifications supplied by Navy SEALs, including special corrosion-resistant finish on internal parts and contrast sights. The slides are engraved with an anchor to designate them as Naval Special Warfare pistols. (Photo: Greg E. Mathieson Sr. / NSW Publications, LLC)*

BOTTOM, RIGHT: *Walther PPK pistol: In 1978, Ranger Manufacturing of Gadsden, Alabama, was licensed to manufacture the PPK and PPK/S; this version was distributed by Interarms of Alexandria, Virginia. This license was eventually canceled. Starting in 2002, Smith & Wesson began manufacturing the PPK and PPK/S under license. (Photo: Greg E. Mathieson Sr. / NSW Publications, LLC)*

M-1911A1 .45-caliber pistol. With the coming of USSOCOM, the urge to standardize became paramount. It was difficult to explain to the USSOCOM commander why he needed to buy separate pistol systems for each group of SEAL teams based on geographical location. Also in the mid-1980s, a push was under way within the DoD to standardize all services on the Berretta 9-mm. At the time, some Army special operations organizations were determined to stick with the Colt .45. Pistols used one time or another by SEALs were made by Smith & Wesson, Heckler & Koch, Glock, Sig Sauer—all had competing 9-mm handguns. Then around 1989, the Navy's weapons center at Crane, Indiana, had a requirement for a unique USSOCOM .45-caliber maritime pistol system, later termed the Mk 23 Mod 0 after it was developed by Heckler & Koch. In 1996, it was adopted as a service pistol under the Mk 23 Mod 0 designation. The Mk 23 provides match grade accuracy while exceeding the most stringent operational requirements for a combat handgun. NAVSEA sponsors a mobile weapons repair van that visits each group location to perform maintenance checks with team armories. Local SEAL team armorers are outstanding in their knowledge and expertise at maintaining and refurbishing small arms.

With the exception of the occasional AK-47, SEAL weapons inventories have been streamlined. Suffice it to say that operators train with the arms they will deploy with. Accuracy and complete familiarity with a reasonable suite of arms is the philosophy today, especially in the GWOT.

Demolitions

"Demo" has always been the hallmark of Navy frogmen—from the original combat demolition units, to UDTs, to present-day SEAL teams. Demolition training sets the SEAL teams apart from other SOF organizations. Every team, every operator, is demolitions qualified, unlike, for example, Army Special Forces. From the days of World War II, the NCDUs used hand-emplaced explosives to demolish beachfront obstacles, natural and artificial. Demolitions were used in Vietnam by UDT elements to flatten sand bars and create canals in the delta. Explosive breaching techniques matured with the coming of terrorism and hostage taking; flash bang grenades—essentially, stun shockers—are used in hostage situations. Other explosive configurations are used to take down secured doors prior to a room clearance operation—an integral part of which is exceptional accuracy in discriminatory shooting. (SEALs rank

THE SOPMOD M-4 ACCESSORY KIT

AN/PVS-14
Universal Pocketscope

EoTech M553
Holographic Weapon Sight

Trijicon ACOG
4x32 TA01NSN

AN/PEQ-15
Advanced Target Pointer,
Illuminator, Aiming Light (ATPIAL)

AN/PAQ-4C
Infrared Aiming Light (IAL)

AN/PVS-17A
Mini Night Vision Sight

M68 Aimpoint CompM2
Close Combat Optic

Trijicon RX01-14
Reflex Sight

AN/PEQ-5
Carbine Visible Laser (CLV)

AN/PEQ-2A
Target Pointer,
Illuminator, Aiming Light (TPIAL)

LMT SOPMOD
Crane Buttstock

Knight's Armament
Backup Iron Sight

A.R.M.S #40
Backup Iron Sight

U.S. Rifle
5.56 mm
M4A1 Carbine

Knight's Armament Rail Interface System (RIS)

Knight's Armament
QD Flash Suppressor

Surefire M962XM07
Millennium Universal
WeaponLight System

Knight's Armament QD NT-4
Sound Suppressor

LMT
Backup Iron Sight

Matech
Backup Iron Sight

M203
Leaf Sight

Surefire Millenium M900A
Vertical Foregrip
WeaponLight System

A3 Detachable Carrying Handle

M203A1 40 mm Grenade Launcher with Knight's Armament QD Mount

Knight's Armament
Forward Pistol Grip

ABOVE: *The Special Operations Peculiar MODification (SOPMOD) accessory kit shows all the various attachment systems that the SEALs could use with the M-4 carbine. The attachments are made by various contractors such as ITT Night Vision, Aimpoint, Trijicon, Colt, Surefire, and Knights Armament. (Graphic illustration by Phil Nguyen)*

LEFT: *This SEAL is carrying the new SOF Combat Assault Rifle, or SCAR, which is a modular rifle made by FN Herstal for the U.S. Special Operations Command (SOCOM). This variant is the 7.62-mm version, long barrel. (Photo by Dave Gatley)*

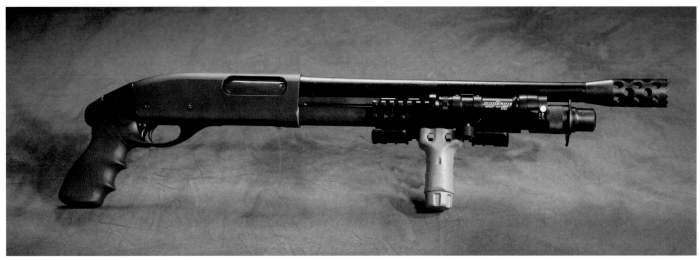

TOP: The M4 carbine is a converted M-16 semiautomatic assault rifle and the most common weapon in the SF inventory. The M4 features a collapsible stock and is readily adaptable to accommodate scopes, night vision devices, and add-ons such as M203 grenade launchers or even shotguns. Firing the standard NATO 5.56-mm round, the M4 is the preferred weapon on the close combat battlefield. (Photo: Greg E. Mathieson Sr. / NSW Publications, LLC)

CENTER: One of the most popular models of submachine gun/machine pistol weapons used by the SEALs is the 9-mm Heckler & Koch MP5-N machine pistol. This one is sporting a silencer. (Photo: Greg E. Mathieson Sr. / NSW Publications, LLC)

BOTTOM: The original AK-47 was one of the first true assault rifles. Even after six decades, the model and its variants remain the most widely used assault rifles in the world because of their durability, low production cost, and ease of use. The SEALs have them in their inventory in the event they need to work in an environment where AK ammo is in abundance and resupply of U.S. ammo is impossible. They are also used periodically in covert operations to better blend in. (Photo: Greg E. Mathieson Sr. / NSW Publications, LLC)

ABOVE, TOP: SEAL teams have always loved the M14 rifles used during the Vietnam War. Though the M14 was replaced by the M16, SEALs have continued their use of the updated M14 Enhanced Battle Rifle (EBR). A 7.62-mm x 51-mm NATO round sniper rifle with silencer and scope was specially made for them at the request of USSOCOM in cooperation with the Naval Special Warfare Center Crane Division and assistance of various weapons manufactures. (Photo: Greg E. Mathieson Sr. / NSW Publications, LLC)

CENTER: A specially modified 12-gauge shotgun, modified by Naval Air Weapons Station, China Lake, which for many years produced unique modifications for the SEAL teams. Here the shotgun has been modified with a pull-back charging lever and a special muzzle on the end of the barrel to help in breaching doors. (Photo: Greg E. Mathieson Sr. / NSW Publications, LLC)

RIGHT: A SEAL carrying an M249 lightweight machine gun (LMG). (Photo: Greg E. Mathieson Sr. / NSW Publications, LLC)

among the foremost shooters in the world.) We will let the photos display some of the bulk demolitions; not much to see, really—C4 is white-looking putty, bulk demo looks like a FedEx package, Bangalore torpedoes (highlighted in the movie *Saving Private Ryan*) look like long, five-inch-wide poles. The haversack demolitions that SEAL swimmers use are interesting: they tie them onto underwater obstacles, tie it all in with detonating cord, fuse it with double-waterproof firing assemblies, and, with the famous line, "Fire in the hole!"—*Boom!*—mission accomplished.

COMMUNICATIONS AND ELECTRONICS

A very important element of NSW operations is the communications and electronics gear SEALs use across the mission spectrum, from peace to war. As was true with the weapons, we would exhaust the allotted pages of this chapter covering it all in technical detail. Communications and electronics—called

SEAL Group-1 conducts a Field Training Exercise (FTX) for COMMS (Communications) that also involves photo and recon training, where scenes are set up that each student is tested and trained to observe, photograph, and communicate to a TOC (Tactical Operations Center). (Photo: Dave Gatley)

The control trailer for the MQ-1 Predator-A and the MQ-9 Reaper Predator B UAV (Unmanned Aerial Vehicle) has two operators manning its flight and targeting at a remote base in Afghanistan. (Photo: Dave Gatley)

comm-ET in the teams—covers the radios, positioning and signaling gear, and cryptologic systems used throughout NSW. These systems are high maintenance. Gone are the UDT days when the AN/PRC-6 walkie-talkie radios from the Korean War made up the communications suite of a platoon. Today, equipment covers all the radio frequencies—HF, VHF, and UHF—and includes man-pack satellite receivers and sensitive GPSs accurate to within a few yards. The importance of communications is seen in operations from Grenada to Afghanistan; from the former conflict came tales of soldiers using pay telephones to connect with the States for air cover. SEAL Lt. Michael Murphy gave his life while making connections with his tactical operations center for urgent support, for which he received the Medal of Honor.

In the not-too-distant past, NSW communicators operating from remote locations would string antennas from trees in order to make HF connections. Later, VHF radios permitted vehicular and aircraft exchanges. UHF radios on

The WARCOM communications team travels around the globe, providing local communications in some of the most austere places in the field, keeping in touch with a variety of locations back in the U.S. and elsewhere. (Photo: Greg E. Mathieson Sr. / NSW Publications, LLC)

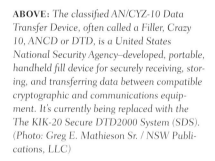

ABOVE: The classified AN/CYZ-10 Data Transfer Device, often called a Filler, Crazy 10, ANCD or DTD, is a United States National Security Agency–developed, portable, handheld fill device for securely receiving, storing, and transferring data between compatible cryptographic and communications equipment. It's currently being replaced with the The KIK-20 Secure DTD2000 System (SDS). (Photo: Greg E. Mathieson Sr. / NSW Publications, LLC)

RIGHT: The aiming and control screen of the CROWS or XM153 Common Remotely Operated Weapons Station system. SEAL operators can sit inside an MRAP and zoom in on a moving target and put the cross-hairs on the enemy and pull the trigger with great accuracy under both day and night conditions. Depending on the configuration, the system can also control grenade launchers and a number of other weapons systems. The CROWS sensor suite includes both video and thermal cameras, as well as a laser rangefinder. Its sensor suite and fire control software permit on-the-move target acquisition and first-burst target engagement. (Photo: Greg E. Mathieson Sr. / NSW Publications, LLC)

the individual operator provide short-range connectivity of a few miles to room-to-room reporting in Close Quarters Battle (CQB) scenarios. The NSW communications vans with satellite connectivity now provide an extended reach for task groups and units in communicating with extended elements on land or at sea. The old picture of a frogman or SEAL breaking down his radio is nearly obsolete; highly skilled fleet technicians are attached to teams today to keep equipment working. Communications are a vital element in successful NSW.

PERSONAL GEAR AND UNIFORMS

Personal SEAL team outfits would fill an L. L. Bean catalog! SEALs operate in the tropics, in the desert, in mountains, and in forests, both Alpine and jungle. The footwear alone is exhaustive. Arctic operations combine science and art, requiring specialized equipment unsuited for temperate zones. Load-bearing vests, ammo pouches, slings of varying dimensions, rappelling harnesses, helmets with integrated communications fixtures, binoculars, eye protection, gloves, thermal and lightweight socks, thermal underwear, layers of clothing, canteens, cooking utensils, tents, sleeping bags, rain gear—in this case the picture is worth

ABOVE: *LOGSU-STORE. JPGNSW Group One's LOGSUG-1 issues a huge amount of high-tech hardware, survival tools, and clothing. This is just a portion of the gear assigned to both advanced trainees and SEAL operators. This is valued at well over $10,000. Flexibility in some of the kits allow the operators to tailor the gear to his way of working. (Photo: Dave Gatley)*

BELOW, LEFT: *SEALs conduct Mountain Warfare operations in camouflaged cold weather gear. (Photo: Chris Desmond / USN)*

BELOW, RIGHT: *Batteries, large and small, pens, pads, locks, compasses, climbing gear, be it something very small or as large as a boat, the LOGSU (Logistical Support Unit) is Naval Special Warfare's one stop shopping store for the specialized gear that the SEALs, SWCC and staff need at any time. (Photo: Greg E. Mathieson Sr. / NSW Publications, LLC)*

RIGHT, TOP: *Wet suits and other dive gear, Gore-Tex, cold weather gear, knives, packs, canteens, NOMEX flight suits, sleeping bags, and every type of personal item for training and missions. This gear is issued to those entering the Basic Underwater Demolition / SEAL (BUD/S) training course. (Photo: Greg E. Mathieson Sr. / NSW Publications, LLC)*

RIGHT, CENTER: *This is a small sampling of the equipment issued to those entering the Basic Underwater Demolition / SEAL (BUD/S). (Photo: Greg E. Mathieson Sr. / NSW Publications, LLC)*

RIGHT, BOTTOM: *A LOGSU staffer taking inventory of personal gear being shipped out of a SEAL base in Iraq. (Photo: Greg E. Mathieson Sr. / NSW Publications, LLC)*

BELOW: *Tactical pants developed and tested by DEVGRP with removable knee pads. Future versions may be utilizing material that is resistant to infrared and thermal imaging. (Photo: Greg E. Mathieson Sr. / NSW Publications, LLC)*

a thousand words. SEALs learn to use all this gear in the year it takes to become qualified operators. Experience from actual operations finds its way back into the NSWCEN and teams in near real time—as soon as the after-action report has been filed. Lessons learned are taken seriously by those preparing to deploy. You want to hit the ground running, so knowledge of what gear to emphasize is critical. Operational procedures are rehearsed extensively week to week, day to day, and hour by hour. The clothing necessary to a particular area of operations is vital, so those deploying want it right. Too late when you are in eight feet of snow in an Afghan mountain pass to miss the right pair of gloves! Great effort at the team and staff levels is expended ensuring NSWRONs are ready to deploy in all respects—equipment, armament, communications, and personal operating gear. The SEAL platoon leadership is responsible for ensuring every man is outfitted correctly.

Fleet Support

Rear ADM (SEAL) George Worthington
USN (Ret)

CHAPTER 10

FLEET SUPPORT

Rear Adm. (SEAL) George Worthington, USN (Ret.)

PAGES 252–253: *SEALs sit ready in the doorways with their Zodiac suspended below a U.S. Army HH-60H Seahawk belonging to the 160th Special Operations Aviation Regiment (SOAR) Night Stalkers, as they prepare for a water insertion. (Photo: Greg E. Mathieson Sr. / NSW Publications, LLC)*

BELOW: *A SEAL Delivery Vehicle Team (SDV) perform a fast-roping exercise from a MH-60S Seahawk helicopter to the topside of Los Angeles–class fast attack submarine USS Toledo (SSN 769). (Photo: Journalist 3rd Class Davis J. Anderson, USN)*

N SW TRADITIONALLY RELIED ON THE FLEET FOR SUPPORT, BUT the terrorist attacks of 9/11 changed that. The bulk of NSW forces operate on shore—first in Afghanistan, today in Iraq—with little contact with the operational fleets.

In addition to the blue-water surface and subsurface capabilities, naval aviation assets are an increasingly important element in the Navy SEAL support package. Since the dark days of Vietnam, today's improved helicopter capabilities remain integral in the air component of SEAL team capabilities. These unique naval assets perform a myriad of missions for the fleet—in addition to providing service support for embarked SEAL platoons. The backbone of the fleet is a standard HH-60 variant helicopter, the same basic airframe as the Army Black Hawk. These fantastic choppers are workhorses of the fleet and are at home at sea and

inserting over water. We will discuss these platforms in detail and display their unique configurations for supporting Navy SEAL operators.

SURFACE SHIPS IN SUPPORT OF SEALS

The 2006 QDR stated, "Special Operations Forces will exploit Afloat Forward Staging Bases (AFSB) to provide more flexible and sustainable locations from which to operate globally." The 2008 DoD "Guidance for Developing the Force" stated that one of the key global posture priorities for DoD was to "Develop options to support strengthened presence of SOF and other expeditionary forces in the operating regions." Staging SEALs, SWCCs, and other SOF afloat is not a new concept.

In the years before establishment of USSOCOM, SEALs and their NSWG commanders reported administratively to the Navy surface force commanders in the Atlantic and Pacific Fleets. Until 1983, the UDTs were doctrinally tied to Surface Amphibious Force and operationally and routinely deployed with the ARGs to the Pacific and Mediterranean areas. The SEAL teams had no amphibious responsibilities and routinely conducted joint and combined training and exercised frequently overseas with foreign counterparts. All UDTs were eliminated in April 1983, and reestablished and reorganized as SEAL and SDV teams; thus, SEAL platoons continued to deploy with the ARGs to satisfy the traditional UDT mission of pre-assault reconnaissance and demolition of obstacles. This nontraditional mission resulted in

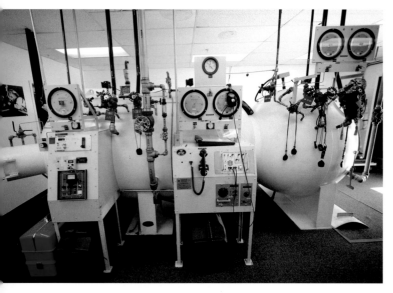

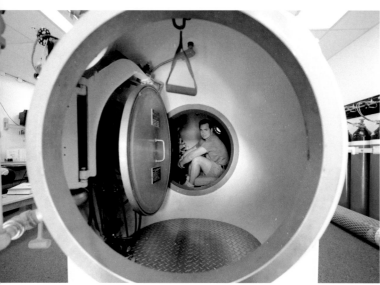

ABOVE, TOP: *The decompression chamber of the Naval Special Warfare Training Center, also known as a recompression or hyperbolic oxygen therapy chamber, is a device used to allow divers to readjust to normal atmospheric pressure. As with any organization utilizing a number of SCUBA divers, there is also a dive medicine section to monitor divers and stand ready in the event an emergency arrises. (Photo: Greg E. Mathieson Sr. / NSW Publications, LLC)*

CENTER: *The hyperbaric chamber at the Naval Special Warfare Training Center in Coronado, California, is used in the event of decompression sickness during dive training with new recruits. (Photo: Greg E. Mathieson Sr. / NSW Publications, LLC)*

RIGHT: *The MQ-1 Predator is an unmanned aerial vehicle (UAV), described as a MALE (medium-altitude, long-endurance) UAV system. The Predator conducts reconnaissance and can fire two AGM-114 Hellfire missiles in support of all military missions. It is protected here in an older hardened aircraft shelter. (Photo by Dave Gatley)*

the SEALs becoming weak in many of their air and land warfare skills because of nonuse while they were deployed afloat. Many efforts were made to shore base the SEALs at the NSWUs or other locations, where they could train and respond when the ARG commander needed them; this concept met with considerable resistance from amphibious commanders, however, and was rejected.

From a historical perspective, SEALs—in the form of the original NCDUs and later UDT operators—became a part of the U.S. Navy's amphibious force in 1943, during World War II, where they would go ashore in advance of the main assault to perform beach reconnaissance at night checking for obstacles and mines and demolishing them as necessary prior to the assault. This became doctrinal in the postwar period and continued throughout the Korean and Vietnam conflicts, where the UDTs also operated as part of the amphibious force. UDT platoons participated in numerous amphibious operations during Korea, including the impressive Inchon landing. In the early days of Vietnam, UDT operators participated in a series of amphibious landings named Dagger Thrust—earmarked to pin down VC units operating in the coastal areas. The force would rehearse in the Philippines prior to each operation; these landings were always unopposed until later, inland, when Marines would encounter token resistance.

On 25 October 1983, SEALs accompanied amphibious forces to the Caribbean for Operation Urgent Fury in Grenada. Alongside other SOF, they performed their historic amphibious reconnaissance mission; in the ensuing years after this mission, however, their amphibious reconnaissance tasks were eventually divested and assumed by others.

Upon formation of USSOCOM in 1987, a flag-level NSWC was simultaneously established by the U.S. Navy as the SOF maritime component. This action changed the entire command and control arrangement because SEALs, under their respective NSWG commanders, now reported to the NSWC admiral and

not to the surface force admiral. SEALs under each NSWG continued to support the ARGs for several more years; because of USSOCOM, however, Navy SEALs no longer work for or directly support the U.S. Navy.

Concurrent with formation of USSOCOM and NSWC, each geographical combatant commander (GCC) simultaneously established a subunified TSOC, and all NSW SEAL, SWCC, or other NSW detachments deploying overseas to the Pacific Command (PACOM), Atlantic Command (LANTCOM), European Command (EUCOM), Latin American Command (SOUTHCOM), or Central Command (CENTCOM, with area of responsibility in Middle East–North Africa–Central Asia) was employed by the TSOC commander. These special operations commands were called SOCPAC, SOCLANT, SOCEUR, SOCSOUTH, and SOCCENT for the respective regions. There was also a TSOC established in Korea—SOCKOR, and most recently SOCAF in Africa. In time of crisis, these TSOCs generally become task organized to form a JSOTF and direct SEAL and SOF war planning and tasking for their particular GCC.

SEAL operations are conducted in all environments, but are particularly well suited for denied and politically sensitive maritime environments. SEAL capabilities can be tailored to achieve not only military objectives through application of all SOF capabilities for which there are no broad conventional force requirements, but also to support the application of the diplomatic, informational, and economic instruments of national power. SEAL operations are typically low visibility or clandestine operations that are applicable across the range of military operations. They can be conducted independently or in conjunction with operations of conventional forces or other government agencies; or with host nations or partner nations. They may include operations with or through indigenous, insurgent, or irregular forces. SEAL and other SOF operations differ from conventional operations in the degree of physical and political risk, operational techniques, modes of employment, and dependence on detailed operational intelligence and indigenous assets. SEAL operations are often conducted at great distances from major operating bases, which support the continuing need for sea basing or AFSB options in maritime areas of interest. Moreover, SEALs employ sophisticated communications systems and special boat assault force and helicopter assault force means of infiltration, support, and exfiltration to penetrate and return from hostile, denied, or politically sensitive areas.

If SEALs or SWCCs are ever needed to support an amphibious commander,

the ARG commander can request their capabilities and assignment from the GCC and regional TSOC. That is not to say that SEALs will no longer have need for amphibious or other ships. In fact, SEALs and USSOCOM have a standing requirement for the sea basing of SOF during known or preplanned operations in hostile or denied areas—generally for short durations. When deployed, a Navy-provided ship or ships will support SEAL and other SOF mission as an AFSB. Ideally, the AFSB will be dedicated to the SOF mission during its period of embarkation and provide support for a boat assault force and helicopter assault force; provide persistent intelligence, surveillance, and reconnaissance; provide UAS capabilities or support; and of course provide hotel services for the onboard detachments. The embarked JSOTF will be task organized depending on the mission and capabilities of the ship or ships assigned. Mission tasking, planning, and intelligence support may be provided by the shore-based TSOC.

This may appear eerily reminiscent of the Marine Corps mission, staging afloat off a potential hot spot; the AFSB for SOF is a substantially different concept, however. This was demonstrated by SOF during the Haitian crisis in 1994, when a JSOTF with Army helicopters and assault forces deployed on board the carrier USS *America*, and again in October 2001 when USS *Kitty Hawk* deployed to the North Arabian Sea in support of OEF. The ship served as an afloat forward staging base for SEALs and other SOF.

There will be times when the SOF mission must dominate and, thus, when AFSBs and other fleet assets primary tasking will be dedicated to a JSOTF commander. The U.S. Navy has been instrumental in supporting SEAL operations throughout the globe; this partnership will only strengthen as the need and demand for all SOF capabilities continue.

THE SUBMARINE CONNECTION

U.S. Navy submarines operate worldwide. SDVTs are integrated into submersible operations more directly than are direct-action SEALs. With the introduction of the DDSs, SDV operations achieved full-time global reach into littoral regions. Both of these capabilities are discussed in other chapters.

Submarine DDSs make up the major capability that SEAL and SDVTs bring to the operational table. The submarine force is arguably the major Navy support agent for NSW, owing to the preponderance of the SEALs being involved in OIF.

Submarines with embarked Navy SEALs continue to figure in national defense planning strategy. As the development program for ASDS proceeds, we can reasonably expect to see more involvement.

The submarine force is the brightest light in fleet support of NSW. When the Berlin Wall came down and the Soviet Union "changed orientation," the mission of the Navy submarine force was altered. Lengthy missile patrols faded into history, and the Soviet submarines were pretty much tied up at their piers. A new era was emerging as the Cold War evaporated. U.S. submarines went looking for a new mission, and NSW figured high on their list. In the late 1980s, submarine services were to be had with a phone call as compared with the previous detailed scheduling requiring months of "standing in line." But even as submarine services for lock-in/lock-out services increased, the anticipated peace dividend did not end up in the DoD, to the chagrin of Navy shipbuilding, submarines included. Submarines will be constructed from keel up with NSW requirements incorporated. This is a major acknowledgement to the growing importance of SOFs. Submarines have had service lives extended and interiors modified to support upward of sixty SOF personnel—Navy SEALs, Army Special Forces and Rangers, and Marine Corps special operations troops. SDVT-1 is co-located with the submarine forces in Pearl Harbor, Hawaii. It is

ABOVE AND BOTTOM, RIGHT: *The USS Ohio SSGN 726 is an old strategic ballistic missile submarine converted to a tactical cruise missile and joint task force submarine platform. Pier side at Pearl Harbor, the Ohio awaits the load-in of SEAL hardware and mission gear. It has been heavily modified to handle SOF (Special Operations Forces) and serve as a host for the SEALs, their SDV (SEAL Dive Vehicle), a new Battle Management Center (the first such ever), and stowage of a considerable amount of SOF gear along with its normal complement of Tomahawk missiles. (Photo: Dave Gatley)*

BOTTOM, LEFT: *The Los Angeles–class submarine USS Dallas (SSN-700) departs Souda Bay harbor following a brief port visit. Dallas is home ported in Groton, Conn., and currently on a routine deployment. Dallas was the first Los Angeles–class submarine to have a dry deck shelter (DDS). Dry Deck Shelters provide specially configured nuclear-powered submarines with a greater capability of deploying Special Operations Forces (SOF). DDSs can transport, deploy, and recover SEAL team Combat Rubber Raiding Crafts (CRRS's) or SEAL Delivery Vehicles (SDVs), all while remaining submerged. (Photo: Paul Farley / USN)*

259

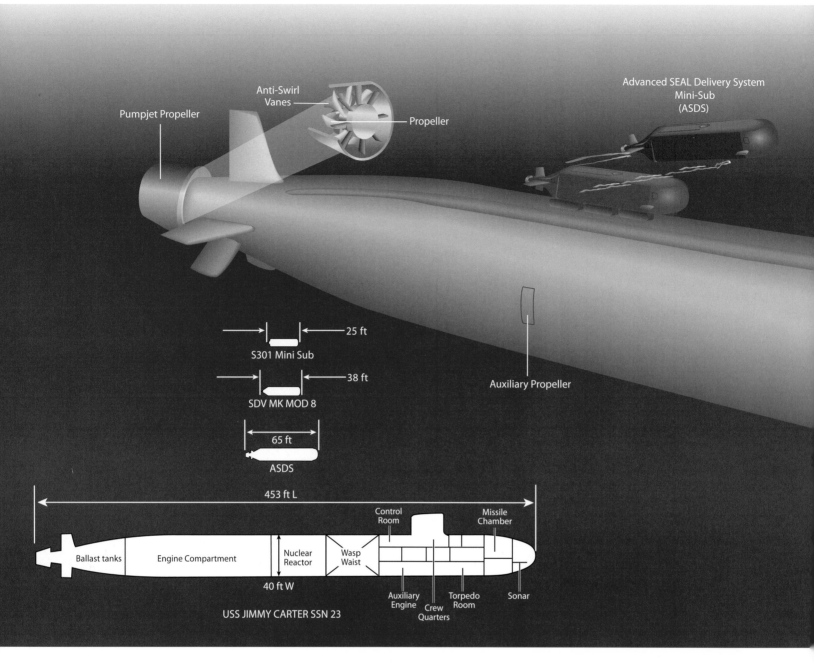

Pumpjet Propeller

Anti-Swirl Vanes

Propeller

Advanced SEAL Delivery System Mini-Sub (ASDS)

Auxiliary Propeller

25 ft
S301 Mini Sub

38 ft
SDV MK MOD 8

65 ft
ASDS

453 ft L

40 ft W

Ballast tanks

Engine Compartment

Nuclear Reactor

Wasp Waist

Control Room

Missile Chamber

Auxiliary Engine

Crew Quarters

Torpedo Room

Sonar

USS JIMMY CARTER SSN 23

RIGHT: *The USS Ohio (SSGN 726) is one of four Trident submarines that have undergone conversion to a new class of guided-missile submarines. The SSGN conversion program took Ohio-class ballistic missile submarines through an extensive overhaul that improved their capability to support and launch up to 154 Tomahawk missiles. They also provide the capability to carry other payloads, such as unmanned underwater vehicles (UUVs), unmanned aerial vehicles (UAVs), and special forces equipment. This new platform also has the capability to carry and support more than 66 Navy SEALs and insert them clandestinely into conflict areas. (Photo: Wendy Hallmark / USN)*

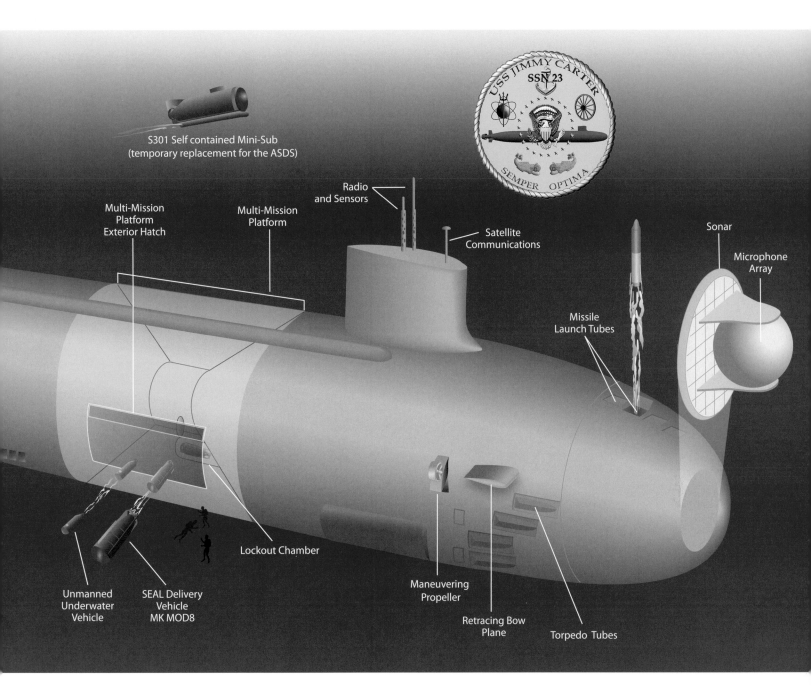

S301 Self contained Mini-Sub
(temporary replacement for the ASDS)

Multi-Mission
Platform
Exterior Hatch

Multi-Mission
Platform

Radio
and Sensors

Satellite
Communications

Sonar

Microphone
Array

Missile
Launch Tubes

Lockout Chamber

Unmanned
Underwater
Vehicle

SEAL Delivery
Vehicle
MK MOD8

Maneuvering
Propeller

Retracing Bow
Plane

Torpedo Tubes

ABOVE: USS *Jimmy Carter* (SSN23) Seawolf-class submarine. Built by Electric Boat Division of General Dynamics, the USS *Jimmy Carter* is unlike any submarine in the U.S. Navy; in fact to some degree, it's not part of the U.S. Navy. Though it is manned and operated by the U.S. Navy, the submarine is not under the Navy's control and is responsible to another entity. With its unique one-of-a-kind design enhancements, the *Jimmy Carter* is designed from the ground up for special operations, the Navy SEALs, and high-tech espionage. Near the midsection, behind the mast, the Multi-Mission Platform (MMP), designed like a wasp waist, was inserted into the length of the submarine, allowing it to flood with water and then open to the ocean, like an underwater garage door allowing for SEALs, unmanned underwater vehicles, and other items to be launched under the sea while still allowing the crew to pass through the ships inside via the shaped passageway. The sub's four retractable electric duct propellers are for "parallel parking." The propellers are similar to that of the ASDS, but much larger, allowing the submarine to maneuver at speeds down to a fraction of a knot. The boat can spin around on its own axis for special operations such as divers exiting to tap undersea fiber-optic cables. With state-of-the-art satellite communications, missile launching, silent running propellers, and other classified features, the USS *Jimmy Carter* adds another weapon system into the arsenal of today's special operations. (Graphic illustration by Susan Coons)

the only SDV team, and it maintains a detachment at the JEB, Little Creek, Virginia. Submarines exercise with embarked SDVTs more than any other naval or joint service. Here are some representative exercises that SDV personnel are required to complete from a host submarine: underwater demolition of an offshore facility, interdiction of a port facility, ship attacks using limpet mines, DDS mass swimmer operations, and personnel and equipment transfer. These operations will be conducted underwater; action at an objective may require inland patrolling on the part of SEAL personnel; extraction by SDV remains the egress option.

The most aggressive program to date has been the conversion of Ohio-class

(SSGN) submarines to host SEALs and SDVTs. These new boats provide an operational capability heretofore unheard of. To reiterate, each submarine will be able to transport upward of sixty special operations operators, including a number of SDVs. Each boat will host two DDSs. The SSGN program will eventually replace Los Angeles–class submarines; the new Virginia-class boats will attract SEALs as well.

The current aggressive approach to special operations by the submarine force is a challenge for NSW, a historically small community. There are currently six DDSs in active service. A modernization program has been planned, where additional DDSs may be procured. Here's the updated situation from NSWG-3:

> The Navy is converting four SSBN Trident missile submarines to SSGN guided missile nuclear submarines with two primary mission areas: Strike (with cruise missiles) and SOF Support. The new Virginia class submarine is also designed to have a significant SOF capability. This is a huge capital investment in SOF by the Navy, and NSW is working to ensure that this robust NSW–Submarine partnership is properly aligned and sustainable. The need and demand for SOF-unique undersea capabilities is growing and the SOF-Submarine Master Plan that aligns the complex array of submarine availability, maintenance, training, and deployment cycles to deliver these critical assets to the fleet has required a Herculean effort across Navy and NSW.

ABOVE: SEALs fly in during a nighttime exercise to attack a Middle Eastern terrorist desert training site. The exercise includes insertion by heliocopter, live/real ammunitions and explosions, along with rocket (LAWS) missiles upon the site and simulated counterattack (or enemy fire) during the extraction portion of exercise. A Navy Seahawk helicopter approaches the insertion site in total darkness, with sand particles kicked up and hitting its rotors, producing a light trace above the copter which is only visible by night vision optics. (Photo:Dave Gatley)

RIGHT: Flying through rain, this special operations variant of the HH-60H Seahawk comes in "hot," firing from two GAU-17A miniguns mounted on either side in this demonstration of air support. (Photo: Dave Gatley)

Balancing submarines and DDS interoperability is a full-time job and a complete accounting would make the reader's eyes glaze over. But very quickly: NSW SOF operates off three Los Angeles 688–class boats: the USS *Dallas* on the East Coast, and USS *Los Angeles* and USS *La Jolla* in Hawaii, all of which will be replaced by the Virginia class. The ASDS operates off two submarines, USS *Greenville* and USS *Charlotte*. There are fourteen SSNs in the Ohio class, and the Navy has started a program to convert them to SSGNs or ballistic missile submarines by inserting a new section behind the ship's sail. The same conversions will make these SSBNs capable of supporting SDV and other SOF operations. The Navy' newest class submarine is the Virginia class, and it will support a dual DDS configuration. The lead ship, USS *Virginia* (SSN-774), entered commissioned service on 23 October 2004.

THE AVIATION CONNECTION

Aircraft of Navy SEALs has grown since the combat lash-up in Vietnam in the 1960s. SEALs are required to be static-line- and free-fall-qualified parachutists. Next we look at the aircraft frames the Navy provides NSW.

The most important aircraft are the HH-60s assigned to the HSCs. These squadrons have an included mission to "conduct Naval Special operations in sup-

RIGHT, TOP: *An MH-6 Little Bird of the U.S. Army's 160th SOAR, known as the Night Stalkers, flies in fast and quiet to deliver an SOF team to the target area. Outfitted with miniguns, the Little Birds can move between small buildings, fast and with stealth. (Photo: Greg E. Mathieson Sr. / NSW Publications, LLC)*

RIGHT, BOTTOM: *SEAL operators conduct a mock mission by fast roping from a SH-60 Seahawk as a quick means of insertion of forces onto the beaches of a training area. (Photo:Dave Gatley)*

BELOW: *The OH-58D Kiowa Warrior is a two-seat, single-engine, four-bladed single main rotor light helicopter with a low light television, thermal imaging system, and laser rangefinder/ designator incorporated into an above-the-rotor Mast Mounted Sight (MMS). The Kiowa Warrior can designate targets for precision-guided munitions carried by Apache helicopters, other airborne weapons platforms, or ground-based systems. (Photo: Dave Gatley)*

BELOW: *U.S. Navy ships and aircraft support the members of Naval special warfare, the SEALs, and SWCC teams and operators around the globe. (Photo: Greg E. Mathieson Sr. / NSW Publications, LLC)*

port of other strike operations." These are the choppers the SEALs spend the most time with, inserting, extracting, fast roping, and, sometimes, CSAR. Pulling friendlies out of tough situations is a strong motivating point for SEALs. (Combat rescue operations in Afghanistan accounted for the largest number of SEAL casualties since World War II.)

During the Vietnam era SEALs conducted most of their airborne operations—insertions and extractions—during daylight hours. The SEALs flew in helicopter attack (light) squadrons: HA(L)-1 from the West Coast and HA(L)-2 from the

264

East Coast. These light choppers could carry eight combat-laden men. In addition to the Navy HA(L)s, SEALs could rely on Army Huey choppers—the troop carriers termed Slicks. Armed helicopters were called gunships and flew in support of the insertion aircraft. By the late1980s, Hueys were phased out as HH-60s were introduced.

In addition to Navy aviation, SEALs often rely on Army and Air Force aviation, notably the Night Stalkers, headquartered at Fort Campbell, Kentucky. Army sup-

ABOVE: SEALs tethered to the bottom of a U.S. Army 160th SOAR helicopter via a Special Patrol Insertion / Extraction (SPIE) rigging. (Photo: Greg E. Mathieson Sr. / NSW Publications, LLC)

RIGHT, TOP: SEAL operators are lifted using a Special Patrol Insertion / Extraction (SPIE) rigging. The SPIE rope is lowered into the pickup area from a hovering helicopter. Patrol personnel, each wearing a harness with an attached carabiner, hook up to a D-ring inserted in the SPIE rope. A second safety line is attached to a second D-ring located above the first. The helicopter lifts vertically from an extract zone until the personnel are clear of obstructions. (Photo: Greg E. Mathieson Sr. / NSW Publications, LLC)

RIGHT, BOTTOM: NSW Group II conducts their annual demonstration at Little Creek, Virginia, for the annual NSW / UDT / SEAL reunion with a display of the GAU-17A mini-guns firing from the sides of the Navy's helicopter. (Photo: Greg E. Mathieson Sr. / NSW Publications, LLC)

port is essential in Iraq and, formerly, in Afghanistan. Navy helicopters have over-water flying capabilities. This skill is obviously necessary for fleet operations such as intercepting, boarding, and searching suspect commercial shipping for contra-band, usually United Nations–prohibited war matériel. This flying is extremely exacting and dangerous. Navy pilots are trained to approach ships and land on moving decks—essential to inserting a SEAL squad using fast-roping techniques. Often, a Navy gunship will fly shotgun for the inserting chopper.

FUTURE SUPPORT

Things are moving in naval aviation with regard to NSW support. Reorganiza-tion is currently under way in the aviation helicopter squadrons. New upgrades

ABOVE, LEFT: *Flying at high speeds, low altitudes, and in total darkness and rain, this special operations variant of the HH-60H Seahawk belonging to the 160th Special Operations Aviation Regiment (SOAR), Night Stalkers, comes in "hot," firing from two GAU-17A miniguns. (Photo: Greg E. Mathieson Sr. / NSW Publications, LLC)*

ABOVE, RIGHT: *Raining thousands of spent shell casings from the two GAU-17A miniguns, this HH-60H Seahawk helicopter, being flown by the 160th Special Operations Aviation Regiment (SOAR), Night Stalkers, provides cover during a SEAL training mis-sion. (Photo: Greg E. Mathieson Sr. / NSW Publications, LLC)*

LEFT: *Team members of Special Boat Team 20 practice fast roping and recovery opera-tions, utilizing the CV-22 Osprey of the U.S. Air Force 8th Special Operations Squadron (SOS), based in Hurlburt Field, Florida. The Osprey is a tilt-rotor aircraft that can hover like a helicopter and tilts its rotor blades while in the air to take off and then fly like a fixed-wing plane. The primary mission of the 8th SOS is insertion, extraction, and resupply of unconventional warfare forces. (Photo: Greg E. Mathieson Sr. / NSW Publications, LLC)*

ABOVE: *In this night vision photo a SWCC operator of SBT-20 is recovered from a lake into the back of an CV-22 Osprey of the USAF 8th Special Operations Squadron during a training exercise in near total darkness. (Photo: Greg E. Mathieson Sr. / NSW Publications, LLC)*

TOP: *A SWCC operator of SBT-20 fast ropes out the back of an CV-22 Osprey of the USAF 8th Special Operations Squadron. (Photo: Greg E. Mathieson Sr. / NSW Publications, LLC)*

RIGHT: *Two Special Boat Team SWCC operators of SBT-20 are lifted up into the back of a CV-22 Osprey of the USAF 8th Special Operations Squadron during a joint special operations training exercise. (Photo: Greg E. Mathieson Sr. / NSW Publications, LLC)*

ABOVE: *A Chinook helicopter inserts a SOC-R craft into the waters of Iraq in support of WARCOMs Special Boat Teams. (Photo: USN)*

LEFT: *SEALs prepare to jump into the surf as their Zodiac is released from the underside of a U.S. Army 160th (SAOR) helicopter. (Photo: Greg E. Mathieson Sr. / NSW Publications, LLC)*

are migrating into the fleet, as are training capabilities. For example, helicopter pilots are now training with night vision goggles for fully blacked-out deck recovery. The legacy systems required extensive deck lighting; this is undergoing improvement to low-level capture. Special operations Army and Air Force helicopter pilots have been night-vision-device capable for years. Adding naval aviation to the U.S. SOF mix would add a dimension to NSW maritime capabilities that is currently missing.

THE GLOBAL WAR ON TERROR

This effort will be long term and has already taxed the U.S. military beyond expectations of a generation ago. Still, current operational evidence overwhelmingly indicates that special operations will be center stage in the foreseeable future. The future for NSW is secure, and new naval developments, such as those seen in the submarine community, will surely reflect the emphasis on it. The present example of submarine conversions to support special operations is a fine example of vision. As mentioned, NSW is itself in a catch-up mode with the number of host submarines under development.

ABOVE: *As the evening moon rises, so does a U.S. Army AH-64 Apache helicopter gunship in support of an SWCC riverine mission. (Photo: Greg E. Mathieson Sr. / NSW Publications, LLC)*

BOTTOM, LEFT: *A tight fit when being loaded aboard one of the largest transport cargo airlift planes in the world, the Air Force C-5A; The Mk V special operations craft is a high-speed waterborne transporter for naval special operations forces. Capable of speeds in excess of 50 knots and a range of 500 nautical miles, the Mk V was designed to get Navy SEALs and other special warfare forces close into shore in a low-to-medium-threat environment. (Photo: DoD)*

BOTTOM, RIGHT: *Loading of the large SEALs ASDS (Advanced SEAL Delivery System) midget submarine is conducted at night, under sodium vapor lighting, aboard the huge C-5A Air Force transport cargo aircraft. The ASDS was conceived to address the need for stealthy long-range insertion of Special Operations Forces. Previous minisubs were of the wet variety, exposing combat swimmers to long, cold waits during transit that impeded combat readiness and had limited blind underwater navigational capability. (Photo: DoD)*

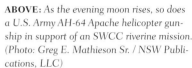

REAR ADM (SEAL) GEORGE WORTHINGTON
USN (RET)

Training and Techniques for the Global War on Terror

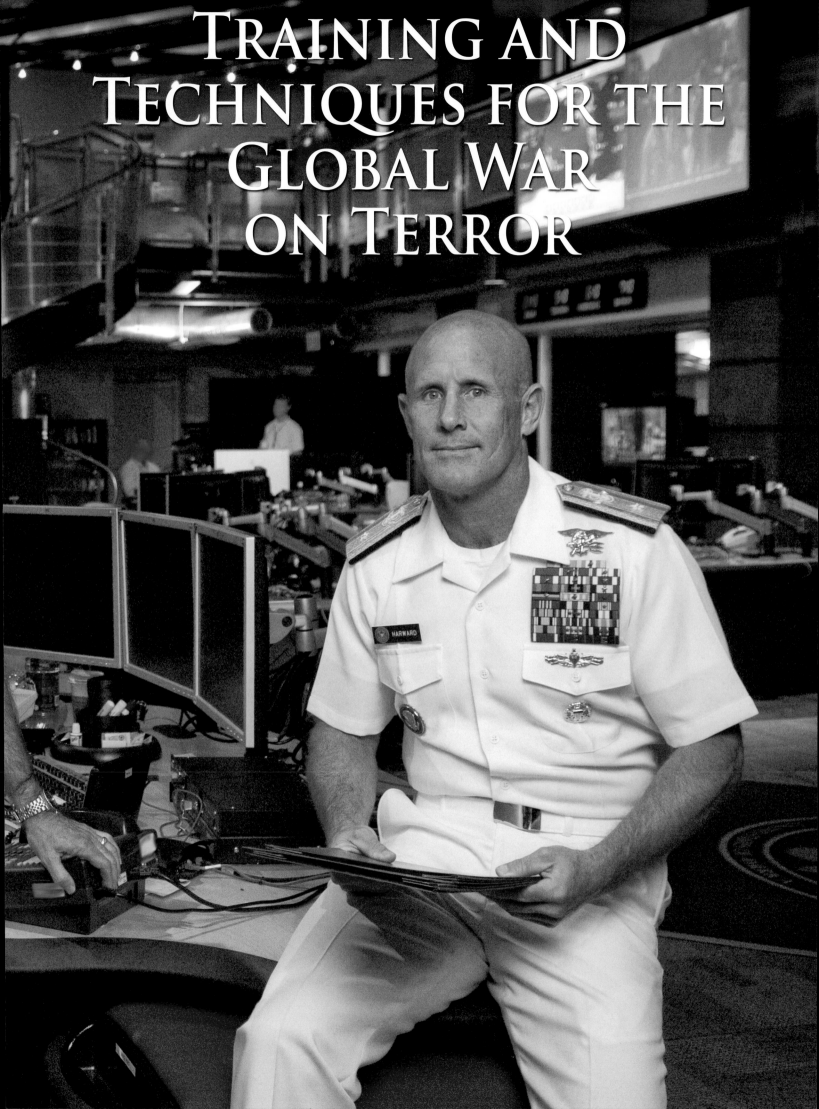

CHAPTER 11

NAVAL SPECIAL WARFARE TRAINING AND TECHNIQUES FOR THE GLOBAL WAR ON TERROR

Rear Adm. (SEAL) George Worthington, USN (Ret.)

PAGES 272–273: *(L–R): Vice Admiral Bert Calland, USN (SEAL), former Deputy Director of Strategic Operational Planning and Deputy Director of the CIA; Vice Admiral Joseph Maguire, USN (SEAL), former Deputy Director of Strategic Operational Planning; and Rear Admiral Bob Harward, USN (SEAL), former Senior Interagency Strategy Team Member for the Joint Staff, brought together for this photo in the Operations Center of the National Counterterrorism Center (NCTC), which is the center for joint operational planning and joint intelligence. The NCTC's operations include but are not limited to leading interagency task forces designed to analyze, monitor, and disrupt potential terrorist attacks. Having experienced SEALs at the top in national planning, knowing the threats and how SEALs work, better assists the operators when risking their lives in the field. (Photo: Greg E. Mathieson Sr. / NSW Publications, LLC)*

BELOW: *Members of the U.S. Army's 160th Special Operations Aviation Regiment (SOAR) pose in front of one of their MH-47G Chinook helicopters stationed in Afghanistan. (Photo: USA)*

TERRORISM IS AS OLD AS TIME ITSELF. TODAY'S GWOT STARTED well before the 9/11 airliner attacks on the World Trade Center and the Pentagon, and United Airlines Flight 93 that crashed into a field near Shanksville, Pennsylvania, which reportedly had the White House as a target. But the war was not recognized as such until American armed forces became operationally engaged. At home, restructuring of the intelligence services was undertaken; a Department of Homeland Security (DHS) was established; overseas, American

ABOVE: *U.S.-led coalition forces successfully intercepted and boarded four Iraqi vessels containing nearly 100 mines in the Khor Abd Allah waterway. Each vessel was equipped with devices made of hollowed-out 50-gallon barrels lined in rows to simulate a cargo barge and tug. One vessel carried uniforms and small arms. Upon intercept, the mines were transported to Camp Patriot by coalition vessels under the protection of seaward security forces for further analysis and destruction. (Photo: USN)*

TOP: *SEAL operators practice on domestic Gas and Oil Platforms (GOPLAT) to prepare for future attacks on world oil production facilities. They operate in small numbers, infiltrating their objective areas by fixed-wing aircraft, helicopters, Navy surface ships, combatant craft, and various underwater crafts. (Photo:. Photographer's Mate 2nd Class Eric S. Logsdon / USN)*

LEFT: *SEALs conduct a (VBSS) Visit, Board, Search, and Seizure, where they board a suspected vessel at sea which may contain contraband or wanted individuals. (Photo: USN)*

SOFs were going after the Taliban that were charged with sheltering the Islamic terrorist organization al Qaeda and its titular leader, Osama bin Laden.

In actuality, the terror war against America and the West goes back before September 2001. Eighty years before, a bomb went off on New York City's Wall Street in 1920, killing thirty-five. Bolsheviks were blamed at the time, but the crime remains unsolved. Closer to our time, attacks against America have become almost commonplace. Only the Oklahoma City bombing is not of suspected or proven radical Islamist origin.

Answers to "Why do they hate us?" are best left to others. What is germane here is the response the nation came up with in employing U.S. Navy SEALs and other SOF in mere weeks following 9/11. This is not new, however, as SEALs were among the first U.S. combatants into Saudi Arabia following the Iraq incursion into Kuwait City in 1990. Commander NSWG-1, Capt. Raymond C. Smith, USN (later rear admiral), mounted out with a detachment of SEALs and special boat personnel and reported to CENTCOM special operations command, while the Kuwait operations were part of the effort to expel the armed forces of Saddam Hussein. But the presence of Westerners in the Saudi kingdom was apparently a raison d'être for Osama bin Laden's political quest to control all Islam by establishing Islamic governments throughout the Middle East with the ultimate goal of expelling the West. From the end of the first Persian Gulf War to the present time, CT operations have been oriented against al Qaeda and its adherents. OIF, collaterally oriented against terror, counts the civil militias as an extension of al Qaeda currently operating throughout Iraq.

The Army and Marine Corps clearly make up the bulk of U.S. forces in Iraq. Congressional testimony by senior military leaders from time to time has barraged the airwaves with plans and strategies. SOF were engaged in Afghanistan and Iraq from the first months following 9/11. From operations in Iraq's al-Anbar province to current operations in Afghanistan, SEALs have been constantly engaged in the GWOT overseas. In addition, Navy SEALs are participating in CT training operations in the Philippines (although they are not permitted in combat).

ONGOING TRAINING AND OPERATIONS

What, exactly, are the SEALs doing in the war? What specific skills do they need to develop to sustain years of continuous deployment to a war zone? How is their training relevant? How does continental United States training prepare teams and squadrons for the Middle East—or anywhere else NSW troops serve? How is training amended as intelligence comes in? How does modern-day training differ from, say, Vietnam-era preparation—apart from jungle versus desert versus mountainous regimes?

A CH-47 helicopter attached to the 159th Aviation Regiment lifts a Naval Special Warfare 11-meter Rigid Hull Inflatable Boat (RIB) during a maritime external transportation system training exercise. The SWCC operators aboard the RIB climb the ladder into the helicopter. (Photo: MC3 Robyn Gerstenslager / USN)

To answer these questions in an unclassified mode requires looking at the training that SEALs and special crewmen undergo preparing for deployment. But more: we need to look at the specific courses offered by the ATC and ULT even before a predeployment squadron is formed up. This training is conducted within the individual SEAL and SBTs as coordinated by the NSWGs, both East and West Coasts. A look at the training cycle is a good place to begin. The standard schedule is two years: six months of individual training—specific rating schools, such as electronics; six months of ULT in platoons; six months of squadron form-up; then six months of deployment to several geographic locations. Today, the preponderance of forces is earmarked for OEF and OIF, as once SEALs were tasked into Vietnam.

There are a couple of support organizations today that directly support NSW and SOF and their families. One, the Navy SEAL Foundation, gives direct, immediate support to NSW families in need for many reasons, but especially for those families affected by a combat (or other) death. Direct emergency support is available to them. Another foundation is the Special Operations Warrior Foundation, established expressly to provide college scholarships to the children of SOF members that have been killed in training or combat—all costs, tuition, board, and books. This is not a loan; it is a gratis endowment. As soon as a member is confirmed deceased, the spouse is contacted. All children are tracked in the foundation database, no matter what age, and tracked through elementary, middle, and

high school—with commensurate encouragement to prepare for college. (Some elect technical schools instead.) Combined, these two foundations cooperate to ensure support for families left behind. Much could be added on the subject of family support. For the interested reader, both foundations have websites, and you are invited to check them out.

During individual training and ULT periods (one year), members can attend courses offered by the ATC discussed earlier. Here are courses offered that we will look at: SEAL Sniper, Lead Breacher, Close Quarters Defense, Helicopter Rope Suspension Training (fast rope/cast), Photo Intelligence Capture, SEAL Delivery Vehicle Operator, and Static-Line Jumpmaster.

ABOVE: *The remains of the World Trade Center and the images produced in those days had an effect on the motivation of SEALs and others in their determination to seek out the terrorists responsible. Here, FEMA Urban Search and Rescue teams work to clear rubble and search for survivors.(Photo: Andrea Booher / FEMA)*

RIGHT: *The airplane alert antenna sits firmly in the ground amidst the rubble. Originally it was on the roof of the World Trade Center. (Photo: Andrea Booher / FEMA)*

BELOW: *President George W. Bush arrives back at the White House after the terrorist attacks at the Pentagon and World Trade Centers in New York City on September 11, 2001. (Photo: © 2001 Greg E. Mathieson Sr. / NSW Publications, LLC)*

SEAL Snipers

SEAL Snipers are a unique breed even among SEALs. Snipers must get into position first. This requires a review of approaches, cover, extraction routes, and lay-up logistics. Prior to beginning a sniper event, an operational decision has to be made concerning the efficacy of such an operation. This is performed above the individual sniper's purview. After an initial assessment is made, the sniper team is brought into the planning process and ingress routes are studied. Depending on the environment, these lay-ups could be deep in enemy territory, or, alternatively, from a rooftop location in a city. The shooting tactics are difficult.

Lead Breacher

Breaching uses a variety of demolition techniques. Most times, breaching entryways is a surprise to the occupants—or so it is hoped. During this training the men learn about explosive loads and about a variety of materials. Flat and shaped demolitions are used over a range of architectural structures.

Close Quarters Defense

CQD—the most popular course among SEALs—trains the individual SEAL in personal defense and how to incapacitate an adversary with a range of force options, starting at the low end, talking, through physical aggression, up to and including deadly force. The idea is to "give 'em what he asks for." While the low end is preferred in capturing an individual, the SEAL has to be prepared to make an immediate decision about what level of aggression to use. The most important

LEFT, TOP: *First responders arrive at the crash site of the Pentagon moments after American Flight 77 was crashed into the five-story building, killing all 58 passengers, four flight attendants, and both pilots, as well as 125 occupants in the Pentagon. (Photo: © 2001 Greg E. Mathieson Sr. / NSW Publications, LLC)*

LEFT, CENTER: *President George W. Bush leads America in the response against the terrorist attack from Camp David, Maryland, on September 22, 2001. (Photo: Eric Draper)*

LEFT, BOTTOM: *The President of the United States receives what's known as the President's Daily Brief (PDB), which contains classified top secret and sometimes eyes-only documents for the President. Many of the briefs include the actions and missions of the US Navy SEALs. This classified document is on the Resolute Desk in the Oval Office. (Photo: Pete Souza)*

BOTTOM, LEFT: *President George W. Bush and Prime Minister Tony Blair of the United Kingdom participate in a video teleconference Thursday, May 17, 2007, in the Situation Room of the White House with the U.S. and U.K. Iraq teams. Secure teleconferences using this new technology grew during the years of the Global War on Terror. The U.K. was one of the strongest allies of the United States. (Photo: Eric Draper)*

BOTTOM, RIGHT: *President George W. Bush is seen at a National Security Council meeting in the White House Situation Room Monday, March 24, 2008. A video teleconference is underway with Gen. David Petraeus, Commander of the Multi-National Force—Iraq, and Ryan Crocker, U.S. Ambassador to Iraq. Also in the room are National Security Adiviser Condoleezza Rice, Secretary of Defense Robert Gates, CENTCOM Cdr. Admiral Fallon, and others. (Photo: Eric Draper)*

STOP THE FLOW OF BLOOD MONEY!

International terrorism is financed by money sent to terrorists from sources around the world. To avoid future incidents, the U.S. Government is offering a reward of up to $5 million for information leading to the dismantling of any system used to finance a terrorist organization and information leading to the arrest or conviction of those who planned or aided in any act of terrorism against U.S. persons or property.

If you have any information about individuals or organizations that finance terrorists, please call 1-800-877-3927 in the U.S.; outside the U.S. contact the nearest U.S. embassy or consulate.

E-mail: RFJ@state.gov

Up to $5 Million Reward • Responses Kept Strictly Confidential

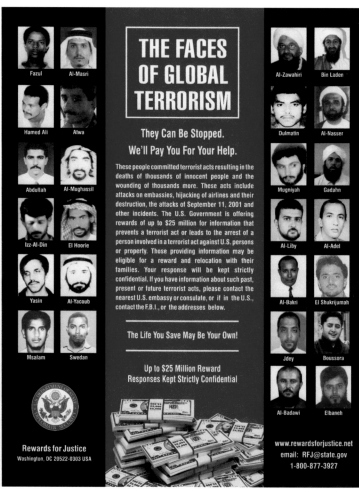

THE FACES OF GLOBAL TERRORISM

Fazul — Al-Masri — Hamed Ali — Atwa — Abdullah — Al-Mughassil — Izz-Al-Din — El Hoorie — Yasin — Al-Yacoub — Msalam — Swedan

Al-Zawahiri — Bin Laden — Dulmatin — Al-Nasser — Mugniyah — Gadahn — Al-Liby — Al-Adel — Al-Bakri — El Shukrijumah — Jdey — Boussora — Al-Badawi — Elbaneh

They Can Be Stopped. We'll Pay You For Your Help.

These people committed terrorist acts resulting in the deaths of thousands of innocent people and the wounding of thousands more. These acts include attacks on embassies, hijacking of airlines and their destruction, the attacks of September 11, 2001 and other incidents. The U.S. Government is offering rewards of up to $25 million for information that prevents a terrorist act or leads to the arrest of a person involved in a terrorist act against U.S. persons or property. Those providing information may be eligible for a reward and relocation with their families. Your response will be kept strictly confidential. If you have information about such past, present or future terrorist acts, please contact the nearest U.S. embassy or consulate, or if in the U.S., contact the F.B.I., or the addresses below.

The Life You Save May Be Your Own!

Up to $25 Million Reward
Responses Kept Strictly Confidential

Rewards for Justice
Washington, DC 20522-0303 USA

www.rewardsforjustice.net
email: RFJ@state.gov
1-800-877-3927

Work of Evil

The United States Government is offering a reward for information leading to the arrest or conviction of those persons who planned or aided in the attacks of September 11, or any act of international terrorism against U.S. persons or property. A reward of up to $25 million may be paid for information leading to the arrest, or conviction of, any member of al Qaeda or those who support al Qaeda.

To date, the U.S. Government has paid over $9.5 million to individuals providing such information.

Individuals providing information may be eligible for a reward, protection of their identities, and relocation with their families. If you have information, please contact the F.B.I. at 202-323-3300 in the U.S. Outside the U.S., contact your nearest U.S. embassy or consulate or write:

REWARDS FOR JUSTICE
Washington, D.C. 20522-0303 U.S.A.
www.rewardsforjustice.net • 1-800-877-3927

Up to $25 Million Reward • Responses Kept Strictly Confidential

MURDER

Nairobi & Dar es Salaam bombings, 1998
224 killed and 5,000 wounded

MURDERER
Usama Bin Laden
UP TO $25 MILLION REWARD

Usama Bin Laden, Muhammad Atef, and Ayman Zawahiri have been indicted for the August 7, 1998 bombings of the U.S. embassies in Kenya and Tanzania. These brutal attacks killed more than 224 innocent Americans, Kenyans and Tanzanians and seriously injured more than 5,000 men, women and children.

Bin Laden, Atef, Zawahiri, and their organization, al Qaeda, also allegedly conspired in the killings of American military personnel in Saudi Arabia and Somalia.

To preserve the peace and save innocent lives from further attacks, the U.S. Government is offering a reward for information leading to the arrest or conviction of Bin Laden, Atef, and Zawahiri. Persons providing information may be eligible for a reward of up to $25 million, protection of their identities, and may be eligible for relocation of themselves and their families. Persons wishing to report information on Usama Bin Laden, Muhammad Atef, Ayman Zawahiri or other terrorists, should contact the authorities or the regional security officer at the nearest U.S. embassy or consulate or write, email or call:

REWARDS FOR JUSTICE
Washington, DC 20522-0303 USA
Email: mail@rewardsforjustice.net
www.rewardsforjustice.net
1-800-877-3927

**UP TO $25 MILLION REWARD
STRICT CONFIDENTIALITY**

aspect is safety of the warriors, which is paramount. Risk is high in all encounters, but we want to bring them all home.

Helicopter Rope Suspension Training

Helicopter rope suspension training helps SEALs get to the target from rotary wing aircraft in hover. Using hawsers and thick gloves, SEALs slide down to the ground (or rooftop). It is a fast way of getting a squad on the objective, but it requires practice.

Photo Intelligence Capture

The Photo Intelligence Capture course teaches SEALs to use photography. It is an in-depth course on the cameras used by SOF for recording targets and approaches.

SEAL Delivery Vehicle Operator

SDV operator is arguably the most difficult assignment in NSW. SDV operations are arduous, technical, dangerous, long, conducted in harsh conditions, cold, and hazardous. Extra monies are earned by SDV SEAL operators. In addition to normal diving pay (and jump and demolition pays), fully qualified SDV operators earn an extra $340 a month. One specific example of an SDV operation that can be discussed involved a combined training exercise with the French navy and U.S. Navy that took place in Toulon. The American SDV departed its host submarine with DDS some distance from the French port, ingressed into the harbor, turned ninety degrees left, placed simulated limpet mines against the hull of an anchored vessel, reversed course, rendezvoused with the submarine, and was taken back into the DDS. The entire mission was conducted submerged. That operation was in 1991; SDVs are even better today.

Static-Line Jumpmaster

SEALs use static-line and free-fall parachutes. The new course, taught in San Diego, includes both. After men are qualified, it takes more training to develop jumpmasters at the Advanced Training Center.

A book of matches, distributed by the U.S. Department of State around the world by the "Rewards for Justice" program, offering rewards for information leading to the capture of Osama bin Laden, Ayman al-Zawahiri, and Sif al-Adel. Bin Laden is now dead, but al-Zawahiri and Sif al-Adel are still alive as of June 2015 and both are active in the upper echelons of al Qaeda. (Photo: Greg E. Mathieson Sr. / NSW Publications, LLC)

This huge fireball explosion clears the deck with over-pressure from the blast. An EOD (explosive ordnance device) team with nearly 325 pounds of ordinance (friendly and enemy) required destruction. This was the resulting fireball. (Photo: Dave Gatley)

FACING PAGE: A series of posters developed by the U.S. Department of State under the "Rewards for Justice" program, which display the terrorists and their actions and offer up to 25 million U.S. dollars to anyone providing information leading to their capture. (Photo: Greg E. Mathieson Sr. / NSW Publications, LLC)

A SEAL observes munitions being destroyed in eastern Afghanistan during Operation Enduring Freedom. The SEALs discovered the munitions while conducting a Sensitive Site Exploitation (SSE) mission. (Photo: PH1 Tim Turner / USN)

BOTTOM, LEFT: *During a Sensitive Site Exploitation (SSE) mission in the Zhawar Kili area, a U.S. Navy SEAL stands in a cave to give intelligence officials an idea as to the cave's size and scope. Used by al Qaeda and Taliban forces, the caves and other aboveground complexes were subsequently destroyed either by Navy Explosive Ordnance Disposal (EOD) personnel or through air strikes called in by the SEALs. (Photo: USN)*

BELOW AND BOTTOM, RIGHT: *U.S. Navy SEALs discover a large cache of munitions in one of more than 70 caves explored in the Zhawar Kili area during a Sensitive Site Exploitation (SSE) mission. Used by al Qaeda and Taliban forces, the caves and other aboveground complexes were subsequently destroyed either by Navy Explosive Ordnance Disposal (EOD) personnel or through air strikes called in by the SEALs. (Photo: USN)*

AFGHANISTAN

Let's look at some CT operations in Afghanistan. Remember, going after the Taliban in Afghanistan was a first step in hunting Osama bin Laden.

The attacks of 9/11 happened on a Tuesday morning. SOFs were under way for OEF in Afghanistan the following month. CENTCOM was the warfighting commander responsible for operations. Navy SEALs reported to the special operations command, CENTCOM. It was headed up by Rear Adm. Albert ("Bert") M. Calland, USN, a former Naval Academy football wide receiver. Calland had the initial influx of SEALs from NSWG-1, in Coronado, at that time commanded by Capt. Robert S. Harward, USN (later rear admiral), a former BUD/S honor man and personal aide to the commander of USSOCOM, Gen. Wayne Downing, USA. Harward had an interesting childhood growing up in Tehran, Iran; he speaks fluent Farsi, a skill that helped him out more than once in Afghanistan.

Calland's mission was to coordinate SOF throughout Afghanistan—no mean task. He had to coordinate with CIA agents sent to liaise with the Northern Alliance warlords, troops who opposed the Taliban. In addition, Calland had to coordinate with the presidents of all surrounding countries. In terms of military play,

he had Army Special Forces and Navy SEALs at his disposal. To eliminate the possibility of mutual interference, he split the Afghanistan SOF operational area into northern and southern regions: Army north, Navy south. This worked pretty well; conventional forces had their operation areas, too, notably Marines. But before we discuss the present, let's take a look at the technical and operational influence of global terrorism on SOFs and the Navy SEALs.

TRAINING, EQUIPMENT, AND TECHNIQUES

Terror is a tactic that has been around for thousands of years. Our focus is on the relatively recent past, however, going back only a quarter of a century, with Operation Eagle Claw, the Iranian hostage rescue attempt, and the crisis at Desert One, when the rescue attempt failed. This disaster pushed Congress into a review of all special operations, which resulted in establishment of the USSO-COM and bulking up of all service special operations capabilities. Even before this formal stand-up in 1987, efforts were under development that would place a lasting mark on service special operations. Many of the techniques remain classified, yet quite a few have been adopted by all special operations and some conventional units.

Fast Roping

Fast roping from helicopters has evolved into a universally accepted form of ingress. Local police SWAT units use it. It is a requirement in training. Our focus here is on the SEAL maritime use of such techniques; VBSS (Visit, Board, Search, and Seizure) tactics use fast roping to gain access to ships in order to search for contraband.

Fast roping uses heavy ropes that dangle from hovering helicopters. Men wear thick gloves to avoid burning their hands as they slide down the rope. The tactic is used to get operators into tight locations where the chopper cannot land, such as a rooftop or a tossing ship deck—or an offshore oil platform. During the first Persian Gulf War, embarked SEALs used fast roping to inspect a noncompliant merchantmen that would not stop to be searched when directed. The technique was also used in the Grenada operation. Since the 1980s, it has been routinely rehearsed by all SEALs.

As the maritime component of USSOCOM, NSW SEALs and SWCCs are responsible for CT techniques on the high seas. In this regard, surreptitiously boarding oceangoing ships is a technique first developed in the early1980s. This tactic was very closely held until the early 1990s. It spurred development of high-speed boats, which are operated and maintained by SBTs. The tactics involve closing a suspected ship at sea from the stern. Lightweight scaling ladders are

RIGHT: *A wanted poster offering a reward of $25 million for Iraqi insurgent leader Abu Musab al-Zarqawi, who had been responsible for much of the resistance U.S. forces were encountering in Iraq. On June 7, 2006, two U.S. Air Force F-16C jets dropped two 500-pound laser-guided bombs on his safe house. (Photo: Greg E. Mathieson Sr. / NSW Publications, LLC)*

BELOW: *Admitted al Qaeda terrorist Zacarias Moussaoui, convicted of conspiring to kill American citizens as part of the September 11, 2001, attacks, is transported by heavily armed U.S. deputy marshals under the cover of darkness from the site of his trial in Alexandria, Virginia, to the U.S. Penitentiary, Administrative Maximum Facility (ADX), better known as a "supermax prison" in Fremont County, Colorado. (Photo by: Greg E. Mathieson Sr. / NSW Publications, LLC)*

ABOVE: *Camp Delta and Echo at the Joint Task Force detention center at Guantánamo Bay, Cuba. Camp Delta formerly contained terrorist detainees and prisoners and is now used for medical and other support services for the detainees and prisoners living in a more permanent high-security center nearby. (Photo: Greg E. Mathieson Sr. / NSW Publications, LLC)*

LEFT: *Many of the terrorists that the SEALs captured are at Guantánamo Bay, Cuba. Camp VI houses the communal living of compliant detainees, while Camp V is more like a maximum security facility housing the noncompliant detainees. Here a U.S. naval officer speaks though the port on the cell door to a detainee. (Photo: Greg E. Mathieson Sr. / NSW Publications, LLC)*

"shot" up the ship's hull, and SEALs ascend to the main deck. This is rigorous climbing. Climbing walls are requirements of all SEAL military construction. BUD/S has one, so trainees are introduced to scaling from the first weeks of basic training. What this has done for the individual SEAL is to reinforce upper-body weight training. Pull-ups have always been an integral part of BUD/S; rope climbing has been added, and the climbing walls are permanent fixtures on the NSW architectural landscape. Even SBT inductees are expected to climb; it is superb physical training.

ABOVE: *A blast in a residential area in Fallujah, Iraq—this type of occurrence unfortunately became the norm for many in the area for a number of years, with car bombs going off daily and roadways unsafe to drive. (Photo: DoD)*

RIGHT, TOP: *A SEAL team helps secure the airfield of Al Asad Air Base, Iraq, as Air Force One lands. President George W. Bush, Secretary of State Condoleezza Rice, Secretary of Defense Robert M. Gates, and others met at Al Asad to meet with Iraqi government leadership, sheiks from Al Anbar province, and U.S. service members deployed to Iraq. (Photo: Cherie A. Thurlby)*

RIGHT, BOTTOM: *A SEAL operator, shown in night vison, stands before the MRAP (Mine Resistant Ambush Protected) vehicles they used on missions in Fallujah, Iraq. (Photo: Greg E. Mathieson Sr. / NSW Publications, LLC)*

BELOW: *SEALs operate Desert Patrol Vehicles (DPV) while preparing for a mission. Each dune buggy is outfitted with complex communication and weapon systems designed for the harsh desert terrain. (Photo: Photographer's Mate 1st Class Arlo Abrahamson / U.S. Navy)*

Close Quarters Battle

Another important technique—arguably the most important operational technique and now a universally accepted tactic—is CQB. This technique is the essence of CT takedowns. German, Israeli, and U.K. special operations teams were first to develop the tactic. CQB involves breaching a building or room where hostages are held, shooting the terrorists without hitting the innocents, and extracting from the area. The tactic has to be honed to aircraft, ships, and land structures. Every SOF in the world practices the technique daily. It is taught in BUD/S from the first days and later honed at the ATC—and forever after in operational units.

CQB involves the time-honored skill of inserting to the area, reconnaissance, and action at the objective. CT has forced urban warfare into the military training syllabus. The Marine Corps has constructed mock towns in which troopers rehearse CQB in streets and buildings. "Shooting houses" are now part of the training wherein operators fire live ammunition at target figures—while missing the hostages, of course. A central element of the shooting regime is accuracy, and special schools have cropped up to train the shooters; all SEALs

LEFT, TOP: *CH-46 lifts out of a serious sandstorm in Fallujah, Iraq. This is considered "No Fly" weather that offers absolutely no visibility. This crew takes advantage of a short break in the storm to escape from the base. Sandstorms are common events and can be bad enough to shut down all ground and air mobility in the affected area, and can last for days or more. (Photo: Dave Gatley)*

LEFT, BOTTOM: *SEALs are prepared for any contingency and deployment, thanks to LOGSU. Even here, far out in the yellow dust of a sandstorm in Iraq, the SEALs are not far from their boats. (Photo: Greg E. Mathieson Sr. / NSW Publications, LLC)*

BELOW: *Wooden blocks are used to plan a SEAL mission in an Iraqi town. The yellow is from a recent duststorm. (Photo: Greg E. Mathieson Sr. / NSW Publications, LLC)*

BOTTOM, LEFT: *SEALs in Mine Resistant Ambush Protected (MRAP) vehicles return from a mission in Iraq. The RG-33 USSO-COM Armored Utility Vehicle (AUV) was designed specifically for U.S. Special Operations Forces and manufactured by BAE Systems. It's outfitted with a remote-controlled weapon system called the CROWS. (Photo: Greg E. Mathieson Sr. / NSW Publications, LLC)*

BOTTOM, RIGHT: *A Navy communications technician checks out the comm gear in a Mine Resistant Ambush Protected (MRAP) vehicle before a team of SEALs deploy on a mission. (Photo: Greg E. Mathieson Sr. / NSW Publications, LLC)*

participate in these schools at one time or another as part of SEAL team deployment preparation.

Discriminate Shooting

Shooting pistols and short assault rifles in the hostage scenario has brought us the double-tap technique whereby the shooter aims at the head of a terrorist and squeezes off two rounds. Head shots are sought because if the terrorist has a finger on a detonator, the head shot immediately prevents any postmortem twitch that could detonate the explosive—not pretty to discuss, but an awful fact

TOP: *Covered in desert dust, various armored vehicles are parked for use by the SEAL teams in Iraq. (Photo: Greg E. Mathieson Sr./ NSW Publications, LLC)*

CENTER: *Wearing body armor and civilian clothes, these SEAL operators move through the streets of Fallujah, Iraq, in their MRAP. Outfitted with numerous secure radios, GPS, and other devices, this heavily armored vehicle is outfitted for nearly any contingency. (Photo: Greg E. Mathieson Sr./ NSW Publications, LLC)*

BOTTOM, RIGHT: *The inside of a SEAL MRAP as it moves through the streets of Fallujah, Iraq. Outfitted with GPS and numerous communications and weapons systems, the SEALs sit in air-conditioned comfort, though the threat of attack always looms. The operator on the right is operating a CROWs weapon system on top of the vehicle, watching the perimeter via a screen that has night vision / thermal zoom capabilities. (Photo: Greg E. Mathieson Sr./ NSW Publications, LLC)*

BELOW: *An American translator assigned the Office of Naval Intelligence accompanies a SEAL team into the field of Iraq in search of insurgents. Civilians and other support personnel of different skills work directly in harm's way with the teams during many missions. (Photo: Greg E. Mathieson Sr./ NSW Publications, LLC)*

LEFT: *SEAL Qualification Training (SQT) involves marksmanship under many conditions, including the head shot. On this range they practice with their weapon of choice — the M4A1 Carbine (5.56-mm round), and their sidearm, the 9-mm pistol. Practicing Close Quarters Combat with live ammo in two-man teams, they work on their familiarity with their weapons and alternate with practice in the Kill House, where they work on team skills in entering and clearing dwellings. (Photo: Dave Gatley)*

of terrorism. All SEAL team members are expert shots. Tier-1 members spend hours a day honing their CQB shooting skills. It is an expensive and necessary part of CT training. In the early 1980s, one special team used more .45-caliber ammunition than the entire Marine Corps! Before the USSOCOM budget was in place, funding SEAL team pistol ammunition was an annual headache for the CNO staff.

Demolition Breaching

Backing up a moment in the terrorist takedown, another technique developed early on was explosive breaching. With this, demolition shaped charges are used to surgically open an entranceway. Some of the materials remain classified, but generally a specifically worked explosive is attached to the structure (door panel or wall) to be blown. When that occurs, the assaulting team rushes through, guns at the ready, and clears the enclosed space (room, hallway, cave), double-tapping any threat. Often, the second man through the door is an EOD expert whose job it is to "render safe" (the official term) any unexploded munitions the terrorists may have

LEFT: *Local Iraqi village leaders meet with SEAL operators to exchange information and discuss the needs of both sides. (Photo: Greg E. Mathieson Sr. / NSW Publications, LLC)*

BELOW: *SEALs, with locals and a translator, leave a meeting with local leaders in an Iraqi village. As part of their mission in Iraq, SEALs meet with local leaders to find out their needs and seek information on insurgents. (Photo: Greg E. Mathieson Sr. / NSW Publications, LLC)*

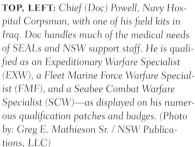

rigged. Dangerous, dirty work: the EOD technicians are today an integral part of CT operations and go through the majority of SEALs training, except they are not BUD/S graduates. They swim, skydive, patrol, dive on submerged ordnance, shoot, and breach. They are among the most highly trained technicians and operators in the world. They are irreplaceable members of the total special operations team in all services. (Some enlisted SEALs, in fact, attend EOD school, but the norm is to recruit full-time EOD members for a tour of duty.)

Snipers

We have already looked at sniper training. Sniping has become an important tool in CT operations and general warfare, as well. This writer was visiting wounded soldiers in Walter Reed Military Hospital in Washington in 2004. A Green Beret sergeant said, "I love SEALs." On further inquiry he related an operation in Afghanistan when his observation team was under attack by mounted Taliban. On a ridgeline two thousand meters (more than a mile) away, a SEAL sniper with a

.50-caliber sniper rifle took them under fire, killing two of the horsemen. The rest bolted. The sergeant appreciates SEAL shooting skills.

SEAL snipers are good. A sniper team is made up of two to three members, all shooters, but ordinarily one snipes, one observes, and one works the communications. SEAL snipers operated in Beirut and are active today in Iraq—just as they were in Afghanistan. The sniper team is an integral part of each SEAL platoon. It goes without saying that it takes a special person to be a sniper. Sniping brings the range into the shooter's retina. It remains close and personal, and the SEAL sniper—or Marine or Army sniper—has to be able to disassociate himself from the act itself. He cannot bring it home. Post-traumatic stress disorder occurs often from battle. Statistics are showing more of it, most recently in Iraq. Still, a sniper has to have the mental stability to function during and more importantly after the engagement. Some snipers accumulate scores of hits or takedowns. It is all part of the battle area and has to be sublimated in the shooter's psyche. In other words,

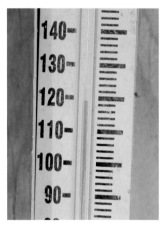

the sniper has to have the mental fortitude to live with the effects of his actions. Without getting too much into psychology, suffice it to say here that SEAL sniper candidates are screened very carefully by command physicians and senior leadership before being accepted for sniper school. A man will usually only spend one tour of duty as a sniper, wartime exigencies depending. Extended tours are unusual and generally not sought. The duty is not for the casual participant. It is a special calling at which SEALs tend to excel.

Parachuting Techniques

Another insertion technique developed alongside fast roping is HAHO (High Altitude High Opening) parachuting. Long practitioners of HALO (High Alti-

ABOVE: *Rear Adm. Edward G. Winters, III, Commander, Naval Special Warfare Command, greets President George W. Bush during the President's final days in office. The President met privately with many of the SEALs to thank them for their efforts and dedication in tracking down terrorists. (Photo: USN)*

LEFT: *Wearing swim fins, a SEAL jumps into the ocean from an aircraft using a static line to join up with his team and their Zodiac. (Photo: USN)*

tude Low Opening) techniques, CT SEALs were looking for means to enter suspected terrorist enclaves or regions without the telltale noise of rotor blades. For many years SEALs had gone to HALO courses offered by the Army; many SEALs were weekend skydivers. In the early 1970s, SEALs brought their own parachutes, then called paracommanders, to team jump days. Brightly colored, multicut steerable parachutes would gently set the fully armed SEAL onto the local drop zone just as his static-line teammate would land in a clump with a controlled parachute landing fall. Of course, the colored rigs were not in operational planning documents; operators were always promised black paracommanders for the real thing. Happily, the real thing never happened.

Today's SEAL trainees attend a contracted static-line and free-fall course right outside San Diego (see Chapter 4). Static-line and HALO techniques are taught; HAHO is not a routinely practiced SEAL team skill. It entails jumping from an aircraft at altitude and immediately deploying the canopy. Such a high opening then allows the parachutist—and associated operators—to glide undetected into a target area miles away from the aircraft exit point. The plane is never detected on radar or heard by the naked ear from the ground. The jumpers,

BOTTOM: *The White House Watch Station is part of the Situation Room (right), or the Sit Room, the complex below the West Wing of the White House, which monitors both classified and unclassified data and video fed in from around the world. Approximately 30 staff of the National Security Council (NSC) Secretariat work five watch teams 24/7 and can connect via live secure video to Air Force One, intelligence agencies, and field commanders around the world. In addition, the President can now conduct secure teleconferencing with world leaders on a moment's notice. (Photos: Eric Draper (bottom, left), Greg E. Mathieson Sr. / NSW Publications, LLC (bottom, right))*

Heavily armed SEALs make their way to a beach on their Zodiac. (Photo: Greg E. Mathieson Sr. / NSW Publications, LLC)

A SEAL flies through the Iraqi desert air over a sand dune using a NSW dirt bike. (Photo: Greg E. Mathieson Sr. / NSW Publications, LLC)

small targets, are not picked up either. The drill is arduous, cold, uncomfortable, and exacting of canopy piloting skills. Steering line extenders are required so the jumper can steer with his feet instead of holding his arms over his head for upward of half an hour. Fun jumping free falls are maybe two or three minutes airborne under canopy with hands overhead in steering toggles. HAHO is not the same, not fun, and is only a precursor to a demanding mission when the SEALs hit the ground—presumably on target and soft. Special areas are required for this training and advance clearance is required with local FAA air controllers. It would not do to have a SEAL jump element collide with a commercial airliner!

New Equipment Upgrades

Guns. A select arsenal is available to SEALs engaged in CT operations. SEAL teams will participate in most of the land warfare developments. Future warriors will sport new power sources, exoskeleton support apparatus that will enable the foot soldier to carry 150 pounds of gear, new observation devices—some developments today can "see" through walls, which is helpful in locating terrorists and hostages—and continued microcommunications and computer-assisted electronics. Of immediate use to SEALs has been the improvement in UAVs. SEALs have several UAV designs to choose from and are currently incorporating more with supporting technicians into all teams. These systems enable the deployed SEAL platoon or element to have real-time confirmation of who is behind the next hill. Sneaking up on a terrorist ambush might become less risky if a SEAL knows who, what, when, and where in advance.

SEALs inspect a container for contraband. (Photo: DoD)

INTELLIGENCE

Team training for the CT mission is just as important as the gear at hand. Small-unit tactics become more decisive as operating areas become more restrictive. Snuggling up against unknown buildings in and around Baghdad is scary stuff; knowing what your closest teammate is doing is essential to room-clearing operations. Doubt has to be eliminated as best as possible, which of course is why intelligence is so important to SEAL missions. Intelligence that supports SEAL team operations comes in many forms . . . .

SEALs in country glean—as opposed to "get"—intelligence from sources, mostly paid informers. In open areas such as Afghanistan, airborne reconnaissance is always helpful, but the word from an individual tribesman or other ideal person on the payroll is more productive. SEALs operated this way in Vietnam with the police special branches that bribed informers. One might argue that this information might be clouded by bias, but nothing replaces so-called ground truth, the on-scene/on-site observation verified by a native. This is true in general combat—where the UAV can provide a lookdown snapshot at an ambush—and is more true in a semi-permissive environment supporting nonuniformed combatants. There is a huge distinction between a flag-bearing enemy and a roadside bomber setting off an improvised explosive device (IED).

COUNTERTERRORISM POSTSCRIPT

The Bush administration established a National Counterterrorism Center (NCTC) in the Washington, D.C., area responsible for collecting and collating all-source intelligence relating to terrorist activities, primarily international. The Center's unclassified website states the following under the title "What we do":

SEALs in the past few years have become closer to the key decision makers in the U.S. government, joining the staff of the Secretary of Defense, the CIA, the National Counterterrorism Center and others. Here the President's Military Aide, a U.S. Navy Lt. Commander and U.S. Navy SEAL, follows the President as they disembark from Marine One, the President's helicopter, on the South Lawn of the White House. The aide is carrying the "football," a case that contains the nuclear release codes in the event of nuclear war and other military response codes and plans which the President keeps at his side at all times. (Photo: Greg E. Mathieson Sr. / NSW Publications, LLC)

ABOVE: *SEALs, under way with the* Truman *Battle Group for Joint Task Force Exercise (JTFEX), fast rope onto the fantail of the guided missile destroyer USS* Oscar Austin *(DDG 79). (Photo: Photographer's Mate 1st Class Michael W. Pendergrass / USN)*

RIGHT: *SEALs conducting a Visit, Board, Search, and Seizure (VBSS) operation, looking for contraband and terrorists. (Photo: USN)*

NCTC serves as the primary organization in the United States Government for integrating and analyzing all intelligence pertaining to terrorism possessed or acquired by the United States Government (except purely domestic terrorism); serves as the central and shared knowledge bank on terrorism information; provides all-source intelligence support to government-wide counterterrorism activities; establishes the information technology (IT) systems and architectures within

Abbottabad Compound

Preconstruction, 2004

Postconstruction, 2011

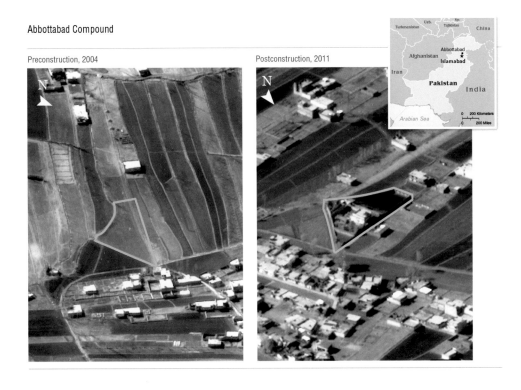

TOP: *The private residence where Osama bin Laden was killed wasn't there a number of years ago. According to neighbors, the new building seemed abnormal both in size and structure. (Graphic: Courtesy of the CIA)*

CENTER, LEFT: *Using advanced imagery and geospatial technology, the National Geospatial-Intelligence Agency built accurate models of Osama bin Laden's compound in Abbottabad for use by the U.S. Navy SEAL / CIA assault teams in planning Operation Neptune Spear. (Photo courtesy NGA)*

CENTER, RIGHT: *A closer look at bin Laden's compound. (Graphic: Courtesy of the CIA)*

Abbottabad Compound, 2005

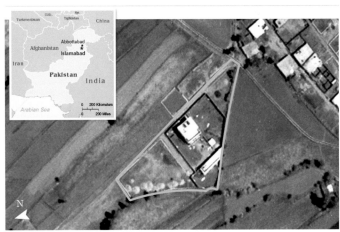

Illustration of Abbottabad Compound

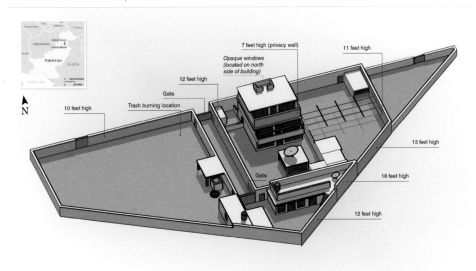

LEFT: *This CIA graphic shows bin Laden's compound. (Graphic: Courtesy of the CIA)*

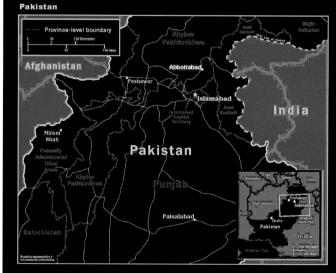

ABOVE: *On May 2, 2011, Osama bin Laden was shot and killed inside a private residential compound in Abbottabad, Pakistan, by Navy SEAL Team 6. (Graphic: Courtesy of the CIA)*

LEFT: *Wanted poster distributed by the FBI placing bin Laden on the FBI Ten Most Wanted list. The word DEAD started to appear on the Internet once he was killed by Navy SEALs. (Photo: Greg E. Mathieson Sr. / NSW Publications, LLC)*

TOP: *President Barack Obama and Vice President Joe Biden in the Situation Room of the White House on May 1, 2011, along with members of the national security team, watch a live satellite feed as members of SEAL Team 6 assault the compound of Osama bin Laden and kill him and others. Please note: a classified document seen in this photograph has been obscured. (Photo: Pete Souza)*

the NCTC and between the NCTC and other agencies that enable access to, as well as integration, dissemination, and use of, terrorism information.

That's a lengthy bit of government "bureau-speak" to describe a very important function: actionable terrorism intelligence is coordinated closely with the JCS, USSOCOM, and the director for national intelligence. Domestic information is passed to the director and the FBI. All USSOCOM subordinate commands are oriented to the CT mission and the GWOT. Historical service training roles are maintained—Navy ships at sea, Army motorized and artillery units, Air Force tactical and strategic command, and the Marine Corps—all services stay ready for general war but are today specifically oriented on defeating terror wherever it crops up. The underlying fact of CT operations is the joint nature of the mission. It is not just SOFs involved.

A remarkable operation occurred on 2 May 2011. On that night was the culmination of many years of collaboration of several military-civilian agencies to track and identify the hiding place of Osama bin Laden. A joint SOF–interagency operation was launched against this international criminal, who was hiding out in Pakistan, and he was cornered and taken down by Navy SEALs. The tactics are in place and used frequently against Taliban forces in Afghanistan. The bin Laden operation was not any different except for the notoriety of the target. Ten years after the tragedy of 9/11, the mastermind had been brought to justice.

Regrettably, CT operations are not without friendly casualties. On 6 August 2011, a conventional Army CH-47 helicopter was downed by a Taliban shoulder-fired missile with the loss of life of thirty Americans, the bulk Navy SEALs—but a conventional flight crew and other supporting SOF operators lost their lives as well. It was the single heaviest U.S. loss in the entire Afghanistan war. The SEALs went out two nights later and killed the Taliban member that fired the missile and his leadership.

The final chapter in the GWOT remains to be written. U.S. SOFs will remain on point for the duration. Even with planned troop drawdowns, SOF will remain engaged—at least for the time being—until the terrorist scourge is finally eliminated.

Naval Special Warfare Operations

Rear Adm (Seal) George Worthington
USN (Ret)

CHAPTER 12

NAVAL SPECIAL WARFARE OPERATIONS

Rear Adm. (SEAL) George Worthington, USN (Ret.)

PAGES 300–301: *A SEAL sniper takes aim in the dusty desert environment of Iraq. (Photo: Greg E. Matheson Sr. / NSW Publications, LLC)*

BELOW: *Pilots of the U.S. Army 160th (SOAR) Night Stalkers prepare to move SEALs and other SOF personnel into an urban area. The Night Stalkers are the primary air transport for the SEALs. (Photo: Greg E. Mathieson Sr. / NSW Publications, LLC)*

NSW OPERATIONAL TEAMS ARE ASSIGNED WORLDWIDE TO THE geographical combatant commands: EUCOM, SOUTHCOM, NORTH-COM, AFRICOM, CENTCOM, and PACOM—Europe, Latin America, North America, Africa, Central (with area of responsibility in Middle East–North Africa–Central Asia), and the Pacific, respectively, which are responsible for U.S. forces in their assigned regions. Now and for more than a decade, the GWOT has occupied center stage, specifically, OIF, where operations are culminating; and OEF, where operations have expanded. In short, NSW forces have not participated in this level of OPTEMPO since the conflict in Vietnam. During the years since Vietnam, teams were engaged in a variety of regional operations such as

those in Grenada, Panama, and Bosnia. Following the Iraqi invasion of Kuwait in 1990, SEALs were among the first combat troops into the region as part of America's effort to expel the Iraqi forces and restore the Kuwaiti government.

In addition to Iraq and Afghanistan, SEALs and other NSW forces are routinely deployed to the European and Pacific theaters and to Latin America. In every geographic location, SEALs and SWCCs, and supporting elements work with other U.S. forces and in combined exercises and operations with Allied forces.

To prepare for operational assignments—in peacetime and wartime—NSW personnel train to precise standards. While numerous official, joint, and service publications describe special activities, operations, and missions, perhaps the refined definition given by Rear Adm. William H. McRaven, USN, in his 1996 book, *Spec Ops: Case Studies in Special Operations Warfare: Theory and Practice*, is the most direct: "A special operation is conducted by forces specially trained, equipped, and supported for a specific target whose destruction, elimination, or rescue (in the case of hostages), is a political or military imperative."

"Trained, equipped, and supported" defines the ingredients behind effective SOFs and NSW teams, in particular. Honing combatant skills in operational units is the meat and potatoes of worldwide NSW employment. Training, training, and training—the cycle is endlessly repetitive, challenging, and seldom boring. SEALs, SDVs, and SBTs participate in training exercises at home and abroad. They participate in Navy fleet exercises in home waters and on deployment. They train and operate with allies, mostly overseas. And then there is the high percentage of operations since 9/11 that have involved actual combat or other real-world special operations, actions, or activities. Normally, training is a two-year cycle: six months each of professional development, ULT, SIT, and an overseas deployment—this last primarily in support of OIF and OEF.

The professional development phase is oriented on the individual Sailor: leave, technical schools, and personal professional courses, several of which are offered at the ATC in Coronado and its detachments. Following this phase, ULT is conducted at the individual SEAL team, SDVT, and SBT, where emphasis is placed on team drills and specific NSW operational techniques. For example, SEAL personnel will hone warfighting techniques in air operations, underwater swimming, personal and crew-served weapons, small-unit tactics (ambushes, patrolling, rapid

reaction drills), communication, and demolition. A great deal of time is spent out of home base areas to conduct this training. This still equates to time away from families, but does not figure in the dwell time definition that is supposed to balance deployments with home presence. Being apart from loved ones is a fact of NSW life. Unfortunately, ranges and training topography are not part of the Coronado or Little Creek landscape, and SEALs have to leave San Diego and Little Creek to benefit from hands-on warfare training. The training facility at Niland, California, provides a desert environment and the Chocolate Mountain firing ranges. East Coast SEALs go north to Fort A. P. Hill, Virginia, for ranges and maneuver areas. On the West Coast, SEALs can use ranges on San Clemente Island, California, when that island is not occupied by BUD/S classes.

To help teams determine what capabilities to train for, certain precise inputs are acknowledged. First, given the present importance of the GWOT, information coming back from Iraq and Afghanistan was central to predeployment training. "Lessons learned" were incorporated into ULT and shared with all operators. To facilitate learning, the NSWGs have established training detachments that serve to instruct team platoons on tactics, current operational techniques, and overall employment guidelines required for the regions in which they are expected to operate. Aiding in this effort are METLs that are specific to each team—that is, SEALs, SDVs, and SBTs. METLs are upgraded routinely as new technology enters or additional missions are assigned. We will discuss some representative METLs in a moment. Now let's look at the group training detachments.

SEAL teams have always had a discrete training cell to put "new guys" through the ropes and train up new and deploying platoons. In the 1960s, a team training department was responsible for imparting this information and running the platoons through their paces. Before deploying to Vietnam, heavy training emphasis was focused on small-unit tactics, weapons familiarization and firing, night patrols, clandestine boat infiltration techniques, and the setting of ambushes. This predeployment training usually lasted six to eight weeks, and was in addition to other work-up tasks that the teams believed were necessary to a successful combat deployment. Time at home back then was hard to come by. Often, platoons would snatch six months back before shipping out for repeat tours. A common saying was that SEAL team members passed each other in the night going to and coming from Vietnam. The same OPTEMPO sensation is being seen again because of the constant deployments to Iraq and Afghanistan, except that command emphasis and attention now equates to a two-year training-deployment cycle. Still, some individuals find themselves redeploying on a more frequent basis; multiple tours into Iraq and Afghanistan are now the rule rather than the exception.

TIME BETWEEN THE WARS

"Time between the wars" is a relative term for NSW. Since direct involvement in the Vietnam conflict ended, Navy SEALs and SBTs have been employed in every combat engagement the United States has accepted. Overseas deployments with the amphibious forces were routine for the UDTs after Vietnam—and later SEALs after all UDTs were reestablished as SEAL or SDV teams in 1983. A SEAL Team 4 platoon supported the amphibious commander by conducting pre-assault reconnaissance in Grenada—that would be the last time SEALs would be in an amphibious direct-support role. Several years after formation of USSOCOM in 1987, SEALs were removed from the Navy's chain of command and placed under USSOCOM for mission tasking, where they were deployed to Panama, Desert Storm, Haiti, Bosnia, and Kuwait. And after the 9/11 attacks they were deployed to Iraq and Afghanistan, where they remain committed today and for the immediate future. Space in this book limits in-depth analysis of these combat engagements, but a thumbnail overview will illustrate NSW's continuing involvement in national defense year after year.

A major maritime undertaking was the 1987 Operation Earnest Will, an effort to protect neutral oil tankers transiting the Persian Gulf. The mission was to thwart Iranian aggression in the Gulf against these ships. As summed up in a USSOCOM history, "To stop these attacks, the U.S. needed surveillance and patrol forces in the northern Persian Gulf . . . SOF, including Army helicopters and Navy SEALs and special boat units (SBUs), had the best-trained personnel and most capable equipment for monitor-

BELOW, TOP: *During Operation Desert Shield and Storm, Navy SEALs trained Kuwaiti special forces. They set up naval special operations groups in Kuwait, working with the Kuwaiti navy in exile. Kuwaiti forces took part in combat operations such as the liberation of the capital city. Here some of those fighters move through the burning oil fields outside of Kuwait City. (Photo: Greg E. Mathieson Sr. / NSW Publications, LLC)*

BELOW, BOTTOM: *Navy SEALs carried out special reconnaissance missions along the Kuwaiti coastline in the buildup to the ground war. When Allied ground operations began, SEALs swam ashore and planted a series of explosive devices. The detonation of these explosives, coupled with machine gun fire from Special Boat Teams, convinced the Iraqi defenders that an amphibious landing was imminent, causing them to commit men to defend the coast. This deception resulted in the USMC thrust, coming over land instead of from the sea, to be met with fewer troops than otherwise. Here U.S. forces begin flying into Kuwait airport amid burning oil wells and fleeing Iraqi troops. (Photo: Greg E. Mathieson Sr. / NSW Publications, LLC)*

FACING PAGE

TOP: *Afghanistan Regular Army cross training in Afghanistan next to U.S. troops serve as guides and translators on some missions. Manning an outpost guard tower, they check out all newcomers to the Multinational Force base near the Pakistani mountains. (Photo: Dave Gatley)*

BOTTOM: *SEALs routinely train foreign nationals in tactics to help defend their country and train others. (Photo: DoD)*

ing hostile activity, particularly at night when the Iranians conducted their missions. Shallow-draft NSW patrol boats could ply waters that had not been swept for mines." To accomplish the SOF mission, two oil service barges, *Hercules* and *Wimbrown VI*, were converted and stationed in the northern Gulf. Each mobile sea base housed 150 men, ten combatant craft, and three helicopters. Supported by Navy surface forces, these forward at-sea bases tracked Iranian warships and intercepted mine-laying operations, sinking several. In addition to the barges, Navy SOF operated from surface ships farther south attacking Iranian oil platforms. SOF participation in Earnest Will ended in September 1989. The Navy had safely escorted 259 ships.

Just as Earnest Will was winding down, USSOCOM prepared to execute Operation Just Cause against strongman Manuel Noriega of Panama. All SOF were engaged: Army Special Forces and Rangers, Air Force Air Commandos, and NSW SEALs and SWCCs. The major mission was to capture Noriega and neutralize the Panamanian defense forces. As part of the overall joint task force, spearheaded by the JSOTF, NSWTUs were assigned to Task Force White, which included Navy SEALs and SWCCs. NSWTUs were divided into four subordinate task elements with separate H-hour missions. The largest task element was assigned to secure Paitilla Airfield, another to attack a Panamanian patrol boat, with the last two units assigned the mission of securing Atlantic and Pacific entrances to the Panama Canal.

The first task element departed Rodman Naval Station at 11:00 p.m. on 19

SEALs routinely train in Close Quarter Combat in Kill Houses around the U.S. to keep their skills sharp. (Photo: MC1 Aaron Peterson / USN)

December en route to Balboa Harbor to conduct an underwater demolition attack against the *Presidente Poras*, a Panamanian Defense Force patrol boat. Slipping over the side of a Zodiac CRRC, a SEAL swim pair using a pure-oxygen, closed-circuit (no bubbles) SCUBA began their attack. They set demolition haversacks on the patrol boat propeller shafts and exfiltrated successfully. This attack marked the first time SEALs had conducted a real-world combat underwater demolition ship attack, although they routinely practice the mission.

The Paitilla task element came ashore at 12:45 a.m., but the element of surprise had been lost due to opening fires in other parts of the city. As the SEALs patrolled toward the airfield tower, a brief verbal exchange was initiated with one member of the guard force. This resulted in a firefight, where eight SEALs were wounded, four of whom later died. The airfield was secured by 2:00 a.m. and medical evacuation effected. The SEALs held Paitilla for more than a day before the Army Rangers relieved them on 21 December.

Operation Desert Shield and Operation Desert Storm, 1990–1991, were major military engagements involving NSW. Iraq had invaded Kuwait on 2 August 1990, and was threatening Saudi Arabia. CENTCOM was the regional commander; SOCCENT deployed to Saudi Arabia on 10 August along with an initial NSWTU comprising NSWG-1 units. The SEALs immediately began training Saudi armed forces engaged in coalition warfare. It took nearly half a year to build up coalition forces to attack north. As reported by USSOCOM, Navy SEALs trained three Saudi sea commandos in maritime special operations, and SBT personnel worked with Saudi boat crews. As part of the CENTCOM deception plan, SEALs performed beach reconnaissance off Kuwait City prior to D-Day (day of the invasion), leaving time-detonated charges in the water to create a diversion. The operational feint convinced the Iraqi command that a Marine Corps amphibious landing was imminent—keeping an entire

Navy SEALs provide Executive Protection for Adm. Leighton "Snuffy" Smith at Eagle Base in Bosnia while he was commander of the Implemenaton Force (IFOR) in Bosnia-Herzegovina. (Photo: Greg E. Mathieson Sr. / NSW Publications, LLC)

division away from the primary invasion, which was a "left hook" thrust from the southeast.

Other operations involving SOF and NSW are best summarized:

- Operation Restore Hope (1992–1995)—Somalia relief, on which the movie *Blackhawk Down* was based
- Operation Uphold Democracy (1994–1995)—Haiti
- Operation Joint Endeavor (1995–1996)—Bosnia-Herzegovina, with subordinate Operation Joint Force
- Operation Provide Comfort (1991)—Iraq, protection of the Kurds
- Operations Focus Relief, Silver Anvil, Assured Response, Shadow Express, Silver Wake, Noble Obelisk, Firm Response, and a host of other named operations that represent deployments for humanitarian assistance around the world. All SOF find great satisfaction in performing these missions. Good examples are SOF efforts in tsunami relief and Hurricane Katrina relief.

As the reader can see from the foregoing, SOF and NSW forces are occupied full-time. As mentioned previously, platoons feel like they are passing each other

A Navy SEAL armed with a 5.56-mm M4 carbine equipped with the Knights Armament Company (KAC) Modular Weapon System (MWS), gives commands in a downed pilot extraction training exercise, Desert Rescue XI. The exercise is the premier Search and Rescue (SAR) training exercise involving all branches of the military and is conducted on various ranges at Fallon Naval Air Station (NAS), Nevada. (Photo: SSGT Arron Allmon II / USAF)

in the night—just as they did during the Vietnam conflict. In today's operating environment, it would be rare for an entire team to be present at home base. It would be no exaggeration to expect that it could be years before some teammates get to meet each other! But they're all training to the same tasks, conditions, and standards, and must be prepared to fulfill team mission-essential tasks, to which we now turn.

MISSION-ESSENTIAL TASKS

Mission-essential tasks are enumerated for NSW operational teams in their METLs, which are classified documents. The METL sets a baseline for ULT exercises. They specify tasks, conditions, and standards. These criteria define the job, all conditions under which it will be performed, and levels of achievement. For example, and not to belabor these definitions, a beach hydrographic reconnaissance would not be conducted during a hurricane. Similarly, a parachute insertion can only occur if weather permits. Small-craft operations are weather limited, as well. And, as always, human endurance is taken into account, especially in arctic conditions. While accompanying photography illustrates many skills and capabilities, here are several examples of METLs to describe how teams train up for various missions.

The most fundamental mission from a historical context is the hydrographic reconnaissance. It has been an essential task ever since 1943, and was the reason for standing up the Pacific UDTs. Hydrographic reconnaissance is conducted before every major amphibious landing. SEAL combat swimmers can survey the offshore approaches to a beach landing site with a variety of new technical tools—from satellite reconnaissance, drone overflights, manned aircraft surveillance, and underwater SDV sweeps launched from a submerged submarine. The task states all the climatological elements to be considered—tides, temperature, moonrise, currents, sea state, hinterland buildup, beach gradient (which is actually determined by the reconnaissance), and the like. And let's not forget length of beach frontage to be surveyed: more beach takes more men. A hundred swimmers are required to support a Marine Corps division OTB landing.

The next important mission task SEALs developed during the Korean War was the inland demolition raid. This involved identification of a target inland from the beach landing area, or of merely an ingress point from the sea. Other mission sets grew out of the inland demolition raid: small-unit tactics, ambushes, personnel snatches, prisoner rescues, and hostile interdictions, for example. The mission-essential task requires a SEAL team to develop skills in land warfare, to include small-arms training, thorough knowledge of a myriad of explosive charges, hand grenades, booby trap avoidance, and patrolling. All these skills are called out in the mission-essential task. Human limitations are noted, as well, such as the amount of time the unit will be engaged—number of hours or days—amount of outside support needed, any combined arms augmentation (e.g., close air support, on-call naval fire support, and artillery, if available), and other operational support. Communications for controlling all support are also identified in the METL; the capability to call in fires is an essential task—controlling aircraft, calling naval gunfire support, or Army or Marine Corps artillery. All of these capabilities are cited in the METL with standards of required effectiveness. As an example, at least one member of the SEAL platoon will have attended a formal school for fire support.

Navy SEALs train Iraqi Army Scouts in gathering tactical intelligence during an advanced Close Quarters Combat course. The training is part of ongoing efforts to increase the Iraqi army's capabilities for providing security. (Photo: MC1 Aaron Peterson / USN)

Specific techniques and communications procedures are standard and are part of the combined arms expertise.

SEAL and SDV platoons have to prove competency in small-unit tactics and land warfare during ULT drills and, later, during squadron work-up for the all-important field training exercise prior to overseas deployment.

Driving the SDV on a reconnaissance and ship attack mission normally involves locking out from a submerged submarine offshore from the target harbor, navigating into the region, conducting the mission, and returning to the submarine totally submerged throughout the operation. This is one of the most difficult missions that SEALs undertake—maybe the *most* difficult. SDV operations can last up to eight hours. The technical skills required to conduct these underwater missions cannot be overstated. Men assigned as SDV operators receive extra hazardous duty pay. They attend several formal schools and spend countless hours underwater honing their piloting and navigational skills. The METL, like all others, calls out the climate, geographic conditions, sea state, current, tide, moon state (for nighttime luminosity should they need to surface), and other regional or tactical considerations. Suffice it to say here that the SDV METLs are highly technical and challenging.

All SWCC operators undergo formal training to serve in an SBT. Their operations primarily involve inserting and extracting SEAL operators in coastal and riverine regions. They have to be able to navigate and maintain their craft, communicate, and, on occasion, man weapons for both offensive and defensive reasons. Often, during operations in Vietnam, the special boat crews engaged in many intensive firefights in order to extract SEAL squads or platoons. During these highly dangerous operations, high levels of warfighting capabilities are mandatory to ensure successful mission accomplishment. A specific METL will call for a crew to launch from a surface ship, navigate clandestinely to the SEAL infiltration point, loiter (depending on length of land operation), extract the SEALs, and return to the host ship. Another SWCC METL might call for the coastal patrol and interdiction of enemy small craft. More often, however, the SBT craft is in direct support of the SEAL element or platoon(s).

We have provided many photos of SEALs and SWCCs during special boat evolutions—all backed up by a METL. Space prohibits covering every potential NSW operational attribute; it is safe to say to say, however, that no SEAL or SWCC unit deploys without having proven itself by demonstration of proficiency as established by the team's METLs. These yardsticks are not frozen. They are continually evaluated in light of overseas lessons learned and evolving missions in theater. The basic METLs discussed here serve only as examples; each specific team has several METLs for which it is accountable and in which the team must prove competency prior to deploying. Individual skill sets required by a specific METL are developed during the professional development phase, either in a formal school (e.g., gunfire support) or in teams through peer contact. Most will be demonstrated during ULT and squadron work-up when all deploying units come together under a deploying SEAL team CO, which we will look at next.

SQUADRON DEPLOYMENTS

NSW forces will generally deploy to the overseas-based NSWTUs, which are positioned as follows: NSWU-1, Guam; NSWU-2, Stuttgart, Germany; NSWU-3, Bahrain; NSWU-4, Little Creek, Virginia; and NSWU-10, Stuttgart, Germany.

Each unit is responsible to a geographic TSOC for NSW operations in the region. During conflict, the TSOCs are used to form the basis of one or more JSOTFs, which organize their combat operations and support. Operational geography ranges from arctic to subtropical, from the ten-thousand-foot snow-capped mountains in Afghanistan to the jungles of Indonesia, Malaya, and the Philippines. Warfare training varies between climates, and proper preparation is indispensable to effectiveness in theater. It is not an easy acclimation. For example, during the Vietnam conflict, SEALs had to enter a theater of average temperatures of more than 90 degrees Fahrenheit from a San Diego norm of 72 degrees; it was a little better coming from summertime on the U.S. East Coast, where the summer temperature and humidity is closer to that found in Southeast Asia. Still, moving to the CENT-COM location in the Middle East today is difficult for most people, including SEALs, who are in superb physical condition.

In addition to the ongoing operations in Iraq and Afghanistan, NSWRONs deploy to the aforementioned locations. Training goes on 24/7. Squadrons participate in joint operations with other SOF units and combined operations with host-nation counterparts. In the European theater, squadron personnel exercise with counterparts from Germany, the United Kingdom, Spain, France, and Italy to "enable European and other partners, particularly NATO, who will support coalition operations in Iraq, Afghanistan, and Africa." East Coast teams work in trans-Sahara Africa to "Deny the Sahara and Sahel as sanctuary for terrorists, their networks, and the criminal activities that directly or indirectly support terrorist networks."

SEALs and SWCCs exercise frequently with counterparts in Thailand, the Philippines, Australia, and Malaysia in the western Pacific. Joint exercises have

A U.S. Air Force HH-60G Pave Hawk helicopter lands to extract personnel as a SEAL team member calls in more air support during a Noncombatant Evacuation Operation (NEO) training exercise conducted during Desert Rescue XI. (Photo: TSGT Scott Reed / USAF)

exotic names: in the Philippines, Exercise Balikatan; in Australia, Talisman Saber; in Thailand, Cobra Gold; and in Korea, Ulchi Focus Lens and Foal Eagle. In addition to these major efforts, the deployed squadrons routinely conduct small joint exercises throughout the year. Ongoing efforts in the Philippines are aimed at training their armed forces to contend with the Islamic threat in the southern islands. Most current operations are being conducted in Mindanao and Zamboanga. The deployed squadron advises on combat to Philippine police units and other government organs.

It is extremely important to keep in mind that, while much of NSW deployments are to regions not directly involved with combat in Iraq and Afghanistan, teams move in and out of combat rotations. One deployment might be to the Philippines, and the next might be to the Middle East. It is a fact that all SEALs will participate in the GWOT with little respite. Normal peacetime rotations are perhaps every two years, but with ongoing combat operations now entering a second decade, personnel can expect to be deployed for six- or eight-month periods and return home for about a year of schools and training in preparation for the next deployment. During Vietnam such deployments were termed "port and starboard" rotations. Not much fun, very hard on families, and to date no let-up in sight, which is not to say there is no light at the end of the tunnel. It is, however, very difficult knowing you will be looking at repeat deployments to a war zone. It cannot be overemphasized how hard this is on families, which fact seemingly goes unremarked in the national media.

POST-9/11 OPERATIONS IN THE GLOBAL WAR ON TERROR

The GWOT has defined the majority of NSW's training focus, and indeed all SOF training. Following the terrorist attacks on September 11, 2001, SOFs started packing their war bags. An operation in Afghanistan was termed OEF, which was in the geographic responsibility of CENTCOM and its component SOCCENT, which was commanded by Rear Adm. Albert "Bert" M. Calland, a Navy SEAL. Much has already been written about this operation, and space limitations in a picture anthology curtail lengthy analysis. By way of summary, OEF was a joint battle—Army, Air Force, Navy, Marines, and other government agencies, notably the CIA, whose field operators provided historic and superb duty. Afghanistan was chosen as a first-strike target owing to the training infrastructure and sanctuary it provided Osama bin Laden, who had vowed war against the West. After years of evading U.S. forces, Osama bin Laden was found and shot dead by U.S. Navy SEALs during a daring cross-border operation in Pakistan on 1 May 2011. Mastermind of several bloody attacks against U.S. and European overseas embassies and assets, bin Laden was the head of a shadow organization termed al Qaeda. This organ was protected by the Afghanistan Taliban government; therefore, Afghanistan was chosen for immediate retaliatory strikes. As stated in the USSOCOM history, "The use of indigenous Islamic, anti-Taliban forces would undermine Taliban legitimacy and reinforce that the fight was between Afghans, and not a U.S. led war against Afghanistan or Islam. In September 2001, the only insurgency opposing the Taliban was the beleaguered Northern Alliance, which controlled about 10 percent of Afghanistan." This set the strategy, but it did not eliminate SOF involvement one iota; in fact, SOF proved predominant in the overall effort. Basically, SOCCENT divided Afghanistan into northern and southern zones. Army Special Forces took the north, NSW took the

A Navy SEAL officer, wearing night vision goggles and armed with his fully tricked out M-4, stands ready in front of his MRAP before heading out on an urban mission in Iraq. (Photo: Greg E. Mathieson Sr. / NSW Publications, LLC)

south. The Army closely advised the Northern Alliance; both services relied on Air Force Combat Controllers for air support. With a respectful nod to Army, Air Force, and CIA operatives, we will concentrate on NSW.

NSW's part of the JSOTF tasking was organized as Task Force K-Bar (TF K-Bar), named after the World War II military knife carried by frogmen. Commanded by the NSWG-1 commander, Capt. Robert Harward, this force established itself in Afghanistan on 22 November 2001, initially at Marine Corps Camp Rhino; soon after it relocated to Kandahar Airfield and coordinated SOF operations throughout southern Afghanistan. TF K-Bar was a combined task force; attached were European forces—from Denmark, Germany, and Norway—as well as forces from Australia, Canada, and New Zealand. Interestingly, this was the first combat deployment outside Germany by German forces since World War II. American attachments included elements of the Air Force Special Operations Command's 720th Special Tactics Group, Army Special Operations Command's 5th Special Forces (Airborne) Group, and somewhat later a company of U.S. Marines.

TF K-Bar began the planning and conduct of direct action missions in January 2002. The first objective turned out to be an extensive cave complex at Zhawar Kili, in Paktia Province, southeastern Afghanistan. Harward expected a reconnaissance of a few hours, but the operation lasted eight days. Thousands of tons of munitions and intelligence documents were turned up. More than 400,000 pounds of ordnance were expended in destroying the cave complex. Several Taliban fighters were killed in action. (In-depth coverage of TF K-Bar operations is to be found in Dick Couch's 2005 book, *Down Range.*)

TF K-Bar performed more than forty-two special reconnaissance and twenty-three direct action missions along the Afghanistan–Pakistan border area, not counting missions associated with the Army's Operation Anaconda. Operation Anaconda took place in early March 2002, when U.S. Army and allied Afghan military forces attempted to destroy al Qaeda and Taliban forces in the Shah-i-Kot Valley and Arma Mountains southeast of Zormat. This was the first operation in the Afghanistan theater to involve a large number of U.S. conventional (i.e., non-SOF) forces participating in direct combat activities.

Many of TF K-Bar missions were conducted in rugged mountains at altitudes exceeding ten thousand feet—far from the usual operating region of littoral coastal haunts. The SEALs definitely proved themselves as effective mountain fighters.

ABOVE: *Vice Adm. Bert Calland (SEAL) (R) commends Capt. Robert Harward (SEAL) (L), U. S. Navy, Commander, Naval Special Warfare Group ONE/Commander, Task Force K-BAR, upon receiving the Presidential Unit Citation. President George W. Bush made a brief stop at Marine Corps Air Station Mira-mar to present the award to Captain Harward and congradulate the troops. (Photo: PH2 Eric S. Logsdon)*

BELOW: *The Operation Iraqi Freedom 2003 Challenge coin given out at the beginning of the war (front). (Photo: Dave Gatley)*

OPERATION IRAQI FREEDOM

Navy SEALs were intimately involved even before the operating phases. Days before the opening shots of OIF, Navy SEALs made a clandestine reconnaissance on southern Iraq oil pumping stations in Basra: the Mina al Bakr and Khor al Amaya offshore oil platforms. An SDV crew approached the installations, tied off the Mk VIII SDV, and swam to the surface to take photographs of the platforms. The entire operation went without a hitch, and the SDV returned to its surface support vessel, an Australian-built high-speed vessel and catamaran, *Joint Venture* (HSV X-1), being leased by the U.S. Navy. The USSOCOM history summarizes this mission:

> On 20 March 2003, a Naval Special Warfare Task Group (NSWTG), consisting of U.S. Navy SEALs, the United Kingdom's 40 Commando Brigade, and Polish SOF, conducted one of the largest direct action missions conducted in OIF. The goal was to simultaneously take control of two offshore oil platforms, Mina Al Bakr (MABOT) and Khor Al Amaya (KAAOT), and secure onshore support valves for each platform and their metering and manifold stations located on the Al Faw peninsula. By taking control of these targets before Iraqi forces could damage them, the NSWTG would avert an environmental disaster and reserve the only oil-export capability in southern Iraq.

The importance of this mission cannot be downplayed, given the history of Saddam Hussein setting fire to Kuwaiti oil wells. Also, the operation represented a unique role for SDVs. On the opening night of hostilities, SEALs and SWCCs infiltrating in NSW eleven-meter RIBs approached and boarded the Mina al Bakr offshore oil platform terminal; Polish Special Forces took down the Khor al Amaya offshore oil platform. Other SEALs secured the onshore pumping stations. The installations were then turned over to British Marines.

As Allied forces marched north to Baghdad, SOF supported operations by moving forward of advancing U.S. Army and Marine Corps elements to provide strategic reconnaissance. Baghdad fell in

mid-2003; SOF—and SEALs—remained to conduct routine direct action missions against suspected Baathist holdouts. In addition, SEALs were assigned to security details protecting high-level Iraqi officials.

CONCLUSION

The representative exercises and operations discussed here are not static. They evolve as conditions dictate. NSW remains a flexible SOF maritime capability that will continue to grow and change as the world situation dictates. Approaching seventy years in existence, the combat swimmers represented by SEAL and SDVTs will continue to be exemplary warriors in the war on terror. Supported by the SBTs and the ever-expanding technical support units—MCT, Support Activities, LOGSUs, imbedded team technicians—SEALs and SWCCs will continue to be at the tip of the USSOCOM spear and, with other SOF, to be a vanguard of U.S. national security.

RESEARCH
AND
DEVELOPMENT

CDR (SEAL) TOM HAWKINS
USN (RET)

CHAPTER 13

RESEARCH AND DEVELOPMENT

Cdr. (SEAL) Tom Hawkins, USN (Ret.)

T HE PROCESS OF ACQUIRING AND DEVELOPING EQUIPMENT IN NSW is fascinating and has been a common ingredient to the success of specialized maritime-focused combat operations from the early days of World War II.

The most noteworthy World War II organizations formed for research, development, and experimentation surrounding maritime special operations were within the OSS, a governmental agency formed specifically for World War II, and within the Joint Army-Navy Experimental and Testing Board and its Navy Demolition Research Unit, which was established at ATB Fort Pierce, Florida, to support the board's combat demolition programs. In fact, the base established for UDT training at Maui, in the then-territory of Hawaii, was called the naval combat demolition training and experimental base, perhaps as a cover name for the UDTs; almost every early operation they conducted was an experiment that provided lessons learned for training.

Before World War II, no one had experimented with the demolition of massed obstacles like those being encountered by amphibious planners in Europe and the Pacific. Beginning in late 1942, experiments were conducted at a temporary site at

Camp Bradford (current location of Joint Expeditionary Base (JEB), Little Creek), near the Atlantic Ocean at the mouth of the Chesapeake Bay. Over the winter of 1942–1943, many different obstacles were tested. Based on this work, preparations were made for establishing a permanent R&D site at Fort Pierce, Florida, which resulted in the formation of the Joint Army-Navy Experimental and Testing (JANET) group and Demolition Research Unit (DRU).

Innovation, however, was not restricted to the formalized developmental initiatives. Probably the earliest and most dynamic capability to come out of the field was the Hagensen Pack, an improvised demolition named after its innovator, Lt. (jg) Carl Hagensen, OIC of NCDU-30, who was part of the Utah Red Beach Demolition Party.

The first NCDUs sent from Fort Pierce arrived in England in November 1943, where they continued to carry out a training program and work in demolition. As a result of participation with their British equivalent (Combined Operations Experimental Establishment), much intelligence in the form of pictures and literature pertaining to obstacles already placed on the coast of France was obtained. Of all the obstacles mentioned, the highest priority was placed on Element C, also called the Belgian Gate. Inasmuch as this was an entirely new obstacle to the NCDUs, considerable time was spent determining the best methods for its destruction.

The greatest difficulty in the process came in the attachment of the charges. From this difficulty came the innovation of the Hagensen Pack, a small canvas sack filled with two pounds of C-2 explosive, which could be fitted and secured to the angle iron regardless of its size or shape by means of a line and V-slot hook of special design. By placing a minimum of sixteen packs in carefully selected positions on an Element C, this large obstacle could be collapsed inward upon itself. The Hagensen Pack was adopted as a standard explosive for the NCDUs for D-Day, and later it was perfected as a standard military demolition pack.

In the Pacific theater, the UDTs had to create almost everything from scratch. For their first operations at Kwajalein in January 1944, UDT-1 and UDT-2 were originally conceived in the fashion of the NCDUs of the Atlantic—not as combat swimmers, but rather as expert assault demolitioneers working from rubber boats in full battle dress at or near the beach.

UDT-2 was actually given the task of experimenting with drone boats called Stingrays. The concept was to fill the drones with ten thousand pounds of explosives and, by remote control, maneuver them to a reef or other obstacle, where they could be remotely detonated. The theory might have been good, but in practice the drone-boat concept proved a miserable failure and the boats were never used again.

In August 1944. a similar ability was given to NCDU men preparing for the invasion of southern France, where they experimented with drone Apex boats. Two kinds of capabilities were attempted: Woofus, a demolition craft whose rockets were supposed to blast underwater obstructions, and Reddy Fish, a torpedo-driven explosive intended for the same purpose. They proved once again that a man with demolitions against individual targets was the only reliable method of accomplishing the task.

The Saipan operation in June 1944 was the first major operation for UDTs after Kwajalein, and the first to use a full-scale swimmer reconnaissance. The UDTs began to realize that development of individual equipment such as face masks, swim fins, compasses, and mine-detecting devices deserved priority. A few men had tried goggles for underwater vision at Kwajalein, but later requested dive masks that covered the eyes and nose. The UDTs were among the first to use the face mask on a large-scale basis. Through experimentation they also adopted a method to pick up men out of the water, while the recovery boat maintained a somewhat constant high speed. Later called the snare method, a man would use a figure-eight rubber-hose-like device to capture a swimmer's outstretched arm and snare him into the recovery boat traveling a full speed.

Many of the UDT developments surrounded creation and refinement of operating tactics and procedures rather than actually developing new hardware.

Many material or hardware innovations surrounding maritime special operations were occurring at the OSS, where activities created a steady demand for devices and documents that could be used to trick, attack, or demoralize the enemy. Finding few agencies or corporations willing to undertake this sort of low-volume, highly specialized work, Gen. William J. Donovan, the organizer of OSS, enthusiastically promoted an in-house capability to fabricate the tools needed for OSS's clandestine missions. By the end of the war, OSS engineers and technicians had formed a collection of labs, workshops, and experts that frequently gave OSS a technological edge over its Axis foes.

The special operations and secret intelligence branches frequently called on the technical prowess assembled in the R&D and related offices. R&D proved adept at inventing weapons and gadgets and in adapting Allied equipment to new missions. The growing number of OSS coastal infiltration and sabotage projects eventually gave rise to an independent branch, the MU, that develops specialized boats, operational equipment, and explosives. The MU fashioned equipment such as underwater breathing gear, fins, face masks, propelled submersibles, waterproof watches and compasses, an inflatable motorized surfboard, and a two-man kayak.

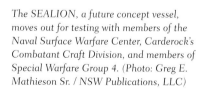

The SEALION, a future concept vessel, moves out for testing with members of the Naval Surface Warfare Center, Carderock's Combatant Craft Division, and members of Special Warfare Group 4. (Photo: Greg E. Mathieson Sr. / NSW Publications, LLC)

The MU formed America's first combat swimmers trained for maritime sabotage, and the Navy's postwar UDTs would later adopt their methods. The MU used the first practical American SCUBA, which was the LARU, a self-contained, pure-oxygen rebreather that allowed men to swim clandestinely underwater emitting no telltale bubbles. In the 1940s, nontethered or self-contained underwater swimming was an obscure and relatively untried concept.

The OSS MU men also experimented with submersibles, and were the first to do so in this country. In June 1943, a Frenchman named Jean de la Valdene contacted the OSS relative to his designs for a new type of one-man submersible vehicle that would be "among man's earliest creations in fiberglass." In many respects Valdene's machine was similar to the British Chariot, inasmuch as the diver wore a breathing apparatus and part of his body was exposed to the water. The OSS MU immediately recognized the possibilities of this new weapon, which they later called the Toy because of its novelty, for its operational swimmer groups. By early 1944, however, the Toy was found to be not suited to MU's purposes and the entire idea was abandoned. OSS MU eventually embraced the British-developed submersible canoe that they called Sleeping Beauty. This one-man submersible was acquired by OSS MU for training. It was later deployed with them to the Pacific theater of operations, where the submersible was used to train for operations against the main island of Japan. OSS and the MU were disbanded in September 1945, after the end of the war with Japan, and much of their work would later be adopted by the postwar UDTs.

UDT men were the first to experiment with thermal protective dress. Here they are seen in a dry suit under which they wore longjohn underwear. They entered the rubber suit from the back, and it was sealed with a clip as seen on the back of this diver. The pressure relief valve seen on the front of the suit allowed excess air to escape as the men descended and the water pressure forced out excess air. (Photo: Courtesy of Tom Hawkins)

The period from 1945, until sometime in 1947, was pretty much a story of simply surviving within the UDTs, which had been left with little manpower and even less money with which to operate after World War II; four fifty-man teams were established, two at NAB, Coronado, and two at NAB, Little Creek.

Because little has been written about this period, there remains an unintended vagueness about UDT activities during the late 1940s and into the Korean War period. Lt. Cdr. Francis Douglass Fane, commander of the UDTs in the Atlantic Fleet, stands out as NSW's foremost and most aggressive innovator during this period. Lieutenant Commander Fane was strongly motivated to get his UDT men involved in just about anything that would continue to get them recognition in magazines, newspapers, books, or anywhere he could lecture in front of an audience. His foremost accomplishment, however, was getting them an expanded underwater capability. His successful actions resulted from a collaboration with Dr. Christian J. Lambertsen, who as we have learned developed and perfected the LARU and tactical-combat-swimming methods used by the OSS MU during World War II. Together, Lieutenant Commander Fane and Dr. Lambertsen brought the full spectrum of MU diving capabilities to UDT during operations on board the submarine USS *Grouper* (SS-214) at St. Thomas, Virgin Islands, in February 1948. The following October, Lieutenant Commander Fane, Dr. Lambertsen, and a UDT detachment from Little Creek were flown to St. Thomas to rendezvous with USS *Quillback* (SS-424), where they conducted operations with the Sleeping Beauty. This was the first time a submersible had been launched and recovered from a submarine.

This was a milestone event for the UDTs, an epoch that introduced the full spectrum of submersible operation capabilities, eventually combining the capabilities of SCUBA, submersibles, and submarines, and perhaps introducing a first real understanding of the need for focused experimentation and research. Whatever the

Italian Pig — minisub. The men of UDT-2 and UDT-4 experimenting with an Italian submersible vehicle in the Chesapeake Bay. The photo was probably taken in the late 1940s. (Photo: Courtesy of Tom Hawkins)

motivation, Lieutenant Commander Fane began a quest to move UDT capabilities forward. It was, however, Dr. Lambertsen, by then a professor at the Perelman School of Medicine of the University of Pennsylvania, who encouraged the U.S. Navy to invest in underwater swimming capabilities and the science and technology needed to attain such capabilities.

Introduction of the LARU into the UDTs led to further development or refinement of swim fins, face masks, and compasses. Introduction of the Sleeping Beauty initiated a long and sometimes challenging marriage of the UDT and U.S. Navy submarine communities, and the beginning of UDT's long and unending pursuit of submersible vehicles.

The potential scope of UDT's new capabilities included the ability to conduct undetected day or night reconnaissance of enemy beaches; underwater demolition of natural and artificial obstacles; day or night observation of enemy surface activities, with photography when conditions were favorable; and demolition attacks on enemy shipping and harbor installations such as docks and net defenses. Each of the new missions was predicated on stealth, using the water for concealment. These new capabilities opened up a vast need for technological advancements in underwater swimming equipment that included: new oxygen diving tables, explosives and demolition devices, diver communication equipment, and power-driven underwater craft.

With the proliferation of sport diving today, it is hard to imagine that in the early 1940s it was a monumental accomplishment to allow men to breathe and move freely without tether underwater. It probably was the equivalent of early powered flight.

At the end of World War II, there was a shift from a wartime acceptance of science and technology serving mission-oriented objectives to a distinction between basic and applied science. The U.S. government, and especially the U.S. Navy, became the guarantor of basic research in oceanography, and this frequently led to sponsorship of research and the physical over the biological sciences. It is fascinating, then, that a large majority of the R&D surrounding the underwater aspects was focused on the UDTs.

At the end of 1949, the U.S. Navy and National Research Council agreed to work together using scientific applications to address problems related to underwater diving. The Navy capability discussion was changing from "underwater demolition team" to the broader term of "underwater swimmers," although the name UDT did not change. In fact, Dr. Lambertsen had written a letter to the CNO in June 1949 outlining the status of underwater operations surrounding the UDTs and made considerable recommendations about a technological path to improving their capabilities. He also recommended that "as soon as practical" a joint conference be arranged to exploit Army and Navy capabilities.

In December 1951, as a direct result of Dr. Lambertsen's letter to the CNO, a swimmer symposium was held at NAB, Coronado, to discuss mutual problems and ideas. This symposium, sponsored by the ONR and largely focused on the UDTs, brought together operational, technical, civilian, and military-subject-matter experts (SMEs) to conduct the Cooperative Underwater Swimmer Project. This project kept the UDTs in the national spotlight and brought their technical and operational issues into the forefront of diving-related research.

Tests were conducted at the Scripps Institution of Oceanography with the cooperation of UDT-1 and UDT-3. The project was aimed to focus "attention on the primitive statue of knowledge in this area." Project objectives were to obtain field data on underwater swimmer performance in open-water conditions; this was groundbreaking research that included respiratory studies involving speed and drag impacts, compressed air and oxygen consumption rates as a function of operational applications, and tests involving diver-thermal protection.

For protection against prolonged exposure to cold water, the UDT men had learned to use woolen underwear in temperatures above 60 degrees Fahrenheit, and a thin rubber suit overtop the underwear in colder water. These so-called dry suits often leaked, which defeated their purpose and made swimming difficult because they filled with water under pressure.

Interestingly, the wet suit had not yet been invented. Dr. Hugh Bradner, a designer and physicist at University of California, had been working on preliminary calculations on the effects of absorptions, or reflection of shock waves on unicellular material. In conjunction with this work, Dr. Bradner was a member of the underwater swimmer project group. His goal was to design a wet suit for the military under-

A UDT operator conducting training and experimentation with advanced technology mine-detection equipment in the early 1950s. (Photo: Courtesy of Tom Hawkins)

General Dynamics Electric Boat moves the third and final Seawolf-class nuclear attack submarine, Jimmy Carter (SSN 23), outdoors for the first time. The move of the 453-foot, 12,139-ton submarine precedes her christening June 5 by former First Lady Rosalynn Carter. Former President Jimmy Carter will also be in attendance and participate in the ceremony. The new submarine honors the thirty-ninth president of the United States, who is the only submarine-qualified man who went on to become the nation's chief executive. Differentiating the Jimmy Carter from all other undersea vessels is her Multi-Mission Platform (MMP), which includes a 100-foot hull extension that enhances payload capability, enabling it to accommodate the advanced technology required to develop and test an entirely new generation of weapons, sensors, and undersea vehicles. A unique feature of the modification was the creation of a flexible ocean interface, referred to as the "wasp waist," which enables the Navy to deploy and recover various payloads without having to use torpedo tubes. (Photo courtesy of General Dynamics Electric Boat)

water swimmer, and the UDTs naturally became his test subjects. The rest, as they say, is history.

The National Research Council in cooperation with the Italian, French, and British governments also consolidated information about the physical, psychological, and physiological effects of underwater blasts on swimmers—an essential study subject from the perspective of a UDT diver.

The UDTs were also the first in the military to use compressed-air or open-circuit SCUBA. Open-circuit SCUBA was reportedly brought to the United States in 1949, when a sporting goods store in Westwood, California, began selling a new UBA called the Aqua Lung, invented in 1943 by French navy captain Jacques Cousteau and Canadian engineer Émile Gagnan. It used a series of multistage regulators with steel bottles containing highly compressed air. Air was inhaled normally through a hose-mouthpiece connected to the regulator and simply exhaled into the water—creating a lot of air bubbles.

Seemingly forgetting the tactical aspects of the LARU, Lieutenant Commander Fane began using the new and easier-to-dive Aqua Lung in place of the LARU, which left no telltale bubbles, and so in effect got rid of UDT's relatively new clandestine diving capability. The LARUs were aging and no longer being produced or supported, and that certainly played into the decision to expand the use of the Aqua Lung. After the Korean War, however, there would be great resurgence of activity to find a replacement for the LARU.

The Italians and Germans had been perfecting closed-circuit pure-oxygen SCUBA technology during the 1950s. In the United States, Dr. Lambertsen had teamed with the J. H. Emerson Company to design and build the follow-on LARU, but no apparatus had been manufactured.

Tactical diving apparatus used by the UDTs throughout the 1950s and into the

The men of UDT-1 and UDT-3 model the various kinds of experimental thermal protective dress utilized in the early 1950s. It was this kind of outfitting that resulted in their being called Frogmen. (Photo: Courtesy of Tom Hawkins)

1960s included the LS-901 Pirelli, manufactured by Pirelli, Milan, Italy, and the Draeger Lt. Lund II, manufactured by Draegerwerk, Lubeck, Germany. These were acquired in various quantities; the Draeger was much preferred by the UDT men, however, because of its simplicity of design and reliability of operation.

At one point the Navy acquired the services of the Scott Aviation Company to reverse engineer the Draeger because of the difficulty in keeping it supported. This was a failed effort; in 1962, however, the UDTs adopted an American tactical oxygen diving apparatus they simply called the Emerson, which was manufactured by the J. H. Emerson Company in the United States. This was derived from design work with Dr. Lambertsen.

The UDTs also used a semiclosed-circuit diving apparatus designed by the Navy and built by the J. H. Emerson Company. It was called the Mk V, and used a calculated premixed percentage of nitrogen and oxygen that permitted the divers to go deep for longer periods and with fewer exhausted bubbles. Owing to maintenance and technical problems, however, the Mk V was withdrawn from use in 1962, and replaced with the Mk VI manufactured by the Scott Aviation Corporation. Only UDT and U.S. Navy EOD divers used the Mk VI, since it was designed with material to make it low magnetic, and thus was suited for operations in and around known and

Personnel man the main control watch aboard the Navy's newest nuclear-powered submarine, the USS Seawolf (SSN 21). The Seawolf uses the latest technology in submarine warfare, making it the fastest and most versatile submarine in the undersea arsenal. She was commissioned on July 19, 1997. (U.S. Navy Photo by Chief Photographer John E. Gay)

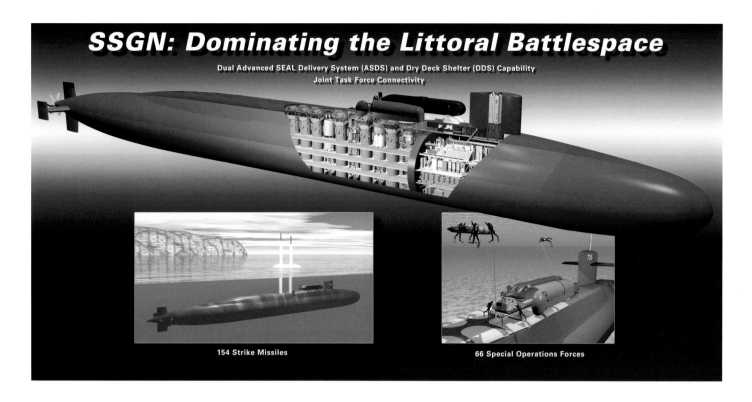

SSGN: Dominating the Littoral Battlespace

Dual Advanced SEAL Delivery System (ASDS) and Dry Deck Shelter (DDS) Capability
Joint Task Force Connectivity

154 Strike Missiles

66 Special Operations Forces

ABOVE: *Puget Sound Naval Shipyard, Washington (August 14, 2003) — Illustration of USS Ohio (SSGN-726), which is undergoing a conversion from a Ballistic Missile Submarine (SSBN) to a Guided Missile Submarine (SSGN) designation. Ohio has been out of service since October 29, 2002, for conversion to SSGN at Puget Sound Naval Shipyard. Four Ohio-class strategic missile submarines, USS Ohio (SSBN-726), USS Michigan (SSBN-727), USS Florida (SSBN-728), and USS Georgia (SSBN-729) have been selected for conversion into a new platform, designated SSGN. The SSGNs will have the capability to support and launch up to 154 Tomahawk missiles, a significant increase in capacity compared to other platforms. The 22 missile tubes also will provide the capability to carry other payloads, such as unmanned underwater vehicles (UUVs), unmanned aerial vehicles (UAVs), and special forces equipment. This new platform will also have the capability to carry and support more than 66 Navy SEALs and insert them clandestinely into conflict areas. (Illustration: USN)*

RIGHT: *Washington, D.C. (June 6, 2003) — Artist conception of the SSGN conversion program. (U.S. Navy graphic)*

suspected minefields. These diving apparatuses remained the mainstay of UDT and SEAL operations throughout the 1960s and early 1970s, when they were replaced with the pure-oxygen Draeger LAR III and the advanced-technology Mk XV closed-circuit, mixed-gas UBA.

In 1947, the UDTs became "sea-air" capable for the first time, when they began extending their at-sea launch and recovery capabilities to include helicopters, which had not been available during World War II. In the postwar period, U.S. Navy and Marine Corps helicopters were used in experiments to drop and recover swimmers in a series of exercises designed to establish the capability. UDT men would simply jump from the helicopters at a low altitude; other men would recover them by winch as the aircraft hovered above. There is no evidence that the capability became a part of routine training or that it was ever deployed with the amphibious forces.

Helicopters also were not widely used in the Korean War, and were not used at all by UDT, since the technology of the time did not permit large passenger or cargo payloads. Experimentation began once more after the war, only this time with helicopters that were more powerful and had more-refined techniques. The men learned to install a swinging bar outside the door of the aircraft, and discovered that if the helicopter pilot were to maintain a constant speed equal to his altitude (e.g., thirty feet at thirty knots), and that if they maintained a rigid feet-first body position, they could swing out and into the water in a single motion with little chance of injury.

Helicopters were never a mainstay for the UDTs, but the capability developed

quickly with the SEAL teams as a method of insertion and extraction during the Vietnam period. Until then, literally all UDT operations were conducted as ship-to-shore maneuvers with dedicated LCPLs carried on board amphibious ships. In Vietnam the majority of SEAL operations were also conducted from boats, but once the value of the helicopter was realized, many more mission capabilities were established, and involved quick-strike operations using U.S. Army "slick" or lightly armed passenger-carrying helicopters. The SEALs also worked very closely with U.S. Navy Seawolf gunship helicopters.

As aircraft got larger and more capable, so did the ingenuity of the SEALs in finding ways to work with them. SEALs did not design carrier-based fixed-wing aircraft, but they did develop the methods to parachute from them. They did not develop the helicopters, but they did develop the methods to work from them, and especially in the maritime environment.

It was in the post–Korean War period that the UDTs began static-line parachuting, first by sending trial groups of men to U.S. Army jump schools, and later by sending all the men to obtain jump qualification as a warfare area specialty. UDT men did not originate parachuting, but they did do what they did best, and that was innovation of water-entry methods using tactical and nontactical diving apparatus. Water jumps were frequently referred to as "Hollywood jumps," because they did not involve hard impacts with the ground. Training water jumps were more complex, however, because they required several support boats in the area to recover the parachutes before they sank. The parachutes also needed to be quickly washed and dried before their next use, and this was time consuming and shortened the life of the parachutes.

ABOVE: *Picture series displays experimentation with technique of casting and recovering from a forward-moving helicopter. A swing-bar was installed and a swimmer would swing into the water as the helicopter maintained equal speed and altitude: 30 knots speed at 30 foot altitude. This put the swimmer in the best position to prevent serious injury. To recover to the helicopter, the men would climb a caving ladder, which required tremendous upper-body strength. (Photo: Courtesy of Tom Hawkins)*

Later, the UDT and SEAL teams were among the first in the military to experiment with the paracommander, a much more controllable parachute developed in France, introduced into the United States in 1961, and adopted by the UDTs in the mid-1960s. Paracommanders allowed introduction of free-fall parachuting, first made popular by sport enthusiasts. The capability emerged as quickly as it did largely because the men went out and bought their own paracommanders and joined civilian sport clubs to jump them. Slowly, the men got permission to jump their own parachutes from military aircraft; later the UDT and SEAL teams adopted a version of the paracommander for tactical use. The paracommander allowed substantially more accuracy for the men to rendezvous at the same landing spot on the ground.

BELOW: *A UDT operator parachutes into the sea near a U.S. naval ship during amphibious training exercises. The men of UDT pioneered the technique of water jumping with static-line parachutes. Note that the man in this photograph is wearing swim fins. (Photo Courtesy of Tom Hawkins)*

Once they began free-fall parachuting, the UDT and SEAL teams went the next step, and developed capabilities to make tactical night jumps on land and in the water. They did this by placing a strobe light on the helmet of the lead jumper. As other jumpers exited the aircraft, they would follow the strobe light, and once all of the parachutes were opened, they would tightly group around the light, and all would land together on the ground. Later they used infrared-capped strobe lights with special goggles to land in total darkness.

Real precision in parachuting was not realized until the advent of the foil or para-wing parachute seen commonly today in sport parachuting and with military free-fall demonstra-

tions—like the U. S. Navy Leap Frogs, which are made up of Navy SEAL and SWCC operators.

In 1965, the Army's Golden Knights parachute team was first to jump para-wings and to demonstrate their unique steerability. By the late 1970s, the para-wing was replaced by the para-foil ram-air parachutes, innovated in the middle 1960s by Domina Jalbert, a kite maker. This system was designed to retard the vertical velocity and provide a relatively soft touchdown. The para-foil, or square parachute, is extremely popular in sport parachuting today, but only sees limited use in the military, and then mainly among Navy SEALs and other SOF units. The majority of military parachutes remain round in shape and have limited steering capability, which is important to large-scale paratrooper operations, since it is undesirable to have several hundred jumpers independently steering their parachutes because of collision risk.

Using free-fall parachute rigs, SEALs can fly under canopy, keeping a tight formation and landing within a few yards of each other. Free-fall jumping evolved substantially in the mid-1970s, when the technique was used to rendezvous with ships and submarines at sea and to glide from high altitude onto distant land targets. Two types of free-fall tactics were perfected: HALO (High Altitude Low Opening) and HAHO (High Altitude High Opening).

Navy SEALs pioneered the use of free-fall jumping with tactical boats and other large operational gear. SEALs perfected HALO jumping from upwards of 36,000 feet on oxygen, where altitude temperatures are subzero and it is common for goggles to freeze and shatter and for the men's eyes to freeze shut. This type of jumping is also very dangerous because of the effects of hypoxia, which is the lack of oxygen.

The UDT and SEAL teams experimented with many kinds of potential air capabilities. Sometimes they were approached to do things only because others figured out that they were crazy enough to try anything once. A prime example of this is the Sky Hook or Fulton recovery system that the Robert Fulton Company of Newtown, Connecticut, developed in the early 1960s with the assistance of the UDTs and Marine Corps. It was a system designed for long-range, high-speed pickup of men and materials described in the company's instructional literature as "a new capability of considerable significance." The idea was to fly a long distance and drop a pick-up kit to someone in need on the ground. Once the pick-up kit was assembled, the airplane would return and simply snatch the soldier in need out of harm's way.

To do this, a man would don a protective suit and a parachute-type harness, which would be attached to a nylon line. The nylon line would be secured to a helium-filled balloon that would be let out to an altitude greater than five hundred feet. The recovery aircraft was equipped with a yoke or wide fork horizontally mounted on its nose. At an altitude of about five hundred feet and traveling at 125 knots (150 miles per hour) or more, the plane would intercept the nylon line and literally snatch the individual into the air and reel him into the airplane with a winch.

The Sky Hook capability was envisioned for land and at-sea rescue, recovery of deep reconnaissance personnel, logistic aerial pick-up, personnel transfers, and more. The UDT and SEAL teams on both coasts demonstrated the capability several times during manned testing. During one of the experiments on the East Coast, UDT Petty Officer Jim Fox was safely snatched into the air

RQ-8B Fire Scout VTUAV, Vertical Takeoff and Landing Tactical Unmanned Aerial Vehicle, produced by Northrop Grumman, Fire Scout, has the ability to autonomously take off from and land on any aviation-capable warship as well as unprepared landing zones close to the forward edge of the battle area (FEBA). It can carry out surveillance, find tactical targets, track and designate targets, and provide accurate targeting data to strike platforms such as strike aircraft, helicopters, and ships. (Photo: Dave Gatley)

LEFT: *The Affordable Weapon System is a U.S. Navy program to design and produce a low-cost off-the-shelf cruise missile launchable from a self-contained solid-propellant rocket booster, mounted in a standard shipping container, and powered by a small turbojet engine. The Affordable Weapon has a range of more than 1,560 kilometers (840 nautical miles), and payload options that include several types of warhead and surveillance packages with a weight of up to 90 kilograms (200 pounds). (Photo: Dave Gatley)*

and reeled toward the recovery aircraft. When he reached the aircraft, however, the nylon line snapped at the winch and he fell away from the airplane to his death in the Chesapeake Bay.

With establishment of the SEAL teams in early 1962, and their parent NOSG staffs in 1963, came formalized R&D programs for the UDT and SEAL teams. NOSG Pacific very early on established a dedicated R&D unit to coordinate developments at the operator level. In spite of the somewhat greater formality of R&D today, this heritage of direct and immediate involvement of the operating teams in development and testing on a day-to-day basis remains active, especially at today's NSW development group.

R&D for the UDT and SEAL teams was best described by Rear Adm. Craig Dorman, a former CO of UDT-11:

> R&D for the teams is very much a personal sport. It's not something we simply hand off to others . . . almost everything SEALs do centers around the individual operator . . . No matter what our missions may require, SEALs must have the physical, physiological, and mental edge. SEALs need to be able to perform and operate at peak efficiency under conditions our opponents can't even tolerate. Because of this, human-centered research, combined with traditionally rigorous training, will continue to be critically important to the teams . . . We [SEALs] care about things on the human dimension. For example, about environmental features like ocean currents, bioluminescence, visibility, temperature, and so forth, on a scale of meters, not kilometers, which are typical for the Navy in supporting things, like aircraft or battle groups.

A program first called the Swimmer Underwater Reconnaissance and Clearance (SURAC) project later resulted in two separate but specific operational requirements (SORs). These were the first formalized R&D programs dedicated solely to the UDT and SEAL teams. SOR 38-01 was called the Swimmer (later SEAL) Weapons System, and SOR 38-02 was called the Swimmer (later SEAL) Support System. The Swimmer Weapons System was a long-range developmental program that envisioned acquisition of more than ninety-five separate line items for development over a period of several years. The SOR 38-01 program, which was later called the Technical Development Plan (TDP), was conceived and organized as early as 1956, by a great American, Charles

BELOW: *The Universal Launch and Recovery Module (ULRM) designed by General Dynamics, Electric Boat Division, allows SEAL SDVs to be stored, deployed and recovered out of missile tubes on the USS Ohio and other Ohio SSGN class submarines. (Photo: Courtesy of Electric Boat)*

Young Jr., who realized that the UDT and SEAL teams had no advocate for instituting developmental programs. The project was established under the old Bureau of Ordnance, which later became the Naval Ordnance Systems Command, and after that NAVSEA. UDT and SEAL developmental programs were accomplished at the Naval Weapons Laboratory, White Oak, Maryland. From Young's own memory (he is now deceased), we have a condensed list of weapons first produced by the swimmer weapons system. Many had multiple and overlapping uses, so interfacing had to be carefully monitored.

Other major items to be acquired under the Swimmer Weapons Program included a family of safety and arming devices, clock timers, a swimmer-launched torpedo, and an SDV-launched torpedo. One item attempted was a sympathetic detonator that would be attached to explosives and so would replace the need to reel out detonation cord in demolition fields.

All demolition firing devices (DFDs) developed for the UDT-SEAL teams had to pass stringent U.S. Navy safety standards, which often made them more complex and expensive. TDP 38-01 delivers many of the explosive and demolition devices used by the SEAL teams today.

A companion program called the Vietnam Laboratory Assistance Program (VLAP) was established during the Vietnam War to provide a more rapid transition of warfighting innovations from the laboratory to the field. The Navy laboratories at White Oak, China Lake, and Panama City provided customized direct support for the NSW community with a selected category of specialty combat items that included booby traps (binoculars, cameras, transistor radios—anything that the VC would try to steal or pick up), weapons (liquid explosives, the Hush Puppy silencer for the 9-mm handgun, multiround magazines, and a crossbow), and everything from nonirritating face-paint sticks, to first-generation night vision devices (Starlight Scopes), to an experimental scout-dog program intended to train German shepherds to detect VC sappers (attack swimmers). The Hush Puppy was unique in that it was not actually conceived to kill the enemy, but rather to eliminate dogs, geese, and ducks that the VC used to warn of approaching SEALs.

Charlie Young's group at the White Oak lab was a major contributor throughout the Vietnam War, as was Bob Forester's group at the Naval Weapons Station, China Lake,

RIGHT: *It is little known that SEALs used combat assault dogs briefly but effectively during the Vietnam period. (Photo: Courtesy of Tom Hawkins)*

BELOW: *Starlite Scope, a first-generation night vision device used by SEALs in Vietnam. These were image intensivers that used reflected light to identify targets at night. They were very low quality and somewhat bulky, but they were always carried and considerd a helpful asset. (Photo: Courtesy of Tom Hawkins)*

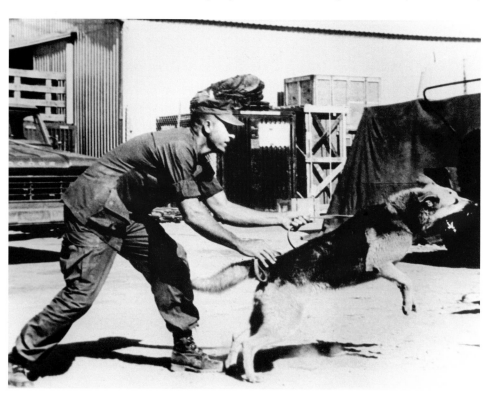

The Seahorse-class Autonomous Underwater Vehicle (AUV) is moved into position with *Sea Fighter's* (FSF-1) stern ramp during launch and recovery testing. At 28 feet, six inches, and weighing 10,800 pounds, *Seahorse* is an untethered, unmanned, underwater robotic vehicle, capable of preprogrammed independent operations. The demonstration was sponsored by the Office of Naval Research (ONR). (Photo: John F. Williams / USN)

Another view of *Seahorse*, an Autonomous Underwater Vehicle (AUV). The *Seahorse* can be used for a number of missions, such as carrying supplies from the mother ship to and from shore. It can travel up to 500 nautical miles at 4 knots. (Photo: John F. Williams / USN)

The Seahorse-class Autonomous Underwater Vehicle (AUV) is maneuvered into position in *Sea Fighter's* (FSF-1) mission bay during launch and recovery testing. (Photo: John F. Williams / USN)

California, and Tom Odum's group at the Navy MDL, Panama City, Florida. These Navy laboratories provided analyses, weapons, support equipment, and operational support—including sending civilian personnel to provide immediate, on-site consulting and liaison that greatly assisted SEALs actively engaged in combat.

Many items for the SEALs also came directly from industry. Probably the most well-known item to come out of the Vietnam era was the Stoner light machine gun. The Stoner 63 and 63A 5.56-mm machine gun has developed a somewhat mythic status as part of the Vietnam-era SEAL armory. It was developed by Eugene Stoner working directly with the SEAL teams. The Stoner weapon's system was unique because it fired belt-fed, 5.56 linked ammunition, whereas most machine guns fired the heavier 7.62 ammunition, hence "light" machine gun. The weapon was manufactured by Cadillac Gage Corporation, and evolved through combat use in Vietnam. Approximately one hundred Mk 23 Mod 0 Stoners were made for Navy SEALs in 1969.

The goal of the Swimmer (later SEAL) Support System, or TDP 38-02, was to develop a Class I and Class II SDV, Class I and Class II UBA, and ancillary equipment. The TDP also called for conversion of previous missile-carrying submarines, USS *Grayback* and USS *Growler*, to carry SDVs. TDP 38-02 was a very revolutionary and very ambitious development program for the UDT and SEAL teams; it was created during a period of active engagement in Vietnam and, thus, progressed somewhat slowly until after the war effort.

Under the direction of the Naval Ships Systems Command, the Naval Coastal Systems Center, Panama City began development of specifications for acquisition of an advanced technology SDV. Two exceptional engineers, Mike Foran and Dick Murdock, headed the UDT and SEAL diving and SDV programs at the Naval Ship Systems Command (NAVSHIP, which later became NAVSEA). Both men were bureaucratic and dedicated. These men deserve a special place in the history of NSW since they developed SDV and UBA contract specifications and oversaw the awarding of contracts and execution of contracting efforts once they were awarded.

The Class I and Class II SDVs were six-man and two-man SDVs, respectively. Their developmental effort was contracted to the Aerojet General Corporation, Azusa, California, and the UBA contract was awarded to the Scott Aviation Corporation, Buffalo, New York. Neither contract effort was successful. SDV development

The pointed nose of the SEALION cuts through the waves and produces minimal wake. (Photo: Greg E. Mathieson Sr. / NSW Publications, LLC

was eventually relocated under government control at the Naval Weapons Center, China Lake, California, and the UBAs were acquired from commercial vendors.

The Class I UBA was a closed-circuit, pure-oxygen diving apparatus, and it was satisfied by the German Draeger LAR III UBA, which remains in use today as the Mk 25 Mod 2. The Class II UBA was a closed-circuit, mixed-gas rebreather, which was a high-technology diving apparatus that was eventually satisfied by the Bio-Marine Corporation, and remains in service today as the Mk 16 Mod 1 UBA. The Mk 16 is used by the SDVTs because of its ability to operate at deeper depths for longer durations, allowing significant mission capabilities, which remain classified.

The SDV effort at China Lake resulted in the Mk VIII (six-man) and Mk IX (two-man) SDVs. Other SDV activities occurring in China Lake were improvements and modernizations to the in-service Mk VII SDV. In addition, considerable work was being done at the Applied Research Laboratory, Austin, Texas, on ahead-looking sonars that were later incorporated to all of the SDVs. Also, Dr. Bill Vaughan and the ONR accomplished several human-performance studies relating to diver performance in SDVs during this period. The SDV program was eventually moved to the Navy laboratory at Panama City, Florida, where it remains today. An expanded discussion about SDV development can be found in Chapter 6.

By the mid-1970s, much of the development foreseen under TDP 38-02 had been accomplished or was significantly under way. A follow-on program simply called the "mission support package" was crafted to supplement the work already accomplished. Some of the mission support package programs involved SDV and diver communication systems, improved ahead-looking and side-looking sonars, passive and active (heated) diver thermal-protection systems, a closed-cycle combustion engine for the SDV, a diver's full-face-mask, a diver's decompression computer, and a diver handheld sonar, among others.

From the late 1970s, until formation of USSOCOM in 1987, much of the R&D activity revolved around improving or modernizing capabilities already in the SEAL team inventory. In 1983, all of the remaining UDTs were reorganized as SEAL or SDVTs.

ABOVE: *Hidden within the hull of SEALION is an SOF version of a Jet-Ski ready for launch. (Photo: Greg Mathieson Sr. / NSW Publications, LLC)*

TOP: *State-of-the-art navigation hardware in the cockpit of the SEALION. (Photo: Greg Mathieson Sr. / NSW Publications, LLC)*

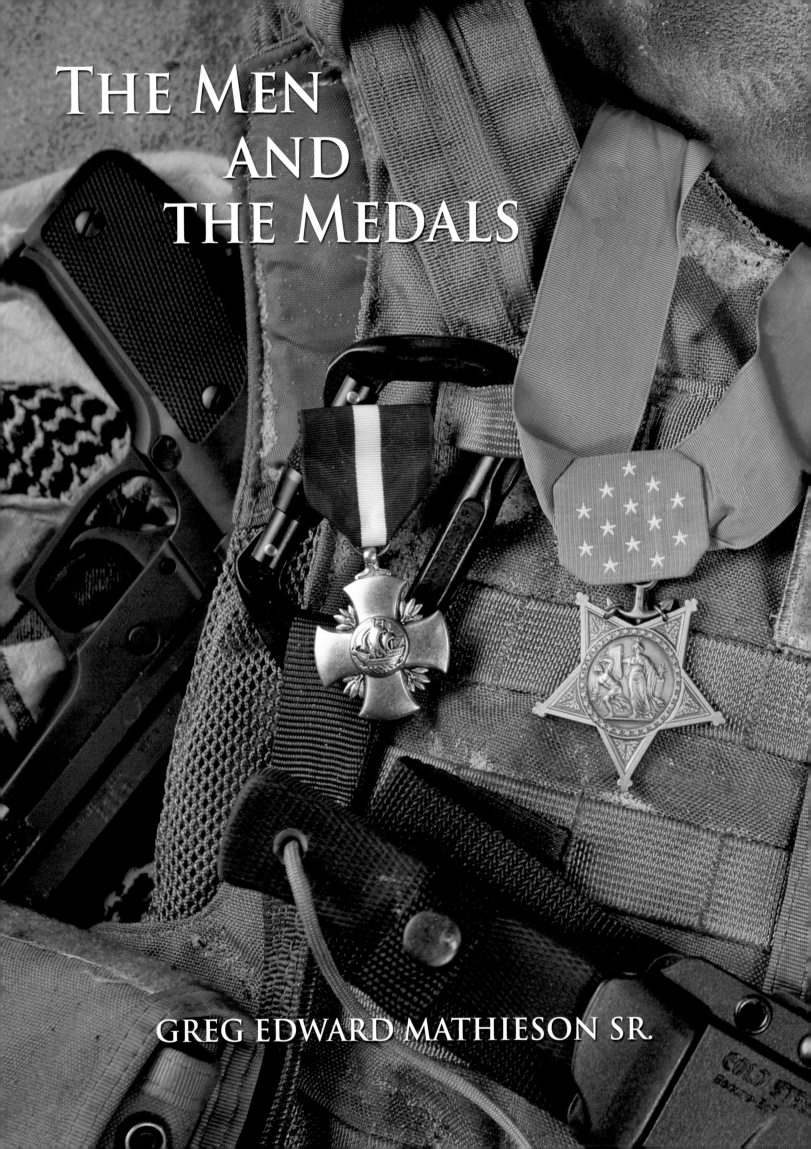

THE MEN
AND
THE MEDALS

GREG EDWARD MATHIESON SR.

CHAPTER 14

THE MEN AND THE MEDALS

Greg Edward Mathieson Sr.

YOU WILL NOTICE THAT THIS CHAPTER WAS NOT WRITTEN BY A Navy SEAL or someone else in the Naval Special Warfare community, though initially it was. I decided to write this chapter myself. Simply put, with great respect for the SEAL family, a hero, or those close to the dramatic, heart-wrenching stories that follow finds it hard to write about the brotherhood of warriors of which they are a member. They see their exploits as just a cut above routine and just doing their job.

As you will read below, extraordinary acts of courage and sacrifice are anything but routine duty. Also, no published work about the SEALs can be complete without the selfless acts of those who work on the ground both in support of a SEAL team's mission and to care for the fallen and their families after the smoke clears. The actions of the SEAL Foundation are, like the SEAL teams, extraordinary labors of charity and love.

Love is not a word commonly associated with the Navy SEALs. But, again, as you will read, the toughest, the most decorated warriors of our time demonstrate that loving their brothers and those left behind are interwoven in the SEAL culture.

These tales are not about the advanced hardware or the mind-numbing, mus-

cle-sapping training. It is about the men of Naval Special Warfare, their unbelievable accomplishments, the stunning sacrifices of them and their families and their bond to one another and the nation they serve. This is important history, much of which the average American has little or no knowledge. In fact, many of the heroics are known to only a few within the highest ranks of government who have a "Top Secret clearance and higher and a need to know."

So I will begin with the most common act of valor and brotherhood which epitomizes the Navy SEALs and the bonding of warriors. This gripping report was told by the forty-third president, George W. Bush, on Memorial Day 2008 at a ceremony at Arlington National Cemetery.

The headstones of Navy SEAL Nathan H. Hardy and Navy SEAL Michael E. Koch stand side by side in Arlington National Cemetery. The brotherhood of both of these SEALs, who trained together, worked together and died together was remembered by President George W. Bush during his speech on Memorial Day 2008 at the cemetery. (Photo: Greg E. Mathieson Sr. / NSW Publications, LLC)

We remember two Navy SEALs—Nathan Hardy of Durham, New Hampshire, and Michael Koch of State College, Pennsylvania. Nate and Mike were partners in the field and they were close friends in the barracks. Through several missions together, they had developed the unique bond of brotherhood that comes from trusting another with your life. They even shared a battlefield tradition: They would often head into battle with American flags clutched to their chests underneath their uniform. Nate and Mike performed this ritual for the last time on February the 4th—they both laid down their lives in Iraq after being ambushed by terrorists. These two friends spent their last few moments on earth together, doing what they loved most—defending the United States of America. Today, Nathan Hardy and Mike Koch lay at rest next to each other right here on the grounds of Arlington.

During the solemn ceremonies we were privileged to attend, we were struck by how ordinary the men of Naval Special Warfare seemed. These highly trained, highly educated men, whose heroism is only understood by their families and fellow Sailors, were decked out in standard uniforms, clean-shaven, and, well, normal. Yet they are so far from normal that I am humbled trying to convey their deeds and dedication.

The clues are pinned to their chests. Displayed below the gold SEAL trident breast insignia are the ribbons honoring their achievements and acts of heroism. Many of the ribbons are rewarded for actions the men cannot speak of. These are medals you don't see on ordinary Sailors. But how does a simple Sailor adorned in dress blue or white uniforms get awarded Silver Stars, Bronze Stars, and Purple Hearts with clusters and V devices signifying "Valor." How does a simple Sailor earn the highest citation of all, the hallmark of ground combat, the Congressional Medal of Honor?

In 1782, General George Washington created a "badge of military merit" for enlisted soldiers who performed bravely in combat. That was the first Purple Heart. It did not get that name officially until 150 years later when the War Department created the purple-colored heart with Washington's bust at its center and a coat of arms at the top. Any soldier, Sailor, or airman is entitled to that badge if he or she is even slightly wounded in combat. But, not to take away from importance of a Purple Heart, the Medal of Honor, the nation's highest decoration, must pass the

muster of the entire military chain of command. First, the act of heroism must be witnessed by two other combatants and then reviewed by the entire chain of command, right to the Commander in Chief. It is a process that can sometimes take years, but those are years during which hundreds investigate and read the exploits of a simple WARRIOR who is about to become a giant among men.

Five U.S. Navy SEALs have been recipients' of this rare and distinctive award; three of those presented for action in Vietnam, where each survived the war, and one each for valor on the battlefields of Iraq and Afghanistan, where both SEALs made the ultimate sacrifice

The most widely known and public of SEAL honorees is Joseph Robert "Bob" Kerrey. Kerrey, after his meritorious service, went on to become the Governor of Nebraska, a United States Senator, and then until 2010 served as the President of New York City's New School. Since 2013, Kerry has worked with Carmen Group, a government affairs lobbying firm.

It is amazing to me how a farm-born kid from the wheat fields of Lincoln, Nebraska, whose sole ambition was to be a pharmacist, became one of the most celebrated heroes in naval history. Then, after his combat tour, he goes on to demonstrate that the recognition of his leadership on the battlefield was justified as he became his home state's governor and a much respected member of the nation's most exclusive club, the US Senate.

It could be argued that Bob Kerrey's stellar career in politics and education found its roots in the jungles of the Republic of Vietnam. Because it were there that he showed the kind of can-do initiative and will to succeed that were to become the guideposts of his later service to a grateful nation. Following is the actual citation that led to his receiving the highest recognition bestowed on a serviceman.

For conspicuous gallantry and intrepidity at the risk of his life above and beyond the call of duty while serving as a SEAL team leader during action against enemy aggressor (Viet Cong) forces. Acting in response to reliable intelligence, Lt. (j.g.) Kerrey led his SEAL team on a mission to capture important members of the enemy's area political cadre known to be located on an island in the bay of Nha Trang. In order to surprise the enemy, he and his team scaled a 350-foot sheer cliff to place themselves above the ledge on which the enemy was located. Splitting his team in 2 elements and coordinating both, Lt. (jg.) Kerrey led his men in the treacherous downward descent to the enemy's camp. Just as they neared the end of their descent, intense

enemy fire was directed at them, and Lt. (jg.) Kerrey received massive injuries from a grenade that exploded at his feet and threw him backward onto the jagged rocks. Although bleeding profusely and suffering great pain, he displayed outstanding courage and presence of mind in immediately directing his element's fire into the heart of the enemy camp. Utilizing his radio, Lt. (jg.) Kerrey called in the second element's fire support, which caught the confused Viet Cong in a devastating crossfire. After successfully suppressing the enemy's fire, and although immobilized by his multiple wounds, he continued to maintain calm, superlative control as he ordered his team to secure and defend an extraction site. Lt.(jg.) Kerrey resolutely directed his men, despite his near unconscious state, until he was eventually evacuated by helicopter. The havoc brought to the enemy by this very successful mission cannot be over-estimated. The enemy soldiers who were captured provided critical intelligence to the allied effort. Lt. (jg.) Kerrey's courageous and inspiring leadership, valiant fighting spirit, and tenacious devotion to duty in the face of almost overwhelming opposition sustain and enhance the finest traditions of the U.S. Naval Service.

What the citation for the Medal of Honor does not state is that Bob Kerrey's wounds were so grave that he later lost his leg. One can only imagine how high up in the Navy's ranks he would have climbed had he be able to pursue a military career rather than one in politics.

And here it is fitting to tell the story of another Medal of Honor recipient who was not a SEAL but a member of the Special Warfare community that supports the SEALS. I call this "fitting," because James Elliott Williams is the most highly decorated enlisted man in the history of the United States Navy.

His story epitomizes the fact that NSW is not just about the heroics of SEALs.

At the age of sixteen, Williams joined the Navy in 1947 and served for twenty years in both Korea and Vietnam. As a petty officer he was assigned to a River Patrol Force to intercept Viet Cong arms shipments in the Mekong Delta. There, on October 31, 1966, he and his men on another boat were caught up in a fierce ambush by two Viet Cong sampans. They destroyed one boat and gave chase to the other, which led them into a horrendous trap with the VC firing on them with machine guns and RPGs from both sides of the riverbank. Instead of retreating, Williams called in Navy attack helicopters and then attacked again.

The bloody three hours that followed that attack became legend in the U.S. Navy. Williams and his men killed numerous Viet Cong and destroyed over 67 armed vessels which disrupted a major VC logistics operation. Two years later, President Lyndon Johnson presented Williams the Medal of Honor.

He had already received the Navy Cross, Silver Star (with one gold award star), the Legion of Merit with "V" device, the Navy and Marine Corps Medal with gold award star, Bronze Star with "V" device and two gold award stars, Purple Heart with two gold award stars, Navy and Marine Corps Commendation Medal with "V" device and gold award star, Navy and Marine Corps Presidential Unit Cita-

Navy Medal of Honor recipients at the U.S. Navy Memorial in Washington, D.C. for the presentation ceremony of the Medal of Honor flag to the family of Lt. Michael P. Murphy on October 22, 2007. (L–R) Capt. Thomas G. Kelley, Joseph Robert (Bob) Kerrey (SEAL), Thomas R. Norris (SEAL), Col. Harvey C. (Barney) Barnum Jr. (USMC). (Photo: Greg E. Mathieson Sr. / NSW Publications, LLC)

tion with bronze service star, the Navy Good Conduct Medal with four bronze service stars, the Navy Expeditionary Medal, the National Defense Service Medal with bronze service star, the Korean Service Medal with two bronze stars, the Armed Forces Expeditionary Medal, and the Vietnam Service Medal with two bronze service stars. His foreign decorations include the Korean Presidential Unit Citation, Vietnam Cross of Gallantry with Gold Star and Palm, United Nations Korean Medal, the Republic of Vietnam Campaign Medal, and the Korean War Service Medal.

The honors did not stop even after his passing in 1999. Today, the USS *James E. Williams (DDG-95)* is an *Arleigh Burke*–class destroyer in the United States Navy. She was named for Petty Officer 1st Class James Elliott Williams.

The next award to come from the Southeast Asian AO is the stuff of which movies are made. Indeed, the exploits of **Thomas R. Norris** reads like a movie script or an action novel. In fact, it was made into one of the most stirring war rescue movies of the last half of the twentieth century, BAT 21 starring Gene Hackman and Danny Glover, is loosely based on a rescue mission lead by Norris, and one that is still talked about in SEAL team offices and corridors.

Norris was born in Jacksonville, Florida, in 1944, and received his college education at the University of Maryland. He got a degree in sociology, specializing in criminology. It seems he knew his life's work would be to go after bad guys. That may have motivated him to become a Navy SEAL. He was assigned to SEAL Team TWO in Little Creek, Virginia, but soon found himself in Quang Tri province as an advisor when an incredible dangerous assignment came his way.

U.S. Air Force Lt. Col. Iceal Hambleton, an Electronic Warfare Officer, who had the kind of top secret information in his brain the enemy dreams of acquiring, was shot down and attempting to evade capture in April 1972 along with another pilot.

For Norris, that mission to rescue two pilots in two different actions took on Hollywood-like scope, when he was asked to infiltrate the escape and evasion area with Vietnamese commandos, find the first pilot and return him to safety, and then return to locate

Simple pieces of colored ribbon and metal only cost pennies to produce but represent much more. (L–R) Silver Star, Medal of Honor, Purple Heart. (Photo: Greg E. Mathieson Sr. / NSW Publications, LLC)

ABOVE: *The Navy Color Guard marches off as the family of Lt. Michael P. Murphy stand behind with senior U.S. Navy officials during the presentation of the Medal of Honor flag at the U.S. Navy Memorial in Washington, D.C. A law was created on October 23, 2002, for the awarding of the flag to each person to whom the Medal of Honor was awarded after the date of the enactment. (Photo: Greg E. Mathieson Sr. / NSW Publications, LLC)*

RIGHT: *Chief of Naval Operations (CNO) Adm. Gary Roughead presents the Medal of Honor flag to Maureen Murphy, mother of Lt. Michael P. Murphy, recipient of the Medal of Honor, during a ceremony at the U.S.Navy Memorial in Washington, D.C. (Photo: Greg E. Mathieson Sr. / NSW Publications, LLC)*

Lieutenant Colonel Hambleton and bring him out safely. One can almost hear Norris saying, "Yeah, no problem."

He and his Vietnamese partners disguised themselves as fishermen complete with a jungle sampan and set out to locate the evading airman. That's the part that turned out to be not such a problem. The first pilot was rescued was ease right underneath the searching enemy noses. It was getting Hambleton out alive two days later that prove a tad more difficult and the citation for the Medal of Honor does read like a screenplay treatment:

> *For conspicuous gallantry and intrepidity in action at the risk of his life above and beyond the call of duty while serving as a SEAL Advisor with the Strategic Techni-cal Directorate Assistance Team, Headquarters, U.S. Military Assistance Command, Vietnam. During the period 10 to 13 April 1972, Lieutenant Norris completed an*

LEFT: *This is a copy of the classified document that was removed from the National Archives. Capt. Christian Lambertsen's family had this document in his personal records even after the government withdrew it from public records and classified it. (Document: Courtesy of the Lambertsen family)*

BELOW: *Much of what the UDTs, SEALS, and SWCC do is classified. Here is an example of when even many of the medals they receive are classified. This is a notice in the files of Capt. Christian Lambertsen, inventor of the LARU breathing unit, in which his Legion of Merit citation was classified as recently as 2008. (Photo: Greg E. Mathieson Sr. / NSW Publications, LLC)*

unprecedented ground rescue of two downed pilots deep within heavily controlled enemy territory in Quang Tri Province. Lieutenant Norris, on the night of 10 April, led a five-man patrol through 2,000 meters of heavily controlled enemy territory, located one of the downed pilots at daybreak, and returned to the Forward Operating Base (FOB). On 11 April, after a devastating mortar and rocket attack on the small FOB, Lieutenant Norris led a three-man team on two unsuccessful rescue attempts for the second pilot. On the afternoon of the 12th, a Forward Air Controller located the pilot and notified Lieutenant Norris. Dressed in fishermen disguises and using a sampan, Lieutenant Norris and one Vietnamese traveled throughout that night and found the injured pilot at dawn. Covering the pilot with bamboo and vegetation, they began the return journey, successfully evading a North Vietnamese patrol. Approaching the FOB, they came under heavy machine gun fire. Lieutenant Norris called in an air strike, which provided suppression fire and a smoke screen, allowing the rescue party to reach the FOB. By his outstanding display of decisive leadership, undaunted courage, and selfless dedication

There is no better example of the brotherhood that SEALSs share than these two American heroes, U.S. Navy SEAL Lt. Thomas R. Norris (L), and U.S. Navy SEAL PO Michael E. Thornton (R). PO Thornton saved the life of fellow SEAL Lientenant Norris, for which he received the Medal of Honor. Three years later, Lientenant Norris received the Medal of Honor for actions that saved a USAF pilot. (Photo: Greg E. Mathieson Sr. / NSW Publications, LLC)

in the face of extreme danger, Lieutenant Norris enhanced the finest traditions of the United States Naval Service.

Lientenant Norris was later seriously wounded and discharged from the Navy. He went on to the career he had planned at the University of Maryland, becoming an FBI agent. A Special Warfare building is named in his honor at the Naval Amphibious Base, Little Creek, Virginia. And, to almost no one's surprise, the Hollywood movie, BAT 21, is more about the downed pilot than the SEAL who rescued him. The unassuming Thomas Norris would have wanted it that way.

Remarkably, the third Medal of Honor awarded in Vietnam went to the Navy SEAL who, six months after Lientenant Norris's BAT 21 exploits, rescued Norris, when he was severely wounded in action and in mortal danger. What an extraordinary grouping of heroes!

Petty Officer **Michael E. Thornton** was five years younger than his squad leader, Tom Norris. Thornton was part of a five-man team that included two Vietnamese SEALs who were assigned to capture an enemy soldier—a common enough

Five Navy SEALs have received the Medal of Honor, the highest award the United States can bestow on a individual in the U.S. military. (Photo: Greg E. Mathieson Sr. / NSW Publications, LLC)

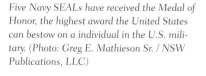

mission for a SEAL Team. Norris led Thornton and the others into enemy territory to snatch a North Vietnamese regular. The mission went bad almost immediately after insertion. It became worse when Thornton was told by one of his retreating Vietnamese SEALs that Norris was dead. Not good enough for Thornton, who reversed course directly into the path of danger to see for himself. Only the citation could capture the flavor of the calamitous mission:

> *For conspicuous gallantry and intrepidity at the risk of his life above and beyond the call of duty while participating in a daring operation against enemy forces in the Republic of Vietnam on October 31, 1972. Petty Officer Thornton, an assistant U.S. Navy advisor, along with a U.S. Navy lieutenant serving as senior advisor, accompanied a three-man Vietnamese patrol on an intelligence gathering and prisoner capture operation against an enemy-occupied naval river base. Launched from a Vietnamese Navy junk in a rubber boat, the patrol reached land and was continuing on foot toward its objective when it suddenly came under heavy fire from a numerically superior force. The patrol called*

in naval gunfire support and then engaged the enemy in a fierce firefight, accounting for many enemy casualties before moving back to the waterline to prevent encirclement. Upon learning that the senior advisor had been hit by enemy fire and was believed to be dead, Petty Officer Thornton returned through a hail of fire to the lieutenant's last position, quickly disposed of two enemy soldiers about to overrun the position, and succeeded in removing the seriously wounded and unconscious senior naval advisor to the water's edge. He then inflated the lieutenant's life jacket and towed him seaward for approximately two hours until picked up by support craft. By his extraordinary courage and perseverance, Petty Officer Thornton was directly responsible for saving the life of his superior officer and enabling the safe extraction of all patrol members, thereby upholding the highest traditions of the United States Naval Service.

One can only wonder what other exploits of those SEALs back in 1970s remain classified. Mike Thornton retired as a lieutenant in 1992.

Sadly, the fourth and fifth Congressional Medal of Honor was awarded posthumously. Again, the valiant deeds are extraordinary—which by now should not be a surprise.

Lieutenant **Michael P. Murphy**, who grew up on Long Island, New York, went on to graduate from Penn State University in 1998 with two degrees, political science and psychology, a testament to his intelligence and quite standard for those who choose to be officers with the SEALs.

Murphy was to go down in Navy history for his actions in Afghanistan in 2005. In June of that year, Murphy was leading a four-man reconnaissance team in Operation Red Wing in the Hindu Kush of that war-torn country, patrolling at an alti-

LEFT: *The Medal of Honor certificate of Lt. Michael P. Murphy. (Photo: Greg E. Mathieson Sr. / NSW Publications, LLC)*

RIGHT: *The Medal of Honor citation of Lt. Michael P. Murphy. (Photo: Greg E. Mathieson Sr. / NSW Publications, LLC)*

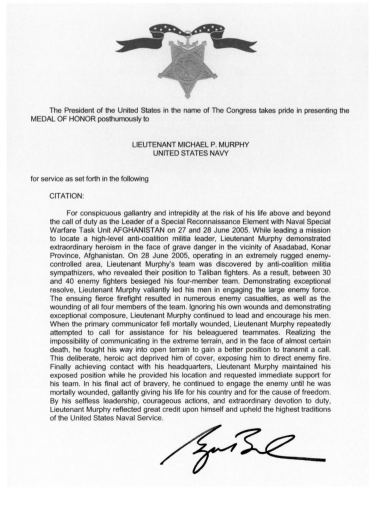

Commemorative coin (front) honoring SCPO Daniel R. Healy, 36, of Exeter, New Hampshire. With four members of his team having been ambushed, he insisted that he be on the rescue mission. Eight of his fellow SEALs on board the helos, as well as the Army 160th Night Stalkers that staffed them, lost their lives in that rescue mission during Operation Redwing. There was only one survivor, Marcus Luttrell (author of the book Lone Survivor). On that day, June 28, 2005, eleven Navy SEALs and eight Army Night Stalkers were lost.

Commemorative coin (front) honoring Medal of Honor recipient Lt. Michael P. Murphy, 29, of Patchogue, New York, who was killed by enemy forces during a reconnaissance mission, Operation Redwing, along with two of his SDVT-1 (SEAL Delivery Vehicle—Team 1) mates. The SEAL team, led by Lieutenant Murphy and consisting of Petty Officers Matthew Axelson, Danny Dietz, and Marcus Luttrell, was on a mission to kill or capture Ahmad Shah, a Taliban leader who commanded a group of insurgents known as the "Mountain Tigers," west of Asadabad.

Commemorative coin (front) honoring PO2 Matthew Axelson, 29, of Cupertino, California, who was killed by enemy forces during a reconnaissance mission, Operation Redwing, along with two of his SDVT-1 mates. Matthew Axelson and DannyDietz were posthumously awarded the Navy Cross; even after being wounded, both men "continued to fight the enemy with undiminished zeal, covering the extraction of the rest of their team while they stayed and fought. Putting the safety of their teammates ahead of their own, they displayed extraordinary heroism in combat." Matt Axelson deployed to Afghanistan in April 2005 and was part of a four-man SEAL reconnaissance team that secretly infiltrated into the Hindu-Kush mountains along the border of Afghanistan on June 27. This unit, led by Lt. Michael P. Murphy, was tracking a high-ranking terrorist leader near 10,000-foot peaks when they were ambushed by overwhelming Taliban forces. Two helicopters of Navy SEALs and Army commandos answered Murphy's electronic call for help. Eight SEALs and eight Army Night Stalker commandos in the lead helicopter perished after it was hit by a rocket-propelled grenade. Three of the original four-man SEAL reconnaissance squad (Matt Axelson, Michael Murphy, and Danny Dietz) were killed in the firefight. A fourth squad member, Marcus Luttrell, survived. He was knocked down by a blast and wounded in both legs. He walked several miles and was hidden and protected by an Afghan shepherd until U.S. commandos rescued him July 3, 2005.

Commemorative coin (front) honoring PO2 Shane E. Patton, 22, of Boulder City, Nevada, who was killed by enemy forces during a reconnaissance mission, Operation Redwing, along with two of his SDVT- 1 mates. Shane Patton was one of 16 troops killed when an MH-47 Chinook helicopter was shot down in Afghanistan on June 28 on a daring daylight mission to reinforce a four-man SEAL reconnaissance squad in 10,000-foot mountainous terrain. Patton, seven other SEALs, and eight Army 160th Night Stalkers died in their heroic

attempt to rescue their fellow SEALs. Michael Murphy, Matthew Axelson, and Danny Dietz fought on courageously and were killed in the firefight against overwhelming Taliban forces. A total of 11 SEALs died that day, the biggest single loss of life for Naval Special Warfare forces since World War II.

Commemorative coin (front) honoring PO2 James E. Suh, 28, of Deerfield Beach, Florida, who was killed by enemy forces during Operation Redwing, along with two of his SDVT-1 mates. Suh was part of a dedicated Naval Special Warfare team fighting Afghanistan's Taliban.

Commemorative coin (front) honoring PO2 Danny Dietz, 26, of Littleton, Colorado, who was killed by enemy forces during the reconnaissance mission, Operation Redwing, along with two of his SDVT-1 mates. Dietz was part of an elite team of four SEALs on a reconnaissance mission "tasked with finding a key Taliban leader in mountainous terrain near Asadabad, Afghanistan," according to a Navy news release. On June 28, 2005, SEAL Team 10 was assigned to kill or capture a high ranking Taliban leader in the Hindu-Kush mountains. The SEAL team was made up of Michael P. Murphy, Marcus Luttrell, Danny Dietz and Matthew Axelson. Luttrell and Axelson were the team's snipers while Dietz and Murphy were the spotters. They were spotted by anticoalition sympathizers, who immediately reported their position to Taliban fighters. A fierce gun-battle ensued between the four SEALs and a much larger enemy force with superior tactical position." The SEALs radioed for help, and a responding Chinook helicopter was shot down by a rocket-propelled grenade, killing eight more SEALs and eight Army Night Stalkers.

ABOVE: *The back of each coin is inscribed "In memory of our fallen bothers." (Photos: Dave Gatley)*

tude of ten thousand feet. His mission was to capture a high-value target, a Taliban leader. The operation went awry when locals tipped off the enemy.

Murphy and his four men were eventually surrounded by the enemy. Every man was wounded during the continuous firefight. To save his men, at one point in the battle Lieutenant Murphy moved into open terrain to get better radio reception with Bagram Air Force base. Within two hours Lieutenant Murphy was to die of his wounds along with Petty Officers Danny Dietz and Mathew Axelson. The

TOP, LEFT: *Daniel Murphy, father of Navy SEAL Lt. Michael Murphy, touches the face of his son's photograph during a ceremony at the Pentagon's Hall of Heroes in which those who have received the Medal of Honor are displayed. (L–R) Secretary of the Navy Gordon England, Secretary of the Navy Donald C. Winter, Maureen Murphy, mother of Lieutenant Murphy, Daniel Murphy, and Chief of Naval Operations Adm. Gary Roughead. (Photo: Greg E. Mathieson Sr. / NSW Publications, LLC)*

TOP, RIGHT: *President George W. Bush hugs Dan Murphy, father of Navy SEAL Lt. Michael Murphy, after the Medal of Honor ceremony as his wife, Maureen Murphy, looks on. Lieutenant Murphy received the Medal of Honor posthumously in a White House ceremony on October 22, 2007. (Photo: Eric Draper)*

RIGHT: *Daniel Murphy and Maureen Murphy, parents of U.S. Navy Lt. Michael Murphy, receive the Medal of Honor on behalf of their son from President George W. Bush in an East Room ceremony at the White House on October 22, 2007. The Medal of Honor was presented to Lieutenant Murphy posthumously for his actions in Operation Redwing. (Photo: Greg E. Mathieson Sr. / NSW Publications, LLC)*

remaining team member who was seriously injured, Petty Officer Marcus Lutrell, was later rescued.

The rescue attempt ended in the single worst mass casualty of that conflict. An Army MH-47 from the Army's elite 160 Special Operations Aviation Regiment, the Night Stalkers, with eight SEALs and eight U.S. Army Special Operation soldiers, was shot down by a Taliban rocket-propelled grenade. It was the largest loss of life for NSW personnel since World War II as well one of the greatest for Regiment 160.

But it was the selfless sacrifice of Lieutenant Murphy that makes that heroism in the Hindu Kush memorable as related by this citation:

> *For conspicuous gallantry and intrepidity at the risk of his life and above and beyond the call of duty as the leader of a special reconnaissance element with Naval Special Warfare task unit Afghanistan on 27 and 28 June 2005. While leading a mission to locate a high-level anti-coalition militia leader, Lieutenant Murphy demonstrated extraordinary heroism in the face of grave danger in the vicinity of Asadabad, Konar Province, Afghanistan. On 28 June 2005, operating in an extremely rugged enemy-controlled area, Lieutenant Murphy's team was discovered by anti-coalition militia sympathizers, who revealed their position to Taliban fighters. As a result, between 30 and 40 enemy fighters besieged his four-member team. Demonstrating exceptional*

Sally and George Monsoor, the parents of Medal of Honor recipient U.S. Navy SEAL Michael A. Monsoor, stand with Navy leadership during ceremonies of the presentation of the Medal of Honor flag at the U.S. Navy Memorial in Washington, D.C. (Photo: Greg E. Mathieson Sr. / NSW Publications, LLC)

With SEAL teammates and Monsoor family members looking on, the Medal of Honor flag is folded in a ceremony held at the U.S. Navy Memorial and presented to the parents of Navy SEAL Michael A. Monsoor. (Photo: Greg E. Mathieson Sr. / NSW Publications, LLC)

Sally Monsoor holds the Medal of Honor flag presented to her and her husband, George Monsoor, the parents of Medal of Honor recipient U.S. Navy SEAL Michael A. Monsoor as Chief of Naval Operations Gary Roughead looks on at a ceremony at the U.S. Navy Memorial in Washington, D.C. (Photo: Greg E. Mathieson Sr. / NSW Publications, LLC)

resolve, Lieutenant Murphy valiantly led his men in engaging the large enemy force. The ensuing fierce firefight resulted in numerous enemy casualties, as well as the wounding of all four members of the team. Ignoring his own wounds and demonstrating exceptional composure, Lieutenant Murphy continued to lead and encourage his men. When the primary communicator fell mortally wounded, Lieutenant Murphy repeatedly attempted to call for assistance for his beleaguered teammates. Realizing

ABOVE, LEFT: *U.S. Navy Master-At-Arms 2nd Class (SEAL) Michael A. Monsoor participates in a patrol in support of Operation Iraqi Freedom. Monsoor has been awarded the Medal of Honor posthumously for diving onto a grenade to save his teammates in Ramadi, Iraq, on September 29, 2006. Monsoor also received the Silver Star for his actions in May during the same deployment in 2006 when he exposed himself to heavy enemy fire to rescue and treat an injured teammate. (Photo: Courtesy of the Monsoor family / USN)*

ABOVE, RIGHT: *Navy SEAL Lt. Michael P. Murphy, from Patchogue, New York. Murphy was killed by enemy forces during a reconnaissance mission, Operation Red Wing, June 28, 2005. (Photo: USN)*

RIGHT: *Navy file photo of Navy SEALs operating in Afghanistan in support of Operation Enduring Freedom. From left to right, Sonar Technician (Surface) 2nd Class Matthew G. Axelson, of Cupertino, California; Senior Chief Information Systems Technician Daniel R. Healy, of Exeter, New Hampshire; Quartermaster 2nd Class James Suh, of Deerfield Beach, Florida; Hospital Corpsman 2nd Class Marcus Luttrell; Machinist's Mate 2nd Class Eric S. Patton, of Boulder City, Nevada; and Lt. Michael P. Murphy, of Patchogue, New York. With the exception of Luttrell, all were killed June 28, 2005, by enemy forces while supporting Operation Redwing. (Photo: USN)*

the impossibility of communicating in the extreme terrain, and in the face of almost certain death, he fought his way into open terrain to gain a better position to transmit a call. This deliberate, heroic act deprived him of cover, exposing him to direct enemy fire. Finally achieving contact with his headquarters, Lieutenant Murphy maintained his exposed position while he provided his location and requested immediate support for his team. In his final act of bravery, he continued to engage the enemy until he was mortally wounded, gallantly giving his life for his country and for the cause of freedom. By his selfless leadership, Lieutenant Murphy reflected great credit upon him and upheld the highest traditions of the United States Naval Service.

The second SEAL to receive the Medal of Honor also gave his life during the War on Terror.

Programs handed out to the guests in the East Room of the White House during the presentations of the Medal of Honor by President George W. Bush to the families of Navy SEALs Lt. Michael P. Murphy on October 22, 2007, and Master-at-Arms 2nd Class Michael A. Monsoor on April 8, 2008. (Photo: Greg E. Mathieson Sr. / NSW Publications, LLC)

Master-at-Arms Second Class **Michael A. Monsoor** was with other SEAL team members in a sniper position in the badlands of Ramadi, Iraq, in 2006, when an enemy grenade hit him directly in the chest and bounced to the floor of their hut.

Monsoor, a Garden Grove, California, native, whose father and brother were Marines, was described by his comrades as a humble and modest man who drew his strength from his family and his faith. And he gave his life to save those around him. The citation for the Congressional Medal describes an ordinary combat situation that turned into and extraordinary act of sacrifice.

For conspicuous gallantry and intrepidity at the risk of his life above and beyond the call of duty while serving as Automatic Weapons Gunner for Naval Special Warfare Task Group Arabian Peninsula, in support of Operation IRAQI FREEDOM on 29 September 2006. As a member of a combined SEAL and Iraqi Army sniper over watch element, tasked with providing early warning and stand-off protection from a rooftop in an insurgent-held sector of Ar Ramadi, Iraq, Petty Officer Monsoor distinguished himself by his exceptional bravery in the face of grave danger. In the early morning, insurgents prepared to execute a coordinated attack by reconnoitering the area around the element's position. Element snipers thwarted the enemy's initial

attempt by eliminating two insurgents. The enemy continued to assault the element, engaging them with a rocket-propelled grenade and small arms fire. As enemy activity increased, Petty Officer Monsoor took position with his machine gun between two teammates on an outcropping of the roof. While the SEALs vigilantly watched for enemy activity, an insurgent threw a hand grenade from an unseen location, which bounced off Petty Officer Monsoor's chest and landed in front of him. Although only he could have escaped the blast, Petty Officer Monsoor chose instead to protect his teammates. Instantly and without regard for his own safety, he threw himself onto the grenade to absorb the force of the explosion with his body, saving the lives of his two teammates. By his undaunted courage, fighting spirit, and unwavering devotion to duty in the face of certain death, Petty Officer Monsoor gallantly gave his life for his country, thereby reflecting great credit upon himself and upholding the highest traditions of the United States Naval Service.

These incredible stories of courage and valor are not the only episodes for which SEALs are known. The exploits reach into space exploration. Many recognize the name of Navy Capt. William M. Shepherd as the first commanding officer of the International Space station, but few know that before becoming an astronaut he was a Navy SEAL. He was followed into NASA by Lt. Cdr. Chris

Cassidy, who had graduated from the Naval Academy with degrees in mathematics and ocean engineering, the latter from MIT. He then became a SEAL and went on receive the Bronze Star for his actions in Afghanistan. He was selected as an astronaut by NASA in 2007, and flew on the Space Shuttle Endeavour mission STS-127 to the International Space Station on July 15, 2009.

But almost no one knows that in the decades before there was an international space station and many years before rocketships flew to the moon, that Navy SEALs were used in laboratory tests to see what punishment a man could take during space travel.

Master Chief Bill Bruhmuller's history as a Navy SEAL is the stuff of legend. An average kid from Walden, Massachusetts, he joined the Navy to "see the world" in 1953, and became one of the Navy's and the world's hidden heroes.

In 1957, space experts at the United States Air Force, charged with getting America ready for space, felt that all astronauts had to be men with high technical skills; physical conditioning became a secondary trait for the endurances needed in space. But space scientists at the Air Force's Wright-Patterson base in Ohio disagreed.

Along came Third Class Petty Officer Bill Bruhmuller and others of his underwater demolition team to prove the scientific theory that physical training was

ABOVE: *A memorial started outside SDV One in Hawaii. (Photo: Greg E. Mathieson Sr. / NSW Publications, LLC)*

TOP, LEFT: *Rear Adm. Joseph D. Kernan, USN (SEAL), receives the flag from the casket of Navy Cryptologic Technician 1st Class Steven Phillip Daugherty at Arlington National Cemetery. Steven Daugherty was killed as a result of enemy action while conducting combat operations near Baghdad on July 6, 2007. Also killed that day were Mass Communications Specialist 1st Class Robert Richard McRill and Special Warfare Operator 1st Class (SEAL) Jason Dale Lewis. (Photo: Greg E. Mathieson Sr. / NSW Publications, LLC)*

TOP, RIGHT: *Rear Adm. Joseph D. Kernan, USN (SEAL), presents the American flag from the casket of Navy Cryptologic Technician 1st Class Steven Phillip Daugherty to his family at Arlington National Cemetery. Support personnel travel and experience many of the same risks as the SEALs and SWCC teams. (Photo: Greg E. Mathieson Sr. / NSW Publications, LLC)*

357

essential for space flight. Bruhmiller and his UDT mates become human guinea pigs. For over three weeks, for twelve hours a day, scientists abused their bodies. After Bruhmiller endured hours at 130-degree heat, his body would be plunged into subzero temperatures. He and his teammates worked in altitude chambers and were subjected to conditions of eleven g-forces.

All those experiments, as just about everything SEALs did was secret for many years. Even when astronauts returned to earth by hitting the ocean in a space capsule, the "Navy divers," as the media was told, pulling them to safety were actually SEALs, but that could never be mentioned. So many secrets!

Bill Bruhmuller's career was a tightly held book of secrets. Just a few years later, he said, "I was one of the first SEALs to be told to turn in my identification and temporarily work for the CIA."

Bruhmuller then told of something historians have been trying to substantiate for decades, "I slipped into a Cuban port with a team of twelve Cuban exile combat divers, in the late winter of 1964, and we blew up a few Russian missile boats."

He had helped train the Cuban exiles. He trusted them. He remembers clearly how loyal they were to Cuba but also to the United States. He sadly remembers November 22, 1963, where he and the Cubans were watching TV at a safe house

LEFT: *SEALs stand at attention for the National Anthem during a capabilities demonstration at the annual UDT—SEAL reunion. (Photo: Greg E. Mathieson Sr. / NSW Publications, LLC)*

BOTTOM: *Navy SEAL Master Chief Bill Bruhmuller was one of the first in the early NASA program used to see what the human body could endure. Bruhmuller graduated with BUD/S Class 13 and was the first SEAL dog handler. Bill's dog Prince was awarded the Purple Heart in Vietnam. (Photo: Courtesy of Tom Hawkins)*

on an island off of Key Biscayne, Florida, and all of them were crying at the news of President John F. Kennedy's assassination.

He calmly and confidently explains that working for the CIA was "pretty neat," that SEALs seconded to the CIA, trained many teams to infiltrate the Communist island. But he says he was the only one that actually became involved in explosive action, and that the combat divers went on twelve missions under his supervision. Blowing up the Russian missile boats was the only mission in which he was in the water, "to make sure it went well."

He remembers the infiltration mission clearly, because they were almost discovered. He began the mission sailing out of a Fort Lauderdale port on the Rex, a Panamanian flagged freighter, to within a few miles of the Cuban coast. He and his team of 13 Cuban exile frogmen took a couple of rubber boats to within a few hundred yards of a Cuban naval port. The mission was to blow up four Kormar-class Soviet missile boats. Bruhmuller admits he was supposed to stay on the freighter, but decided at the last minute to participate in the mission. His Cuban exile mates were attaching limpet mines to hulls of the Komars, while he observed an armed guard on the pier. The limpet mines "made a hell of a racket as they were slammed onto the boats," recalls Bruhmuller. He watched as the guard called for help on his radio, knowing that someone was sabotaging the missile boats.

Bruhmuller, then an E-5, says that three of the four boats blew high into the sky as he and his team made their way back to the CIA mother ship.

That kind of unassuming bravery under fire beyond all imagination is what awards the SEALs more medals per capita than any other military unit.

Another example is the kind of courage and determination exemplified by Senior Chief Petty Officer Douglas Day on a really nasty day in Fallujah, Iraq. Day was awarded the Silver Star after he breached an enemy building while under heavy fire. He was shot 17 times, hit by an enemy grenade, and had his service rifle shot from his hand. All that was not enough to cause him to withdraw: he drew his sidearm and killed three more insurgents without injuring the women and children in close proximity.

And that kind of heroism is not just the hallmark of SEAL shooters. Even their doctors are warriors first:

Medical officer Lt. Mark L. Donald was on a mounted patrol conducting combat operations in Afghanistan against al Qaeda and Taliban forces in October of

FACING PAGE

BOTTOM, LEFT: *Navy Capt. William Shepherd, shown wearing his space suit and SEAL Trident on the front, graduated the U.S. Naval Academy and later earned a graduate degree from MIT. He served in the UDTs, SEAL teams, and Special Boat Units and was selected by NASA in 1984 for the astronaut program. Having flown four space flights and logging in some 159 days in space, Shepherd commanded the first mission to the International Space Station (ISS) from October 2000 till March 2001. (Photo: Courtesy of NASA)*

BOTTOM, RIGHT: *Navy SEAL and astronaut Chris Cassidy graduated from the U.S. Naval Academy, then went on to earn his graduate degree at MIT. Cassidy served 10 years as a SEAL and was deployed to Afganistan two weeks after 9/11 and did a second tour there. He also accumulated over 200 hours as a DDS Commander with SDV2 before being selected by NASA for astronaut training. Here he's outside the Space Shuttle on mission STS-127. (Photo: Courtesy of NASA)*

RIGHT: *Secretary of State Condoleezza Rice with SEAL operators from SEAL Team Ten during during the last two weeks of the Bush administration.*

BOTTOM, RIGHT: *Secretary of State Condoleezza Rice meets with members of a SEAL team before flying back to Washington for the final two weeks of the Bush administration.*

BELOW: *This commemorative coin was created to honor the first SEAL to die in combat in Afghanistan: Petty Officer 1st Class Neil C. Roberts, 32, who died during Operation Anaconda in early March 2002. For weeks U.S. forces had been watching as Taliban and al Qaeda fighters gathered south of Kabul. Code-named Operation Anaconda, the battle plan aimed at this force was a hammer-and-anvil strategy. Friendly Afghans, assisted by U.S. special forces, would flush the enemy from the north and north-west toward three exits of the Shah-i-Kot valley, where American troops waited. Neil Roberts had been aboard one of two MH-47 Chinooks, double-headed helicopters that were responding to this huge and intense battle. While they were preparing to set down, they came under heavy fire from small arms and rocket-propelled grenades, one of which bounced, without exploding, off the armor of a Chinook. In the same bird, a hydraulic line was cut. Roberts, who was the rear gunner and had been returning fire from the open back hatch, had apparently slipped on the draining oil, and had been jolted out when the chopper banked hard to the north. Surviving the 5-10 foot fall, Roberts was able to evade the enemy for a while. By aerial surveillance, Roberts was seen trying to flee. About three hours after the first incident, two more Chinooks set off from Bagram on the dual mission to rescue Roberts and insert more troops. One of the choppers took heavy machine-gun fire. It shuddered and spiraled toward the ground but managed to crash-land less than a mile from the place the first pair had come under attack. As the troops clambered out of the wrecked MH-47, they were ambushed. An AC-130 gunship was ordered into the battle to provide close air support, but the enemy barrage was so intense that U.S. troops couldn't be lifted out during daylight. Fighting continued through the day, as the first team searching for Roberts fought its way to the downed Chinook. It was not until midnight that the last U.S. soldier was evacuated. The choppers also carried 11 wounded and the bodies of seven Americans: Roberts and six of his rescuers. (Photo: Dave Gatley)*

2003. He and the patrol were ambushed by extremely heavy fire from rocket-propelled grenades and small arms. Two RPGs exploded in front of his vehicle. While returning fire, Lieutenant Donald pulled the Afghan commander to safety and with the battle raging around him extracted the wounded American driver to the side of the destroyed vehicle. As withering incoming fire racked their position, Donald covered his two wounded comrades with his own body. Then, seeing two other Afghans badly wounded in two other destroyed vehicles, he fought his way to their rescue and under heavy fire gave medical treatment.

After treating the wounded, he then took charge of the Afghan squad and deployed them to break the ambush while continuing to treat numerous critically injured comrades.

Later that same day, while sweeping an area of earlier combat, he and his element were again ambushed by a platoon-sized enemy force. Knowing personnel

were gravely wounded, Lieutenant Donald without hesitation and with complete disregard for his own safety ran two hundred meters between opposing forces exposing himself to withering and continuous heavy-machine-gun and small-arms fire to render medical treatment to two of the wounded, one Afghan and one American.

It does not end there. While still under intense enemy fire, wounded by shrapnel and close to Apache helicopter rocket targets, he organized the surviving Afghan soldiers and led a two-hundered meter fighting withdrawal to friendly positions.

Only after he evacuated his wounded men and returned to base did he treat his own wounds. For extraordinary valor, Lt Mark L. Donald, a medical officer, received the Navy Cross for actions that October 25, 2003. A few weeks later, Lieutenant Donald received the Silver Star for additional actions on November 10, 2003.

Again, that is the stuff of legend.

Finally, there is the almost unbelievable story of Lieutenant (j.g.) Jason Redmon. He did not regale President Bush with his exploits when being visited at Bethesda Naval Hospital, but it is almost certain the Commander in Chief was told of this inspiring SEAL.

In a log kept by Redmon he recounted with honor what caused his injuries and how he was recovering: "3 x 7.62 by 54mm PKC rounds, 5 blood transfusions, 1 tracheotomy, 7 months 2 days with Trach, approximately 1150 stitches, approximately 200 staples, 3 plates, 1 titanium orbital floor, 15 screws, 8 pins, 12 skin grafts, 2 external fixators, 1 fibular bone graft, 11 weeks jaw wired shut for 11 weeks, 40 pounds of weight loss, approximately 120 hours of surgery, 20 surgeries, 59 days in hospital and sill counting."

And, if for a moment you think Redmon is keeping a tally of his misery, think again. This is what is affixed to his door at the hospital:

Attention !!– Please Read
Attention to all who enter here:

If you are coming into this room with sorrow or to feel sorry for my wounds, go elsewhere. The wounds I received, I got in a job I love, doing it for people I love, supporting the freedom of a country I deeply love. I am incredibly tough and will make a full recovery. What is full? That is the absolute utmost physically my body has the ability to recover. Then I will push that about 20% further though sheer mental tenacity. This room you are about to enter is a room of fun, optimism, and intense rapid regrowth. If you are not prepared for that, go elsewhere."

LEFT: *Medical Officer Lt. Mark L. Donald was awarded the Navy Cross and then a few weeks later received the Silver Star for another heroic act. (Photo: Courtesy of Jeannie Hobbs)*

BELOW: *This note was posted on the door of wounded Navy SEAL Lt. Jason Redman at Walter Reed National Medical Center. (Photo: USN)*

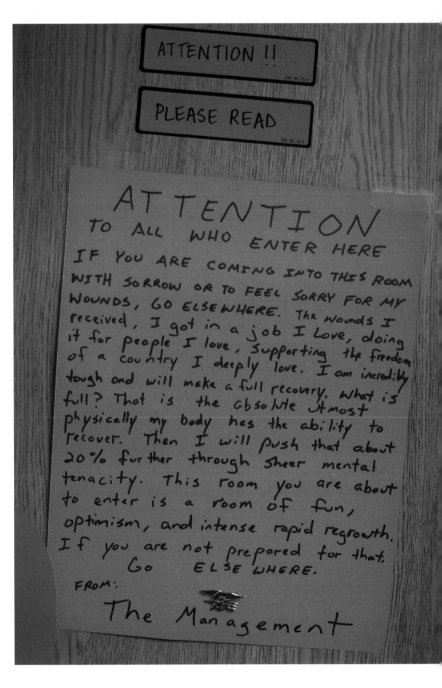

361

LEFT, TOP: *President George W. Bush and Vice President Dick Cheney meet with members of SEAL Team Ten one last time before they leave office in a few weeks.*

LEFT, CENTER: *President Bush, behind closed doors and out of sight of the public and the media, addresses the U.S. Navy SEALs, SWCC, and NSW staff in thanking them for their sacrifice.*

LEFT, BOTTOM: *Vice Adm. Robert Harward (SEAL) Deputy Commander, U.S.* Central Command; Adm. Eric T. Olson (SEAL), Commander of U.S. Special Operations Command; President George W. Bush; Rear Adm. Edward G. Winters II (SEAL) Commander, U.S. Naval Special Warfare Command; Capt. Brian L. Losey (SEAL), Director Combating Terrorism, National Security Council; Vice Adm. Joseph D. Kernan (SEAL), Senior Military Assistant to the Secretary of Defense; Vice President Dick Cheney.

In those simple words you will find the heart and soul of ALL SEALs, all those in the NSW community. We owe them a debt we will never be able to pay.

We could go on and on into a series of books about the exploits and acts of the sacrifice, bravery, and heroism of the men of Naval Special Warfare, SEALs, and their forefathers. It is not our intent to slight anyone by not listing their names, actions, and those sacrifices here; there are many, both known and unknown, some only known to God. And not all actions receive medals or accolades. For, as they see it, it was simply their job.

Not all of the men and their medals are stories of SEALs. So many more in support of the SEAL missions give their limbs and their lives, too. They, the SEALs and the cryptologists, the communications specialists, the explosive ordnance men, the masters-at-arms, and others leave behind grieving families so proud of their lost sons, fathers, brothers, and husbands. Those families are all cared for by the various groups and foundations whose charitable work keeps the NSW and SEAL family together during years of grief and growth. They are there for them as a brotherhood well after their service to our country is over and in times of need, during peace and war.

If your heart is filled with pride after reading these stories and viewing these photographs then join the team, the family of Naval Special Warfare. These organizations can use your assistance in supporting the families of those left behind and to help those that need

RIGHT: *On September 11, 2012, the anniversary of the terrorist attack of 9/11, President Barack Obama made an unscheduled visit to Arlington National Cemetery on the way to a ceremony at the Pentagon. Outside of the view of news cameras, the media, and bystanders, the President walked over to the headstones of the Navy SEALs killed in the mission Extortion 17 and placed a Presidential Challenge Coin on the headstones of each of the SEALs, the three Air Force personnel, and the headstone marked as Unidentified Remains. This quiet act of reverence and respect was never reported. (Photo: Greg E. Mathieson Sr. / NSW Publications, LLC)*

LEFT: *In a private moment outside the view or knowledge of anyone on the anniversary of 9/11, President Barack Obama placed his Presidential Challenge Coin on the head-stone of Navy SEAL Lt. Cdr. Jonas Kelsall in Arlington National Cemetery. (Photo: Greg E. Mathieson Sr. / NSW Publications, LLC)*

it most. These organizations were established to ensure the great NSW warriors of today and tomorrow will be perpetually honored and supported.

These vital campaigns aim at raising millions of dollars for the benefit of U.S. Navy SEALs, special boat operators, and support personnel; warriors of the Naval Special Warfare who are at the forefront of the Global War on Terror and quietly go about their jobs around the world, so that we can live free from terror attacks on our shores.

Please visit their website at www.NavySEALFoundation.org and help a hero.

BELOW: *The son of Navy Cryptologic Technician 1st Class Steven Phillip Daugherty places his hand on the casket of his father one last time in Arlington National Cemetery. (Photo: Greg E. Mathieson Sr. / NSW Publications, LLC)*

The Future of Naval Special Warfare

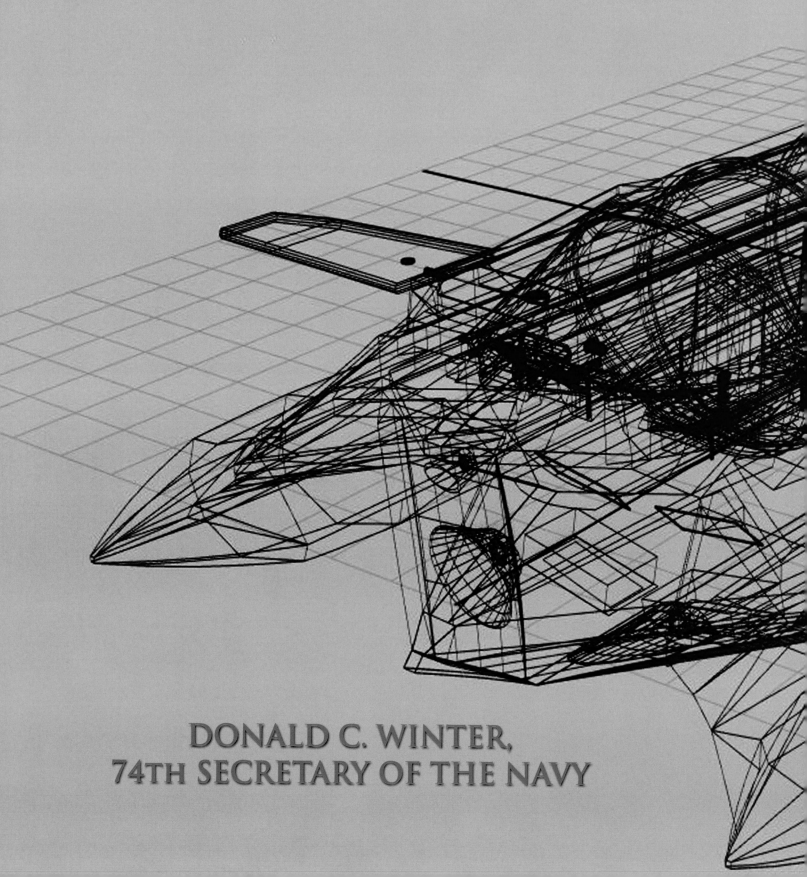

DONALD C. WINTER,
74TH SECRETARY OF THE NAVY

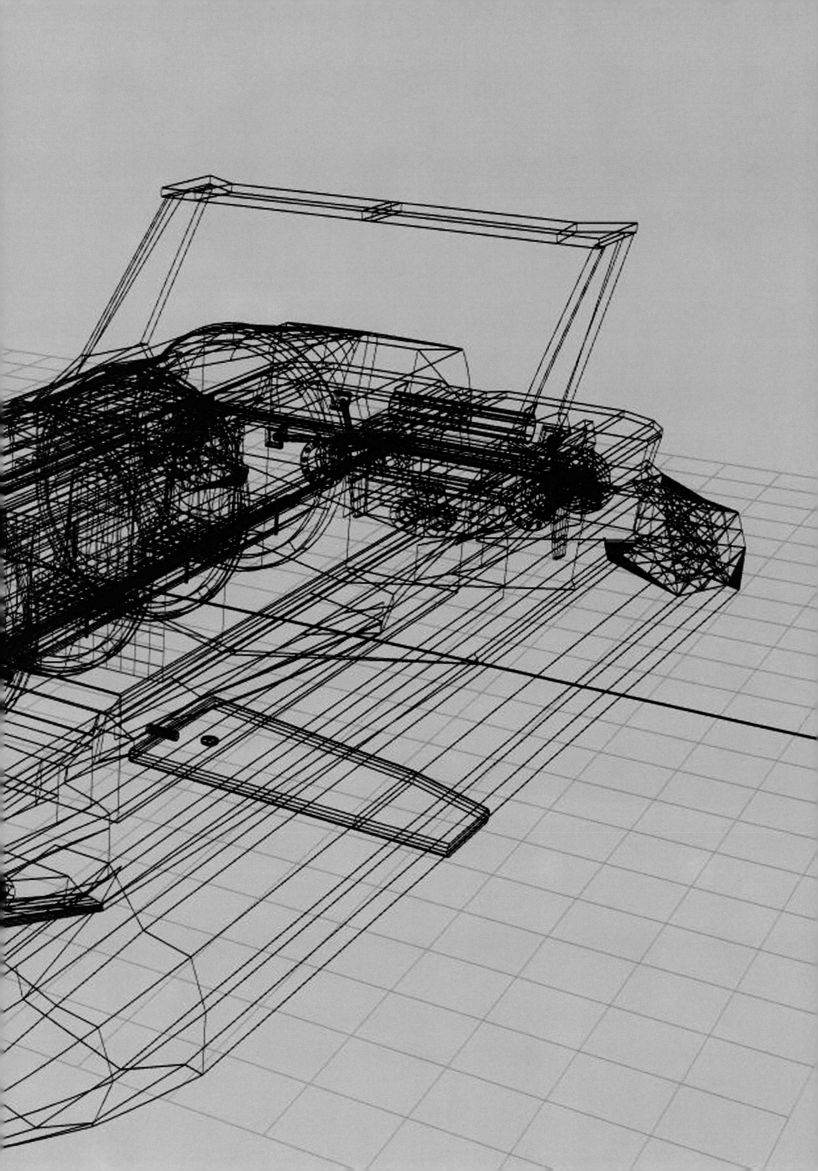

CHAPTER 15

THE FUTURE OF NAVAL SPECIAL WARFARE

The Honorable Donald C. Winter,
74th Secretary of the Navy

PAGES 364–365: *The Marion Hyper-Sub prototype "Fathom" is one of many concepts and products that corporations are developing on their own to pitch to SOCOM and the U.S. Navy to help in fighting the new age of terrorism, drug trafficking, and littoral security. Some Hyper-Subs are capable of being air-dropped into the ocean, have a length of over 30 feet, and can carry 8 personnel and dive to depth of 600 feet. Having a surface speed of 45 knots, some can travel 1,000 miles without refueling. (Graphic courtesy of Marion Hyper-Sub)*

BELOW: *SEAL operators may fly and drive in military vehicles like this one in the future. D-Star Engineering presented this concept of their AurAayan V/STOL Experimental (AVX-17) at a Defense Advanced Research Projects Agency (DARPA) conference with other companies developing "flying vehicles" for the military. (Photo courtesy: D-Star Engineering)*

In times of war or uncertainty, there is a special breed of warrior ready to answer our nation's call, a common man with uncommon desire to succeed. Forged by adversity, he stands alongside America's finest special operations forces to serve his country, the American people, and protect their way of life. I am that man.

U.S. Navy SEAL Creed

THE U.S. AND MANY OF ITS ALLIES WERE FACED WITH AN UNPRECedented global security challenge following the attacks on the World Trade Center and the Pentagon on September 11, 2001. These attacks did not go unanswered; the global war against terrorism was engaged. In the years since 9/11, NSW has been engaged in special operations on a global scale that both demonstrated the efficacy of special operations and underscored gaps in our ability to confront an asymmetric enemy operating on a global basis. As combat

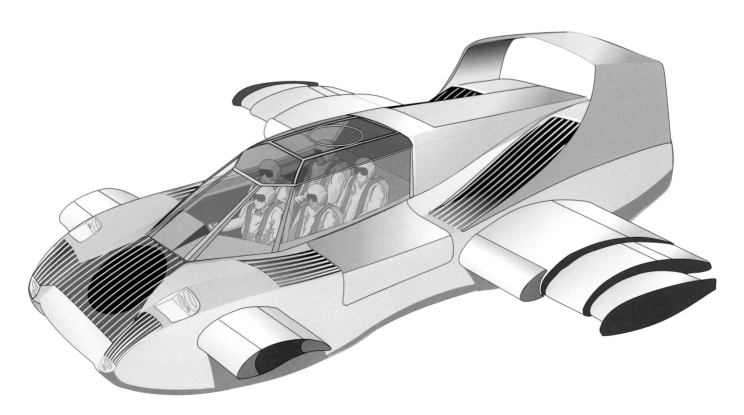

A Navy SEAL takes aim on a rocky mountainside. He uses an SOF Combat Assault Rifle, or SCAR, which is a modular rifle made by FN Herstal for the U.S. Special Operations Command. (Photo: USN)

The Special Operations Forces Combat Assault Rifle (SCAR), manufactured by FN Herstal. The SCAR is currently being phased into service with the U.S. Navy SEALs, where it will replace multiple other weapons. There are two rifle variants, the Light—5.56-mm, and the Heavy—7.62 CAL, with a short and a long barrel options to fit both rifles. Fitting both rifles is the MK19 Grenade launcher that snaps onto the rail system. Mk16—Light here—with the Mk19 and suppressor. (Photo: Dave Gatley)

and other special operations progressed, U.S. and partner nation special operations forces rapidly transformed to engage and counter this threat. Confronted by a dynamic, adaptive, and ruthless enemy, NSW has been fully engaged in the global war on terrorism, and will be for the foreseeable future. Couple this with long-standing requirements to support major combat operations in conventional warfare, and the demands on NSW and the entire Special Operations communities have never been greater . . . nor the potential consequences of failure as profound.

History is replete with military forces that focused on past conflicts in preparing for the future, and that were insufficiently prepared when subsequently confronted by evolutions (and revolutions) in warfare. One of the U.S. Special Operations community's foremost objectives is to constantly prepare for the next conflict—whenever and wherever it should occur and whatever form that engagement may take.

How NSW is positioning itself for success and relevancy into the future is the subject of this final chapter. While the future is unknowable, there are objectives, trends, and realities that govern the future roles, missions, and direction of NSW. Understanding this, one gains a better sense of what may lie ahead for NSW, how and why NSW operators must prepare for that future, and—where reality and

expectation collide—how this warrior culture that stresses vigilance, readiness, and adaptability will persevere.

UNDERSTANDING THE FUTURE OPERATING ENVIRONMENT

The U.S. faces a broad spectrum of potential security challenges. From pirates operating off the coast of Somalia, transnational terrorists such as al Qaeda, and rogue nations, to potential peer competitors, threats range greatly, both geographically and militarily. Furthermore, while our investments over the past 60 years in strategic and tactical forces have successfully deterred conflict with near-peer competitors, such as the former Soviet Union, the same cannot be said about rogue nations, terrorists, or pirates. Hostilities with rogue nations, like the former Iraqi regime of Saddam Hussein, often stem from miscalculations, notwithstanding the overwhelming capabilities of U.S. and Allied forces. Terrorists are emboldened by fanatical beliefs and a willingness to sacrifice themselves and their families for a cause, while pirates tend to be motivated by desperate economic environments, and are often facilitated by a lack of governance in the region. In these latter cases, armed conflict is not just a possibility we hope to be deterred, but likely a continuing reality.

The nature of such "limited" conflicts requires the surgical application of proportionate force. No one questions our capability, for example, to wipe out the Somali towns that harbor pirate activities. However, the collateral casualties that

On May 10, 2006, the Naval Special Warfare leaders receive the Presidential Unit Citation from Secretary of the Navy, the Honorable Dr. Donald C. Winter, for actions during Operation Iraqi Freedom. (Photo: USN)

would result from such an attack make such an option untenable. Special operations provide the flexibility of force application that both is appropriate and is necessitated by the political realities of the modern era.

Special operations, and NSW in particular, are easily adapted to the geographical uncertainties associated with such conflicts. The geographic certainties of the Cold War, which enabled NATO forces to focus on areas such as the Fulda Gap, are largely absent in today's environment and are unlikely to return in the foreseeable future. A naval-based force provides a flexible means of accessing most future potential conflict areas since the seas cover 70 percent of the globe, and 80 percent of the world's population lives within 250 miles of the sea. Furthermore, access from the sea minimizes the political risks associated with the use of fixed bases on foreign soil, such as the delicate situation we experienced in 2003 regarding U.S. bases in Turkey. Nonetheless, the ongoing conflict in Afghanistan points out the need to project and maintain special operations forces hundreds of miles inland.

The face of a future SEAL—Class 261. (Photo: Dave Gatley)

Additionally, it is important to note that, while irregular forces have historically depended on their local knowledge of geography and terrain to achieve an asymmetric advantage, we are now seeing such forces look toward other means to enhance their capabilities. In particular, we are now seeing them use and adapt technology in ways that provide new and unique means of leverage. With the growth of the Internet and global commerce in electronics, capabilities that heretofore were limited to the forces of highly developed nations are now available worldwide. The Internet alone provides mechanisms for recruiting, training, and coordinating the actions of terrorists in ways that were not even envisioned until recently. Coupled with global availability of cellular and satellite communications, these technologies enable a wide range of capabilities from command and control of complex attacks to improvised explosive devices.

As the mechanisms of global connectivity evolve, so, too, will the leveraging of technology. We are already seeing the evolution from e-mail and Web posting to Twitter and other electronic technologies. Furthermore, there is no reason to expect these technology adaptations will be limited to the realm of command and control. Prolifera-

tion of weapons technology is evident today with the use of explosively formed projectiles in the Middle East. Proliferation and availability of chemical, biological, or radiological weapons to terrorists and other irregular forces may well be upon us shortly.

The proliferation, adaptation, and application of advanced technologies by our enemies will continue to change the nature of irregular warfare. In the future, we will not be able to count on having an overwhelming technical advantage in all tactical situations. We will have to learn how to adapt and offset these changes because, once more, the stakes of irregular warfare have been raised.

The implications of terrorism and other forms of irregular warfare were made evident on 9/11 and continue to evolve as terrorist organizations develop their concepts of war. The changing nature of the threats the U.S. faces is reflected in the changing view of Special Operations Forces. Prior to 9/11, SOF was typically described as a force multiplier, an adjunct force to conduct pre–D-Day operations and then assume a minor role in follow-on surgical operations—all in support of a larger conventional force. Post-9/11, SOF has been transformed into one of the key implements of U.S. national strategy execution.

Furthermore, where possible, U.S. strategy is employing indirect approaches—building the capability and capacity of partner nations—to prevent festering problems from evolving into crises that pose great risks to the U.S. and Allied nations and thereby require costly (and potentially controversial) direct military intervention. In doing so, the capability and will of U.S. Allies and partners are as important as our own.

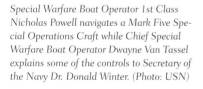

MK-IA | MK-IC

MK-IA
- Lightweight
- Full Body Load Distribution
- Conformal Structure Allows Dynamic Motion
- Integrates with Current Kit

MK-IC
- Full Body Load Distribution
- Lower Body Powered Augmentation
- Mitigates Fatigue, Stress & Injury
- Increases Ballistic Protection to 3x Coverage

The U.S. Special Operations Command (USSOCOM) displayed promotional images at a recent trade show, detailing some concepts of the new Tactical Assault Light Operator Suit, known as TALOS. (Greg E. Mathieson Sr. / NSW Publications, LLC)

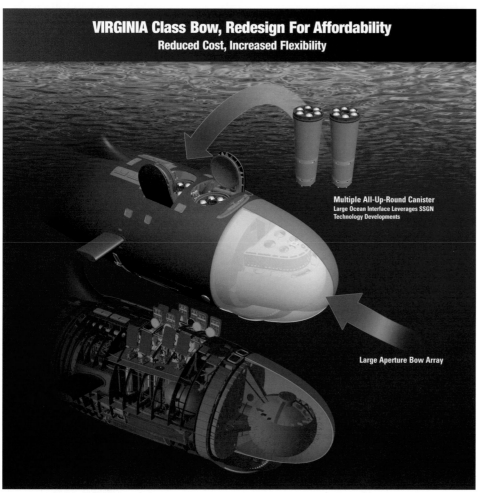

VIRGINIA Class Bow, Redesign For Affordability
Reduced Cost, Increased Flexibility

Multiple All-Up-Round Canister
Large Ocean Interface Leverages SSGN
Technology Developments

Large Aperture Bow Array

The most impressive success was the "bow bundle." Designers are dramatically simplifying the bow, working to replace the traditional sonar sphere with a hydrophone array and change the configuration for the Tomahawk missile launchers mounted behind the sphere. Instead of 12 individual tubes, the design would include two six-missile magazines. Not only will this save more than $40 million per ship, it will increase the payload flexibility of the Virginia class. The new missile tubes are based on the 7-foot diameter D-5 Trident ballistic missile tubes, with changes similar to those done in the four Ohio-class SSGN submarine conversions. The tubes, which will be newly manufactured and somewhat shorter than the Ohio-class tubes, will each carry a Multiple All-Up-Round Canister (MAC) with six Tomahawks. The Virginia installation omits the seventh missile in the center, leaving room for an access tube. The missile canister will be removable from the new Virginia payload tubes, allowing flexibility to fit different weapons or underwater vehicles. Since the connectors and dimensions are the same as the Ohio SSGN tubes, new payloads designed for those ships will be compatible with the Block III and later Virginias. The new tubes nearly double the amount of payload space compared with the former VLS installation, going from 1,200 cubic feet to 2,300. The new missile tubes will reduce construction and life-cycle costs, and save an estimated $8 million per ship beginning with the 2012 ship. (Illustration courtesy of General Dynamics, Electric Boat)

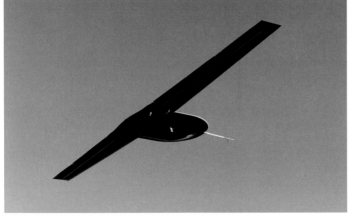

TOP, LEFT: *The RQ-3A DarkStar Tier III Minus was one of two high-altitude-endurance UAVs being developed for the Defense Airborne Reconnaissance Office (DARO) by the Advanced Research Projects Agency (ARPA) joint UAV program. The DarkStar is optimized for reconnaissance of low observables in highly defended areas. Physically, it is a little over half the span and a third the length of the Global Hawk aircraft. (Photo: DoD)*

TOP, RIGHT: *A Pterodactyl ultralight is one of the systems that the Naval Special Air Warfare Center Weapons Division at China Lake has been working on in hopes of developing an ultralight military aircraft. China Lake has developed many of the unique weapons for the SEALs and the rest of the Navy. (Photo: Courtesy of NAWS China Lake)*

BOTTOM, LEFT: *Recently approved by the FDA, the XSTAT is a first-of-its-kind hemostatic device for the treatment of gunshot and shrapnel wounds on the battlefield. XSTAT works by injecting a group of small, rapidly expanding sponges into a wound cavity using a syringe-like applicator. Each sponge contains an x-ray detectable marker. In the wound, the XSTAT sponges expand and swell to fill the wound cavity within 20 seconds of contact with blood. This creates a temporary barrier to blood flow and provides hemostatic pressure. (Photo courtesy of REVMEDX)*

BOTTOM, RIGHT: *The Naval Special Warfare Development Group tests and develops new products and equipment. Here Secretary of the Navy Dr. Donald C. Winter (white shirt on the right) listens to a brief on the "Sentry HP" unmanned aerial vehicle (UAV) developed by DRS Technologies while touring the Naval Special Warfare Development Group. (Photo: USN)*

Catalysts of future wars can be as varied as their potential participants. Whether caused by religious, ethnic, or territorial disputes; economic strife; failed governments; hegemonic dreams; or international instability, crises inviting U.S. engagement will likely see NSW involvement. NSW's role may include monitoring and quietly influencing situations across a broad spectrum of national security efforts to prevent hostilities, or bringing an arsenal of special operations capabilities to the fight, or some combination of both.

PAST AS PROLOGUE: THE SEAL LEGACY

Much has been written of the SEALs' illustrious heritage and how the legacy established by their forebears influences and informs SEAL and NSW operations of today and tomorrow. From the beaches of World War II through current conflicts, SEALs and their predecessors participated in every U.S. conflict and forged an indisputably colorful, valorous, and unique reputation. The SEAL Creed, developed in 2004, provides an excellent window into the mind-set of SEALs. The expression "earn your Trident every day" reflects a warrior ethos founded on challenging oneself to be mentally, physically, and professionally prepared at all times. (Note: The Trident is how the SEALs refer to their gold warfare breast insignia.) The ethos speaks of loyalty to country, unit, and teammate; integrity and taking responsibility for actions on and off the battlefield; excelling as a warrior; self-discipline; and never quitting. The history of the SEALs proves these are not hollow words, but rather words that embody what a SEAL is, does, and believes.

Exhaustive studies and analyses have been conducted to determine who can successfully become a SEAL and identify attributes common to SEALs. While the merit of these studies is a source of some debate, a number of identifiable characteristics have been borne out over the past forty-five years as contributing directly to the success of SEAL operations and advancement of the SEAL community. Understanding the thread of NSW history, traditions that mold SEALs and the

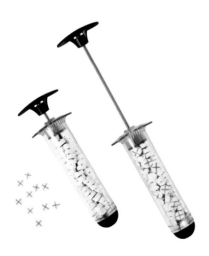

commonality between that individual and his predecessors is key to understanding the future of NSW. Were one to place a World War II–era UDT and an OIF/OEF SEAL in the same room, age, operational experience, and equipment would contrast sharply. The two, however, would have far more in common than they would have differences. Neither pursued a career in NSW to fight for himself; rather, each did so in service of a greater cause . . . one he feels privileged to serve. The words of the SEAL Creed would resonate equally with both, particularly the following:

The Nano Air Vehicle (Hummingbird) (NAV) by AeroVironment is a flying prototype being developed under a contract with DARPA. With a wingspan of 16 cm (6.5 in) and a weight of only 19 grams, it can fly at 10 meters per second and can withstand 2.5 meter per second wind gusts. It can send a live video signal to a palmtop controller/ monitoring station. (Photo: Courtesy of AeroVironment)

> I serve with honor on and off the battlefield. The ability to control my emotions and my actions, regardless of circumstance, sets me apart from other men. Uncompromising integrity is my standard. My character and honor are steadfast. My word is my bond . . . We expect to lead and be led. In the absence of orders I will take charge, lead my teammates and accomplish the mission. I lead by example in all situations. . . . I will never quit. I persevere and thrive on adversity. My nation expects me to be physically harder and mentally stronger than my enemies. If knocked down, I will get back up, every time. I will draw on every remaining ounce of strength to protect my teammates and to accomplish our mission. I am never out of the fight.

One of the unspoken responsibilities of each generation of SEALs is to guard and advance the legacy inherited from their predecessors. In short: to leave "the Teams" better than they found them, and to enrich—and, in turn, be enriched by—their service with an august group of warriors.

Special Forces Combat Assault Rifles (SCAR), manufactured by FN Manufacturing, a U.S. subsidiary to the Belgian company FN Herstal. The FN SCAR is currently being phased into service with the SEALs, where it will replace other weapons. The Mk 19 grenade launcher fits both rifles, snapping onto the rail system. (Photo: Courtesy of FN Manufacturing)

Consistent with their constant drive for self-improvement—and contrary to popular opinion and myth—SEALs are by nature self-critical. This self-criticism is leveraged heavily within the NSW community to improve unit effectiveness by focusing extensively on operational tactics, techniques, and procedures (TTPs). The lifeblood of NSW, TTPs are continually developed and/or refined in order to stay ahead of enemy capabilities, leverage technological advances, and optimize operational success. *After Action Reports* and *Lessons Learned* catalogue a constant cycle of self-evaluation wherein SEALs critique themselves, their operations, and their TTPs. Tactics are studied, modified, and incorporated into basic and advanced training. Lessons learned come back to NSW training commands on a near-daily basis, where they are reviewed by experienced NSW officers and senior enlisted SEALs. Owing to the rigor and constancy of this ongoing process, professional stagnation is mitigated.

From his earliest association with NSW, a

TOP, LEFT: *The latest "nano" drone aircraft being used today is the Proxdynamics PD-100 Black Hornet PRS. Quiet as a fly, it has a range of nearly 1.5 km and can hover as three cameras transmit live video to the operator. Its size relative to SEAL Trident pin is shown here. (Photo: Greg E. Mathieson Sr. / NSW Publications, LLC)*

TOP, RIGHT: *The Proxdynamics PD-100 Black Hornet Personal Reconnaissance nano helicopter drone hovers in flight while its three cameras transmit live video and HD snapshots back to the operator. (Photo: Greg E. Mathieson Sr. / NSW Publications, LLC)*

BOTTOM: *The Proxdynamics PD-100 Black Hornet Personal Reconnaissance System (PRS) is a complete "nano" unmanned aircraft system (UAS) consisting of two nano helicopters, a base station, a controller, and a display unit. (Photo: Greg E. Mathieson Sr. / NSW Publications, LLC)*

BELOW: *The Proxdynamics PD-100 Black Hornet Personal Reconnaissance nano helicopter drone transmits live video and HD snapshots back to the operator's screen 1.5 km away. (Photo: Greg E. Mathieson Sr. / NSW Publications, LLC)*

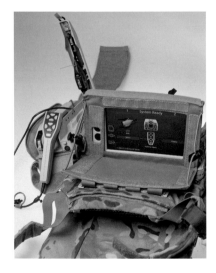

SEAL is taught to expect and plan for the unexpected. As the community matured, NSW came to recognize the value of distinguishing between (1) *what we know*, (2) *what we don't know*, and (3) *what we don't know we don't know*. SEALs must be able and willing to go beyond recognition of facts and unknowns to anticipate variables that cannot be predicted. In doing so, operational planning realistically accommodates the fog and friction of war and the SEAL is both mentally and operationally better prepared to deal with unplanned events. Further, SEALs apply a similarly enlightened mind-set to NSW strategic planning. In doing so, NSW has come of age and embarked on a path of strategic concept development that will prove critical to its readiness, relevance, and continuing ability to adapt to a rapidly evolving global environment.

SEALs are frequently described by others as *family men, just "regular guys," highly motivated*, and *clannish*. Such observations—often delivered with an expression of surprise—are indicative of the strong sense of family within the SEAL community as well as the role family support plays in the health of the community. Familial rapport may be common to small, self-selecting groups, but it is unique within NSW. That uniqueness stems from its dual-edged nature: the support a SEAL receives from his family, and the support NSW renders to the family of a SEAL. With an esprit de corps second to none within the U.S. military, SEALs aspire to excellence on the battlefield and view their preparation for same as never ending. To commit the requisite time and energy to excel, SEALs must be willing to entrust the welfare of their family to others. This bond of trust—forged in the crucible of BUD/S, tempered by the trial of battle and shared adversity, and shared with their brothers-in-arms and their extended SEAL family—is seldom spoken of, innately understood, and girds every aspect of the SEAL community's interactions. Nurtured by tradition, this trust is cross-generational and perhaps the strongest unifying factor within NSW.

As the NSW community has expanded, these sentiments and support have been extended to the broader NSW family encompassing SWCC and NSW Combat Support and Combat Service Support (CS/CSS) personnel. In addressing the future of NSW, confidence among NSW operators that their family will be well cared for in the operator's absence is a key operational readiness and retention issue. Absent such confidence, the community would suffer heightened attrition and/or decline in readiness due to operator distraction over family matters. One example of the importance NSW places on family support: in recognition of the emotional adjustments associated with an operator's return from combat, NSW instituted an en route decompression program that permits a phased readjustment before the operator—returning from combat—is reunited with his family.

Having emphasized that SEALs of all eras are cut from the same cloth, it would be imprudent to ignore significant generational differences. One in particular is the "millennial" generation and the culture it brings to NSW. This generation of SEALs, SWCC, and CS/CSS personnel will influence how NSW conducts business in the future. As a whole, the millennial generation is more technologically astute and sensitive to globalization than its predecessors. Social networking is second nature, a powerful tool, and will change how NSW trains and operates.

Conversely, social networking comes with vulnerabilities such as operational security risks, because the ubiquity of information has the potential to cause harm. Consistent with NSW's well-deserved reputation for adaptability and innovation, this technology will—like hand-to-hand combat—be leveraged to turn it to NSW's advantage and against the enemy.

REDEFINING THE NAVAL SPECIAL WARFARE OPERATOR

The direct action SEAL of yesteryear has evolved into the warrior diplomat of today. Still fully capable of kinetic operations, today's SEAL has broadened significantly and is increasingly called upon to understand and exercise the role of statesman. In a combat situation, he must be able to temper violence of action with situational awareness and reasonable restraint. In choosing a course of action, he must balance the impulse to "run to sound of guns" with an understanding of the greater long-term investment associated with diplomacy. SEALs understand the value of being able to manipulate and influence the environment in order to create conditions conducive to achieving U.S. national objectives, whether this is required on the battlefield, in briefing congressional staffs, as part of a country team, or in dealing with remote tribal leadership. The national security implications of special operations require a thinking man who recognizes that far more can be achieved through nonkinetic than kinetic means, and that the actions of tactical SOF units can and have affected strategic outcomes.

In one of the more significant evolutions within the NSW community, NSW CS/CSS personnel have evolved from the shadows to become fully integrated members of the NSW team. Recognizing the growing sophistication and ubiquity of technology across all areas of engagement and the increasing demands placed on SEALs, NSW instituted a concept of developing and integrating technological and combat support personnel directly into SEAL and Special Boat Team operations. As a result, NSW expanded its organic capability extensively to integrate—at the tactical level—critical interlocking disciplines and capabilities that support finding, fixing, and finishing the enemy; exploiting and analyzing information derived from operations; and then—based on that analysis—beginning planning and preparation for follow-on operations. This Find-Fix-Finish-Exploit-Analyze or F3EA cycle, supported largely by an in-house contingent of specially trained and integrated CS/CSS personnel, has yielded unprecedented results in OIF and OEF. Much has been achieved through integration and

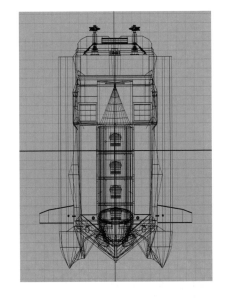

inculcation of non-SEALs and SWCCs as NSW enablers; considerably more is required in the future to maximize this synergistic effort, however. One need look no further than other SOF organizations to understand the value of this initiative; they are endeavoring to replicate the NSW model.

The operational role and capabilities of SWCC have also been expanded. As with the SEALs, SWCC maturation stemmed from both an expanded NSW charter and the creativity and proven effectiveness of the operators themselves. The future of the boat teams is evolving beyond the current craft in the inventory and planned replacement craft. SWCCs

The Marion Hyper-Sub prototype "Fathom" is one of many concepts and products that corporations are developing to pitch to SOCOM and the U.S. Navy to help in fighting the new age of terrorism, drug trafficking, and littoral security. Some Hyper-Subs are capable of being air-dropped into the ocean, have a length of over 30 feet, can carry eight personnel, and can dive to depth of 600 feet. With a surface speed of 45 knots, some can travel 1,000 miles without refueling. (Graphics courtesy of Marion Hyper-Sub)

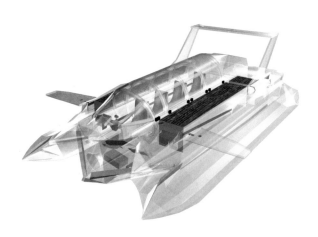

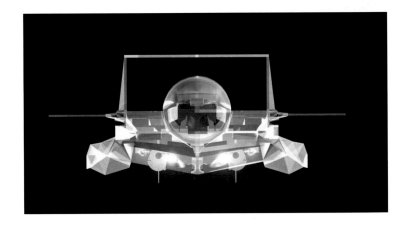

The introduction of the Barrett 98B®/ MRAD® will be viewed as a new era of the precision sniper rifle. The rifle departs from the traditional barreled action with its modular upper and lower receiver, with user-changeable calibers/barrel system and trigger assembly. Fully field serviceable, it has familiar controls and assault rifle ergonomics. (Photo: Courtesy of Barrett)

BELOW, RIGHT: *The Ops-Core® Advanced Combat Helmet (ACH) Upgrade Kit and Survivability Kit (shown attached) transform the standard issue ACH into a platform capable of easily integrating system components and accessories. Providing leading helmet protection for many SOF units and regular forces, the kits consist of a visor and mandible for added eye and face protection from blunt threats and blast shockwaves to help increase survivability in high threat operations. The design is also one that can be seen in many of the new TALOS concepts. (Photo courtesy of Ops-Core. Ops-Core Inc., a wholly owned subsidiary of Gentex Corporation)*

are broadening their expertise to become "master mariners" capable of adapting to changing environments and utilizing different craft as circumstances dictate.

NSW and the conventional Navy continually look for ways to improve interoperability. In addition to modification of Navy platforms to support NSW—commissioning of Littoral Combat Ships (LCS), conversion of SSBNs to SSGNs and capabilities to support special operations, and mobile sea-basing—NSW and the conventional Navy have expanded areas of mutual cooperation. Formation of the Naval Expeditionary Combatant Command (NECC) is viewed as a significant step toward enhanced NSW/USN expeditionary interoperability. Further, relationships and synergy between the U.S. Navy,

LEFT: *Elbit Systems of America's QuadEye™ is a Panoramic Night Vision Goggle (PNVG) with advanced features and performance so pilots and aircrew can accomplish difficult night missions successfully and safely. QuadEye™ provides a central 40° binocular field of view plus monocular vision with an additional 30 degrees to either side.*

This extended view is similar to the normal eye's peripheral vision and reduces the degree to which panning the head is needed when wearing goggles. QuadEye™ is designed around four advanced 16mm image intensifier tubes. Its modular construction permits the user to select between using only the two inner channels or four panoramic channels. Additionally, QuadEye™ provides for projection of Avionics HUD symbology or the aircraft's targeting sensor's video image into the goggle's eyepiece through a miniature, high-resolution display. A miniature debriefing camera is also integrated to the eyepiece to record what the user sees in the central channel and the display. The camera's video output can be recorded on an aircraft video recorder for later mis-

sion debriefing or user training. SEALs are now looking at using these on the newer FAST helmets. (Photo: Courtesy of Elbit Systems of American, LLC)

CENTER: *The FAST (Future Assault Shell Technology) helmet was recently introduced by Ops-Core . It represents a paradigm shift in military helmet protection. While distinguished by its unique mounting features and a non-salad-bowl appearance, its true capabilities as the first modular and fully integrated ballistic helmet were more subtle. It was not until the FAST helmet was adopted by most of the elite Special Forces units around the world—including the U.S. Navy SEALs—that the true potential of the helmet was recognized. With its fully integrated features for configuring night vision, communication devices, eye and face protection, the FAST helmet was the first military helmet to give soldiers the flexibility to customize their headborne equipment setup based on a particular mission objective. This capability allowed them to choose the optimal balance between weight, threat*

protection, and situational awareness for a given task. The appeal of the integrated features would have been short lived had it not been for one of the most important aspects of the helmet: its weight. The FAST helmet was engineered from the ground up to utilize new ballistic materials and manufacturing processes. This resulted in shell weight that was 32 percent lighter than anything that had come before it, while retaining the same level of protection and durability. Once coupled with a liner and suspension system that was equally comfortable and significantly more stable than its counterparts, the FAST helmet's ability to redistribute load, dynamic momentum, and helmet center of gravity offered a significant reduction in neck fatigue over extended time frames. By keeping an "open" mounting architecture on rails and shroud for industry to use without license fees or limitations, the FAST helmet quickly became the desired platform for many equipment manufacturers to build upon and further enhance the soldiers' options for optimal setup and increased situational awareness. (Photo: Courtesy of Ops-Core)

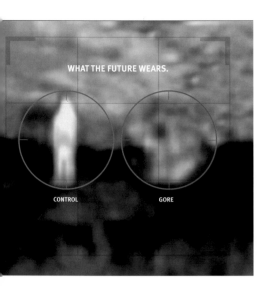

LEFT: *Some military sensors pick up signatures that are invisible to the naked eye. The figure on the right is wearing the new W.L. Gore multispectral camouflage material, which defeats short-wave infrared range (SWIR) and helps conceal the operator against sensor surveillance in the field. (Photo courtesy W.L. Gore and Associates)*

CENTER: *W.L. Gore and Associates, widely known for developing GORTEX, is also a leader in next-generation concealment capabilities products. Their new camouflage deflects ultraviolet and infrared surveillance. (Photo courtesy of W.L. Gore and Associates)*

RIGHT: *Remotely operated gun mounts with infrared and thermal lens on the bows of special boats allow for less risk to the gunner and better sighting of the target. (Photo. DoD)*

U.S. Marine Corps, NSW, and Marine Corps Special Operations Command are continuously improving as each comes to a better understanding of the capabilities of the others and the value of their common cause. Perhaps most significant is acceptance of the concept that—depending on the operational situation—conventional naval units may be in a supporting role to NSW, NSW may support other naval components, or the supported/supporting roles may shift as an operation evolves. Improved interoperability has yielded excellent results as supported/supporting lines of demarcation across the continuum of SOF-conventional operations grow increasingly flexible . . . a significant improvement in keeping with DoD's growing emphasis on Irregular Warfare.

NSW will increasingly emphasize operations *by*, *with*, and *through* partner and Allied nations, thereby reducing the U.S. footprint and fingerprints on operations and strengthening partners' capabilities, will, and self-sufficiency. Doing so requires identifying and developing the people, skills, and capabilities required to operate effectively outside declared war zones, and the ability to develop and maintain access in politically sensitive and ambiguous environments.

NAVAL SPECIAL WARFARE TRAINING— PAST, PRESENT, AND FUTURE— AND ITS IMPACT

Subscribing to the adages "the more you sweat in peace, the less you bleed in war" and "train as you will fight," SEALs are relentless in their pursuit of realistic training. The NSW thought process: when one is not in combat, one should train in an environment replicating combat as closely as possible. There is no substitute for realistic training that toughens the mind, body, and spirit. With the fuller integration of CS/CSS personnel into SEAL and SWCC operations, training has broadened to encompass the full spectrum of NSW combat and combat-related operations. This integration of technology, analysis, and Subject Matter Experts (SMEs) begat development of an entire new series of TTPs, which, similar to SEAL and SWCC TTPs, are constantly reviewed, revised, and incorporated into training. In the past, battle staff training was not something NSW perceived as being within its purview. Now, training in preparation for battle, staff, TOC, and other forward operating support is viewed as essential.

In 2007, NSW Squadrons began assigning and deploying with dedicated cadres of select CS/CSS SMEs. These cadres (1) were trained by NSW to fuse their diverse capabilities into an integrated, synergistic package and (2) underwent NSW indoctrination and training to incorporate their individual and collective expertise

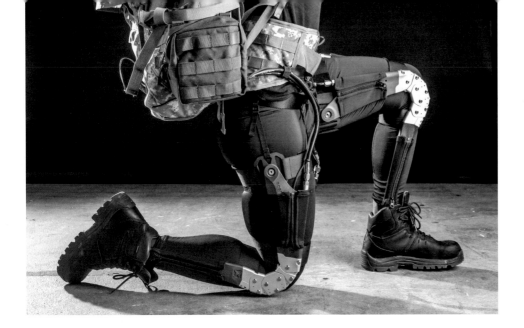

into the NSW F3EA cycle. Adding to the strength of this concept is the ability of each discipline to "reach back" to its parent organization and network to stay abreast of the most recent technological advancements, seek subject matter expertise, and identify ways to further enhance support to NSW. As a result, each NSW Squadron has a dedicated, responsive, and fully integrated capability that vastly improves the Squadron's capabilities and frees SEALs and SWCCs to focus more effectively on their primary roles. This model will continue to mature and increasingly expand integration of non-SEALs into NSW doctrine and organizations.

A fundamental SEAL mantra states, "The only easy day was yesterday." This is universally accepted among both BUD/S candidates and career SEALs. Subject to a number of interpretations, it is fundamentally accepted as meaning a SEAL's day will never get any easier, he must prepare for the worst, and never give less than his best. Again, strive to earn the Trident every day.

Beyond tactical skills, NSW increasingly emphasizes training in language, regional expertise, and culture (LREC) awareness for SEALs, SWCC, and CS/CSS personnel. As NSW's role in the broader spectrum of operations short of war expands so must individual and group study of culture and related social sciences. Cultural understanding, a minimum of rudimentary skill in languages, and political situational awareness are keys to appreciating and working within the operational environment. To optimize its global effectiveness, NSW regularly reviews and revises LREC awareness in order to maintain a healthy regimen of cultural education, training, and cross-training. Additionally, NSW is constantly exploring ways to expand and strengthen the force's cultural diversity.

Nonetheless, for all the developments and progress in NSW training and regardless of the necessity of evolving training to meet current and future threats,

there are basic elements of that training which will remain largely untouched as their value has been continuously substantiated over sixty-five years of operations. By recognizing and retaining legacy training such as Hell Week, cold ocean endurance swims, and rock portage during BUD/S, core strengths—upon which much of a SEAL's follow-on training and operations will build—are not compromised. That which served to mold the frogman of World War II will similarly screen and mold the SEAL of tomorrow.

NAVAL SPECIAL WARFARE AND FUTURE CHALLENGES

Moving beyond its role today and into the foreseeable future, NSW will balance engagement between counter-asymmetric and other national security threats. Iraq and Afghanistan may well cease to dominate NSW priorities, and evolving national interests will dictate NSW engagement globally. In the future NSW is likely to shift its attention to even more diverse and widely distributed strategic locations around the globe, whether in support of overseas contingency operations or of other national security policy. To do so, NSW must continu-

TOP: *Navy SEALs use the latest cold weather equipment to train in snow-capped mountain terrain. Advanced technologies and weapons increase the SEALs' ability to withstand extreme conditions and maximize safety and efficiency in the field. (Photo: Chris Desmond / USN)*

BOTTOM: *A Raven B being launched over the desert sands. (Courtesy of AeroVironment)*

ally reassess its force, organizational structure, and operational priorities . . . and do so according to a viable and flexible strategic plan. Security Force Assistance (SFA) is a case in point.

SOF involvement in and leadership of SFA activities around the world is growing. SFA is a critical tool among U.S. policy initiatives to reduce government failures and global disenfranchisement—both of which provide fertile breeding ground for terrorism, violent extremist organizations, and criminal activities that threaten national activities. SFA combined with SOF core capabilities also provide near-immediate, visible, and significant respite in support of emergency humanitarian relief. Refugee situations create an atmosphere ripe for extremists to exploit. Emergency response often requires the ability to deploy highly trained, self-sufficient forces with a small footprint to remote areas on extremely short notice. With proven maritime, cultural, and joint interoperability prowess, NSW is uniquely suited to respond to such crises and establish a humanitarian beachhead awaiting arrival of conventional assistance. The "hearts and minds" value of such action is inestimable, dramatically decreasing the potential for destabilization and fostering a positive U.S. image.

RELISHING A CHALLENGE

Naval Special Warfare is uniquely positioned to play a vital role in the years ahead as a force of choice to further U.S. national security interests. As the demand for NSW expertise expands and evolves, NSW will undergo change and organizational

FACING PAGE

Transformer gunship concept by TEXTRON, as part of a DARPA (Defense Advanced Research Projects Agency) program of developing a flying Humvee. The race to build the world's first flying military jeep just moved a step closer to the finish line. DARPA has selected two companies to proceed with the next stage of its Transformer, a fully automated four-person vehicle that can drive like a car and then take off and fly like an aircraft. Lockheed Martin and AAI Corp., a unit of Textron Systems, are currently in negotiations with DARPA for the first stage of the Transformer project. (Graphic courtesy of TEXTRON)

redefinition. The community will mature into an increasingly accomplished, culturally fluent irregular force. Given the multitude of issues that constrain growth, the NSW community will continue to struggle to produce sufficient numbers of the much-in-demand SEAL and SWCC operators without compromising standards; increasingly, they will compete with other DoD and U.S. government organizations to recruit and retain personnel possessing the skill sets necessary to execute a broad irregular charter. Cultivation of the warrior diplomat as a core NSW competency will increase without diminishing core competencies in direct action and surveillance and reconnaissance tasks. Foreign Internal Defense (FID) and SFA will occupy a greater percentage of the NSW operator's time as greater emphasis is placed on influencing environmental change rather than the United States directly implementing it. FID and FSA will occupy a greater percentage of the NSW operator's focus because greater emphasis will be placed on influencing host nation government military, diplomatic, economic, and other actions and activities. Successful FID and FSA actions will aim to prevent hostilities. When combat is warranted, it will best be accomplished by host nation personnel with appropriate NSW–SOF influence and support, often working with and through the interagencies.

Transition of this nature requires a clear course and steady hand at the helm. It must be viewed as an investment requiring uncommon patience on the part of operators, senior leaders, and elected officials to endure lengthy gestation periods before such influence can clearly be seen as contributing to national security objectives. As with any investment, it involves risk . . . but if history is any indication, investment in NSW is its own reward.

While the SEAL Creed eloquently describes the U.S. Navy SEAL, the terse description offered by a retired SEAL captures the essence of NSW:

NSW builds to moving goal posts. There is no end of game. Constantly adapting and never relaxing its vigilance, NSW welcomes challenge and is all about solving problems. Physical and mental toughness equate to readiness. There are no timeouts or replays. The team is always poised to take the field. Every scrimmage is played like the Super Bowl. Second place is for losers.

NSW comprises a fraternity of warriors, each generation building on the legacy of its predecessor. Beginning with SEALs, this fraternity has expanded to encompass a broad array of operators whose support of and integration into the NSW community have been indispensable in advancing maritime special operations and successful engagement of twenty-first-century enemies.

As this last page is turned, Naval Special Warfare is already writing a new chapter in the annals of special operations.

Brave men have fought and died building the proud tradition and feared reputation that I am bound to uphold. In the worst of conditions, the legacy of my teammates steadies my resolve and silently guides my every deed. I will not fail. [U.S. Navy SEAL Creed]

TOP, LEFT: *RADM Robert S. Harward Jr. (R), to his left Captain Herbert—Commanding Officer of the training facility Center NSWC—exchange salutes with a new SEAL graduate (Class 259). (Photo: Dave Gatley)*

TOP, RIGHT: *The Trident. (Photo: Dave Gatley)*

LEFT: *Specially engraved KA-BAR knifes (the traditional SEAL's knife) are arranged before a ceremony in which they are presented to new SEALs at SEAL Qualification Training course graduation ceremony, where SEALs finally receive their Tridents. Engraved upon the blade of the weapon is the name of a fallen SEAL teammate Killed in Action along with date and location of the action that claimed their brother. A homage that connects their personal celebration of achievement to the legacy of those teammates who have gone before and paid the ultimate price for their nation. (Photo: Dave Gatley)*

BOTTOM: *Before the SEAL Qualification Training course graduation ceremony, where SEALs receive their Tridents in front of family and friends, there is a more somber, private ceremony. Taking place behind closed doors, each new SEAL warrior is presented a specially engraved KA-BAR Knife engraved with the name of a fallen SEAL teammate Killed in Action. (Photo: Dave Gatley)*

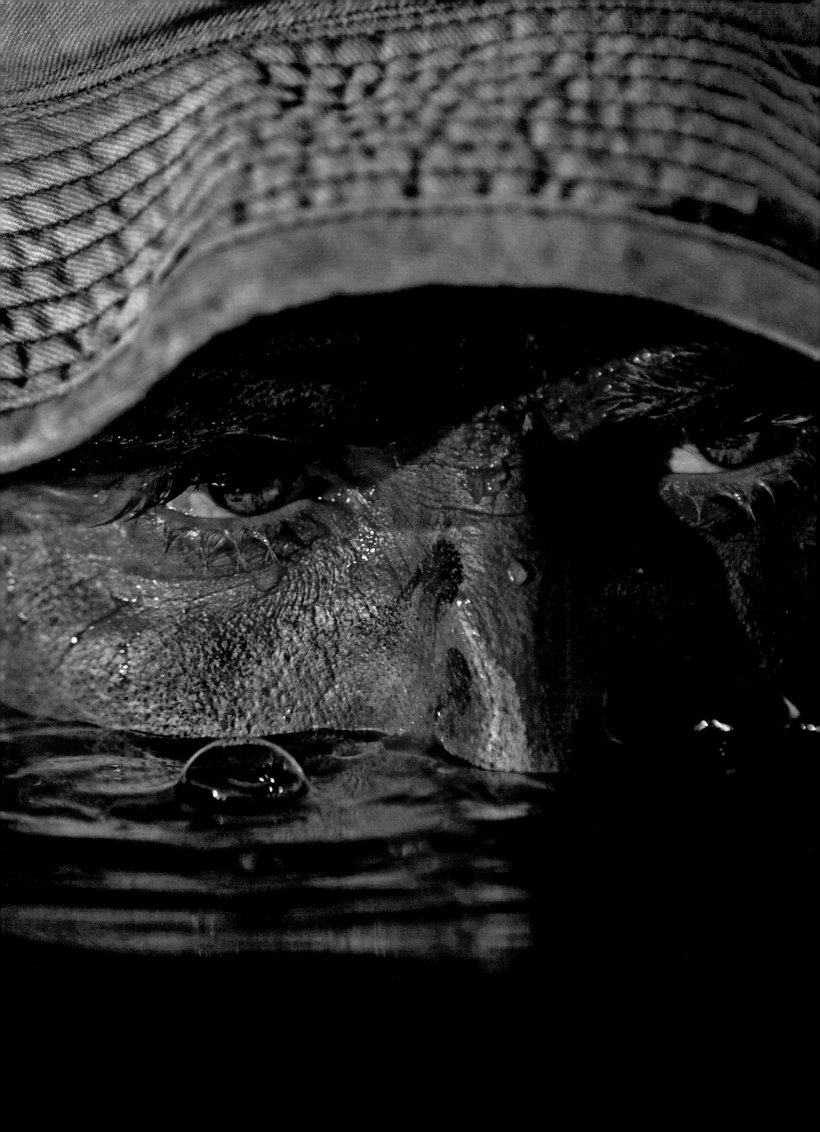

CHRONOLOGY
THIS DATE IN NAVAL SPECIAL WARFARE

AUGUST 1942 – Amphibious Scouts and Raiders (Joint) formed at ATB, Little Creek, Virginia. With Army and Navy personnel; commanded by Army 1st Lt. Lloyd Peddicord and Executive Officer Navy Ens. John Bell, they train for Operation Torch, the first Allied amphibious invasion of World War II at North Africa.

AUGUST 1942 – Area "D" established on the Maryland side of the Potomac River to train OSS operatives in clandestine maritime sabotage and small-boat operations.

SEPTEMBER 1942 – Led by Navy salvage officers Lts. Mark W. Starkweather and James W. Darroch, 15 Navy divers trained at ATB, Little Creek, Virginia, for a directed underwater demolition mission in Operation Torch.

NOVEMBER 1942 – Operation Torch, North Africa. Scouts and Raiders and Navy demolition men complete successful missions. Most are awarded the Navy Cross.

JANUARY 1943 – Scout and Raider school formed at Fort Pierce, Florida.

JANUARY 1943 – A Marine Section established within the Special Operations Branch of OSS with responsibility for planning covert infiltration operations from the sea. On 10 June they are reorganized as the OSS Maritime Unit (MU) with branch status.

APRIL 1943 – First Naval Combat Demolition group formed under Navy Lt. Fredrick Wise with 13 Seabees from the Construction Battalion School at Camp Peary, Virginia, and trained at ATB, Solomons Island, Maryland, for Operation Husky in Sicily.

APRIL 1943 – Secretary of the Navy Frank Knox signs articles leading to the formation of the Sino-American Special Technical Cooperative Organization (SACO); directed by U.S. Navy Cdr. (later Adm.) Milton E. "Mary" Miles.

MAY 1943 – Adm. Ernest J. King issues orders for permanent "Naval Demolition Units." Training relocated from ATB, Solomons Island, Maryland to ATB, Fort Pierce, Florida.

JUNE 1943 – Naval Combat Demolition Unit (NCDU) School formed at ATB, Fort Pierce, Florida, under Navy Lt. Cdr. Draper Kauffman as Officer in Charge. Only volunteers were taken. Hell Week established.

JUNE 1943 – The Marine Section established within the Special Operations Branch of OSS reorganized as the Maritime Unit (MU) with OSS branch status.

JULY 1943 – Commander, Amphibious Force, Pacific 7 Fleet directs establishment of a school for Amphibious Scouts in the vicinity of Cairns, Australia and calls them Special Services Unit #1. Members are from Australia and U.S. Navy and U.S. Army.

AUGUST 1943 – NCDU #1 under Ens. Edwin S. Williams deploys on secret orders for reoccupation of Kiska, Aleutian Islands. Upon completion of the unopposed assault on the islands, the U.S. embarrassingly discovers that the enemy had already departed.

SEPTEMBER 1943 – NCDU #2 and NCDU #3 under Lts. (j.g.) Frank Kaine and Lloyd Anderson shipped to the Southwest Pacific. Later joined by NCDU 19, 20, 21, and 24. Would be the only NCDUs to remain organized through World War II.

NOVEMBER 1943 – NCDU #11, led by Lt. (j.g.) Lawrence L. Heidman, is the first NCDU to arrive in England in preparation for the invasion of Europe.

NOVEMBER 1943 – NCDU Lt. (j.g.) Carl Hagensen develops the Hagensen pack, a demolition used extensively during the invasion of Normandy. Hagensen was OIC of NCDU #30 and part of the Utah Red Beach Demolition Party.

NOVEMBER 1943 — OSS-MU Operational Swimmer Groups 1 and 2 begin training in November 1943 at Camp Pendleton, California, later moved to Catalina Island off the coast of California in January 1944, and finally to warmer waters in the Bahamas in March.

NOVEMBER 1943 — During the Tarawa landing at the Gilbert Islands on 22 November, a submerged reef caused amphibious landing craft to founder far offshore resulting in the loss of hundreds of U.S. Marines from enemy fire and by drowning.

NOVEMBER–DECEMBER 1943 — Because of Tarawa, Adm. Kelly Turner, Commander, Fifth Amphibious Force, directed that 30 officers and 150 enlisted men be moved to Waimanalo Amphibious Training Base to form UDT-1 and UDT-2 with U.S. Army, Navy, and Marine Corps volunteers. It is here that the Underwater Demolition Teams Pacific were born.

JANUARY 1944 — UDT-1 under Cdr. E. D. Brewster begins early-morning operations at Kwajalein in the Marshall Island group. Ens. Lew Luehrs leads UDT's first daylight swimming reconnaissance.

JANUARY 1944 — OSS-MU L-Unit #1 and #2 deployed to England for cold water training and infiltration of enemy harbors along the coast of France with the aim of destroying shipping and U-boat pens. The unit was not deployed, and returned in June.

MARCH 1944 — Naval Combat Demolition Training and Experimental Training Base formed at Maui, Hawaiian Territory, with UDT training under the direction of Lt. Cdr. John T. Koehler; former Commanding Officer of UDT-2, who devised an organization plan for a 100-man team consisting of 13 officers and 87 enlisted men.

APRIL 1944 — UDT-3, UDT-4, and UDT-5 are formed at Maui entirely of men from the Fort Pierce NCDU training course.

6 JUNE 1944 — D-Day. Thirty-four NCDUs combined with U.S. Army engineers form Gap Assault Teams to clear obstacles at Omaha and Utah beaches at Normandy, France. Thirty-one NCDU men killed and 60 wounded, making this the bloodiest day in the history of NSW. NCDUs at Omaha receive the Presidential Unit Citation (one of three given that day), and NCDUs at Utah receive the Navy Unit Commendation.

JULY 1944 — During the invasion of Guam on the morning of 21 July, UDT-4 Platoon Commander Ens. Thomas D. Nixon is killed by a Japanese sniper while guiding small craft ashore, becoming the first UDT casualty of World War II.

JULY 1944 — Twenty U.S. Navy officers and 150 enlisted men begin training at the Scout and Raider school in Fort Pierce, Florida, under a classified project called "Amphibious Group Roger." These "Rice Paddy Navy" sailors were trained to work with Chinese counterparts to conduct reconnaissance operations along the Yangtze River with SACO.

JULY 1944 — OSS-MU OSG-1 loaned to the U.S. Navy to become the nucleus of UDT-10 in the Pacific. Five men from this group and several UDT operators from Maui were assigned a special mission and participated in the first UDT submarine operation conducted during the war; from USS *Burrfish* (SS-312) at the island of Yap in the Caroline Islands. Three members of the special-mission group were captured and later killed by their Japanese captors, and their bodies were never recovered. They were: Chief Petty Officer Howard "Red" Roeder (from UDT) and Petty Officers Bob Black and John MacMahon (from OSS).

AUGUST 1944 — Code-named *Anvil* and later *Dragoon*, several of the NCDUs from Utah Beach were augmented with new units from Fort Pierce and participated at the landing in southern France; the last amphibious assault in Europe during World War II.

NOVEMBER 1944 — Commander, Amphibious Force, U.S. Pacific Fleet named Capt. B. Hall Hanlon, USN the first Commander of Underwater Demolition Teams, Amphibious Force, U.S. Pacific Fleet (known as "Mud Pac" by the men).

JUNE 1945 — Capt. Robert H. Rodgers, USN assumed command of UDTs at Pearl Harbor. All 28 UDTs are sent to ATB, Oceanside, California, for a month-long period of cold water training in preparation for the invasion of Japan. A UDT Flotilla is organized with two subordinate UDT Squadrons.

AUGUST 1945 — Training at Oceanside abruptly curtailed on 14 August after President Harry S. Truman ordered the use of nuclear weapons at Hiroshima, Japan, on 6 August 1945 and at Nagasaki, Japan, on 9 August. UDTs are sent to Japan for occupation duties.

OCTOBER 1945 — UDTs move to Coronado, California, for reorganization. Thirty-one UDTs were formed. UDT-1, UDT-2, and Team Able were disbanded. The most teams at any one time numbered 28. All teams were Fort Pierce–trained except UDT-1, UDT-2 (the "provisional" teams), and UDT-14, UDT-16, and UDT-17, which were made up largely of fleet volunteers trained in Hawaii.

JANUARY 1946 — Rapid demobilization at the conclusion of the war left only four active-duty UDTs, each with a complement of seven officers and 45 enlisted men. Postwar UDT-1 and UDT-2 at Coronado, California, were commanded by Lt. Cdr. Walter Cooper. UDT-3 and UDT-4 at Little Creek, Norfolk, Virginia, were commanded by Lt. Cdr. Francis Douglas "Red Dog" Fane.

WORLD WAR II FOOTNOTE – It is a little known fact that UDT men were the most decorated Navy combat veterans of World War II. They were awarded 750 Bronze Stars, 150 Silver Stars, two Navy Crosses, and an undetermined number of Purple Hearts—quite remarkable for men who went into combat carrying no weapon other than a K-Bar knife.

JUNE 1947 – UDTs become "sea-air"–capable for the first time when they began experimentation with at-sea launch and recovery capabilities from helicopters, which were not available during World War II. This capability never became a part of routine training, because early helicopters could not carry enough personnel or their equipment.

FEBRUARY 1948 – UDTs begin submersible operations. Lieutenant Commander Fane and Dr. Chris Lambertsen bring the full spectrum of OSS-MU diving capabilities to UDT during diving operations aboard the submarine USS *Grouper* (SS-214) at St. Thomas, USVI.

OCTOBER 1948 – A UDT detachment from Little Creek embarked USS *Quillback* (SS-424) and conducted operations with the British submersible "Sleeping Beauty." This was the first time a submersible had been launched and recovered from a U.S. submarine.

JUNE 1950 – Korean War begins. A 10-man UDT detachment from UDTs Pacific led by Lt. (j.g.) George Atcheson was in Japan and quickly dispatched to Korea.

AUGUST 1950 – UDT-1 arrives under the command of Lt. Cdr. D. F. "Kelly" Welch. They were committed to a somewhat new mission – night coastal demolition raids against railroad tunnels and bridges. On the night of 5 August, a UDT detachment departed USS *Diachenko* (APD-123) to conduct a demolition raid against a train bridge-tunnel near Yosu. Lt. (j.g.) Atcheson and Boatswain Mate 3rd Class Warren "Fins" Foley lead the group. During the ensuing operation 10 North Korean soldiers opened fire and Foley was hit and fell over the seawall. The men returned safely, and it was later determined that Petty Officer Foley was the first U.S. Navy casualty of the Korean War.

SEPTEMBER 1950 – On 15 September, UDT-1 and UDT-3 support Operation Chromite, the amphibious landing at Inchon.

OCTOBER 1950 – UDTs support mine-clearing operations at Wonsan Harbor. U.S. minesweepers USS *Pirate* (AM-275) and USS *Pledge* (AM-277) hit mines and sink within miles of each other. UDT men rescue 25 sailors. UDT operator William Giannotti completes the first U.S. combat diving operation using an Aqua Lung, when he dove on *Pledge* to mark its location.

NOVEMBER 1950 – UDT-3 conducts hydrographic reconnaissance at Song Jin, Korea.

DECEMBER 1950 – UDT 3 conducts beach reconnaissance at Chawol-To, Yong Hung Do, and Wolmi Do and So. On Christmas Eve an eight-man squad sets off over 20 tons of explosives to demolish waterfront facilities at the port city of Hungnam. The largest nonnuclear explosion since World War II and largest of the Korean War.

JANUARY–AUGUST 1951 – UDT-3 conducts reconnaissance of Chinhea, Masan, Pusan Harbor, Susaki Ko, and numerous others during the ensuing months.

JULY 1951 – UDT-3 conducts mine reconnaissance and clearance at Wonsan Harbor.

AUGUST 1951 – UDT-3 and Marine Corps Reconnaissance Division personnel begin raids along east and west coasts of Korea.

FEBRUARY 1952 –UDT-5 established and continues supporting minesweeping operations until midsummer, when Operation Fishnet conducted, aimed to disrupt North Korea's fish-based economy.

OCTOBER 1952 – UDT-3 conducts reconnaissance at Kangnung.

JULY 1953 – Armistice ends fighting on 27 July 1953.

FEBRUARY 1954 – UDT-1, UDT-3, and UDT-5 redesignated UDT-11, UDT-12, and UDT-13 respectively. UDT-2 and UDT-4 on the East Coast become UDT-21 and UDT-22. This is to conform to the odd-number prefix used to designate Pacific Fleet units and even numbers in the Atlantic. Soon thereafter, UDT-13 disestablished.

SPRING 1955 – UDTs begin static-line parachuting, first by sending trial groups of men to U.S. Army jump schools, and later all men to obtain a jump qualification specialty. UDT men did not originate parachuting, but did innovate water-entry methods using tactical and nontactical diving apparatus.

MARCH 1961 – In a SECRET memorandum dated March 10 on general concept of the Development of an Improved Naval Guerrilla / Counterguerrilla Warfare Capablility, Capt. William E. Gentner Jr., Director of Strategic Plans Division, suggests, "An appropriate name for such units could be SEAL units, SEAL being a contraction of SEA, AIR, LAND, and thereby indicating an all-around, universal capability."

APRIL 1961 – Brigade 2506 lands at Playa Girón (Bay of Pigs), Cuba, in a failed attempt to overthrow communist government of Fidel Castro. UDT men provided advisory elements to train assault swimmers and raiders. No direct combat actions were undertaken by UDT personnel and none were planned.

MAY 1961 – SECRET CNO Memo for OP-1 in which Adm. Arleigh Burke asks for a list of names of Navy Personnel, particularly officers, and a list of equipment to start a "Guerrilla Warfare" program, later to become the SEAL teams.

JANUARY 1962 – SEAL Team ONE and SEAL Team TWO established. Formation of the SEAL teams was an evolutionary process, and not accomplished by any single group or individual, but the result of U.S. national policy surrounding world events.

OCTOBER 1962 – Cuban Missile Crisis confrontation between the U.S. and Soviet Union. UDT and SEAL Teams conduct planning and prepare for conflict.

NOVEMBER 1963 – Naval Operation Support Groups, Pacific and Atlantic, established at Coronado and Little Creek to command the UDT and SEAL Teams, Navy Beach Jumper Units (BJUs).

FEBRUARY 1964 – Boat Support Units established as components of Naval Operation Support Groups Atlantic and Pacific. BSU-1 organized Mobile Support Teams to support SEAL and Military Assistance Group operations in Vietnam. BSU-2 provided boat support and maintenance for the East Coast UDT and SEAL Teams.

FEBRUARY 1964 – Capt. Phil Bucklew, Commander, Naval Operations Support Group, Pacific heads the Vietnam Delta Infiltration Study Group tasked to study the problem of enemy infiltration of men and supplies into South Vietnam's Mekong Delta. The Bucklew Report concludes that border infiltration problems are significant and that the U.S. needs to develop an extensive riverine operations capability to assist the South Vietnamese military.

WINTER 1964 – Members of SEAL Team TWO lead a team of 13 Cuban exiled frogmen into a Cuban naval port to sink three of four Russian Kormar-class missile boats while working for the CIA.

APRIL 1965 – UDT and SEAL teams support Operation Powerpack, the U.S. invasion of the Dominican Republic undertaken to protect American lives and prevent a possible Castro-type takeover by communist elements.

OCTOBER 1965 – UDT Commander Robert J. Fay hit by a mortar round and becomes the first Naval Special Warfare operator killed during the conflict in Vietnam.

FEBRUARY 1966 – A SEAL Team ONE detachment arrives in the Rung Sat Special Zone (south of Saigon) in Vietnam to conduct direct-action missions.

AUGUST 1966 – On 19 August, SEAL Team ONE suffers its first combat fatality. Radarman 2nd Class Billy Machen becomes the first SEAL killed while engaged in a fierce gunfight in the Rung Sat Special Zone, South Vietnam. He was posthumously awarded the Silver Star.

APRIL 1967 – Naval Operations Support Groups ONE and TWO renamed Naval Special Warfare Groups Pacific and Atlantic.

APRIL 1967 – Helicopters were never a mainstay for the UDTs, but the capability developed quickly with the SEAL teams as a method of insertion and extraction during the Vietnam period. The U.S. Navy activated Helicopter Attack (Light) Squadron (HAL) 3 at Vung Tau, South Vietnam. When working together, SEALs and SEALWOLFs became a dominating operational team.

MARCH 1969 – On 14 March, SEAL Team ONE Lieutenant Joseph R. "Bob" Kerrey leads his SEAL platoon on a mission to capture important members of the enemy's political cadre on an island in the bay of Nha Trang. He would later be awarded the Medal of Honor for his leadership on this day.

EARLY 1969 – UDT-13 in the Pacific and UDT-22 in the Atlantic established.

JULY 1971 – Boat Support Units established as Coastal River Squadrons and become the repository of many Navy combatant craft returning from Vietnam. Coastal River Divisions 11, 12, and 13 formed as subordinate commands under CRS-1. Coastal River Divisions 20, 21, 22, and 24 organized under CRS-2.

DECEMBER 1971 – On 7 December, Mike Platoon from SEAL Team ONE commanded by Lt. Shannon McCrary return to their homeport in Coronado, California. This was the last SEAL platoon deployed for combat in Vietnam. SEAL advisors remain.

FEBRUARY 1972 – UDT and SEAL Team breast insignia are approved by the Navy Uniform Board. About one year later, a single gold "Trident" insignia is approved for wear by officer and enlisted. It is the only gold insignia worn by enlisted members in the Navy (all others are silver). This action was accomplished to recognize that, as they did at the first class at Fort Pierce in June 1943, officers and enlisted personnel complete the same training for warfare area qualification.

APRIL 1972 – SEAL Team TWO Lt. Tom Norris completes an unprecedented ground rescue of two downed pilots deep within heavily controlled enemy territory in Quang Tri province. For his heroic actions he is later awarded the Medal of Honor. He is accompanied by South Vietnamese SEAL Petty Officer 3rd Class Nguyen Van Kiet, who will later be awarded the U.S. Navy Cross, one of only two from his nation to receive this award.

JUNE 1972 – On 6 June, Lt. Melvin "Spence" Dry leads a SEAL Delivery Vehicle (SDV) detachment to assist in POW recovery operations off the coast of North Vietnam. He is killed when performing a water entry from a helicopter for rendezvous with his host submarine. He is the last Navy SEAL killed in the Vietnam conflict.

MARCH 1973 – Last advisors from SEAL Team ONE and SEAL Team TWO depart Vietnam, ending NSW's formal involvement in Southeast Asia.

OCTOBER 1973 – SEAL Petty Officer 1st Class Michael E. Thornton, an assistant U.S. Navy advisor, along with Navy SEAL Lt. Tom Norris accompany a three-man Vietnamese patrol on an intelligence-gathering and prisoner-capture operation against an enemy-occupied naval river base. Through a hail of fire, Thornton rescues his badly wounded lieutenant, and will later receive the Medal of Honor. He is the last non-posthumous recipient of the Medal of Honor during the Vietnam conflict, and perhaps the only Medal of Honor recipient to rescue another Medal of Honor recipient.

MAY 1975 – Less than two weeks after the fall of South Vietnam, forces of the communist Khmer Rouge in Cambodia attack and seize the American merchant ship *Mayagüez,* capturing its crew and removing them to Kaoh Tang Island. Navy SEALs prepare for reconnaissance in advance of a Marine Corps helicopter assault.

OCTOBER 1978 – Coastal River Squadron ONE in San Diego reorganized as Special Boat Squadron ONE as a Navy Major Command. Component Special Boat Units 11, 12, and 13 formed as subordinate commands. CRS-2 becomes SBR-2 with SBU-20, 22, 24 as components. SBU-26 in Panama will later be organized.

OCTOBER 1980 – Navy formally establishes a special mission unit called SEAL Team SIX.

OCTOBER 1983 – SEAL and SEAL Delivery Vehicle Team task elements support Amphibious Force operations in Beirut, Lebanon. On October 23, the U.S. Marine barracks are bombed, killing hundreds of Marines.

OCTOBER 1983 – Operation Urgent Fury, the invasion of Grenada in response to the illegal deposition and execution of Grenadian prime minister Maurice Bishop. SEALs killed during a nighttime parachute jump were Senior Chief Engineman Robert R. Schamberger, 1st Class machinist Mate Kenneth J. Butcher, Quartermaster 1st Class Kevin E. Lundberg, and 1st Class Hull Technician Stephen L. Morris.

1985 – SEAL Capt. Cathal "Irish" Flynn is the first Navy SEAL ever promoted to flag rank. He was selected for promotion to rear admiral and assigned as Commander, Naval Security and Investigative Command and Assistant Director of Naval Intelligence for Counterintelligence and Anti-terrorism.

APRIL 1987 – Naval Special Warfare Command is established at Naval Amphibious Base, Coronado. It is the naval component to U.S. Special Operations Command, and the first flag officer billet designated for a SEAL officer. The first commander is Rear Adm. (SEAL) Charles Le Moyne, the second SEAL officer selected for flag rank.

SEPTEMBER 1987 – Operation Prime Chance. During the Persian Gulf War, NSW forces conduct their first operations under the U.S. Special Operations Command. NSW SEALs and Special Boats and Army AH-6/MH-6 helicopters begin operations from an afloat operating bases, barges called *Hercules* and *Wimbrown 7.*

SEPTEMBER 1987 – Operation Prime Chance, a largely secret effort to stop Iranian forces from attacking Gulf shipping. A SEAL team lands aboard the the *Iran Ajr*, an Iranian ship converted for use as a minelayer vessel and seizes it. Several Iranian sailors are rescued after leaping overboard during the attack. SEALs scuttle the vessel.

OCTOBER 1987 – Operation Earnest Will. On 17 May, Iran fire two Exocet missiles, killing 37 Sailors and wounding 21 others aboard USS *Stark* (FFG 31). On several occasions, Tehran fires Chinese-made Silkworm missiles on Kuwait from Al Faw Peninsula and U.S.-flagged tanker *Sea Isle City.* Washington retaliates by deploying U.S. Navy SEALs to blow up an oil platform in the Rostam field.

DECEMBER 1989 – Operation Just Cause, the U.S. invasion of Panama that deposed general, dictator, and Panamanian military leader Manuel Noriega. SEALs insert at Paitilla airfield to prevent Noriega from leaving Panama. Lt. John Connors, Engineman Chief Petty Officer Donald McFaul, Torpedoman's Mate 2nd Class Issac Rodriguez, and Botswain's Mate 1st Class Chris Tilghman are killed during the operation. Eight other SEALs are seriously wounded.

EARLY 1990 – The first Special Warfare Combat Craft-crewman (SWCC) qualification course established resulting in formal training for personnel desiring a career in special boats.

AUGUST 1990 – The Persian Gulf War (2 August 1990 – 28 February 1991), also called Operation Desert Storm or referred to simply as the Gulf War, was essential to getting Saddam Hussein out of Kuwait. U.S. Navy SEALs provide a diversionary "landing," involving only a small SEAL element, but succeeding in shifting the bulk of Iraq's forces in the wrong direction. SEALs and U.S. Army helicopter teams capture 75 Iraqi troops on and around Qurah Island.

MARCH 1992 – The war in Bosnia and Herzegovina becomes an international conflict. Navy SEALs are routinely deployed through November 1995 to conduct special operations. SEALs continue the hunt for war criminals for several more years.

OCTOBER 1993 – Operation Gothic Serpent. A military operation conducted by SEALs and other special operations forces of the U.S. with the primary mission of capturing Somali warlord Mohamed Farrah Aidid. One officer and three enlisted

SEALs are awarded the Silver Star for actions during the rescue of a downed Black Hawk helicopter crew.

1994 — SWCC personnel are designated by Naval Enlisted Classification Code (NEC) 9533 and "closed-looped" detailed, meaning that they can manage their entire navy career in special boats.

SEPTEMBER 1994 — Operation Uphold Democracy begins September 1994 with the deployment of the U.S.-led Multinational Force. The operation officially ends on 31 March 1995 when it is replaced by the United Nations Mission in Haiti (UNMIH). SEALs, SWCCs, and NSW Coastal Patrol (PCs) ships participate.

SEPTEMBER 1998 — Operation Shadow Express: SEALs and other U.S. Special Operations Forces (SOF) deploy to Liberia in fall 1998 after violent civic unrest in Monrovia threatens the U.S. embassy. Within 12 hours, a command and control element and 20 SEALs, Coastal Patrol ship USS *Chinook*, and SWCCs with an 11-meter NSW RIB deploy off the coast to provide an in-extremis response.

SEPTEMBER 2001 — The events of September 11, 2001, focused the world's attention on radical Islamic terrorism and U.S. Navy SEALs immediately proceed to the source of the attack: Afghanistan. Since 9/11, SEAL teams have constantly been in Iraq, Afghanistan, and elsewhere, working with military and intelligence agencies to target the leadership of terrorist groups, primarily al Qaeda, as well as providing training and support for local forces.

SEPTEMBER 2001 — Operation Enduring Freedom begins in Afghanistan. Navy SEALs support Task Force K-Bar under a Combined Joint Special Operations Task Force (CJSOTF). Navy SEAL Capt. Robert Harward commands the CJSOTF-SOUTH, which was established in response to the terrorist attacks of September 11, 2001. TF K-Bar is comprised of U.S. Navy SEALs and SWCCs, U.S. Army Special Forces, U.S. Air Force Combat Controllers, and Coalition special operations forces from Canada, Norway, Denmark, Germany, Australia, New Zealand, and Turkey. In December 2004, President Bush awarded the Presidential Unit Citation to members of TF K-Bar during a private ceremony to recognize their heroic efforts from October 2001 to March 2002. The event marked the first time since Vietnam that any NSW unit received this award.

MARCH 2002 — A short but intense military engagement between U.S. Special Operations Forces and Taliban insurgents was fought on March 3, 2002, atop Takur Ghar Mountain in Afghanistan. The battle proved the deadliest engagement of Operation Anaconda, an effort early in the war to rout Taliban forces from the Shahi-Kot Valley and Arma Mountains. The mountain is eventually taken; however, eight U.S. service members are killed and many wounded. Navy SEAL Petty Officer Neil C. Roberts is the first casualty of the battle, which has become known as the Battle of Roberts Ridge.

OCTOBER 2002 — Special Boat Squadrons 1 and 2 reorganize as Naval Special Warfare Groups 3 and 4 respectively. Special Boat Units become Special Boat Teams.

APRIL 2003 — On 23 March 2003, a convoy of a U.S Army Combat Support Battalion element makes a wrong turn and is ambushed near Nasiriyah, a major crossing point over the Euphrates northwest of Basra, Iraq. Pvt. Jessica Lynch, a supply clerk, is wounded and captured by Iraqi forces. Eleven other soldiers in her company are killed in the ambush. On 1 April 2003, U.S. Navy SEALs, with support from U.S. Marines and other U.S. Special Operations Forces, launch a nighttime raid on the hospital where she is being held and successfully retrieve her and the bodies of eight American soldiers.

DECEMBER 2004 — USS *James E. Williams* (DDG-95) is commissioned. The ship is named in honor of the Vietnam-era sailor and most-decorated enlisted man in Navy history. In addition to the Medal of Honor, Williams's many awards include the Navy Cross, Silver Star, Navy and Marine Corps Medal, Bronze Star, Purple Heart, and the Navy Commendation Medal with combat distinguishing devices. James Elliott Williams passed away in 1999.

JUNE 2005 — Operation Redwings. Late in the night of 27 June 2005, a team of four Navy SEALs, tasked for surveillance and reconnaissance falls into an ambush just hours after inserting from an MH-47 helicopter. Three of the four SEALs are killed in the ambush; a Quick Reaction Force helicopter sent in for their aid is subsequently shot down with a rocket propelled grenade, killing all on board—eight Navy SEALs and eight U.S. Army Special Operations aviators. The SEALs returned some nights later and killed the individuals responsible for shooting down the helicopter.

JUNE 28, 2005 — Three of four SEALS on the ground (Murphy, Dietz, Axelson) are killed during combat operations in support of Operation Redwing. On the same day, a QRF of eight Navy SEALs and eight Army Night Stalkers are also killed when the MH-47 helicopter that they were aboard was shot down by enemy fire in the vicinity of Asadabad, Afghanistan in Kumar province. Lieutenant Murphy is awarded the Medal of Honor posthumously for his actions that day.

SEPTEMBER 2006 — Navy SEAL Michael A. Monsoor gives his life on September 29 by throwing his body on an enemy grenade during Operation Iraqi Freedom to save the lives of his fellow SEALs. He is awarded the Medal of Honor posthumously in a White House Ceremony.

NOVEMBER 2006 — The new SEAL Special Warfare Operator (SO) and SWCC Special Warfare Boat Operator (SB) ratings are approved by the Navy.

JULY 2007 – Admiral Eric T. Olson becomes the first SEAL qualified officer to attain the rank of Vice Adm. (three Stars) and later Admiral (four Stars), and the first Naval officer to command U.S. Special Operations Command.

AUGUST 2008 – In a ceremony in Little Creek, Virginia, SEAL Delivery Team Two is disestablished.

APRIL 2009 – Somali pirates seize the cargo ship MV *Maersk Alabama* 240 nautical miles southeast of the Somali port city of Eyl. This was the first successful pirate seizure of a ship registered under the American flag since the early nineteenth century. A standoff subsequently ensues between the USS *Bainbridge* and the pirates aboard a lifeboat from the *Maersk Alabama*, where they hold the captain of the ship, Richard Phillips, hostage. On 12 April 2009, U.S. Navy SEAL snipers on the fantail of *Bainbridge* open fire and kill the pirates remaining in the lifeboat with a three-shot volley.

MAY 2011 – Operation Neptune Spear U.S. Navy SEALs perform a cross-border raid and kill Osama bin Laden in his compound in Abbottabad, Pakistan. The killing of the 9/11 mastermind had been years in the making. As the SEALs moved inside the compound, the national security team at the White House listened for "Geronimo," the code name for bin Laden. "We knew when we heard Geronimo KIA," President Obama said. The raid was later described by the president as "the most important single day of his presidency."

AUGUST 2011 – The crash of a CH-47D helicopter in Wardak province, Afghanistan on 6 August 2011 results in the death of all 38 persons on board. The helicopter and its crew, call sign Extortion 17, carried an Immediate Reaction Force (IRF) that included 17 U.S. Navy SEALs and their combat assault dog, five NSW Sailors, eight U.S. Army aircrew, and U.S. Air Force para-rescue and combat controllers, as well as eight members from an Afghan security element. While landing to assist U.S. Army Rangers in combat, the CH-47D was hit with an enemy rocket-propelled grenade and crashed killing all on board. The loss of 17 of these brave SEAL warriors on this mission represented the largest single loss of life in the history of the SEAL Teams.

GLOSSARY

AA&E – Arms, ammunition, and explosives

ADCOM – Administrative Control Command

ADMIRAL – A Navy officer rank: Rear Admiral, Vice Admiral, Admiral

AFSB – Afloat Forward Staging Base

AFSOC – Air Force Special Operations Forces Command

AIS – Automated Information System

AK-47 – A Russian assault rifle produced in 1947 by Mikhail Kalashnikov

AO – Area of Operations – A specific area, zone, or sector in which a unit is assigned to operate.

AOR – Area of Responsibility

AFSOF – Air Force Special Operations Forces

ASDS – Advanced SEAL Delivery System

ASDSTU – Advanced SEAL Delivery System Task Units

ASO – Advanced Special Operations

BAIL-OUT BOTTLES – An alternate reserve short-term emergency air supply

BCD / BC – buoyancy control device BCD, sometimes referred to as buoyancy control (BC)

BDA – Budget damage assessment

BDU – Battle dress uniform

BEACH JUMPERS – A special warfare unit specializing in deception and psychological warfare during World War II.

BUD/S – Basic Underwater Demolition / SEAL training

BLACKWATER – Commercial military training and service company

BSU – Boat Support Unit

BROWN-WATER NAVY – Slang term used to refer to riverine or inland waterway Special Boat Units

BUDWEISER – The SEAL badge or insignia known as the Trident is sometimes referred to as the **BUDWEISER.**

C2 – Command and Control

C2W – Command and control warfare

C-4 – A plastique military grade explosive

C4I – Command, Control, Communications, Computers, and intelligence

CAMP PEARY – A Navy training base located near Williamsburg, Virginia

CAO – Crisis action planning

CAR-15 – Colt Automatic Rifle-15 Military Weapons System

CB – Construction Battalion

CBRNE – Chemical, biological, radiological, nuclear, and high-yield explosives

CCDR – Combatant commander

CDRTSOC – Commander, Theater Special Operations Command

CDRUSCENTCOM – Commander, United States Central Command

CDRUSPACOM – Commander, United States Pacific Command

CDRUSEUCOM – Commander, United States European Command

CDRUSSOCOM – Commander, United States Special Operations Command

CDRUSSOUTHCOM – Commander, United States Southern Command

CENTCOM – Central Command

CESE – Civil engineering support equipment

CFFC – Combined Fleet Forces Command

CHUTING STARS – An earlier parachute demonstration team

CI – Counterintelligence

CIA – Central Intelligence Agency

CJCS – Chairman, Joint Chiefs of Staff

CMC – Command Master Chief

CMS – Cryptologic material security

CNO – Chief of Naval Operations

CNSWC – Commander, Naval Special Warfare Command, also COMNAVSPECWARCOM

CNSWG – Commander, Naval Special Warfare Group, also COMNAVSPECWARGRU

CNSWTF – Commander, Naval Special Warfare Task Force

CNSWTG – Commander, Naval Special Warfare Task Group

CO – Commanding Officer

COA – Course of action

COCOM – Combatant Command

COMNAVSPECWARCOM – Commander, Naval Special Warfare Command

COMSEVENTHFLT – Commander, SEVENTH Fleet

COMSIXTHFLT – Commander, SIXTH Fleet

COMSOCCENT – Commander, Special Operations Command, United States Central Command

COMSOCEUR – Commander, Special Operations Command, United States European Command

COMSOCPAC – Commander, Special Operations Command, United States Pacific Command

COMSOCSOUTH – Commander, Special Operations Command, United States Southern Command

CONOP – Concept of operations

CONPLAN – Concept plan

CONUS – Continental United States

COMMODORE – An informal title used by the U.S. Navy for captains in charge of several commands

COMPASS BOARD – Attack board, used for underwater navigation. The newer electronic version is known as the HMU, Hydrographic Measuring Unit

COVERT OPERATIONS / ACTIONS – The word "covert" refers to actions nonattributable to the United States

CP – Counter-profileration

CPI – Coastal patrol and interdiction

CRRC – Combat Rubber Raiding Craft

CRS – Coastal river squadrons

CSAR – Combat search and rescue

CSG – Carrier strike group

CSL – Cooperative security location

CSS – Combat service support

CSSD – Combat service support detachment

CT – Counterterrorism

CTF – Commander, task force

CTG – Commander, task group

DA – Direct action

DCI – Director Central Intelligence

DDCI – Deputy Director Central Intelligence

DDO – Deputy Director of Operations, CIA

DDS – Dry Deck Shelter, used to house and transport SDVs on the backs of submarines

DDSO – Deputy Director Special Operations (Joint Staff J3)

DESERT SHIELD / STORM – 1990–1991, Military buildup of U.S. and Coalition forces in Saudi Arabia and area countries for the purpose of repelling the invasion of Iraqi forces into Kuwait

DET – Detachment

DEVGRP – DEVGROUP, Development Group, Based in Dam Neck, Virginia, is responsible for the research, testing, and development of new equipment utilized by SEALs, SWCC, and NSW members.

DIA – Defense Intelligence Agency

DoD – Department of Defense

DPV – Desert Patrol Vehicle or Fast Attack Vehicle (FAV) all-terrain dune buggy designed by Chenowth

DRAEGER – Mark V, Mark XV, closed and semiclosed diving apparatus (SCUBA)

DRONE – Unmanned aerial vehicle (UAV) controlled autonomously by computers in the vehicle

DZ – Drop zone

E&R – Evasion and recovery

ELINT – Electronic Intelligence, such as those of the National Security Agency, NSA

EOD – Explosive Ordnance Disposal

EPW – Enemy prisoner of war

ESG – Expeditionary Strike Group

EUCOM – European Command

EXORD – Execute order

FAST ROPING – A tactic of lowering operators to the ground from hovering helicopters

FID – Foreign internal defense

FORT PIERCE – A U.S. Navy amphibious base in

Florida during World War II; home of the UDT –SEAL Museum

FOS – Forward Operating Site

FREE-FALL – A civilian skydiving term referring to parachuting without a static line attached to the aircraft.

FROGMAN – An informal term first used to describe Underwater Demolition Team (UDT) swimmers

FULL MISSION PROFILE – A term used describing the preparation, planning, sequestering, movement to (inserting) actions at an objective, and with withdrawal (extraction)

FYDP – Future Years Defense Plan, a Department of Defense budget planning document

GCC –Geographic combatant commander

GLTD – Ground laser target designator

GMV-N – Ground Mobility Vehicle — Navy

GPF OR GPMF – General purpose (military) forces

GPS – Global Positioning System

GRINDER – The workout area at BUD/S where students perform physical training

GROUP 1 – West Coast SEAL Command located in Coronado, California, which commands Seal Teams 1,3,5,7

GROUP 2 – East Coast SEAL Command of Seal Teams 2,4,8,10 located in Little Creek, Virginia

GROUP 3 – Based in Coronado, California, has overall command for Swimmer Delivery Teams, SDV-1 located at Pearl Harbor, Hawaii, and SDV-2 located at Little Creek, Virginia, until it was disestablished in August of 2008.

GROUP 4 – Based at Little Creek, Virginia, has overall command of Special Boat Teams 12, of which Special Warfare Combatant-Craft Crewmen (SWCC) operate a variety of crafts, from the Mk V, RHIB, Zodiac, and the newer Sealion.

GROUP 11 – A newly established group responsible for the administration of Naval Special Warfare reserves.

HAHO - High Altitude High Opening – A military parachute technique whereby a jumper deploys his canopy at high altitude and glides horizontally to the landing zone

HALO – High Altitude Low Opening – A military parachute technique whereby the jumper falls free from altitude to a predetermined altitude above the ground; civilian term is skydiving

HELL WEEK – An intense week of training at the end of BUD/S phase to test students' commitment and determination under pressure

HHQ –Higher headquarters

HLZ –Helicopter landing zone

HMU – Hydrographic Measuring Unit

HN –Host nation

HUSH PUPPY – Noise-suppressed pistol used to silence dogs and small animals from alerting the enemy

HSB – High Speed Boats, used during Desert Shield / Storm to intercept small attack boats

HSSC – Heavy SEAL Support Craft

HYDROGRAPHIC SURVEYS – Hydrographic Mapping Unit (HMU)

HYPERBARIC CHAMBER – Decompression chamber

IAW –In accordance with

ICW – In coordination with

IED – Improvised explosive device

IMINT – Image intelligence

INTEL – Intelligence

INFLATABLE BOATS – Rubber raiding craft used by all Special Operations Forces for amphibious maneuvers

IO – Information operations

IPB –Intelligence preparation of the battlefield

ISIC – Immediate superior in command

ISO – In support of

JCO – Joint commission observers

JCS – Joint Chiefs of Staff

JFC – Joint force commander

JIC – Joint Intelligence Command

JOC –Joint Operations Center

JOPES –Joint Operations Planning and Execution System

JOPP –Joint operation planning process

JP – Joint publication

JS – Joint Staff

JSCP –Joint strategic capabilities plan

JSOC – Joint Special Operations Command – Headquartered at Pope Air Force Base in North Carolina and Fort Bragg. It falls under the command of SOCOM

JSOTF –Joint Special Operations Task Force

JSPS –Joint Strategic Planning System

JTF – Joint Task Force

KA-BAR KNIFE – A World War II utility / fighting knife used by U.S. Marines and UDT

LCM – Landing Craft Mechanized, also known by the nickname "Mighty Mo"

LCPL – Landing Craft Vehicle, Personnel

LDO –Limited duty officer

LEAP FROGS – The current U.S. Navy parachute demonstration team. Formerly known at the U.S. Navy UDT / SEAL Exhibition Parachute Team

LIC –Low-intensity conflict

LIMPET MINE – Underwater mine attached to ships magnetically or by other means

LIO – Leadership interdiction operations

LITTLE CREEK – The homeport in Virginia of East Coast Naval Special Warfare Teams

LNO –Liaison officer

LOC – Line of communication

LOGSU – Logistics Support Unit - LOGSU 1, located on the West Coast and LOGSU 2, located in Little Creek, Virginia, provide for the purchasing, maintaining, and inventory of nearly all the equipment, vehicles, boats, and weapons being used by SWCC and SEAL operators and other support personnel.

LSSC – Light SEAL Support Craft

M203 – Grenade launcher

M82 – A SASR, "Light Fifty," 50.-caliber developed by Ronnie Barrett of American Barrett Firearms

M-79 – A infantry grenade launcher

MACV – Military Assistance Command Vietnam

MARCIRAS – Maritime-Combat Integrated Releasable Armor System designed by Eagle Industries

MARSOC – Marine Special Operations Command

MBB – Mission brief back

MCC – Mission Coordination Center, located in Coronado, California, to monitor and support Naval Special Warfare operations and exercises

MCD –Mobil Communications Detachment

MCM – Mine countermeasure

MCO –Major combat operations

METL – Mission essential task list

MFP – Major force program

MIO – Maritime interception operations

MK 8 – Flexible linear demolition charge, 25-foot explosive hose, filled with TNT

MK V – Mark Five, Special Operations craft

MOH – Medal of Honor

MOOTW –Military operations other than war

MP 5 – Heckler & Koch 9-mm submachine gun

MPK –Multipurpose knife

MRAD – Multi-Role Adaptive Design, sniper rifle designed by American Barrett Firearms

MSC –Mission Support Center

MSD –Maintenance Support Detachment

MSR –Mission support request

MSSC – Medium SEAL Support Craft

MST – Mobile Support Teams

MTT – Mobile Training Team

NAVSCIATTS – Naval Small Craft Instruction and Technical Training School

NAVSOF – Naval Special Operations Forces

NAVSOTF – Naval Special Operations Task Force

NAVSPECWARCEN – Naval Special Warfare Center; also NSWCEN, BUD/S

NAVSPECWARCOM – Naval Special Warfare Command; also NSWC

NAVSPECWARGRU – Naval Special Warfare Group; also NSWG

NAVSPECWAROPSUPPGRU – Naval Special Warfare Operational Support Group

NAVSPECWARUNIT – Naval Special Warfare Unit; also NSWU

NCDU –Naval Combat Demolition Unit

NCTC – National Counter Terrorism Center

NEO – Noncombatant Evacuation Operation

NRO – National Reconnaissance Office, responsible for maintaining the fleet of U.S. spy satellites and producing intelligence imagery from space

NSW – Naval Special Warfare, Navy SEALs, SWCC operators and support personnel that are part of WARCOM

NSWC – Naval Special Warfare Command

NSWCEN – Naval Special Warfare Center

NSWG – Naval Special Warfare Group

NSWRON – Naval Special Warfare Squadron

NSWTE – Naval Special Warfare Task Element

NSWTF – Naval Special Warfare Task Force

NSWSTG – Naval Special Warfare Task Group

NSWTU – Naval Special Warfare Task Unit

NSWU – Naval Special Warfare Unit

OCONUS –Outside the continental United States

OGA –Other Government Agency, sometimes referring to NSW, CIA, DIA, FBI, U.S. Treasury, Secret Service, Department of State, or others

OIC – Officer in Charge

ONI – Office of Naval Intelligence

OPCON –Operational Control

OPE – Operational preparation of the environment

OPLAN – Operational Plan

OPORD – Operation Order

OPS – Operations

OPSEC – Operational Security

OSD – Office of the Secretary of the Defense

OSG – Operational Support Group

OSPREY – V-22 aircraft

OST – Operational Support Team

OSU – Operational Support Unit

OTB – Over-the-beach, operations in which SEALs come in from the sea by various means to cross over the beach to move inland.

P11 ZUB – Heckler and Koch underwater firing pistol

PAO – Public Affairs Officer /Office – Responsible for military interface with the public and news media

PBR – Patrol boat, riverine

PE – Preparation of the environment

PGH – Patrol Gunboat Hydrofoil

PHOTINT – Photographic Intelligence

PLT – Platoon

PMS – Preventive maintenance system

POM – Program objective memorandum

PSD – Personal Security Detail

PSYOP – Psychological operations

PTF –Patrol Torpedo Fast

QRF – Quick Reaction Force

RDT&E – Research, Development, Testing, and Evaluation

RED CELL – Program designed to test security of the U.S. Navy, its ships, and its bases against a terrorist attack

RIB – Rigid Hull Inflatable Boat, NSW

RSO&I – Reception, Staging, Onward Movement, and Intergration

SA – Security Assistance

SASR – Special Application Scoped Rifle

SBD –Special Boat Detachment

SBR – Special Boat Squadron

SBT – Special Boat Team

SBU – Special Boat Unit

SCAR – Special Forces Combat Assault developed by FN Herstal. The military nomenclature for the rifles is that of the MK-16 and MK-17 representing some 40 different configurations.

SCUBA – Self-Contained Underwater Breathing Apparatus

SCI – Sensitive Compartmented Information

SDV – SEAL Delivery Vehicle, formerly known as Swimmer Delivery Vehicle. A covert flooded submersible, where swimmers ride exposed to water, breathing on the SDV's compressed air supply

SDVT – SEAL Delivery Vehicle Team

SDVTU – SEAL Delivery Vehicle Task Unit

SEABEES – Navy Construction Battalions

SEAL – Acronym for Sea, Air, and Land

SEAL TEAM 6 – Counterterrorist team established in 1980

SEALION – SEAL Insertion, Observation, and Neutralization. A new 71-foot fast boat designed by Carderock Division of the Naval Surface Warfare Center (NSWC)

SEAWOLVES – Informal term for Vietnam-era Navy attack helicopter squadrons that supported SEAL tactical operations

SECDEF – Secretary of Defense

SECNAV – Secretary of the Navy

SIPRNET –Secret Internet Protocol Router Network

SIT – Squadron Interoperability Training

SO – Special Operations

SOC – Special Operations Craft or Special Operations Command

SOCCENT – Special Operations Command, Central

SOCEUR – Special Operations Command, Europe

SOCOM – Special Operations Command – Located in Tampa, Florida, at McDill Air Force Base. Commands and encompasses all Special Operations of the U.S. Navy, U.S. Marines, U.S. Army and U.S. Air Force. Most notably, Navy SEALs, Army Green Berets, Air Force Special Operations, U.S. Army 160th Night Stalkers, Delta Force, and Rangers

SOCPAC – Special Operations Command, Pacific

SOC-R – Special Operations Craft—Riverine

SOCSOUTH –Special Operations Command, South

SOF – Special Operations Forces

SOG – Special Operations Group

SOMPE-M – Special Operations Mission Planning Environment-Maritime

SOMPF – Special Operations Mission Planning Folder

SOT – Special Operations Technician

SR –Special Reconnaissance

SSGN – Nuclear-powered guided missile submarine

SSN – Nuclear-powered attack submarine

ST – SEAL team

STAR – Fulton Surface-to-air Recovery

STONER LIGHT MACHINE GUN – A lightweight Vietnam-era submachine gun used by SEAL teams

SUPPACT – Support activity

SUROB – Surf observation

SWCC – Special Warfare Combatant-Craft Crewman

TACON – Tactical control

TCS – Tactical cryptologic support

TE – Task element

TF – Task force

TG – Task group

TIP – Target intelligence package

TOC – Tactical operations center

TRADET – Training detachment

TS – Top Secret

TSOC – Theater Special Operations Command

TTP – Tactics, Techniques, and Procedures

TU – Task unit

UAV – Unmanned aerial vehicle

UDT – Underwater Demolition Team

ULT – Unit Level Training

UW – Unconventional Warfare – Used to describe irregular operations. It has undergone many interpretations over the years and is today a stand-alone activity of Special Operations.

USAFSOC – U.S. Air Force Special Operations Command, headquartered in Pensacola, Florida

USASOC –U.S. Army Special Operations Command, headquartered at Fort Bragg, North Carolina

USCENTCOM – United States Central Command

USEUCOM – United States European Command

USPACOM – United States Pacific Command

USSOCOM – United States Special Operations Command

USSSOUTHCOM – United States Southern Command

UUV – Unmanned underwater vehicle

UW – Unconventional warfare

VAS – Visual Augmentation System

VBSS – Visit, Board, Search and Seizure

WARCOM – Headquarters for the U.S. Naval Special Warfare Command, located in Coronado, California. Though no longer a command of the U.S. Navy, it comes under the command of SOCOM, a stand-alone command dealing with all areas of U.S. Special Operations.

WARNORD – Warning order

WMD – Weapons of mass destruction

ZODIAC – The formal name of the French company that provides Combat Rubber Raiding Craft (CRRC) for all Special Operations Forces.

Authors and Editors

Greg Edward Mathieson Sr.

Author / Photographer / Videographer / Soldier

Greg Mathieson is as comfortable working in war zones as he is at the White House. For more than thirty-three years he has chronicled the epic lives of our heroic men and women in uniform, our star-crossed national celebrities and the media-focused, often chaotic lives of those who make the decisions on American policy.

Born and raised in Glen Cove, Long Island, this ten-year U.S. Army veteran's stellar reputation has allowed him to repeatedly cross the line working for hard news organizations as well as the federal government with equal objectivity. His work has ranged from public portraits of the famous to intimate portrayals of their the private lives.

Few photographers working today have covered as many traumatic current events, political watersheds, and cultural and historical milestones as Mathieson. Since establishing his agency, MAI Photo News Agency, in 1981, Mathieson has been called on by such agencies as the Secret Service, FEMA, the U.S. Department of Justice, and the military services to create images that capture the core values of those agencies in service to the American people. His editorial images have appeared on the covers of *Life, Time, Newsweek, U.S. News and World Report, The New York Times, Paris Match*, and thousands more around the globe in sixty-four countries.

Mathieson is not only well known in the corridors of political power and the halls of the Pentagon. This veteran of the Vietnam era has used his deep knowledge of the American military to photograph the jungles of Panama and Honduras, the Korean DMZ, and the wars in the Persian Gulf, including Desert Storm and the invasion of Iraq. He is highly experienced on the front lines, having spent 15 years in and out of Iraq for months at a time, depicting the difficult struggle of the Kurdish and Iraqi people. He lived with the Contra rebels on the jungle borders of Nicaragua fighting the Sandinistas and was the first into Kuwait City, recording the U.S. Marines entering the city, pushing out the Iraqi Army during Desert Storm. He was also on the snow-covered shores of the Sava River as the first U.S. M1 tanks crossed into Bosnia and Herzegovina.

Those dangerous and extraordinary experiences reached a zenith when Greg Mathieson was selected as the videographer by NBC News to sneak into Iraq two months before the 2003 war as one of a five-member covert team traveling across the snow-covered mountains of Iran into the future war zone. Working unilaterally and not embedded with U.S. troops like other members of the media, his team was the first to reach Saddam Hussein's palace in Tikrit prior to U.S. forces arriving. His video has appeared on both NBC and ABC News networks. He is so trusted by his clients—many of whom are kings, queens, prime ministers, heads of state, corporate chieftains, and government agencies—that he is routinely privy to critical briefings; he is instantly a member of the team.

During the past twenty-two years, Mathieson has never given up his efforts to create the ultimate photo book chronicling the activities of the U.S. Navy SEALs and the closed community of Naval Special Warfare in which they live. Now, for the first time, much of that veil will be lifted for a peak at America's greatest secret warriors and the people who support them.

DAVE GATLEY

PHOTOJOURNALIST

Dave Gatley is an independent photojournalist who has worked assignments around the world. Based in the southwestern corner of the United States, his skills and reputation necessitate his travel all over the country and overseas for hard-news organizations, corporations, the U.S. military, and other U.S. government agencies.

Dave has been a professional photographer for over thirty-nine years and is the former chief photographer for the *Los Angeles Times*, working there eighteen years and as a freelance commercial/editorial photographer for over twenty-one years. Prior to the *Los Angeles Times*, Dave worked eight years as a senior computer programmer / analyst with the RAND Corporation specializing in military logistics, weapon systems, and large government databases.

Nationally recognized as an award-winning photojournalist and nominated for the Pulitzer three times, he has served hundreds of international and domestic news magazines and newspapers and has been published in over three dozen books.

Few photographers working today have had the breadth of experience covering current events and natural or man-made disasters marking cultural and historical milestones. Few in his field have the technical background or the experience. He has brought digital photography and imaging solutions, consultation, design, direction, and implementation to the Digital Archiving Project with the Zoological Society of San Diego (ZSSD), as well as the Federal Emergency Management Agency (FEMA) where he set up a News Photo Desk operation while working as lead photographer for FEMA's National Emergency Response Team (ERT-N).

Mr. Gatley's assignments have taken him to nearly every

U.S. state and over thirty countries. To date, he has completed dozens of tours into the war-torn Middle Eastern countries of Afghanistan, Iraq, Kuwait, Pakistan, Bahrain, Qatar, UAE, Turkey, Uzbekistan, and Kyrgyzstan. In addition, he has had many assignments throughout Western Europe and the western Pacific.

Some of his commercial and corporate clients include General Motors, General Dynamics, ITT, Lockheed, Motorola, Pacific Bell, Panasonic, Raytheon, Zoological Society of San Diego, numerous pharmaceutical companies, and many more.

His accomplishments have included Board and Vice President of both the Los Angeles and San Diego Chapters of the American Society of Media Photographers (ASMP) and President of the San Diego News Photographers (SDNP). Dave teaches photojournalism at Point Loma Nazarene University, lectures, and been an instructor with Panasonic for their nationally advertised Digital Photo Academy.

REAR ADMIRAL (SEAL) GEORGE WORTHINGTON, USN (RET.)

Rear Admiral George R. Worthington was born in Louisville, Kentucky, and was commissioned from the U.S. Naval Academy in June 1961. His initial tour of duty was in destroyers with an early staff tour as Aide-de-Camp and Flag Lieutenant for a Flotilla Commander. He applied for Underwater Demolition Team training and graduated with Class 36 in December 1965.

Following graduation he served as operations and executive officer in Underwater Demolition Team ELEVEN, completing two combat deployments to Vietnam. He graduated from the Naval Destroyer School Department Head course and served as operations officer in USS *Strong* (DD-768). He was later assigned to Naval Special Warfare commands and served a year in Saigon on the Naval Special Warfare Group (Vietnam). School tours followed at the U.S. Marine Corps Command and Staff College and National War College.

Worthington served command tours commensurate with rank with SEAL Team ONE, Inshore Undersea Warfare Group ONE, operating the Navy marine mammal program, and Naval Special Warfare Group ONE, responsible for West Coast SEAL Teams and Special Boat Squadrons. He served as Naval Attaché to the American Embassy, Phnom Penh, Cambodia, during the last days of the Khmer Republic. Staff tours included assignments with the Chief of Naval Operations as program sponsor for Naval Special Warfare, Chief of Staff for the Special Operations Command (Europe), Stuttgart, Germany, and as a Flag Officer, with the Secretary of Defense as Deputy Assistant Secretary of Defense (Special Operations and Counterterrorism). He commanded the Naval Special Warfare Command as his last active tour.

Since retirement, Worthington has served on the board of directors of ZODIAC North America, makers of operational rubber raiding craft; WESCAM-Sonoma, makers

of high-resolution stabilized camera systems used on the Predator UAV; and the special operations Warrior Foundation, a nonprofit foundation providing college scholarships for orphans of deceased Special Operations personnel. He is a member of the board of advisors to High Technol-

ogy Solutions in San Diego, a government services firm. He worked two years with WarRoom Research (Maryland) on war room design and security. He currently consults with IFG Ltd. for littoral warfare craft requirements. (The Office of Naval Research has just authorized construction of the Littoral Support Craft, Experimental, or "X-Craft," which he promoted with several articles for the Naval Institute *Proceedings* on littoral warfare and combatant craft.) He has written the SEAL chapters for anthologies titled "The Navy" and "United States Special Operations Forces."

Worthington is a current sport parachutist with over 1,200 skydives, an avid skier, and Masters swimmer. He is a member of various professional societies. His interests are in National Defense and Naval Special Warfare littoral warfighting capabilities.

COMMANDER (SEAL) THOMAS L. HAWKINS, USN (RET.)

Commander Tom Hawkins retired from the U.S. Navy after twenty-four years active service as a career SEAL and Naval Special Warfare officer. Born and raised in Philippi, West Virginia, he entered the Navy in February 1966 and was commissioned the following May. He completed Underwater Demolition Team Replacement training with Class 38 in Little Creek, Virginia, and subsequently completed operational tours in UDT-21, UDT-22, and SEAL Team TWO, where he deployed to the Republic of Vietnam as a Platoon Commander. He commanded UDT-22 for thirty-three months during the period of its reorganization and establishment as SEAL Delivery Vehicle Team TWO. At the time of his Navy retirement he was serving as Director, NSW Programs at the Naval Sea Systems Command. His military decorations include the Bronze Star and Navy Commendation Medal with Combat "V" and the Combat Action Ribbon. He is currently serving in the

Combat Development Directorate at the Naval Special Warfare Development Group. From 1995 to 2005 Tom Hawkins served as President of the UDT-SEAL Association—the national fraternal organization of U.S. Navy Frogmen and SEALs. During the same period he served as President of the UDT-SEAL Memorial Park Association, served on the Board of Directors of the UDT-SEAL Museum Association and in 2000 was founding President and Chairman of the Board of Naval Special Warfare Foundation, where he continues to serve as Director, History and Heritage. Since 1994, he has served as editor and publisher of the UDT-SEAL Association and NSW Foundation's quarterly publication, *The BLAST: The Journal of Naval Special Warfare*. Tom and his wife, Carol, reside in Virginia Beach, Virginia, and will soon relocate to their home in West Virginia.

ACKNOWLEDGMENTS

The Honorable George W. Bush,
43rd President of the United States

The Honorable Donald C. Winter,
Secretary of the Navy

The Honorable John F. Lehman Jr.,
Secretary of the Navy

Capt. Kevin Wensing, USN (Ret.),
Special Assistant for Public Affairs, DOSD

Col. Barney Barnum Jr., USMC (Ret.),
Deputy Assistant Secretary of the Navy

The Honorable Christopher M. Lehman

Adm. Eric T. Olson, USN (SEAL)

Adm. William H. McRaven, USN (SEAL)

Vice Adm. Joseph Maguire, USN (SEAL)

Vice Adm. Bert Calland, USN (SEAL)

Vice Adm. Bob Harward, USN (SEAL)

Rear Adm. Garry J. Bonelli, USN (SEAL)

Rear Adm. Joseph D. Kernan, USN (SEAL)

Rear Adm. Edward G. Winters III, USN (SEAL)

Rear Adm. Tom Brown, USN (SEAL)

Rear Adm. Sean A. Pybus, USN (SEAL)

Capt. Charles Heron, USN (SEAL),
USSOCOM NSWG-2

Capt. Colin Kilrain, USN (SEAL),
USSOCOM NSWG-2

Capt. Gardner Howe, USN (SEAL),
USSOCOM NSWG-3

Capt. Evin Thompson, USN (SEAL),
USSOCOM NSWG-4

Capt. Charles Wolf, USN (SEAL),
USSOCOM NSWG-4

Capt. Roger Herbert, USN (SEAL),
NSW Training Center

Capt. Duncan Smith, USN (SEAL), WARCOM

Capt. Beci Brenton, USN, Special Assistant for PA,
Office of the Secretary of the Navy

Capt. Wesley Spencer –
CO NSWG-1 Advance Training Command

Capt. C. R. Lindsay – COS NAVSPECWARCOM

Cdr. Greg Geisen, Force Public Affairs Officer,
Naval Special Warfare Command

Cdr. Michael Wilson – USSOCOM NSWLSU1

Cdr. Sass – NSWG3 – SDVT1 (Pearl Harbor, Hawaii)

Capt. Wesley Spencer –
CO NSWG-1 Advance Training Command

Cdr. Gordon Howe – NSWG-3 Commodore

Cdr. Christopher J. Cassidy, USN, SEAL, NASA

Lt. Cdr. Joseph P Burns – USSOCOM NSWLSU1

Lt. Cdr. Joe Fuller. SEAL, USN (Ret.)
NSW/O Motivator-Mentor

Lt. Cdr. Teri Alexander, NSW Group One

Lt. Cdr. MacDonald –
NSWG3 – SDVT1 (Pearl Harbor, Hawaii)

Lt. Cdr. Eric Rehberg – USSOCOM NAVSOC

Lt. Cdr. Michael Bennett, USCG

Ken McGraw. USSOCOM

CWO2 Chad Clement, SEAL

WO Peter Sagasti –
NSWG3 – SDVT1 (Bangor–Keyport,Washington)

Fred Francis, Senior NBC News Correspondent

Bob Rieve, Commodore, SEAL, USN (Ret.) NSW Foundation

Steve Gilmore, Naval Special Warfare Command

Lina Camello, NSW Group One

Trish O'Connor, APAO, Naval Special Warfare Command

Lt. Tommy Crosby, PAO, NSW Group One

Lt. Linda Sweeney – PAO NSWG-1

Lt. Nathan Potter

Lt. Steve Schultz (Kodiak, Alaska)

Lt. Jacob Booher – San Clemente Island, California

Lt. Russel Aldridge – USS *Ohio*

Lt. Joe Kochera – USS *Ohio*

Lt. Schultz – OIC USSOCOM NSWG1 (Det Kodiak)

Lt. Jonathan Macaskill –
    USSOCOM NAVSOC – NSWSBT-12 NAB –
    SWCC

Lt. Mickaila Johnston, M.D. – NSWG Four

Lt. Dana DeCoster

Lt. Bauer – OIC SWCC Combat Qual Trg

Mark Wertheimer, Naval History and Heritage Command

Gordon Hatchell, NAVSEA-NSWC Carderock Division

Greg E. "Chip" Mathieson Jr.

SCPO Scott D Williams – NAVSPECWARCOM

(SOC) CPO Darren Anderson – USSOCOM NAVSOC
    – NSWSBT-12 NAB – SWCC

PO2 Kevin Beauchamp –
    USSOCOM NSWCEN – APAO

MC2 Brian Billar – NAVSPECWARCOM

SCPO Boychuk – USSOCOM NSWG-1

MCC Scott Boyle, NSW Group Four

Larry Brown, The Boeing Company

Al Bruton, Master Diver and
    International Underwater Photographer

Chief Deborah Carson (Ret.)

Gregg Cook, Submergence Group, LLC

Richard Long, GENTEX Corporation

S. Paul Dev, D-STAR Engineering Corp.

MC 1 Robert M. Dylewski – NSWG-3

Mark Faram, Photographer

Rohan Fernando, Draeger Safety, Inc.

Kathy Gatley

Robert Hamilton, General Dynamics Electric Boat

Capt. Michael R. Howard, SEAL, USN (Ret.),
    Executive Director, Navy UDT-SEAL Museum

R Jason Jadgchew – LOGSU
    Medical Rehab / Hydro-Tank

SCPO Joe Kuhns – Det Kodiak

Dr. Christian J. Lambertsen and Family

Kimberly Laudano, PAO
    160th Special Operations Aviation Regiment

SOC Rico Madaffari – San Clemente Island, California

Reynolds R. Marion, Marion Hyper-Sub

John Carver, Eagle Industries

Wallace Martin, Naval Air Weapons Station, China
    Lake, California

(Ret) SEAL Moki (Philip) Martin –
    Superfrog/Superseal program

SOC Darren M.C. Burnett

Ruth McSweeney, Navy UDT-SEAL Museum

Walter Mess, OSS / MU

SK1 Matt Moore – NSWLSU1

SBC (SWCC) Jarlath O'Brien

SCPO Eric Peters USSOCOM
    NSWCEN (Det Kodiak)

Lt Matthew R. Maasdam – USSOCOM NSWCEN

Lt Stephen H Schultz – USSOCOM NSWCEN

Lt Brian D Ko – USSOCOM NSWCEN

Charles Pinch, The OSS Society, Inc.

CWO Peter Sagasti – NSWG-3
    (CERTEX Keyport, Washington, and USSOCOM)

SCPO Wayne Stansel – San Clemente Island, California

ENS Zack Steinbock – OIC Niland

Marty Strong, Blackwater Worldwide

SCPO Andy Wilkins – Niland

David Wilberding, STIDD Systems, Inc.

WO (SWCC) David Wylie

Lt. Christopher R. Bolton

Mike Hayes, NSC

Kimberly Tiscione, 160th SOAR

Carl Kroft, NCTC

Leslie Jewell, NCTC

**And to all the Operators, MCs, PAOs and staffs and other
government agencies that helped in accomplishing this project**

Terrorists

AYMAN AL-ZAWAHIRI

DESCRIPTION

RESTRICTED ACCESS
TRAINING FACILITY NOT OPEN
FOR GENERAL USE

WARNING
DO NOT **POSITION** FEET
OR STOW EQUIPMENT
UNDER SEAT

IS TODA
DAY
COMPLA
KIL

TOP SECRET

THIS IS A COVER SHEET
FOR CLASSIFIED INFORMATION

ALL INDIVIDUALS HANDLING THIS INFORMATION ARE REQUIRED TO PROTECT
IT FROM UNAUTHORIZED DISCLOSURE IN THE INTEREST OF THE NATIONAL
SECURITY OF THE UNITED STATES.

HANDLING, STORAGE, REPRODUCTION AND DISPOSITION OF THE ATTACHED
DOCUMENT WILL BE IN ACCORDANCE WITH APPLICABLE EXECUTIVE
ORDER(S), STATUTE(S) AND AGENCY IMPLEMENTING REGULATIONS.

(This cover sheet is unclassified.)

TOP SECRET

ALL
Photography
Filming / Sk
Prohibited

OT/SEAL TRAINING
HE ONLY EASY DAY
WAS YESTERDAY

STAY CLEAR 100 METERS
DEADLY FORCE
AUTHORIZED
إبتعد 100 متر ! يصرح

خطر
ابق بعيدا
DANGER
STAY BACK

OFF LIMITS AREA
DO NOT ENTER

NOTICE TO PASSENGERS

following items are considered "PROHIBITED" by the
ansportation Security Administration and may not be
transported aboard the aircraft:

PROHIBITED ITEMS

ms, Swords, Knives, Explosives, Weapons, Martials Arts
Equipment, Pornographic or Offensive Material, War
phies, Harmful Devices or Any Device That May Cause
n. Ammunition, Ammunition Casings, Lighter (all types),
mmable Fluids, Blue Tip (strike) Matches, Soil, Soiled
rticles, Agricultural Products to include Fresh Fruits,
Plants. Meats or Vegetables.

following items are considered "CONTROLLED" by the
Transportation Security Administration and may be
sported aboard aircraft, however; MUST BE DECLARED
passenger Service Baggage Inspection Officials and
Military Customs Inspectors

CONTROLLED ITEMS

y Weapons, Prescription Medication, Professional Gear
(TA-50), Classified and Hazardous Materials.

NAVAL SPECIAL WARFARE
COMBATANT - CRAFT
CREWMAN
CREWMAN QUALIFICATION
TRAINING - CQT

NAVAL SPECIAL WARFARE CENTER
SEAL QUALIFICATION TRAINING

WARNING

NO VIDEO TAPING OR
PHOTOGRAPHING WITHOUT
PRIOR WRITTEN PERMISSION
FROM COMMANDING OFFICER
SEAL DELIVERY VEHICLE TEAM ONE

SECRET

COMBAT STRESS

Most Wanted
Terrorists
CONSPIRACY TO KILL NATIONALS OF THE UNITED ST

KHALID SHAIKH MOHAM

NAVSP
COMBAT
(FOR OFFIC

DESCRIPTION

TRAIN AT
FIREAR
INHERENT

TRAINING AT BL
EACH INDIVIDU
TRAINING FACILI
OF INJURY, LO
THE USE OF BLA

THE PARTICIPATI
TRAINING AT THE
CONSTITUTE A
FOREGOING

CAUTION

REWA

RESTRICTED AREA
ESIDENTS, GUESTS AND
FFICIAL BUSINESS ONLY

GROUND
GUIDE
REQUIRED

DAILY SCHED
ALL TRASH DAILY
WATCH COT PUT UP
ICE/WATER COOLERS
FUEL EVERYTHING
VEHICLE RESPONSIBILITY
TICK CHECK
WATER FOR WATCH (Don't
DUMP LEFTOVER WATER)
INVENTORIES
FUEL BOATS AFTER EVERYTHING ELSE IS
DONE!
DISCREPENCIES
SHAVES,

Pho
Film

MAINTAIN MUZZLE
AWARENESS
TROOPS IN TOWE

WARNING
RESTRICTED AREA - KEEP OUT
AUTHORIZED PERSONNEL ONLY
AUTHORIZED ENTRY INTO THIS RESTRICTED AREA
CONSTITUTES CONSENT TO SEARCH OF PERSONNEL
AND THE PROPERTY UNDER THEIR CONTROL
INTERNAL SECURITY ACT OF 1950 SECTION 2150 USC 797
NO PHOTOS

انتظر لاشارة المرور و نقدم بحذر
WHEN SIGNALED PROCEED
AND PASS WITH CAUTION

منطقة محظورة

RICTED AREA

HOTOGRAPHY

ممنوع التص

G
RE

(C) 2012 GREG E. MATIESON SR. / NSW PUBLICATIONS, LLC

RESTRICTED AREA
NO VIDEO
OR PHOTOGRAPHY
AUTHORIZED

22.95

WITHDRAWN

LONGWOOD PUBLIC LIBRARY
800 Middle Country Road
Middle Island, NY 11953
(631) 924-6400
longwoodlibrary.org

LIBRARY HOURS

Monday-Friday	9:30 a.m. - 9:00 p.m.
Saturday	9:30 a.m. - 5:00 p.m.
Sunday (Sept-June)	1:00 p.m. - 5:00 p.m.

EMERGENCY EXIT
ROUND AND DITCHING
USE ONLY

DRINKING WATER
ONLY
DO NOT USE FOR
CLEANING GEAR

WAR
المطار
REST
نوع علاقة
It is unlawful t
permission ins
Sec. 21 Internal Sec
علاقی ته داخلیدل غیرقانونی دی
٠-٥٠ دامرپکا کود ٧٩٧ پ اساس
داخل شدن ممنوع است
١٩٥ - ٠-٥- کود امريکا ٧٩٧
While in this installation all
their control a
شخص تلاشی سی
چيز تلاشی شود
Use of deadly Force authorized

PERSONNEL ONLY

WARNING

Moving Gate Can Cau
Serious Injury or Dea

KEEP CLEAR! Gate May Move at Any T
Do Not Allow Children To Play In Are
or Operate Gate.
Operate Gate Only When
Gate Area is in Sight

G
RE

The following items
Transportation S
trans

PROH

Firearms, Swords, K
Equipment, Por
Trophies, Harmful D
Harm. Ammunition,
Flammable Fluids,
Articles, Agricul

The following items
Transportation
transported aboard